Principles of Pediatric ICD-10-CM Coding

Editor
Jeffrey F. Linzer Sr, MD, FAAP
AAP Representative, *ICD-9-CM* Editorial Advisory Board
Member, Committee on Coding and Nomenclature
American Academy of Pediatrics

Consulting Editor
Cindy Hughes, CPC, CFPC, PCS

American Academy of Pediatrics
141 Northwest Point Blvd
Elk Grove Village, IL 60007-1019

American Academy of Pediatrics Department of Marketing and Publications Staff
Maureen DeRosa, MPA, Director, Department of Marketing and Publications
Mark Grimes, Director, Division of Product Development
Diane L. Della Maria, MS, Senior Product Development Editor
Carrie Peters, Editorial Assistant
Sandi King, MS, Director, Division of Publishing and Production Services
Leesa Levin-Doroba, Manager, Publishing and Production Services
Kate Larson, Manager, Editorial Services
Peg Mulcahy, Manager, Graphic Design and Production
Marirose Russo, Brand Manager, Practice Management and Professional Publications

Library of Congress Control Number: 2012947274
ISBN: 978-1-58110-738-8
eISBN: 978-1-58110-759-3
MA0630

The recommendations in this publication do not indicate an exclusive course of treatment or serve as a standard of medical care. Variations, taking into account individual circumstances, may be appropriate.

The mention of product names in this publication is for informational purposes only and does not imply endorsement by the American Academy of Pediatrics.

Every effort has been made to ensure that the drug selection and dosage set forth in this text are in accordance with the current recommendations and practice at the time of publication. It is the responsibility of the health care provider to check the package insert of each drug for any change in indications and dosage and for added warnings and precautions.

Copyright © 2013 American Academy of Pediatrics. All rights reserved. No part of this publication may be reproduced, stored in a retrieval system, or transmitted in any form or by any means, electronic, mechanical, photocopying, recording, or otherwise, without prior permission from the publisher. Printed in the United States of America.

Table of Contents

Introduction v

Chapter 1: Guidelines and Conventions of *ICD-10* Coding 1

Chapter 2: Certain Infectious and Parasitic Diseases **(A00-B99)** 15

Chapter 3: Neoplasms **(C00-D49)** 23

Chapter 4: Diseases of the Blood and Blood-Forming Organs and Certain Disorders Involving the Immune Mechanism **(D50-D89)** 33

Chapter 5: Endocrine, Nutritional, and Metabolic Diseases **(E00-E89)** 41

Chapter 6: Mental, Behavioral, and Neurodevelopmental Disorders **(F01-F09)** 53

Chapter 7: Diseases of the Nervous System **(G00-G99)** 65

Chapter 8: Diseases of the Eye and Adnexa **(H00-H59)** 79

Chapter 9: Diseases of the Ear and Mastoid Process **(H60-H95)** 91

Chapter 10: Diseases of the Circulatory System **(I00-I99)** 97

Chapter 11: Diseases of the Respiratory System **(J00-J99)** 107

Chapter 12: Diseases of the Digestive System **(K00-K95)** 119

Chapter 13: Diseases of the Skin and Subcutaneous Tissue **(L00-L99)** 133

Chapter 14: Diseases of the Musculoskeletal System and Connective Tissue **(M00-M99)** 145

Chapter 15: Diseases of the Genitourinary System **(N00-N99)** 157

Chapter 16: Pregnancy, Childbirth, and the Puerperium **(O00-O9A)** 167

Chapter 17: Certain Conditions Originating in the Perinatal Period **(P00-P96)** 177

Chapter 18: Congenital Malformations, Deformations, and Chromosomal Abnormalities **(Q00-Q99)** 189

Chapter 19: Symptoms, Signs, and Abnormal Clinical and Laboratory Findings Not Elsewhere Classified **(R00-R99)** 199

Chapter 20: Injury, Poisoning, and Certain Other Consequences of External Causes **(S00-T88)** 205

Chapter 21: External Causes of Morbidity **(V00-Y99)** 217

Chapter 22: Factors Influencing Health Status and Contact With Health Services **(Z00-Z99)** 227

Appendices

Appendix A: Answer Key for Review What You Have Learned 241

Appendix B: Epilepsy Table 255

Appendix C: Signs and Symptoms 259

Index 263

Introduction

The deadline for transition from *International Classification of Diseases, Ninth Revision, Clinical Modification (ICD-9-CM)* to *ICD-10-CM* is October 1, 2015. This move represents a large undertaking for physicians, providers, and all of the entities who work with health care data in the United States. It is our hope that this book and resources like it will serve as references to help smooth the transition.

As we move to *ICD-10-CM,* there are other changes in the health care system that place greater emphasis on full and correct reporting of patient diagnoses. The information derived from diagnosis codes submitted in health care transactions like health insurance claims is used to detect patients who may benefit from additional services, identify health and safety issues, and compare costs of care. Accurate and complete reporting of diagnoses is needed to guide these activities. This starts with the documentation on which code selection is based.

No matter how specific the codes in a classification system, without supporting documentation the information conveyed by the codes will be incomplete and likely unsupportive of care coordination and management activities and may fail to show the complexity of care necessary for the patient encounter. For this reason, it is important that physicians and providers document diagnoses that can be translated to specific codes whenever possible. This means adopting the terminology that is currently used to describe conditions and clearly indicating any established diagnosis.

For instance, classifications of severity have been developed for many conditions, including asthma. Asthma may be diagnosed as mild intermittent, mild persistent, moderate persistent, or severe persistent, and codes can specify the patient's status at the time of an encounter as uncomplicated, with exacerbation, or with status asthmaticus. However, these codes cannot be reported if the diagnosis on the claim is nonspecific, such as reactive airway disease, which at best translates to unspecified asthma. A diagnosis of unspecified asthma may not only fail to support a level of service billed for the associated encounter, it may result in additional requests for records from payers (an administrative hassle for your practice) and may not alert a private payer that offers support services to families of patients with asthma that your patient is a candidate for those benefits.

Change is hard, and change regarding work that may feel like a burdensome distraction from patient care is even harder. However, advances in patient care and direction of often-limited resources to areas of need are most often based on health care data that are derived from codes assigned to medical records, collected in patient registries, and submitted on health care claims.

For this reason, as you prepare for the transition to *ICD-10-CM,* we hope that you will note the terminology used for diagnoses and consider whether the terminology used in your documentation will support accurate diagnostic code selection.

≡ CHAPTER 1 ≡

Guidelines and Conventions of *ICD-10* Coding

Like its predecessor, *International Classification of Diseases, Ninth Revision, Clinical Modification*, ICD-10-CM has 3 main steps for selection of an accurate code

1. Look up a diagnosis or condition in the alphabetic index first and then in the tabular list.
2. Read all instructional notes in both the alphabetic index and the tabular list.
3. When in the tabular list, be sure to check for instructions at the 3-digit category level in addition to the code level.

Beyond these 3 steps are the official guidelines and conventions of *ICD-10-CM* as established by the Centers for Medicare & Medicaid Services (CMS) and the National Center for Health Statistics (NCHS) and approved by the cooperating parties for *ICD-10-CM*: the American Hospital Association, the American Health Information Management Association, CMS, and NCHS. The guidelines provide additional instruction beyond the conventions (general rules) contained directly within the alphabetic index and tabular list of the code set. Use of the official guidelines of *ICD-10-CM* is required under the Health Insurance Portability and Accountability Act when using the code set. However, conventions take precedence over the guidelines.

In this chapter, we will look at the structure of *ICD-10-CM* codes and review of some key guidelines and conventions that apply to the overall code set. Chapter- and diagnosis-specific guidelines of *ICD-10-CM* will be included later in reviews of each associated chapter.

First, let's note a few key definitions associated with the general conventions and guidelines of *ICD-10-CM*.

Character—a letter or number that serves as the building block of *ICD-10-CM* codes, sometimes referred to as digits

Category—a 3-character unit that may be a complete code when no further subcategories exist but often serves as the base for building a 4- to 7-character code, categories are the main entries of the tabular list

Subcategory—a further defined category of 4 to 6 characters that is not a complete code

Code—a complete set of characters for which there are no further subdivisions, 3 to 7 characters long, describing a condition or reason for an encounter or related factors such as external causes

And—means "and/or" *in ICD-10-CM*

With—means "with" or "due to" in *ICD-10-CM*

Principal diagnosis—in a non-outpatient setting, that condition established after study to be chiefly responsible for occasioning the admission of the patient to the hospital or other non-outpatient setting for care (including home health agencies)

First-listed diagnosis—in an outpatient facility or office setting, the diagnosis, condition, problem, or other reason for encounter/visit shown in the medical record to be chiefly responsible for the services provided

Combination code—a single code that represents either multiple conditions or a single condition and an associated secondary process or complication

Placeholder—*ICD-10-CM* uses the letter "X" as a placeholder. Where a subcategory of less than 6 characters requires 7 characters for a complete code, an "X" must be used as a placeholder filling in any undefined characters.

Sequela—a late effect of an illness or injury that is no longer in the acute phase

These terms are used throughout the *ICD-10-CM* code set and the guidelines for its use.

Code Structure

As shown by the definition above, codes in *ICD-10-CM* are alphanumeric and may be from 3 to 7 characters long. All alphabetic characters except the letter U are used. The pattern of the code structure is 3 characters before a decimal followed by up to 4 more characters.

Pattern: **XXX.XXXX**

The first 3 characters form the code category. The first character is an alphabetic. The second character is numeric. Remaining characters may be alphabetic or numeric. Alphabetic characters are not case sensitive. The code category may then be further expanded on with etiology, severity, site, manifestations, or intent within the fourth through sixth characters. The seventh character is an extension required in some categories to further define the episode of care, status of fracture healing, the number of the fetus in obstetrical conditions, or the site of recording of the Glasgow coma scale.

Examples of complete codes

R05 Cough
R06.2 Wheezing
G43.C0 Periodic headache syndromes in child or adult, not intractable
G40.B01 Juvenile myoclonic epilepsy, not intractable, with status epilepticus
S52.311D Greenstick fracture of shaft of radius, right arm, subsequent encounter for fracture with routine healing
T37.5X5A Adverse effect of antiviral drugs, initial encounter

> Check it out: To further familiarize yourself with code structures, look up each of the codes in the example above in the tabular list. Look at the 3-character category for each and note other codes in each category.

The letter "X" is used as a placeholder embedded in some codes to either provide for future expansion of a code category or where a seventh character is required but a code is less than 6 characters long, the placeholder must be added to fill the those spaces between the end of the code and the seventh character.

Examples

    H60.8X1 Other otitis externa, right ear

    H60.8X2 Other otitis externa, left ear

    M48.52XA Collapsed vertebra, not elsewhere classified, cervical region, initial encounter

    X32.XXXA Exposure to sunlight, first encounter

The codes **H60.8X1** and **H60.8X2** are examples of the placeholder used to maintain the sixth character structure while leaving room for expansion. Codes **M48.52XA** and **X32.XXXA** are examples of codes completed by addition of placeholders to fill the characters between the end of the subcategory listing and a required seventh character.

> Check it out: To further your understanding of the "X" placeholder, look up each of the code categories in the example above and review other codes in each category. Try forming different variations of codes in categories **M48** and **X32**.

Guidelines and Conventions of the Alphabetic Index

The alphabetic index of *ICD-10-CM* consists of an alphabetic list of terms for diseases, injuries, and other reasons for encounters with their corresponding codes or code categories. It also includes an index to external causes of injuries, a table of neoplasms, and a table of drugs and chemicals. The alphabetic index contains main terms followed by a listing of terms that add specificity, such as acute or chronic. When a code appears next to a main term in the index, the code is a default code representing the condition most commonly associated with that term. This is often an "unspecified" code and should be reported only when information needed to arrive at a more specific code is not available.

Each main term in the index may be followed by a listing of subterms that further define the condition. The indents in the alphabetic index serve to guide the reader through the list of subterms, keeping each level of granularity connected back to the main term. Note that "with" is the first subterm in categories where it applies. The remaining subterms are in alphabetic order.

Example   **Adenoiditis** (chronic) **J35.02**
          – with tonsillitis **J35.03**
          – acute **J03.90**
              – recurrent **J03.91**
              – specified organism NEC **J03.80**
                  – recurrent **J03.81**
            – staphylococcal **J03.80**
              – recurrent **J03.81**

In the example above, adenoiditis is the main term with an initial first subterm "with tonsillitis" followed by a second subterm "acute" followed by further levels of subterms to specify the organism involved and whether or not the acute adenoiditis is recurrent.

When consulting the alphabetic index, terms or subterms may be followed by a series of terms enclosed in parentheses. These are nonessential modifiers that may or may not be present in the documentation and do not affect the code number assigned.

Examples **Asthma, asthmatic** (bronchial) (catarrh) (spasmodic) **J45.909**

Agenesis
– adrenal (gland) **Q89.1**

> **Terms to Know**
>
> **Etiology**—the cause or origin of a disease
>
> **Manifestation**—the display or disclosure of characteristic signs or symptoms of an illness

Brackets are used in the alphabetic index to identify manifestation codes.

Example **Amyloidosis** (generalized) (primary) **E85.9**
– with lung involvement **E85.4 [J99]**
– familial **E85.2**
– genetic **E85.2**
– heart **E85.4 [I43]**

Manifestation codes are always sequenced second to the etiology codes. In the example above, code **E85.4** represents organ-limited amyloidosis and secondary codes **J99** or **I43** indicate the manifestation in the lungs or heart. The descriptors for codes **J99** and **I43** include the phrase "in diseases classified elsewhere," indicating they are manifestation codes. In the tabular list, these codes appear with an instruction to code first the underlying disease.

Example **I43 Cardiomyopathy in diseases classified elsewhere**
Code first underlying disease, such as
  amyloidosis **(E85-)**
  glycogen storage disease **(E74.0)**
  gout **(M10.0-)**
  thyrotoxicosis **(E05.0-E05.9-)**

A dash (–) following a code in the alphabetic index indicates that the code is incomplete and that further characters must be located in the tabular list. Even where the dash is not present at the end of a code in the alphabetic index, the tabular list should be consulted for further instructions and possible seventh character requirements.

Example   Index entry—**Kearns-Sayre syndrome H49.81-**
　　　Tabular list—**H49.81** Kearns-Sayre syndrome
　　　Progressive external ophthalmoplegia with pigmentary retinopathy
　　　Use additional code for other manifestation, such as: heart block **(I45.9)**
　　　H49.811 Kearns-Sayre syndrome, right eye
　　　H49.812 Kearns-Sayre syndrome, left eye
　　　H49.813 Kearns-Sayre syndrome, bilateral
　　　H49.819 Kearns-Sayre syndrome, unspecified eye

In the above example, the dash at the end of the index entry for Kearns-Sayre syndrome indicates that **H49.81** is not a complete code. The tabular list provides the necessary sixth characters, indicating the involvement of one or both eyes and instruction to additionally report any manifestation such as heart block. *ICD-10-CM* captures laterality where it applies.

Terms in the index that include the abbreviation NEC for not elsewhere classified correspond to codes representing documented conditions other than those specified in *ICD-10-CM*. Think of NEC in the index as meaning other or other specified.

Example of NEC **Aberrant** (congenital)—see also Malposition, congenital
　　　– artery (peripheral) **Q27.8**
　　　　– basilar NEC **Q28.1**

　　　Q28.1 Other malformations of precerebral vessels
　　　Congenital malformation of precerebral vessels NOS
　　　Congenital precerebral aneurysm (nonruptured)

The abbreviation NOS for not otherwise specified corresponds to unspecified codes representing conditions for which documentation does not support a more specific code selection.

Example of NOS **Birth**
　　　– compression during NOS **P15.9**
　　　P15.9 Birth injury, unspecified

When an unspecified code is not provided in a category, the "other" code option represents both other and unspecified.

The alphabetic index also contains the instructions to "see" and "see also." The instruction "see" will be followed by another term that should be referenced in the index to arrive at the correct code. A "see also" instruction indicates that there is another main term that may provide additional alphabetic index entries related to the condition. It is not necessary to follow the see also note when the original main term provides the necessary code.

Examples   **Abandonment**—see Maltreatment
　　　Abnormal, abnormality, abnormalities—see also Anomaly

It is necessary to follow the instruction to "see Maltreatment" in the first example above. However, if the abnormality to be reported is represented in the subterms of the second example, the "see also Anomaly" instruction can be disregarded.

The instruction "see also" is used to guide selection of the correct column in the neoplasm table and to use of the table of drugs and chemicals for adverse effect, poisoning, underdosing, or toxic effects of drugs or chemicals. These tables are important references to code selection but, as with the alphabetic index, the tabular list remains the final step in code selection.

The neoplasm table lists the codes or code subcategories for neoplasms by anatomical site. For each site, 6 columns provide for selection by type of neoplasm: malignant primary, malignant secondary, carcinoma in situ, benign, uncertain behavior, or unspecified behavior. The alphabetic index provides the "see also" instructions referencing the correct column for the morphological varieties of neoplasms.

Example   Diagnosis documented is neuroblastoma of right adrenal gland

> Notable change from *ICD-9-CM:* The alphabetic index in *ICD-10-CM* does not include morphology codes. Some code descriptors do still include morphology (eg, malignant melanoma).

Alphabetic index   **Neuroblastoma**
– olfactory **C30.0**
– specified site—see Neoplasm, malignant, by site

Neoplasm table   Site—Adrenal, gland
Malignant column **C74.9-**

Tabular list   **C74.9** Malignant neoplasm of unspecified part of adrenal gland
C74.90 Malignant neoplasm of unspecified part of unspecified adrenal gland
C74.91 Malignant neoplasm of unspecified part of right adrenal gland
C74.92 Malignant neoplasm of unspecified part of left adrenal gland

The alphabetic index provides direction to the malignant column of the neoplasm table. The neoplasm table provides the subcategory for the code but indicates the code is incomplete with a dash following the code number, **C74.9-**. The tabular list provides the choices for complete code selection, with **C74.91** representing the right adrenal gland. (Further documentation of the site as capsule, cortex, or medulla of the adrenal gland would have resulted in a more specific code in this example.)

Similarly, the table of drugs and chemicals provides a list of codes or subcategories of codes by substance with columns indicating accidental poisoning, intentional self-harm poisoning, poisoning by assault, undetermined poisoning, adverse effect, and underdosing.

Example   Documentation states overdose of amoxicillin due to parent error in administering dose

Alphabetic index   **Overdose, overdosage (drug)**—see table of drugs and chemicals, by drug, poisoning

Table of drugs   Drug—Amoxicillin, Poisoning, accidental **T36.0X1**

Tabular list   **T36 Poisoning by, adverse effect of and underdosing of systemic antibiotics**

The appropriate seventh character is to be added to each code from category **T36.**
- **A**—initial encounter
- **D**—subsequent encounter
- **S**—sequela

T36.0X Poisoning by, adverse effect of and underdosing of penicillins

T36.0X1 Poisoning by penicillins, accidental (unintentional)

Note that the index listing for overdose refers to the table of drugs and chemicals with a "see" instruction. The table of drugs and chemicals provides subcategory **T36.0X1** but does not provide a complete code. The tabular list instructions at category **T36** note that a seventh character must be added to indicate the type of encounter as initial, subsequent, or sequela to the poisoning. Selection of a code from the table alone would result in an invalid code.

> **Check it out:** To further your understanding of how the table of drugs and chemicals is used, look up amoxicillin and find the code for an adverse effect associated with this drug.

The final part of the alphabetic index is the external cause of injuries index. External cause codes are intended to provide data for injury research and evaluation of injury prevention strategies. These codes capture the cause, intent, place of occurrence, activity of the patient at the time of the event, and patient status (eg, civilian, military). The selection of the appropriate external cause code is guided by the alphabetic index of external causes and by inclusion and exclusion notes in the tabular list. These codes are not required when the external cause is included in the code for the related condition, as in our example above for accidental poisoning by overdosing of ampicillin.

Example   Documentation states this is the initial encounter with a patient who was injured due to being run over by a giraffe while cleaning its pen at the zoo. Codes for injuries sustained would be reported first followed by external cause codes.

External cause of injuries index   **Run over** (accidentally) (by)
– animal (not being ridden) NEC **W55.89**

Tabular list   **W55 Contact with other mammals**

The appropriate seventh character is to be added to each code from category **W55.**
- **A**—initial encounter
- **D**—subsequent encounter
- **S**—sequela

W55.89 Other contact with other mammals

The external cause of injury index leads us to subcategory **W55.89.** The tabular list provides instruction that a seventh character is required to complete this code (ie, **W55.89XA**). The external cause of injury index would be further consulted to locate codes for place of occurrence, activity, and status at the time of the accident based on the documentation in this example.

Guidelines and Conventions of the Tabular List

The tabular list is a chronological listing of *ICD-10* codes composed of 21 chapters based on body system or condition. Chapters are further divided into blocks for ease of reference. These chapters will each be explored in this text but, like the alphabetic index, there are some guidelines and conventions for use of the tabular list that should first be noted.

The structure of the tabular list is an indented listing of categories, subcategories, and codes. Only codes are reported. Categories are the 3-character main entries of the tabular list. Some codes are complete at the 3-character category level. Others will be complete at the fourth or fifth character subcategory, while many codes are composed of 6 or 7 characters. It is important to note instructions at the chapter, block, category, and subcategory levels to achieve a complete code.

Example

Chapter instructions

Chapter 16
Certain conditions originating in the perinatal period (P00-P96)
Note: Codes from this chapter are for use on newborn records only, never on maternal records.
Includes: conditions that have their origin in the fetal or perinatal period (before birth through the first 28 days after birth) even if morbidity occurs later
Excludes 2
congenital malformations, deformations, and chromosomal abnormalities **(Q00-Q99)**
endocrine, nutritional, and metabolic diseases **(E00-E88)**
injury, poisoning, and certain other consequences of external causes **(S00-T88)**
neoplasms **(C00-D49)**
tetanus neonatorum **(A33)**

Note that chapter-level instructions provide information on conditions reported or not reported with codes in the entire chapter. Particularly this chapter does not include any condition based on information in the maternal records and applies only to conditions originating in the fetal or perinatal period.

Block level

Newborn affected by maternal factors and by complications of pregnancy, labor, and delivery (P00-P04)
Note: These codes are for use when the listed maternal conditions are specified as the cause of confirmed morbidity or potential morbidity that have their origin in the perinatal period (before birth through the first 28 days after birth). Codes from these categories are also for use for newborns who are suspected of

having an abnormal condition resulting from exposure from the mother or the birth process but without signs or symptoms, and after examination and observation, is found not to exist. These codes may be used even if treatment is begun for a suspected condition that is ruled out.

The block level instructions apply to all codes in the block, as here where the above instruction applies to codes in the **P00** through **P04** range. Note that codes in this block are reported even when the suspected condition resulting from exposure from the mother or the birth process is not confirmed after examination and observation.

Category level

P00 Newborn (suspected to be) affected by maternal conditions that may be unrelated to present pregnancy

Code first any current condition in newborn

Excludes 2

newborn (suspected to be) affected by maternal complications of pregnancy **(P01.-)**

newborn affected by maternal endocrine and metabolic disorders **(P70-P74)**

newborn affected by noxious substances transmitted via placenta or breast milk **(P04.-)**

Instructions at the category level often advise on sequencing of codes, reporting of additional codes, and conditions included or not included in the category.

Subcategory and/or code level

P00.0 Newborn (suspected to be) affected by maternal hypertensive disorders

Newborn (suspected to be) affected by maternal conditions classifiable to **O10-O11, O13-O16**

At the subcategory and code level, instructions often provide further definition of what conditions are classified there. This is also where instruction to report additional codes for related or underlying conditions is often found.

Before looking further at types of instructional notes used in the tabular list, a review of abbreviations and punctuation will be helpful. As in the alphabetic index, parentheses in the tabular list enclose nonessential modifiers that may or may not be present in the documentation without affecting the code selection. Parentheses are also used with references to codes or code ranges from other categories.

Examples   **F98.0** Enuresis not due to a substance or known physiological condition

Enuresis (primary) (secondary) of nonorganic origin

H53.5 Color vision deficiencies

Color blindness

Excludes 2

day blindness **(H53.11)**

Brackets used in the tabular list enclose synonyms, alternative wording, or explanatory phrases.

Example   **F93.0** Separation anxiety disorder of childhood
                Excludes 2
                mood [affective] disorders **(F30-F39)**

A colon is used in the tabular list after a phrase that needs one or more modifiers following the colon to make it complete as in the example for juvenile osteochondrosis below. The terms listed after "Osteochondrosis (juvenile) of:" provide complete information on the affected site of the pelvis.

Example   **M91.0** Juvenile osteochondrosis of pelvis
                Osteochondrosis (juvenile) of:
                      acetabulum
                      iliac crest [Buchanan]
                      ischiopubic synchondrosis [van Neck]

As in the alphabetic index, the abbreviation NEC is used to indicate other or other specified. This applies when documentation includes specific information that is not identified in *ICD-10-CM* codes.

Example   **P24.80** Other neonatal aspiration without respiratory symptoms
                Neonatal aspiration NEC

The abbreviation NOS indicates unspecified and applies when documentation does not support selection of a more specific code. In *ICD-10-CM*, the same code may sometimes be used to report both other specified and unspecified conditions.

Example   **Q38.6** Other congenital malformations of mouth
                Congenital malformation of mouth NOS

The tabular list includes several instructional notes to guide correct code selection. An includes note provides a list of terms that may include synonyms for the condition reported with a category or code or an informative phrase regarding conditions included. The lists are not exhaustive, and additional terms may be referenced in the alphabetic index.

Examples   **J02** Acute pharyngitis
                Includes: acute sore throat
                P04 Newborn (suspected to be) affected by noxious substances
                      transmitted via placenta or breast milk
                Includes: nonteratogenic effects of substances transmitted via placenta

Codes and categories may also contain lists of synonyms and included conditions without the includes note but with the same intent of providing examples of included conditions. These are called inclusion terms.

Example   **J02.0** Streptococcal pharyngitis
                Septic pharyngitis
                Streptococcal sore throat

Exclusion terms come in 2 forms in *ICD-10-CM*. The tabular list contains excludes 1 and excludes 2 notes. An excludes 1 note means the conditions in the note are not coded here. Codes in an excludes 1 note are not reported in conjunction with the codes to which the note is applied. For instance, congenital conditions are not reported in conjunction with codes reporting the same condition as acquired.

Example   **Q03** Congenital hydrocephalus
Includes: hydrocephalus in newborn
Excludes 1
Arnold-Chiari syndrome, type II **(Q07.0-)**
acquired hydrocephalus **(G91.-)**
hydrocephalus due to congenital toxoplasmosis **(P37.1)**
hydrocephalus with spina bifida **(Q05.0-Q05.4)**

An excludes 2 note is less restrictive. Interpret this to mean "not included here." This note indicates that conditions listed are not represented by this code or category but may be reported in addition to the code or codes when both conditions are present. For instance, a patient may have both acute and chronic infection at the same encounter with both conditions reported.

Example   **J31.1** Chronic nasopharyngitis
Excludes 2: acute nasopharyngitis **(J00)**

> Check it out: To further review the excludes 1 and excludes 2 notes, look up code **J00** in the tabular list and review the exclusion notes associated with this category.

The tabular list also provides sequencing instructions for some codes. These often include conditions that are or may have manifestations.

Examples   **J12 Viral pneumonia, not elsewhere classified**
Code first associated influenza, if applicable **(J09.X1, J10.0-, J11.0-)**
J12.1 Respiratory syncytial virus pneumonia
Q87 Other specified congenital malformation syndromes affecting multiple systems
Use additional code(s) to identify all associated manifestations
J10.83 Influenza due to other identified influenza virus with otitis media
Use additional code for any associated perforated tympanic membrane **(H72.-)**

In the first example, the "code first" instruction advises that pneumonia associated with influenza is reported secondarily to the code for the influenza. The second example shows a "use additional code(s)" note indicating that the **Q87** code is sequenced first and followed by codes for all associated manifestations. This illustrates the sequencing rule that manifestations are always reported secondarily to the code for the underlying condition (etiology). The "use additional code(s)" note in the third example shows that this convention may be used for complications and other code sequencing purposes.

Another sequencing note in the tabular list will likely seldom apply to pediatric conditions as it appears infrequently in the list. "Code, if applicable, any causal condition first" notes indicate that this code may be assigned as a principal diagnosis when the causal condition is unknown or not applicable. If a causal condition is known, then the code for that condition should be sequenced as the principal or first-listed diagnosis. These notes apply to conditions such as sequela of a cerebrovascular accident or difficulties with micturition due to enlarged prostate.

The tabular list instruction "code also" does not give sequencing direction. It instructs that multiple conditions may be required to fully describe a condition but leaves sequencing to the discretion of the physician based on the focus of the encounter.

>**M08 Juvenile arthritis**
>
>**Code also** any associated underlying condition, such as
>
>>regional enteritis [Crohn disease] **(K50.-)**
>>
>>ulcerative colitis **(K51.-)**

General Guidelines for Code Selection

Code selection in *ICD-10-CM* begins with the use of alphabetic index and then the tabular list. The primary guideline to remember is that the tabular list is the end point for code selection. Codes selected from the alphabetic index alone may be incomplete in either the code structure or the ability to fully describe the condition without reporting of additional codes as instructed by the tabular list.

To identify diagnoses, symptoms, conditions, problems, complaints, or other reasons for the encounter/visit, appropriate codes from **A00.0-T88.9** and **Z00-Z99.8** must be reported. Codes for external causes **(V01-Y99)** are never the principle or first-listed diagnosis code. Report external causes codes in addition to codes from **A00.0-T88.9** and **Z00-Z99.8** as indicated.

Report codes for signs and symptoms only when a definitive diagnosis has not been established or the signs and symptoms are not commonly associated with the conditions for which the patient was seen. Unless otherwise directed by *ICD-10-CM* instructions, signs and symptoms that are common to a condition are not separately reported.

There is no time limit on the reporting of sequelae (late effects). Codes for sequelae should be reported as indicated. This may require 2 codes sequenced with first the code representing the nature of the sequela and then a code for the sequela.

>*Examples*
>
>>**L90.5** Scar conditions and fibrosis of skin
>>
>>**T22.351S** Burn of third degree of right shoulder
>>
>>**X12.XXXS** Contact with other hot fluids

Note that the nature of the sequela (scarring) is reported first, with the code for sequela of a burn reported second. This example also includes a third code describing the external cause of the injury that resulted in the sequela. Note that the seventh character on the **X12** code is also an "S," indicating the condition reported is a sequela to an accident involving contact with hot fluids. Codes for place of occurrence, activity, and status were not added because these are only reported at the initial encounter.

The above guidelines do not apply where the code for the sequela is followed by a manifestation code identified in the tabular list and title or the sequela code has been expanded (at the fourth, fifth, or sixth character levels) to include the manifestation(s).

Other few key points from the general guidelines are

- If a condition is stated as both acute (subacute) and chronic and codes for acute and chronic are listed at the same indentation level in the alphabetic index, both codes may be reported for the same encounter.
- When a single code describes more than one condition or a condition and its complication or sequela, report only that code for those conditions.
- Each unique code is reported only once per encounter even if that code represents 2 conditions or the condition is bilateral where *ICD-10-CM* does not provide codes for laterality.
- *ICD-10-CM* provides separate codes for laterality in most conditions where laterality applies. Some categories include a code for bilateral conditions. If a condition is bilateral but only codes for right and left are provided, report codes for both right and left.
- Only report conditions noted as impending or threatened if these subterms are included in the alphabetic listing for the condition. Otherwise, report the underlying condition or symptoms.
- Code a condition as a complication only if the documentation clearly indicates that the condition is a complication. If in doubt, ask the physician or provider for clarification.

These points will be repeated and further clarified in review of chapter-specific guidelines.

> **Check it out:** The *ICD-10-CM Official Guidelines for Coding and Reporting* can be downloaded from the National Center for Health Statistics at **www.cdc.gov/nchs/icd/icd10cm.htm#10update.** While this chapter reviewed the guidelines and conventions, reading Section IA and IB of the official guidelines is recommended.

Review What You Have Learned

1.1 All codes in *ICD-10-CM* are more than 3 characters long.
   A. True
   B. False

1.2 The external cause of injury index is used to find codes for reporting
   A. Cause and intent
   B. Place of occurrence
   C. The activity of the patient at the time of the event
   D. The patient status
   E. All of the above

1.3 Terms found at the same indentation level within the alphabetic index are never reported for the same encounter.
   A. True
   B. False

1.4 The excludes 1 note at code **Q03** (congenital hydrocephalus) indicates that code **P37.1** (hydrocephalus due to congenital toxoplasmosis) may be reported in addition to **Q03**.
   A. True
   B. False

1.5 Code **M48.52A** is a correct code for reporting a collapsed vertebra, not elsewhere classified, cervical region, initial encounter.
   A. True
   B. False

1.6 Which section of *ICD-10-CM* is the final resource used to select a complete diagnosis code for a neoplasm?
   A. Alphabetic index
   B. Neoplasm table
   C. Table of morphology codes
   D. Tabular list
   E. None of the above

1.7 Brackets *are* used in the alphabetic index to enclose synonyms, alternative wording, or explanatory phrases.
   A. True
   B. False

≡ CHAPTER 2 ≡

Certain Infectious and Parasitic Diseases (A00-B99)

Chapter 1 of the *International Classification of Diseases, Tenth Revision, Clinical Modification (ICD-10-CM)* tabular list provides codes for certain infectious and parasitic diseases. This chapter includes most conditions that are generally recognized as communicable or transmittable. It does not include codes for

- Certain localized infections classified in chapters for body systems
- Infectious and parasitic diseases complicating pregnancy, childbirth, and the puerperium
- Influenza and other acute respiratory infections

However, codes from Chapter 1 may be reported in addition to some of these conditions where instructions indicate that an additional code should be used to report the infectious agent.

Chapter 1 also does not include codes for carrier or suspected carrier of infectious disease or for infectious and parasitic diseases specific to the perinatal period. These conditions are identified in an excludes 2 note indicating that they could be reported in addition to codes from Chapter 1 when both conditions are present.

> **Check it out:** To get a better sense of the conditions represented by codes in Chapter 1, look at the 22 blocks for this chapter in the tabular list. Note that *ICD-10-CM* groups infections with a predominantly sexual mode of transmission into one block of codes. Codes in the block **B90-B94** are used to report sequelae of conditions reported with codes **A00-B89**.

The code categories in Chapter 1 range from **A00-B99**. One instruction that applies to this entire chapter of codes is

Use additional code to identify resistance to antimicrobial drugs **(Z16-)**

This instruction should be applied when the documentation states there is drug resistance but the code for the infection does not identify drug resistance.

Examples   **N39.0** Urinary tract infection, site not specified
B96.20 Unspecified *Escherichia coli [E coli]* as the cause of diseases classified elsewhere
Z16.11 Resistance to penicillins

J15.212 Pneumonia due to methicillin-resistant *Staphylococcus aureus*

Note that in the first example, codes **N39.0** and **B96.20** do not include indication of drug resistance, making it necessary to additionally report code **Z16.11** to indicate resistance to penicillins. However, code **J15.212** for pneumonia due to *S aureus* includes "methicillin-resistant" in the description, obviating the need for an additional code.

> **Check it out:** *ICD-10-CM* includes codes for reporting colonization or carrier status for certain conditions. Documentation of a positive screening result in the absence of current infectious process is reported with a code from category **Z22**. If an infectious process, such as pneumonia due to methicillin-resistant *S aureus* (MRSA) is documented in addition to colonization status, a code from category **Z22** may be reported in addition to codes for reporting the infection. Look at codes **Z22.321** and **Z22.322** to see examples for MRSA and methicillin-susceptible *S aureus*.

The first example also illustrates another instruction for reporting infectious conditions. Infections that are classified in chapters other than Chapter 1 and do not specify the organism as part of the infection code will have an instruction to also report a code from one of the following categories:

- **B95** *Streptococcus, Staphylococcus,* and *Enterococcus* as the cause of diseases classified to other chapters
- **B96** Other bacterial agents as the cause of diseases classified elsewhere
- **B97** Viral agents as the cause of diseases classified elsewhere

Because the **N39.0** code for a urinary tract infection did not specify the organism, code **B96.20** is added to indicate *E coli* was documented as the causal organism.

Category or Condition-Specific Guidelines

Section IC of the *ICD-10-CM* guidelines provides chapter-specific guidelines. For Chapter 1, these guidelines provide instruction on reporting of certain infectious diseases. It is important to become familiar with these in order to correctly report the associated conditions.

HIV

HIV is one of the conditions for which there are important guidelines. HIV is reported only when the physician or provider documents that the patient is HIV positive, has an HIV-related illness, or has had an HIV-related illness in the past. Patients for whom documentation states HIV positive or similar indications of HIV without any indication of current or past HIV-related illness should be assigned code **Z21** (asymptomatic human immunodeficiency virus [HIV] infection status).

For patients who may have been exposed to HIV but have not been documented as HIV positive, report code **Z20.6** (contact with and [suspected] exposure to HIV). Use the following codes for screening tests and counseling related to HIV:

Screening
Z11.4 Encounter for screening for human immunodeficiency virus [HIV]
Counseling
Z71.7 Human immunodeficiency virus [HIV] counseling

HIV testing in symptomatic patients should be reported with diagnosis codes for the related symptoms. For patients with high-risk behaviors, also report codes for high-risk behaviors. Code **Z71.7** may be reported for encounters with a patient who returns for test results and receives a negative HIV test result.

A nonconclusive HIV test finding in infants is reported with code **R75** (nonconclusive laboratory evidence of HIV).

> From the guidelines: Once a patient has developed an HIV-related illness, the patient should always be assigned code **B20** on every subsequent admission/encounter. Patients previously diagnosed with any HIV illness **(B20)** should never be assigned code **R75** or **Z21** (asymptomatic HIV infection status).

The alphabetic index lists HIV under the terms Human and HIV with a see also note at HIV, directing to the term "Human" where more subterms are provided. The terms "Acquired," "AIDS" (related complex), and "ARC" (AIDS-related complex) will also lead to the code for HIV. Each term directs that the infection, HIV, is found in the tabular list at **B20**. Below is a copy of code **B20** from the tabular list and its instructions.

B20 Human immunodeficiency virus [HIV] disease

Includes
acquired immune deficiency syndrome [AIDS]
AIDS-related complex [ARC]
HIV infection, symptomatic

Code first
Human immunodeficiency virus [HIV] disease complicating pregnancy, childbirth and the puerperium, if applicable **(O98.7-)**
Use additional code(s) to identify all manifestations of HIV infection

Excludes 1
asymptomatic human immunodeficiency virus [HIV] infection status **(Z21)**
exposure to HIV virus **(Z20.6)**
inconclusive serologic evidence of HIV **(R75)**

The first instruction is an includes note informing of other documented terms that are included in this category. This is followed by the code first note that instructs that HIV disease complicating pregnancy is reported with a combination of a code from category **O98.7-** followed by code **B20**. (Patients with asymptomatic HIV infection status presenting for a health care encounter during pregnancy, childbirth, or the puerperium should receive codes of **O98.7-** and **Z21**.)

The next instruction is to "Use additional code(s)" to report manifestations of HIV infection.

Example   An HIV-positive patient is diagnosed with recurrent HIV-related candidiasis.
B20 Human immunodeficiency virus [HIV] disease
B37.0 Candidal stomatitis

Note that because the candidiasis is noted as HIV-related, code **B20** is sequenced first. If the condition were not documented as HIV-related, code **B20** would be a secondary code.

> From the guidelines: Section IC1a2b—If a patient with HIV disease is admitted for an unrelated condition (such as a traumatic injury), the code for the unrelated condition (eg, the nature of injury code) should be the principal diagnosis. Other diagnoses would be **B20** followed by additional diagnosis codes for all reported HIV-related conditions.

The final instruction is an excludes 1 note indicating the conditions such as asymptomatic HIV status is not reported with codes in this category.

Sepsis

ICD-10-CM guidelines also provide guidance on reporting of sepsis and severe sepsis. Sepsis is reported using codes that identify the underlying systemic infection. If the infectious agent is not specified, code **A41.9** (sepsis, unspecified organism) is assigned. Sepsis may be reported in spite of negative blood cultures when a physician confirms the diagnosis. *ICD-10-CM* does not include a code for urosepsis. This term is considered nonspecific and not equivalent to sepsis. Coders must ask the physician for more information when assigning a code for a condition documented as urosepsis to confirm whether there is septicemia due to a urinary tract infection or a localized infection before coding.

Examples of codes for sepsis
A40.0 Sepsis due to streptococcus, group A
A41.01 Sepsis due to methicillin-susceptible *Staphylococcus aureus*
A41.4 Sepsis due to anaerobes

The codes for sepsis are sequenced first when a patient is admitted with both sepsis and a localized infection (eg, pneumonia, cellulitis). If only the localized infection was present at admission with sepsis developing during the stay, the hospital reports the localized infection first and then the code for sepsis. Sepsis related to noninfectious conditions such as burns may be reported first if it is the condition chiefly responsible for hospital admission, otherwise it is reported after the code for a noninfectious condition meeting the definition of principal condition for admission.

Severe sepsis is reported when documentation indicates organ dysfunction associated with sepsis. Severe sepsis is not reported when documentation indicates that organ failure is unrelated to sepsis. Codes for reporting severe sepsis include

R65.20 Severe sepsis without septic shock
R65.21 Severe sepsis with septic shock

The code for the underlying infection is sequenced before the code for severe sepsis. Additional codes should be reported to indicate the type of organ failure.

Example: A patient admitted with sepsis due to meningococcal meningitis develops related kidney failure.

A39.0 Meningococcal meningitis
R65.20 Severe sepsis without septic shock
N17.9 Acute kidney failure, unspecified

When the underlying infection is documented as due to a procedure, see codes in categories **T80-T88** for complications of surgical and medical care such as

T81.4- Infection following a procedure
T80.2- Infections following infusion, transfusion and therapeutic injection
T88.0- Infection following immunization

Note that the documentation must state a relationship between the infection and the procedure for codes in this category to be reported. Sepsis or severe sepsis would be reported in addition to these codes as indicated. Additional codes from categories **Y62-Y82** may be reported to indicate complications of medical care or medical devices.

> **Check it out:** To further understand the categorizations of sepsis, look up the term "sepsis" in the alphabetic index and note the subterms, including "due to" and "newborn," and the levels of specificity that follow.

Bacterial sepsis of a newborn, including congenital sepsis, is reported with codes from Chapter 16 for certain conditions originating in the perinatal period. Newborn sepsis is reported with codes from category **P36.** Most of the codes in this category include the infectious agent in the code description, including streptococci, staphylococci, *E coli,* and anaerobes. However, code **P36.8** (other bacterial sepsis of newborn) is nonspecific and requires the addition of a code from category **B96** (other bacterial agents as the cause of diseases classified elsewhere) to provide complete reporting.

Examples: A 20-day-old infant is diagnosed with sepsis due to streptococcus B.
P36.0 Sepsis of newborn due to streptococcus, group B

A 20-day-old infant is diagnosed with sepsis due to *Pseudomonas aeruginosa*.
P36.8 Other bacterial sepsis of newborn
B96.5 *Pseudomonas (aeruginosa) (mallei) (pseudomallei)* as the cause of diseases classified elsewhere

Note that only code **P36.0** is required for the first example because the code includes the organism. Two codes are required in the second example to specify the condition and the organism. If applicable, use additional codes to identify severe sepsis **(R65.2-)** and any associated acute organ dysfunction.

> Category **P36** is found in Chapter 16, which includes conditions that have their origin in the fetal or perinatal period (before birth through the first 28 days after birth) even if morbidity occurs later.

Coding Scenarios

A 3-month-old female is brought to the emergency department with fever and upper respiratory symptoms. Radiological examination shows pneumonia. The physician diagnoses pneumonia due to respiratory syncytial virus.

J12.1 Respiratory syncytial virus pneumonia

> From the guidelines: Section IB9—Assign only the combination code when that code fully identifies the diagnostic conditions involved or when the alphabetic index so directs.

A 12-year-old boy is seen in the office for complaints of fever, sore throat, and general malaise for the last 4 days. Examination reveals swollen glands. Monospot and complete blood cell count are positive. The physician diagnoses Epstein-Barr virus mononucleosis.

B27.00 Gammaherpesviral mononucleosis without complication

> From the guidelines: Section IB5—Signs and symptoms that are associated routinely with a disease process should not be assigned as additional codes, unless otherwise instructed by the classification. Because the symptoms of fever, sore throat, malaise, and swollen glands are common to mononucleosis, these are not reported separately or as complications.

A 7-year-old presents to the physician's office with fever, sore throat, and a rash on his chest and neck that appeared 2 days ago. Rapid streptococcal testing is positive. Examination also reveals otitis media in the right ear. Final diagnosis is scarlet fever with streptococcal pharyngitis complicated by otitis media.

A38.0 Scarlet fever with otitis media
J02.0 Streptococcal pharyngitis

> Check it out: Look at the tabular list notes for codes **A38.0** and **J02.0**. What type of excludes note is presented for each? Which type of excludes note indicates that a condition is not reported with a code or category but may be additionally reported when present? (Hint: Section IA12b in the guidelines)

A child has developed a bloodstream infection in the hospital. The pediatric infectious disease specialist previously evaluated the patient and ordered cultures. On this subsequent visit, she documents coagulase-negative staphylococcal sepsis due to an umbilical catheter.

> **T80.211D** Bloodstream infection due to central venous catheter, subsequent encounter
>
> **A41.1** Sepsis due to other specified staphylococcus

> Check it out: Look at block **T80-T88** in the tabular list and you will find the instruction, "Use additional code to identify devices involved and details of circumstances **(Y62-Y82).**" Code **T80.211D** includes the central venous catheter device, and we have no further details of circumstances to report. To fully report the diagnoses for this scenario, one would need to query the physician for more information, such as failure of sterile precautions.

Review What You Have Learned

2.1 When reporting severe sepsis, you should first code the related organ failure.
   A. True
   B. False

2.2 A 7-week-old child is admitted with a diagnosis of sepsis due to streptococcus group B. What codes should be reported?
   A. **P36.0**   Sepsis of newborn due to streptococcus, group B
   B. **P36.0**   Sepsis of newborn due to streptococcus, group B
      R65.20   Severe sepsis without septic shock
   C. **A40.1**   Sepsis due to streptococcus, group B
   D. **A41.9**   Sepsis, unspecified organism
   E. **B95.1**   Streptococcus, group B, as the cause of diseases classified elsewhere

2.3 A 16-year-old female presents to her physician's office for a well visit and asks for contraceptives because she has been sexually active and is concerned about becoming pregnant. In counseling the patient about sexual activity and sexually transmitted infections, the physician recommends and the patient request HIV testing. A rapid test kit is negative for HIV. What is the appropriate diagnosis code for the HIV test?
   A. **Z71.7**   Human immunodeficiency virus [HIV] counseling
   B. **B20**   Human immunodeficiency virus [HIV] disease
   C. **Z11.4**   Encounter for screening for human immunodeficiency virus [HIV]
   D. **Z11.51**   Encounter for screening for human papillomavirus (HPV)

2.4 Codes included in an excludes 2 note are never reported with the codes to which the note applies.
   A. True
   B. False

2.5 Category **Z16** codes could be reported to show resistance to antimicrobial drugs in addition to which of the following codes?
   A. **A41.51**   Sepsis due to *Escherichia coli [E. coli]*
   B. **B95.7**   Other staphylococcus as the cause of diseases classified elsewhere
   C. **B95.2**   Enterococcus as the cause of diseases classified elsewhere
   D. All of the above

2.6 A child is admitted with pneumonia due to infection by respiratory syncytial virus (RSV). A code identifying infection by RSV must be reported in addition to code **J12.1** (RSV pneumonia).
   A. True
   B. False

≡ CHAPTER 3 ≡

Neoplasms (C00-D49)

*I*n *International Classification of Diseases, Tenth Revision, Clinical Modification (ICD-10-CM)*, all malignant and most benign neoplasms are classified in Chapter 2 of the tabular list with code categories of **C00-D49.** Neoplasms are classified first by anatomical site and then by behavior. As noted in the Chapter 1 review of the alphabetic index for those neoplasms documented with histology, such as osteosarcoma, the alphabetic index will provide direction to the correct behavior column in the table of neoplasms. The table of neoplasms is used to locate the code category based on site and behavior. Final code selection is made from the tabular list, where additional instructions and/or code characters may be found.

Table 3-1 displays the first 3 rows of the table of neoplasms, showing the listing of sites in the first column followed by columns for each of the behaviors. The first column begins with an unspecified neoplasm and then proceeds with an alphabetic listing of sites.

Table 3-1. Table of Neoplasms Example

	Malignant Primary	Malignant Secondary	Carcinoma in situ	Benign	Uncertain Behavior	Unspecified Behavior
Neoplasm, neoplastic	C80.1	C79.9	D09.9	D36.9	D48.9	D49.9
abdomen, abdominal	C76.2	C79.8-	D09.8	D36.7	D48.7	D49.89

> From the guidelines: Section IC2k—Code **C80.1** (malignant [primary] neoplasm, unspecified) equates to cancer, unspecified. This code should only be used when no determination can be made as to the primary site of a malignancy. This code should rarely be used in the inpatient setting.

The 6 behavior categories are often included in the description of the neoplasm (eg, benign fibroadenoma of the breast). It is important to distinguish between neoplasms of uncertain behavior and of unspecified behavior. The *ICD-10-CM* guidelines do not provide definitions for these terms. However, the definition for neoplasms of uncertain behavior may be carried over from *ICD-9-CM*.

Uncertain behavior—certain histomorphologically well-defined neoplasms, the subsequent behavior of which cannot be predicted from the present appearance.

Neoplasms of unspecified behavior should be viewed in the same manner as other unspecified codes. Codes titled "unspecified" are for use when the information in the medical record is insufficient to assign a more specific code (not otherwise specified [NOS]). These codes would apply to documentation such as growth NOS, neoplasm NOS, new growth NOS, or tumor NOS. Documentation of a mass should not be reported with codes for neoplasms unless further documentation supports classification as a neoplasm (eg, documentation of malignant mass).

> From the guidelines: Section IC2—To properly code a neoplasm it is necessary to determine from the record if the neoplasm is benign, in situ, malignant, or of uncertain histologic behavior. If malignant, any secondary (metastatic) sites should also be determined.

It is important to differentiate between primary and secondary neoplasms. Reporting of multiple neoplasms of noncontiguous sites should be based on documentation of the status of each as different primaries or primary and secondary (ie, metastatic) neoplasms. In those cases where the patient has advanced metastatic disease and no known primary or secondary sites are specified, code **C80.0** (disseminated malignant neoplasm, unspecified) is reported. Code **C80.0** should not be used in place of assigning codes for a known primary site and all known secondary sites.

A malignant neoplasm of a transplanted organ should be coded as a complication of the transplant. A code from category **T86.-** (complications of transplanted organs and tissue) would be reported followed by code **C80.2** (malignant neoplasm associated with transplanted organ) and the code for the specific malignancy.

All malignant neoplasms, whether functionally active or not, are classified in Chapter 2. Appropriate codes in Chapter 4 (ie, **E05.8, E07.0, E16-E31,** and **E34.-**) may be used as additional codes to indicate either functional activity by neoplasms and ectopic endocrine tissue or hyperfunction and hypofunction of endocrine glands associated with neoplasms and other conditions classified elsewhere. Malignant neoplasms of ectopic tissue are reported with the code for the site of origin mentioned.

Codes for the most common pediatric cancer are not referenced in the table of neoplasms. The codes for leukemia are indexed in the alphabetic index under "leukemia." The codes for leukemia specify whether the patient has or has not achieved remission or is in relapse. If it is unclear from the documentation whether the patient has achieved remission, the physician should be asked to confirm.

Example

Alphabetic index	Leukemia, leukemic **C95.9-**
	– acute lymphoblastic **C91.0-**
Tabular list	**C91 Lymphoid leukemia**
	Excludes 1: personal history of leukemia **(Z85.6)**
	C91.0 Acute lymphoblastic leukemia [ALL]
	Note: Code **C91.0** should only be used for T-cell and B-cell precursor leukemia.

C91.00 Acute lymphoblastic leukemia not having achieved remission
Acute lymphoblastic leukemia with failed remission
Acute lymphoblastic leukemia NOS
C91.01 Acute lymphoblastic leukemia, in remission
C91.02 Acute lymphoblastic leukemia, in relapse

This example provides illustration of the referenced term in the alphabetic index and the necessary instructions and fifth characters for the codes found in the tabular list. Note the exclusion of personal history of leukemia (code **Z85.6**). There is also a note at subcategory **C91.0** advising that codes in this subcategory are only for reporting the 2 common subtypes of acute lymphoblastic leukemia (T-cell and B-cell precursor leukemia). As previously noted, fifth characters are added to designate remission status.

As with codes for leukemia, the alphabetic index is the place to start in finding codes for lymphoma. However, lymphoma codes do not include remission status. Instead these codes are specific to body areas as in the example below for Burkitt lymphoma.

C83.70	Burkitt lymphoma, unspecified site
C83.71	Burkitt lymphoma, lymph nodes of head, face, and neck
C83.72	Burkitt lymphoma, intrathoracic lymph nodes
C83.73	Burkitt lymphoma, intra-abdominal lymph nodes
C83.74	Burkitt lymphoma, lymph nodes of axilla and upper limb
C83.75	Burkitt lymphoma, lymph nodes of inguinal region and lower limb
C83.76	Burkitt lymphoma, intrapelvic lymph nodes
C83.77	Burkitt lymphoma, spleen
C83.78	Burkitt lymphoma, lymph nodes of multiple sites
C83.79	Burkitt lymphoma, extranodal and solid organ sites

Many other childhood neoplasms are best referenced in the alphabetic index. Here are some of the instructions that you will find in the alphabetic index to guide correct code selection. Note the terms that may be classified in more than one of the 6 behavior categories.

Astrocytoma—specified site, see Neoplasm, malignant, by site
    unspecified site **C71.9**
   subependymal, unspecified **D43.2**
   subependymal, giant cell, specified site—see Neoplasm, uncertain behavior, by site

Ependymoma—anaplastic of specified site—see Neoplasm, malignant, by site
   anaplastic, unspecified site **C71.9**
     benign, specified site—see Neoplasm, benign, by site
     benign, unspecified site **D33.2**
   myxopapillary, unspecified site **D43.2**
     specified site—see Neoplasm, uncertain behavior, by site
   papillary, unspecified site **D43.2**
     specified site—see Neoplasm, uncertain behavior, by site

Germ cell—see also Neoplasm, malignant, by site

Glioma—astrocytic, specified site—see Neoplasm, malignant, by site
　　　　unspecified site **C71.9**
　　　mixed, specified site—see Neoplasm, malignant, by site
　　　　unspecified site **C71.9**
　　　nose **Q30.8**
　　　subependymal, specified site—see Neoplasm, uncertain behavior, by site
　　　　unspecified site **D43.2**
Glioblastoma (multiforme) specified site—see Neoplasm, malignant, by site
　　　unspecified site **C71.9**
Hepatoblastoma **C22.2**
Melanoma—skin, see Melanoma, skin, by site or Melanoma, in situ, by site
　　　juvenile—see Nevus
　　　malignant of soft parts other than skin—see Neoplasm, connective
　　　　tissue, malignant
　　　metastatic—see **C79.8-**
　　　spindle cell—with epitheloid, mixed or superficial spreading—
　　　　see Melanoma, skin, by site
　　　type A or B **C69.4-**
Medulloblastoma—desmoplastic **C71.6**
　　　specified site—see Neoplasm, malignant, by site
　　　unspecified site **C71.6**
Neuroblastoma—olfactory **C30.0**
　　　specified site—see Neoplasm, malignant, by site
　　　unspecified site **C74.90**
Neuroectodermal (peripheral)—see Neoplasm, malignant, by site
　　　primitive, specified site—see Neoplasm, malignant, by site
　　　　primitive, unspecified site **C71.9**
Osteosarcoma (any form)—see Neoplasm, bone, malignant
Rhabdomyosarcoma (any type)—see Neoplasm, connective tissue, malignant
Retinoblastoma—differentiated or undifferentiated **C69.2-**
Sarcoma—see also Neoplasm, connective tissue, malignant
　　　Ewing's—see Neoplasm, bone, malignant
Wilms tumor **C64-**

Treatment of Malignancy

Encounters and treatment directed at a malignancy are reported with a diagnosis code for the malignancy except when the encounter is solely for chemotherapy, immunotherapy, or radiation therapy. When primary and secondary malignancies are present but treatment is directed at the secondary malignancy, report the secondary malignancy first followed by the code for the primary malignancy. When a primary malignancy is documented as no longer present (eg, surgically excised, eradicated) with no evidence of continued presence or treatment, the history of the malignant neoplasm is reported with a code from category **Z85** (personal history of neoplasm).

> From the guidelines: Section IC2m—When a primary malignancy has been excised but further treatment, such as an additional surgery for the malignancy, radiation therapy, or chemotherapy, is directed to that site, the primary malignancy code should be used until treatment is completed.

Codes in category **Z51** are reported first for encounters solely for antineoplastic treatments, including radiation therapy, chemotherapy, and immunotherapy. A secondary diagnosis code indicating the condition being treated is also reported.

Z51 Encounter for other aftercare
    Code also condition requiring care
    Excludes 1: follow-up examination after treatment **(Z08-Z09)**
        Z51.0 Encounter for antineoplastic radiation therapy
        Z51.1 Encounter for antineoplastic chemotherapy and immunotherapy
    Excludes 2: encounter for chemotherapy and immunotherapy for non-neoplastic condition—code to condition
        Z51.11 Encounter for antineoplastic chemotherapy
        Z51.12 Encounter for antineoplastic immunotherapy

The code also note for category **Z51** provides the instruction to report both the **Z51** code and a code reporting the condition requiring care but does not give sequencing direction. As previously noted, the **Z51** is reported first when an encounter is solely for the purpose of radiation, chemotherapy, or immunotherapy. When a patient undergoes surgical resection of a neoplasm followed by chemotherapy or radiation therapy at the same encounter, the code for the neoplasm is reported first followed by the code for the treatment. Codes in category **Z51** are reported only for current episodes of treatment and not for follow-up as indicated by the excludes 1 note excluding follow-up codes **Z08-Z09**. It is important to also see the excludes 2 note at subcategory **Z51.1**, indicating that chemotherapy or immunotherapy directed at non-neoplastic conditions should be reported with a code for the condition being treated. Codes in subcategory **Z51.1** are reported only for antineoplastic treatment. Codes for complications occurring in conjunction with an antineoplastic treatment, such as uncontrolled nausea and vomiting, are reported in addition to the code for the treatment.

When an encounter is for management of a complication associated with a neoplasm and the treatment is only for the complication, the complication is coded first, followed by the appropriate code(s) for the neoplasm. The exception to this guidance is anemia due to malignancy, which is reported secondary to the code for the neoplasm.

Examples
    K12.31 Oral mucositis (ulcerative) due to antineoplastic therapy
    C49.0 Malignant neoplasm of connective and soft tissue of head, face, and neck

Y84.2 Radiological procedure and radiotherapy as the cause of abnormal reaction of the patient, or of later complication, without mention of misadventure at the time of the procedure
C91.00 Acute lymphoblastic leukemia not having achieved remission

D63.0 Anemia in neoplastic disease

> From the guidelines: Section IC2c1—When the admission/encounter is for management of an anemia associated with the malignancy, and the treatment is only for anemia, the appropriate code for the malignancy is sequenced as the principal or first-listed diagnosis followed by code **D63.0** (anemia in neoplastic disease).

When an encounter is solely for management or treatment of anemia associated with chemotherapy or immunotherapy, the encounter is reported with a code for the anemia followed by codes for the neoplasm treated and the adverse effect of the treatment. Codes for reporting anemia due to antineoplastic treatment are found in categories **D60–D64**.

Examples

D64.81 Anemia due to antineoplastic chemotherapy
D61.1 Drug-induced aplastic anemia
D61.810 Antineoplastic chemotherapy induced pancytopenia

Each of these codes would be reported first and followed by codes for the neoplasm and a code for the adverse effect.

Example

D64.81 Anemia due to antineoplastic chemotherapy
C91.00 Acute lymphoblastic leukemia not having achieved remission
T45.1X5A Adverse effect of antineoplastic and immunosuppressive drugs

An encounter solely addressing anemia due to radiation therapy is also reported with a code for the anemia followed by codes for the neoplasm treated and code **Y84.2** indicating the adverse effect of radiation therapy.

D61.2 Aplastic anemia due to other external agents
C49.0 Malignant neoplasm of connective and soft tissue of head, face, and neck
Y84.2 Radiological procedure and radiotherapy as the cause of abnormal reaction of the patient, or of later complication, without mention of misadventure at the time of the procedure

Pain associated with a neoplasm is reported with code **G89.3** (neoplasm-related pain [acute] [chronic]). This code may be reported first when the main reason for an encounter is the management or treatment of neoplasm-related pain. The code for the neoplasm would also be reported. Code **G89.3** may also be a secondary diagnosis to the code for treatment of a neoplasm when documented as an additional condition. It is not necessary to also report a site-specific pain code when reporting **G89.3**.

For treatment directed at a pathological fracture due to a neoplasm, report first a code from category **M84.5** (pathological fracture in neoplastic disease). Codes in category **M84.5** must include a seventh character indicating the type of encounter as initial, subsequent, or addressing a sequela. When the focus of an encounter is treatment of the neoplasm with an associated pathological fracture, report first the code for the neoplasm followed by the appropriate code for the fracture.

Follow-up and Surveillance

Encounters with patients seen in follow-up after completion of treatment for malignant neoplasm may be reported with codes for follow-up examination and history of malignant neoplasm. Code **Z08** is specific to reporting follow-up after completed treatment for malignant neoplasm.

> **Z08** Encounter for follow-up examination after completed treatment for malignant neoplasm
> Medical surveillance following completed treatment
> Use additional code to identify any acquired absence of organs **(Z90.-)**
> Use additional code to identify the personal history of malignant neoplasm **(Z85.-)**
> **Excludes 1:** aftercare following medical care **(Z43-Z49, Z51)**

Note that follow-up care is not aftercare, which would include situations when the initial treatment of a disease has been performed and the patient requires continued care during the healing or recovery phase, or for the long-term consequences of the disease. Aftercare codes describe services such as chemotherapy, attention to vascular devices, and care following bone marrow transplant. Follow-up care codes are associated with surveillance after completed treatment of a condition.

Coding Scenarios

A child is diagnosed with anaplastic astrocytoma involving the frontal and temporal lobes.

> **C71.8** Malignant neoplasm of overlapping sites of brain

> From the guidelines: Section IC2—A primary malignant neoplasm that overlaps 2 or more contiguous (next to each other) sites should be classified to the subcategory/code .8 (overlapping lesion), unless the combination is specifically indexed elsewhere. For multiple neoplasms of the same site that are not contiguous, such as tumors in different quadrants of the same breast, codes for each site should be assigned.

A child receiving chemotherapy for acute lymphoblastic leukemia with failed remission develops a related complication of dehydration due to nausea and vomiting. Intravenous hydration is provided in addition to the chemotherapy.

Z51.11 Encounter for antineoplastic chemotherapy
C91.00 Acute lymphoblastic leukemia not having achieved remission
E86.0 Dehydration
R11.2 Nausea with vomiting, unspecified

> From the guidelines: Section IC2e3—When a patient is admitted for the purpose of radiotherapy, immunotherapy, or chemotherapy and develops complications such as uncontrolled nausea and vomiting or dehydration, the principal or first-listed diagnosis is **Z51.0** (encounter for antineoplastic radiation therapy), **Z51.11** (encounter for antineoplastic chemotherapy), or **Z51.12** (encounter for antineoplastic immunotherapy) followed by any codes for the complications.

A 17-year-old who completed treatment for leukemia 7 years ago with complete remission is seen for concerns of flu-like symptoms for about a week. The physician diagnoses an upper respiratory infection with history of leukemia.

J06.9 Acute upper respiratory infection, unspecified
Z85.6 Personal history of leukemia

> From the guidelines: Section IC2d—When a primary malignancy has been previously excised or eradicated from its site and there is no further treatment directed to that site and there is no evidence of any existing primary malignancy, a code from category **Z85** (personal history of malignant neoplasm) should be used to indicate the former site of the malignancy.

A patient who completed treatment for astrocytoma of the right temporal lobe with good results returns for a surveillance visit. The patient continues to do well with no signs of recurrence.

Z08 Encounter for follow-up examination after completed treatment for malignant neoplasm
Z85.841 Personal history of malignant neoplasm of brain

> From the guidelines: Section IC21c8—The follow-up codes are used to explain continuing surveillance following completed treatment of a disease, condition, or injury. They imply that the condition has been fully treated and no longer exists. Follow-up codes may be used in conjunction with history codes to provide the full picture of the healed condition and its treatment. The follow-up code is sequenced first, followed by the history code.

In conjunction with a patient's chemotherapy session for a neuroblastoma of the cortex of the left adrenal gland, a physician manages anemia due to chemotherapy.

Z51.11 Encounter for antineoplastic chemotherapy
C74.02 Malignant neoplasm of cortex of left adrenal gland
D64.81 Anemia due to antineoplastic chemotherapy
T45.1X5A Adverse effect of antineoplastic and immunosuppressive drugs

> Check it out: Look carefully at Section IC2e3 and Section IC2c2 of the guidelines for *ICD-10-CM*. Note that Section IC2c2 instructs that the code for anemia due to antineoplastic therapy is reported first when "the only treatment is for the anemia." What does Section IC2e3 state about complications occurring in conjunction with an encounter for chemotherapy?

Review What You Have Learned

3.1 A patient admitted for chemotherapy for Burkitt lymphoma involving lymph nodes of the neck is also treated for nausea with vomiting. What diagnosis codes should be reported?
   A. **C83.71**   Burkitt lymphoma, lymph nodes of head, face, and neck
      R11.2   Nausea with vomiting, unspecified
      Z51.1   Encounter for antineoplastic chemotherapy and immunotherapy
   B. **Z51.1**   Encounter for antineoplastic chemotherapy and immunotherapy
      C83.71   Burkitt lymphoma, lymph nodes of head, face, and neck
      R11.2   Nausea with vomiting, unspecified
   C. **Z51.11**   Encounter for antineoplastic chemotherapy
      C83.71   Burkitt lymphoma, lymph nodes of head, face, and neck
   D. **Z51.11**   Encounter for antineoplastic chemotherapy
      C83.71   Burkitt lymphoma, lymph nodes of head, face, and neck
      R11.2   Nausea with vomiting, unspecified
   E. **R11.2**   Nausea with vomiting, unspecified
      C83.71   Burkitt lymphoma, lymph nodes of head, face, and neck

3.2 Following complete resection of a medulloblastoma of the cerebellum a pediatric oncology team is consulted for radiation and chemotherapy planning. What diagnosis codes should be reported?
   A. **C71.6**   Malignant neoplasm of cerebellum
      Z51.11   Encounter for antineoplastic chemotherapy
   B. **Z85.841**   Personal history neoplasm of the brain
   C. **Z51.11**   Encounter for antineoplastic chemotherapy
      C71.6   Malignant neoplasm of cerebellum
   D. **C71.6**   Malignant neoplasm of cerebellum
      Z51.0   Encounter for antineoplastic radiation therapy
      Z51.11   Encounter for antineoplastic chemotherapy
   E. **C71.6**   Malignant neoplasm of cerebellum

3.3 You must always start in the table of neoplasms to arrive at the correct code for a neoplasm.
   A. True
   B. False

3.4 *ICD-10-CM* codes for lymphoma include designations of remission or recurrence.
   A. True
   B. False

3.5 After complete excision of a malignant neoplasm, a code for the neoplasm should be reported until all associated treatment is completed.
   A. True
   B. False

3.6 What diagnosis code(s) should be reported for a visit to manage pain in the right lower leg due to an osteosarcoma of the fibula?
   A. **G89.3**   Neoplasm related pain (acute) (chronic)
      C40.21   Malignant neoplasm of long bones of right lower limb
   B. **R52**   Pain, unspecified
   C. **G89.3**   Neoplasm related pain (acute) (chronic)
      C40.21   Malignant neoplasm of long bones of right lower limb
      M79.604 Pain in right leg
   D. **C40.21**   Malignant neoplasm of long bones of right lower limb
      G89.3   Neoplasm related pain (acute) (chronic)

≡ CHAPTER 4 ≡

Diseases of the Blood and Blood-Forming Organs and Certain Disorders Involving the Immune Mechanism (D50-D89)

In *International Classification of Diseases, Tenth Revision, Clinical Modification (ICD-10-CM)*, Chapter 3 of the tabular list includes codes for reporting conditions such as anemias, bone marrow disorders, coagulation defects, purpura, and disorders of the spleen. Code categories in this chapter include **D50-D89.** This chapter does not include codes for neonatal conditions or hematopoietic neoplasms. Endocrine, nutritional, and metabolic disorders are also addressed in other chapters.

The *ICD-10-CM* guidelines do not offer chapter-specific instructions for this chapter, so coding must be guided by instructions in the alphabetic index and tabular list, and by related instructions and guidelines for other chapters.

The first codes in this chapter are for nutritional, hemolytic, and aplastic anemias. Iron deficiency anemia other than that due to blood loss or sideropenic dysphagia is reported with code **D50.8** (other iron deficiency anemias). Vitamin B_{12} anemia due to intrinsic factor deficiency, including congenital intrinsic factor deficiency, is reported with code **D51.0.** Dietary folic acid deficiency or goat's milk anemia is reported with code **D52.0.**

The alphabetic index listing for the subterm "congenital" under the main term "anemia" directs to code **P61.4** (other congenital anemias, not elsewhere classified). However, code **P61.4** should be reported only if no other code reflects the specific condition documented. The alphabetic index provides 8 more specific listings for the term "congenital anemia," including codes from chapters 3 and 16. For instance, "congenital anemia due to isoimmunization" directs to code **P55.9** (hemolytic disease of newborn, unspecified) (from Chapter 16) while "aplastic congenital anemia" directs to code **D61.09** (other constitutional aplastic anemia). Not all potentially congenital anemias are included at this listing in the index. Codes for reporting congenital anemia not indexed at this listing include the following:

D61.01	Constitutional (pure) red blood cell aplasia (Diamond-Blackfan anemia)
D61.09	Other constitutional aplastic anemia (Fanconi anemia)
D55.8	Other anemias due to enzyme disorders
D53.0	Protein deficiency anemia
D64.4	Congenital dyserythropoietic anemia

> Check it out: Review the listings for congenital anemia in the alphabetic index and note the combination of codes from chapters 3 and 16. Then look at the excludes 1 notes for hemorrhagic and hematologic disorders of newborn **(P50–P61)** noting the exclusion of hereditary hemolytic anemias **(D55–D58)**. Note codes **P55.0, P55.1,** and **P61.3** that may be used to report newborn anemia due to isoimmunization or fetal blood loss and code **P61.2** for anemia of prematurity.

Hemolytic anemia codes are found in block **D55–D59**. In this block are codes for many hereditary forms of anemia such as glucose-6-phosphate dehydrogenase deficiency anemia **(D55.0)**, acquired hemolytic anemias, and other hemoglobinopathies. Thalassemia and sickle cell anemia are included here.

When reporting thalassemia, be sure to note the exclusion of sickle cell thalassemia (thalassemia Hb-S) from category **D56**. Sickle cell thalassemia is classified with other codes for sickle cell disorders in category **D57**. Thalassemia minor or thalassemia trait is reported with code **D56.3** regardless of whether the type is α, β, or $\delta\beta$. Code **D56.0** (α-thalassemia) includes hydrops fetalis due to α-thalassemia but does not include hydrops fetalis due to isoimmunization **(P56.0)** or that not due to immune hemolysis **(P83.2)**.

> Check it out: Many hemoglobin disorders are indexed under the term "disease" in the alphabetic index. To further your understanding of how these conditions are indexed, look at the subterms of "disease, hemoglobin" in the alphabetic index. Note that specific codes for thalassemia are included under several subterms of hemoglobin, as are sickle cell anemias. Thalassemia is itself a main term in the alphabetic index, whereas sickle cell disorder is included as a subterm of disease.

Category **D57** (sickle cell disorders) includes codes for sickle trait and sickle cell disorders with and without crisis. Screening for sickle cell trait is reported with code **Z13.0**. Note the instruction to use an additional code to report associated fever **(R50.81)** in addition to codes in category **D57**. Codes for sickle cell disease with crisis include further specificity, indicating acute chest syndrome or splenic sequestration, when applicable.

Example

D57.21   **Sickle-cell/Hb-C disease with crisis**
    D57.211   Sickle-cell/Hb-C disease with acute chest syndrome
    D57.212   Sickle-cell/Hb-C disease with splenic sequestration
    D57.219   Sickle-cell/Hb-C disease with crisis, unspecified

In the example above, code **D57.219** would be used to report other manifestations of crisis in sickle cell/Hb C, such as dactylitis.

Manifestations of sickle cell disease may also be reported in addition to the code for sickle cell disorder. For instance, an encounter with a patient for sickle cell anemia with crisis and glomerulonephritis may be reported with codes

D57.00 Hb-SS disease with crisis, unspecified
N08 Glomerular disorders in diseases classified elsewhere

Anemia in chronic disease (other than enzyme disorders) is reported with codes from category **D63.** The code for the underlying disease is reported before the code for the anemia. Category **D63** provides specific codes for reporting anemia in neoplastic disease and kidney disease. Code **D63.8** (anemia in other chronic diseases classified elsewhere) is used to report anemia in conditions such as hypothyroidism.

> Check it out: Anemia associated with neoplasms and antineoplastic treatments was previously discussed in Chapter 3. If you have forgotten the guidelines for reporting these conditions, review Section IC2c1-2 of the *ICD-10-CM* guidelines.

Secondary autoimmune anemia (cold or warm type) is reported with code **D59.1** (other autoimmune hemolytic anemias). Category **D59** also provides codes for reporting drug-induced hemolytic anemias, hemolytic uremic syndrome, and mechanical or microangiopathic anemia. When reporting hemolytic uremic syndrome, the related infection (eg, *Escherichia coli*) is reported in addition to code **D59.3.**

Codes for drug-induced anemia and anemia due to other external agents are reported first with codes for the external cause (eg, adverse effect of medicine or toxic effect of non-medicinal substance) additionally reported.

Pancytopenia is reported with codes from subcategory **D61.8.** However, pancytopenia is often not separately reported (eg, pancytopenia due to congenital pure red cell aplasia is reported with code **D61.01**). The excludes 1 note at subcategory **D61.8-** should be reviewed when reporting pancytopenia.

Codes for coagulation defects, purpura, and other hemorrhagic defects are found in block **D65-D69.** An abnormal anticoagulation profile without further diagnosis is reported with code **R79.1.** Newborn coagulation defects should be reported with codes in categories **P60-P61.** Neonatal purpura is reported with code **P54.5** (neonatal cutaneous hemorrhage). Coagulation factor defects may be referenced by type in the alphabetic index under "Deficiency, Factor."

Block **D70-D77** provides codes for other disorders of the blood and blood-forming organs, including agranulocytosis, other white blood cell disorders, and disorders of the spleen. Category **D70** (neutropenia) provides codes for congenital, drug-induced, periodic, and infection-related neutropenia excluding transient neonatal neutropenia **(P61.5).** Instructions for category **D70** include reporting of fever or mucositis in addition to a code in the category.

Decreases in white blood cell counts other than neutropenia may be reported with codes in subcategory **D72.81-.** An elevated white blood cell count including bandemia may be reported with codes from subcategory **D72.82-,** with the exception of eosinophilia **(D72.1).**

> **Check it out:** You might expect to find codes for increased or decreased white blood cell counts in Chapter 18 **(R00–R99)** rather than category **D72**. To become more familiar with the classification of increased or decreased blood components, review the alphabetic index entries for decrease and increase, noting the references to blood components.

Splenic disorders are reported with codes from category **D73** except congenital asplenia **(Q89.01)**; congenital splenomegaly **(Q89.09)**; and conditions due to trauma, other diseases, or splenectomy. Splenomegaly without definitive diagnosis is reported with code **R16.1.**

Immunodeficiency

Codes in block **D80–D89** are used to report immunodeficiency with predominantly antibody defects, combined immunodeficiency, common variable, severe immunodeficiency, and immunodeficiency associated with other major defects. Ataxia telangiectasia is not included here but is classified as a systemic atrophy in Chapter 6 of the tabular list.

> **Check it out:** Most congenital malformations are reported with codes **Q00–Q99** from Chapter 17 of the tabular list. To see an example of an exception, look up "hypoplasia, thymus" in the alphabetic index to find the appropriate code for hypoplasia of the thymus with immunodeficiency.

It is notable that unlike antineoplastic immunotherapy that is reported with a specific code **(Z51.12),** immunotherapy for non-neoplastic conditions is reported with the code for the condition being treated. Some codes for encounters related to but not directly addressing disorders of the blood or blood-forming organs or immunodeficiency include the following:

Z28.03	Immunization not carried out because of immune-compromised state of patient
Z48.290	Encounter for aftercare following bone marrow transplant
Z83.2	Family history of diseases of the blood and blood-forming organs and certain disorders involving the immune mechanism
Z90.81	Acquired absence of spleen
Z90.89	Acquired absence of other organs (eg, thymus gland)

Complications of transfusions may be reported with codes from multiple chapters of *ICD-10-CM*. Graft-versus-host disease is reported with codes from category **D89.81-.** Instructions for this category include reporting first the underlying cause, such as complications of transplanted organs and tissue **(T86.-)** or complications of blood transfusion **(T80.89).** Other potential codes for complications associated with transfusion include

D69.51	Post-transfusion purpura
E83.111	Hemochromatosis due to repeated red blood cell transfusions
E87.71	Transfusion associated circulatory overload
J95.84	Transfusion-related acute lung injury (TRALI)
R50.84	Febrile nonhemolytic transfusion reaction

Coding Scenarios

An 18-month-old child is seen for a well-child examination. The child appears pale but is playful. The mother reports that the child does not eat well at mealtime but drinks 6 to 8 bottles of milk each day. A complete blood cell count (CBC) is performed and the results were reviewed by the physician with diagnosis of iron-deficiency anemia due to inadequate dietary intake.

Z00.121	Encounter for routine child health examination with abnormal findings
D50.8	Other iron deficiency anemias

> From the guidelines: Section IC21c13—Some of the codes for routine health examinations distinguish between "with" and "without" abnormal findings. When assigning a code for "with" abnormal findings, additional codes should be assigned to identify the specific abnormal finding(s).

A pediatric hematologist is consulted in the clinic for a 7-year-old child whose pediatrician has diagnosed an idiopathic aplastic anemia. Laboratory results provided by the primary physician indicate aplastic anemia. The child has a history of congenital ventricular septal defect (VSD) repaired at age 1 year. The father indicates that he is concerned because his family history includes severe anemia on his father's side. Following a complete history and physical examination, the physician diagnoses aplastic anemia, rule out Fanconi anemia; repaired congenital VSD; and family history of anemia. Additional tests are ordered, and the patient will be seen again in 1 week.

D61.9	Aplastic anemia, unspecified
Z87.74	Personal history of (corrected) congenital malformations of heart and circulatory system
Z83.2	Family history of diseases of the blood and blood-forming organs and certain disorders involving the immune mechanism

> From the guidelines: Section IVH—Do not code diagnoses documented as "probable," "suspected," "questionable," "rule out," or "working diagnosis" or other similar terms indicating uncertainty. Rather, code the condition(s) to the highest degree of certainty for that encounter/visit, such as symptoms, signs, abnormal test results, or other reason for the visit.
>
> Please note: This differs from the coding practices used by short-term, acute care, long-term care, and psychiatric hospitals.

> Check it out: Both the patient's congenital condition and family history are relevant to the physician's workup of this patient and included in the final diagnoses. To review how the secondary diagnoses were applied to this case, see the guidelines for reporting of personal and family history. Section IC17e3: If a congenital malformation or deformity has been corrected, a personal history code should be used to identify the history of the malformation or deformity. Also see Section IC21c4: History codes are also acceptable on any medical record regardless of the reason for the visit. A history of an illness, even if no longer present, is important information that may alter the type of treatment ordered.

A 5-month-old baby is seen in the emergency department for fever and upper respiratory symptoms. The child has been fussy and not eating well despite wanting to nurse. Family history indicates no related hereditary conditions, but the child is exposed to tobacco smoke in her home. The physical examination shows bilateral acute serous otitis media and mild upper respiratory symptoms. A CBC indicates neutropenia. Records show the neonatal CBC was normal. The physician diagnoses bilateral acute serous otitis media with decreased absolute neutrophil count and advises follow-up with the pediatrician to reevaluate the patient's ears and further investigate potential autoimmune neutropenia.

H65.03	Acute serous otitis media, bilateral
D70.9	Neutropenia, unspecified
R50.81	Fever presenting with conditions classified elsewhere
Z77.22	Contact with and (suspected) exposure to environmental tobacco smoke (acute) (chronic)

> From the guidelines: Section IC18b—Signs or symptoms that are associated routinely with a disease process should not be assigned as additional codes unless otherwise instructed by the classification.
>
> Note the inclusion of code **R50.81** in addition to the codes for otitis media and neutropenia. This is based on the instruction in the classification for category **D70**: "Use additional code for any associated: fever **(R50.81)** mucositis **(J34.81, K12.3-, K92.81, N76.81)."**

A 5-month-old infant, who was born prematurely at 32 weeks, 1 day, is seen for a scheduled follow-up of anemia of prematurity. Despite a prolonged stay in the neonatal intensive care unit, she has had an uneventful posthospital course. The child continues to gain weight as expected and appears healthy. Laboratory results confirm that the patient continues to progress well.

P61.2	Anemia of prematurity

≡ DISEASES OF THE BLOOD AND BLOOD-FORMING ORGANS (D50-D89) ≡ 39

> From the guidelines: Section IV,I—Chronic diseases treated on an ongoing basis may be coded and reported as many times as the patient receives treatment and care for the condition(s).

A 15-year-old patient with Hb-SC disease presents to the ophthalmologist for evaluation of newly diagnosed retinal changes. The physician diagnoses Stage 1, proliferative sickle cell retinopathy.

    D57.20   Sickle-cell/Hb-C disease without crisis
    H36   Retinal disorders in diseases classified elsewhere

> Check it out: Look at the alphabetic index listing for retinopathy. The subterms proliferative and sickle cell will direct to codes **D57.-[H36]**. What do the brackets in the alphabetic index indicate about code **H36**? This was reviewed in Chapter 1, but if you need to refresh your memory, see Section IA,7 of the guidelines.

Review What You Have Learned

4.1 A 3-year-old presents to the pediatrician's office with a new complaint of easily bruising and a rash that seems to be spreading. The physician notes that the patient had an upper respiratory virus a few weeks ago but has seemed to quickly recover from that. A CBC is obtained and results reviewed. The physician diagnoses idiopathic thrombocytopenic purpura and instructs the parents to bring the child in for a repeat CBC in 1 week. What diagnosis code(s) is appropriate for reporting this encounter?

    A. **D69**   Purpura and other hemorrhagic conditions
    B. **P54.5**   Neonatal cutaneous hemorrhage
    C. **J06.9**   Acute upper respiratory infection, unspecified
    D. **D69.3**   Immune thrombocytopenic purpura
    E. **D69.3**   Immune thrombocytopenic purpura
       T14.8   Other injury of unspecified body region

4.2 The physician diagnoses anemia in hypothyroidism without goiter. What diagnosis codes should be reported?

    A. **D64.1**   Secondary sideroblastic anemia due to disease
    B. **D63.8**   Anemia in other chronic diseases classified elsewhere
    C. **E03.1**   Congenital hypothyroidism without goiter
       D63.8   Anemia in other chronic diseases classified elsewhere
    D. **C71.6**   Hypothyroidism, unspecified
       D63.8   Anemia in other chronic diseases classified elsewhere
    E. **C71.6**   Hypothyroidism, unspecified

4.3 Transient hypogammaglobulinemia of infancy is reported with code **P61.4** (other congenital anemias, not elsewhere classified).
   A. True
   B. False

4.4 Reporting of sickle cell trait requires documentation of "with" or "without" crisis.
   A. True
   B. False

4.5 Sickle cell thalassemia is classified in the tabular list category **D57** (sickle cell disorders).
   A. True
   B. False

4.6 A child who has a history of acute lymphoblastic lymphoma in remission is found to be anemic at a checkup. What diagnosis code(s) should be reported?
   A. **D63.0**   Anemia in neoplastic disease
      C83.50   Lymphoblastic (diffuse) lymphoma, unspecified site
   B. **C83.50**   Lymphoblastic (diffuse) lymphoma, unspecified site
   C. **C91.01**   Acute lymphoblastic leukemia, in remission
      D63.0   Anemia in neoplastic disease
   D. **C83.50**   Lymphoblastic (diffuse) lymphoma, unspecified site
      D63.0   Anemia in neoplastic disease

≡ CHAPTER 5 ≡

Endocrine, Nutritional, and Metabolic Diseases (E00-E89)

In International Classification of Diseases, Tenth Revision, Clinical Modification (ICD-10-CM), Chapter 4 of the tabular list includes codes for reporting conditions such as diabetes and other endocrine disorders, malnutrition, overweight and obesity, and metabolic disorders. Code categories in this chapter include **E00-E89.**

The *ICD-10-CM* guidelines for Chapter 4 offer chapter-specific instructions only for diabetes mellitus. Coding is mostly guided by instructions in the alphabetic index and tabular list, and by related instructions and guidelines from other chapters.

> Check it out: Chapter 4 of the tabular list begins with an instruction we reviewed in Chapter 3 of this book regarding neoplasms: "All neoplasms, whether functionally active or not, are classified in Chapter 2. Appropriate codes in this chapter (ie, **E05.8, E07.0, E16-E31, E34.-**) may be used as additional codes to indicate either functional activity by neoplasms and ectopic endocrine tissue or hyperfunction and hypofunction of endocrine glands associated with neoplasms and other conditions classified elsewhere." To further review the conditions in Chapter 4 that may be reported to describe functional activity secondary to codes for neoplastic conditions, look up the codes in parentheses above in the tabular list. These codes may also be applicable to report late effects of cancer treatment.

Chapter 4 of the tabular list includes an excludes 1 note that applies to the entire chapter.

"Excludes 1: transitory endocrine and metabolic disorders specific to newborn **(P70-P74)**"

The tabular list indicates that you should look to codes **P70-P74** for reporting transitory endocrine and metabolic disturbances caused by the infant's response to maternal endocrine and metabolic factors, or its adjustment to the extrauterine environment.

> **Check it out:** To gain further understanding of the endocrine and metabolic disorders represented in categories **P70-P74,** see these categories in the tabular list. Note the exclusions at category **P72** that direct to codes in Chapter 4 for conditions such as congenital hypothyroidism.

Thyroid Disorders

The first block of codes in this chapter of the tabular list represent disorders of the thyroid gland. Category **E00** (congenital iodine-deficiency syndrome) includes an instruction to also report associated intellectual disabilities. Congenital hypothyroidism is reported with codes from category **E03**. Codes in category **E03** distinguish between congenital hypothyroidism with and without goiter. Hashimoto thyroiditis is reported with code **E06.3.**

Codes in category **E04** (other nontoxic goiter) would not be reported for conditions that are more specifically defined, such as conditions in categories **E00-E03.0.**

> **From the guidelines:** Section IA9a—Codes titled "other" or "other specified" are for use when the information in the medical record provides detail for which a specific code does not exist.

Diabetes Mellitus

The block of codes containing categories **E08-E13** includes 5 categories of codes for diabetes.

1. **E08** Diabetes mellitus due to an underlying condition
2. **E09** Drug- or chemical-induced diabetes mellitus
3. **E10** Type 1 diabetes mellitus
4. **E11** Type 2 diabetes mellitus
5. **E13** Other specified diabetes mellitus

This block of codes is not used to report gestational diabetes **(O24.4-)** or, as noted above, transitory endocrine disorders in the neonatal period. Management of preexisting or unspecified diabetes in pregnancy, childbirth, and the puerperium is reported with a combination of codes from category **O24-** and the appropriate category of codes from categories **E08-E13.**

The alphabetic index listing for the terms "diabetes, diabetic" provides a default code of **E11.9** (type 2 diabetes mellitus without complications). This is followed by the subterm (-) and a list of additional subterms (--) representing manifestations of type 2 diabetes. It is important to find the subterm (-) listing for the type of diabetes documented in the patient record to achieve correct coding. The subterms (-) appear in the following order:

Diabetes, diabetic (mellitus) (sugar) **E11.9**
- with
- bronzed **E83.110**
- complicating pregnancy—see Pregnancy, complicated by, diabetes
- dietary counseling and surveillance **Z71.3**
- due to drug or chemical **E09.9**
- due to underlying condition **E08.9**
- gestational (in pregnancy) **O24.419**
- hepatogenous **E13.9**
- inadequately controlled—code to Diabetes, by type, with hyperglycemia
- insipidus **E23.2**
- insulin dependent—code to type of diabetes
- juvenile-onset—see Diabetes, type 1
- ketosis-prone—see Diabetes, type 1
- latent **R73.09**
- neonatal (transient) **P70.2**
- non-insulin dependent—code to type of diabetes
- out of control—code to Diabetes, by type, with hyperglycemia
- phosphate **E83.39**
- poorly controlled—code to Diabetes, by type, with hyperglycemia
- post-pancreatectomy—see Diabetes, specified type NEC
- post-procedural—see Diabetes, specified type NEC
- secondary diabetes mellitus NEC—see Diabetes, specified type NEC
- specified type NEC **E13.9**
- steroid-induced—see Diabetes, due to, drug or chemical
- type 1 **E10.9**
- type 2 **E11.9**

Additional subterms expand this listing to 6 pages in the alphabetic index. Final code selection from the tabular list will help verify the correct selection in the alphabetic index.

The *ICD-10-CM* guidelines do provide guidance on reporting of diabetes mellitus. Key among these guidelines are

- If the type of diabetes is not documented, the default is type 2.
- The type of diabetes is not assumed by age of the patient or insulin use.
- Diabetic manifestations are combined with the codes for diabetes.
- Report as many codes as necessary to include all manifestations.
- Secondary diabetes is always caused by another condition or event (eg, cystic fibrosis, malignant neoplasm of pancreas, pancreatectomy, adverse effect of drug, or poisoning).
- When reporting secondary diabetes, follow the tabular list instructions to sequence the diagnoses.
- Code **Z79.4** (long-term [current] use of insulin) should be reported when appropriate in addition to codes for type 2 or secondary diabetes.
- Code **Z79.4** is reported only for long-term insulin use and not for temporary use during an encounter.
- Codes for diabetes with hyperglycemia are reported for conditions documented as out of control, poorly controlled, or inadequately controlled.

ICD-10-CM does provide a code **(R73.09)** for reporting prediabetes or latent diabetes. Code **R73.09** (other abnormal glucose) does not include neonatal disorders categorized in codes **P70–P70.2.** Patient encounters for dietary counseling related to prevention or management of diabetes or other underlying medical conditions may be reported with **Z71.3** (dietary counseling and surveillance). When reporting code **Z71.3,** use additional codes to report any associated underlying condition and, if known, the patient's body mass index **(Z68.5-).** Report code **Z46.81** for an encounter for fitting and adjustment, instruction and training, or titration of an insulin pump.

Type 1 diabetes is reported with codes from category **E10.** Each category of codes for diabetes contains subcategories indicating specific manifestations. Below are the subcategories for category **E10.** Within each subcategory (except **E10.8** and **E10.9**) are multiple codes that better specify the nature of the complication, such as ketoacidosis with coma **(E10.11)** and without coma **(E10.10).**

E10.1	Type 1 diabetes mellitus with ketoacidosis
E10.2	Type 1 diabetes mellitus with kidney complications
E10.3	Type 1 diabetes mellitus with ophthalmic complications
E10.4	Type 1 diabetes mellitus with neurologic complications
E10.5	Type 1 diabetes mellitus with circulatory complications
E10.6	Type 1 diabetes mellitus with other specified complications
E10.8	Type 1 diabetes mellitus with unspecified complications
E10.9	Type 1 diabetes mellitus without complications

> **Check it out:** To gain further insight into the variety of codes used in reporting diabetes and its associated manifestations, look at codes in subcategory **E10.62-.** Note the instructions found at codes **E10.621** and **E10.622** to also report a code from category **L97** or **L98** to identify the site of the ulcer. Codes in categories **L97** and **L98** identify not only the site of the ulcer, but also the extent (eg, fat layer exposed).

An example of conditions reported with codes in category **E10** is reporting of a patient who is a type 1 diabetic seen for hypoglycemia and poor compliance with diabetes management.

E10.649	Type 1 diabetes mellitus with hypoglycemia without coma
Z91.19	Patient's noncompliance with other medical treatment and regimen

Note that the single code identifies both the underlying type 1 diabetes and the manifestation of hypoglycemia. Code **Z79.4** is not reported to indicate long-term insulin use because this is not required when reporting type 1 diabetes.

Codes in category **E11** (type 2 diabetes mellitus) are similarly structured but include a subcategory for manifestation of hyperosmolarity **(E11.0)** rather than a category for reporting ketoacidosis. Code **Z79.4** is reported in addition to codes in category **E11** when long-term insulin use is documented.

Diabetes due to an underlying condition is reported with codes from category **E08**. The instructions at category **E08** direct that the code for the underlying condition is reported first followed by the code from category **E08**, and if long-term insulin use is documented, code **Z79.4**. This category includes diabetes secondary to conditions such as cystic fibrosis, malignant neoplasms, or malnutrition. It does not include diabetes that is post-procedural, post-pancreatectomy, neonatal, or described by other codes in the **E09-E13** categories.

Example

E84.8	Cystic fibrosis with other manifestations
E08.9	Diabetes mellitus due to underlying condition without complications

Category **E09** is used to report drug- or chemical-induced diabetes mellitus. Reporting services in this category requires a combination of codes to indicate the secondary diabetes with any manifestations, poisoning due to a drug or toxin or an adverse effect of a drug and, if applicable, long-term current insulin use. The tabular list instructions for this category are

Code first poisoning due to drug or toxin, if applicable (**T36-T65** with fifth or sixth character **1-4** or **6**)

Use additional code for adverse effect, if applicable, to identify drug (**T36-T50** with fifth or sixth character **5**)

Use additional code to identify any insulin use **(Z79.4)**

To better understand the above instructions to report codes from categories **T36-T65**, some information on these categories is necessary. The *ICD-10-CM* guidelines tell us that codes in these categories are combination codes that include the substance that was taken as well as the intent. Poisoning includes overdose, reaction to improper use of a medication (eg, interaction of drugs and alcohol), wrong method of administration, or toxicity due to an interaction of a non-prescribed drug taken with a prescribed drug.

> From the guidelines: Section IC19e1—In Chapter 1 of this book, the table of drugs and chemicals was noted as a part of the alphabetic index. As with other portions of the alphabetic index, the guidelines instruct, "Do not code directly from the Table of Drugs and Chemicals. Always refer back to the Tabular List."

Codes in categories **T36-T50** provide for reporting of
- Unintentional poisoning by wrong substance given/taken in error—subcategories end in "1"
- Intentional self-harm poisoning—subcategories end in "2"
- Intentional harm (assault) poisoning—subcategories end in "3"
- Undetermined intent of poisoning—subcategories end in "4"
- Adverse effects of a drug that has been correctly prescribed and properly administered—subcategories end in "5"
- Underdosing by taking less substance than prescribed or instructed whether inadvertent or deliberate—subcategories end in "6"

When no intent of poisoning is indicated, report a code for accidental poisoning. Codes for undetermined intent are reported only when documentation clearly states that intent was undetermined.

Noncompliance **(Z91.12-, Z91.13-)** or complications of care **(Y63.8-Y63.9)** codes are to be used with an underdosing code to indicate intent, if known. No additional external cause code is required for poisonings, toxic effects, adverse effects, and underdosing codes.

Codes in categories **T51-T65** are used to report toxic effects when a harmful substance (chiefly non-medicinal) is ingested or comes in contact with a person. Toxic effect codes also have an associated intent: accidental, intentional self-harm; assault; and undetermined.

The following example shows a combination of codes to report an initial encounter for uncomplicated diabetes as an adverse effect of methylprednisolone.

E09.9 Drug- or chemical-induced diabetes mellitus without complications
T38.0X5A Adverse effect of glucocorticoids and synthetic analogues

Note the seventh character **A** is required to complete subcategory **T38.0X5**, indicating the initial encounter.

T-codes are also used to indicate underdosing or overdosing of insulin due to malfunction of an insulin pump. The codes for various malfunctions include

T85.614- Breakdown (mechanical) of insulin pump
T85.624- Displacement of insulin pump
T85.633- Leakage of insulin pump
T85.694- Other mechanical complication of insulin pump

Each of these codes would be completed with a seventh character **A** (initial encounter), **D** (subsequent encounter), or **S** (sequela).

The following example illustrates use of these codes to report an initial encounter for underdosing of insulin due to leakage from the insulin pump resulting in ketoacidosis.

T85.633A Leakage of insulin pump
T38.3X6A Underdosing of insulin and oral hypoglycemic [anti-diabetic] drugs
E10.10 Type 1 diabetes mellitus with ketoacidosis without coma

This example follows the *ICD-10-CM* guideline instructions to report first the code for the mechanical complication followed by codes for the underdosing and the type of diabetes with any associated complication. Note the inclusion of the seventh character **A** on both T-codes to reflect the initial encounter for this condition.

To report a case of insulin overdose due to an insulin pump malfunction, report first the mechanical complication with a code from subcategory **T85.6-** and then a code from subcategory **T38.3x1-** (poisoning by insulin and oral hypoglycemic [anti-diabetic] drugs, accidental [unintentional]).

Code **T85.72** is used to report the initial encounter for an infection and inflammatory reaction due to an insulin pump. When reporting this code, use an additional code to identify the infection.

Codes in category **E13** provide for reporting of diabetes mellitus due to genetic defects, post-pancreatectomy, post-procedural, and secondary diabetes that is otherwise not classified. The *ICD-10-CM* guidelines provide specific instructions for post-pancreatectomy diabetes mellitus. Sequence first code **E89.1** (post-procedural hypoinsulinemia). Assign a code from category **E13** and a code from subcategory **Z90.41-** (acquired absence of pancreas) as additional codes.

Instructions at code **E89.1** reinforce the guideline instructions.

> **E 89.1 Post-procedural hypoinsulinemia**
>
> **Use additional** code, if applicable, to identify acquired absence of pancreas **(Z90.41-)** diabetes mellitus (post-pancreatectomy) (post-procedural) **(E13.-)** insulin use **(Z79.4)**
>
> **Excludes 1:** transient post-procedural hyperglycemia **(R73.9)**
> transient post-procedural hypoglycemia **(E16.2)**

Categories **E15** and **E16** provide codes for reporting nondiabetic hypoglycemic coma and other pancreatic insulin secretory disorders. Other disorders of carbohydrate metabolism are found in category **E74**.

Disorders of Other Endocrine Glands

Categories **E20-E35** provide codes for reporting disorders of other endocrine glands. This includes conditions of the parathyroid gland, pituitary gland, hypothalamus, adrenal glands, ovaries, testes, and polyglandular conditions. Codes in category **E23** are used to report disorders in either the pituitary or hypothalamus.

Category **E30** provides codes for reporting disorders of puberty. Delayed sexual development is reported with code **E30.0**. Precocious puberty is reported with code **E30.1**, except in cases of central precocious puberty **(E22.8)**. Sexual precocity with adrenal hyperplasia is reported with code **E25.9** or, when congenital, with code **E25.0**. Category **E34.5-** provides for reporting of androgen insensitivity syndromes.

Short stature due to endocrine disorder **(E34.3)** does not include hereditary or idiopathic short stature **(R62.52)** or short stature due to dysmorphic syndromes (code the syndrome). Nutritional short stature is reported with code **E45**.

Category **E36** includes interoperative complications of the endocrine system, such as hemorrhage, hematoma, puncture, or laceration.

Malnutrition and Other Nutritional Deficiencies

Blocks **E40-E46** and **E50-E64** include codes for malnutrition and nutritional deficiencies. These categories do not include pediatric failure to thrive **(R62.51)** or feeding problems in a newborn **(P92.-)**. Intestinal malabsorption **(K90.-)** is also not reported with codes in this block. An excludes 2 note indicates that nutritional anemias **(D50-D53)** and/or starvation **(T73.0)** are not represented by codes in this block but may be additionally reported when indicated. Cachexia due to malnutrition is reported with code **R64**.

Active infantile or juvenile rickets is reported with code **E55.0**. Vitamin D–resistant rickets is reported with code **E83.31** (familial hypophosphatemia).

Category **E64** is to be used to indicate conditions in categories **E43, E44, E46,** and **E50-E63** as the cause of sequelae, which are themselves classified elsewhere. The sequelae include conditions specified as such; they also include the late effects of diseases classifiable to the above categories if the disease itself is no longer present. This category does not include retarded physical development due to protein-calorie malnutrition **(E45)**. Report the condition resulting from malnutrition (sequela) and other nutritional deficiencies first, and then the code from category **E64.**

Overweight, obesity, and other hyperalimentation **(E65-E68)** include codes for overweight, obesity, and morbid obesity due to excess calorie intake, drug-induced obesity, and unspecified obesity. A code from subcategory **Z68.5-** should be additionally reported for the body mass index (BMI) when BMI is documented.

The final block in this chapter is metabolic disorders **(E70-E88)**. Dehydration **(E86.0),** hypovolemia **(E86.1),** and other volume depletion **(E86.9)** are included in this block. It does not include dehydration in a newborn **(P74.1).**

Secondary lactase deficiency **(E73.1)** is also included in this block. Glucose-galactose malabsorption is reported with code **E74.39** (other disorders of intestinal carbohydrate absorption). Report unspecified lactose intolerance with code **E73.9.**

Category **E78** includes disorders of lipoprotein metabolism and other lipidemias. This includes lipoprotein deficiency **(E78.6),** pure hypertriglyceridemia **(E78.1),** and pure hypercholesterolemia **(E78.0).** It does not include sphingolipidosis **(E75.0-E75.3).**

Category **E80** (disorders of porphyrin and bilirubin metabolism) includes codes for Gilbert syndrome **(E80.4)** and Crigler-Najjar syndrome **(E80.5).** It does not include breast-milk jaundice **(P59.3),** jaundice due to isoimmunization **(P55-P57),** neonatal jaundice due to other excessive hemolysis **(P58.-),** or neonatal jaundice from other and unspecified causes **(P59.-).**

Cystic fibrosis is also classified in this block. Codes in category **E84** include combination codes for cystic fibrosis with manifestations. This category includes

E84.0	Cystic fibrosis with pulmonary manifestations
Use additional code to identify any infectious organism present, such as *Pseudomonas* **(B96.5)**	
E84.11	Meconium ileus in cystic fibrosis
Excludes 1:	meconium ileus not due to cystic fibrosis **(P76.0)**
E84.19	Cystic fibrosis with other intestinal manifestations
E84.8	Cystic fibrosis with other manifestations
E84.9	Cystic fibrosis, unspecified

Note that an additional code to identify any infectious agent is required when reporting cystic fibrosis with pulmonary manifestations. Meconium ileus not due to cystic fibrosis is reported with code **P76.0.**

Category **E87** provides codes for other disorders of fluid, electrolyte, and acid-base balance. Metabolic acidosis is reported with code **E87.2** (acidosis) or **E87.4** (mixed disorder of acid-base balance). Alkalosis alone is reported with code **E87.3.** Acidosis in type 1 diabetes is reported with codes **E10.10** and **E10.11.** Acidosis of a newborn is reported with code **P84** (other problems with newborn).

This chapter ends with category **E89** (post-procedural endocrine and metabolic complications and disorders, not elsewhere classified). The category has an excludes 2 note stating intra-operative complications of endocrine system organ or structure **(E36.0-, E36.1-,** or **E36.8)** are not represented by codes in this category but may be additionally reported when applicable.

Coding Scenarios

The parents of a 3-month-old child previously diagnosed with transient neonatal diabetes mellitus are counseled on the results of molecular genetic testing that shows the patient has permanent neonatal diabetes mellitus with mutation of KCNJ11. The child is stable without complications on subcutaneous insulin and will be transitioned to oral therapy.

E13.9	Other specified diabetes mellitus without complications
Z79.4	Long-term (current) use of insulin

> From the tabular list: Note the conditions in category **E13** include diabetes mellitus due to genetic defects.
>
> **E13** Other specified diabetes mellitus
> Includes diabetes mellitus due to genetic defects of beta-cell function
>   diabetes mellitus due to genetic defects in insulin action
>   post-pancreatectomy diabetes mellitus
>   post-procedural diabetes mellitus
>   secondary diabetes mellitus NEC
>
> Though the diabetes mellitus due to genetic defects appears within the neonatal period, it is not transitory as described by codes in category **P70** (transitory disorders of carbohydrate metabolism specific to newborn).

An obese teenager with BMI at the 97th percentile and newly diagnosed type 2 diabetes is seen for counseling regarding disease management and avoidance of complications, including dietary and lifestyle changes. The obesity is found to be due to the patient's excessively high caloric intake and sedentary habits. Goals for diet change and physical activity are agreed to by the patient and his caregiver.

E11.9	Type 2 diabetes mellitus without complications
E66.09	Other obesity due to excess calories
Z68.54	Body mass index (BMI) pediatric, greater than or equal to 95th percentile for age

> From the guidelines: Section IB14—For the BMI, depth of non-pressure chronic ulcers and pressure ulcer stage codes, code assignment may be based on medical record documentation from clinicians who are not the patient's provider (ie, physician or other qualified health care practitioner legally accountable for establishing the patient's diagnosis), since this information is typically documented by other clinicians involved in the care of the patient (eg, a dietitian often documents the BMI and nurses often document the pressure ulcer stages). However, the associated diagnosis (such as overweight, obesity, or pressure ulcer) must be documented by the patient's provider. If there is conflicting medical record documentation, either from the same clinician or different clinicians, the patient's attending provider should be queried for clarification. Please note: This differs from the coding practices used by short-term, acute care, long-term care, and psychiatric hospitals.

A healthy neonate delivered vaginally is seen during the initial hospital stay. The parents have a family history of cystic fibrosis and are carriers of cystic fibrosis, so the child is screened for the disease prior to leaving the hospital with a negative result.

Z38.00 Single live-born infant, delivered vaginally
Z13.228 Encounter for screening for other metabolic disorders
Z83.49 Family history of other endocrine, nutritional, and metabolic diseases

> From the guidelines: Section IC18b—A screening code may be a first-listed code if the reason for the visit is specifically the screening examination. It may also be used as an additional code if the screening is done during an office visit for other health problems. A screening code is not necessary if the screening is inherent to a routine examination, such as a pap smear done during a routine pelvic examination. Should a condition be discovered during the screening, then the code for the condition may be assigned as an additional diagnosis.

A patient with cystic fibrosis who was recently discharged from the hospital after being treated for an infection due to *Pseudomonas aeruginosa* is readmitted to the hospital with respiratory complications. The new infection is diagnosed as methicillin-resistant *Staphylococcus aureus* (MRSA).

E84.0 Cystic fibrosis with pulmonary manifestations
B95.62 Methicillin-resistant *Staphylococcus aureus* infection as the cause of diseases classified elsewhere

> Instructions in the tabular list for code **E84.0** state, "Use additional code to identify any infectious organism present...." In this example, MRSA is identified.
>
> From the guidelines: Section IC1e—When there is documentation of a current infection (eg, wound infection, stitch abscess, urinary tract infection) due to MRSA, and that infection does not have a combination code that includes the causal organism, assign the appropriate code to identify the condition along with code **B95.62** (MRSA infection as the cause of diseases classified elsewhere) for the MRSA infection. Do not assign a code from subcategory **Z16.11** (resistance to penicillins).

A 3-year-old who was adopted from Indonesia is seen in follow-up to assess growth and development, which has been progressing well. This child was first seen 1 year ago for an initial examination after arriving in the United States. The child was diagnosed with protein-calorie malnutrition and showed signs of delayed development due to malnutrition. The parents report a very healthy appetite and progress in toileting, language, and social skills. The child has not yet completed catch-up growth and development, but is progressing well.

E45 Retarded development following protein-calorie malnutrition

> From the guidelines: Section IV—Chronic diseases treated on an ongoing basis may be coded and reported as many times as the patient receives treatment and care for the condition(s).

Review What You Have Learned

5.1 A patient with type 1 diabetes who uses an insulin pump is seen in the emergency department for ketoacidosis. The patient's pump malfunctioned causing leakage and an underdose of insulin delivery. The patient did not become comatose due to early intervention. What is the appropriate first-listed diagnosis code?
   A. **E10.10** Type 1 diabetes mellitus with ketoacidosis without coma
   B. **R73.9** Hyperglycemia
   C. **T85.633** Leakage of insulin pump
   D. **T38.3X1** Poisoning by insulin and oral hypoglycemic [anti-diabetic] drugs, accidental
   E. **T85.633A** Leakage of insulin pump, initial encounter

5.2 How many codes are required to report diabetes due to cystic fibrosis with a non-healing ulcer of the right calf?
   A. 2
   B. 4
   C. 1
   D. 3
   E. None of the above

5.3 Chapter 4 of the tabular list includes codes for reporting transitory metabolic disturbances caused by the infant's response to maternal endocrine and metabolic factors, or its adjustment to the extrauterine environment.
   A. True
   B. False

5.4 There are 2 categories of codes for diabetes mellitus in *ICD-10-CM*.
   A. True
   B. False

5.5 Malnutrition codes in Chapter 4 include codes for reporting anemia.
   A. True
   B. False

5.6 Code **E87.3** is not used to report acidosis in a patient with type 1 diabetes mellitus.
   A. True
   B. False

≡ CHAPTER 6 ≡

Mental, Behavioral, and Neurodevelopmental Disorders (F01-F09)

In *International Classification of Diseases, Tenth Revision, Clinical Modification (ICD-10-CM)*, Chapter 5 of the tabular list includes codes for reporting a variety of conditions that may be mental, behavioral, or neurodevelopmental disorders. The blocks in this chapter include

- Mental disorders due to known physiological conditions **(F01-F09)**
- Mental and behavioral disorders due to psychoactive substance use **(F10-F19)**
- Schizophrenia, schizotypal, delusional, and other non-mood psychotic disorders **(F20-F29)**
- Mood and affective disorders **(F30-F39)**
- Anxiety, dissociative, stress-related, somatoform and other non-psychotic mental disorders **(F40-F48)**
- Behavioral syndromes associated with physiological disturbances and physical factors **(F50-F59)**
- Disorders of adult personality and behavior **(F60-F69)**
- Intellectual disabilities **(F70-F79)**
- Pervasive and specific developmental disorders **(F80-F89)**
- Behavioral and emotional disorders with onset usually occurring in childhood and adolescence **(F90-F98)**
- Unspecified mental disorder **(F99)**

The *ICD-10-CM* guidelines for Chapter 5 offer chapter-specific instructions for reporting pain associated with psychological disorders and pain disorders with related psychological factors. There is also guidance on reporting of psychoactive substance use. Coding for other conditions is mostly guided by instructions in the alphabetic index and tabular list, and by related instructions and guidelines from other chapters.

Chapter 5 of the tabular list includes an excludes 2 note that applies to the entire chapter.

> "Excludes 2: symptoms, signs and abnormal clinical laboratory findings, not elsewhere classified **(R00-R99)**"

> From the guidelines: Section IB5&6—Signs and symptoms that are associated routinely with a disease process should not be assigned as additional codes unless otherwise instructed by the classification. Additional signs and symptoms that may not be associated routinely with a disease process should be coded when present.

Mental Disorders Due to Known Physiological Conditions

This block of codes begins with the following note

> This block comprises a range of mental disorders grouped together on the basis of their having in common a demonstrable etiology in cerebral disease, brain injury, or other insult leading to cerebral dysfunction. The dysfunction may be primary, as in diseases, injuries, and insults that affect the brain directly and selectively; or secondary, as in systemic diseases and disorders that attack the brain only as one of the multiple organs or systems of the body that are involved.

One category in this block that may be reported in relation to pediatric sports injuries or brain injury due to infection is **F07.8** (other personality and behavioral disorders due to known physiological condition). This category includes codes for post-concussional and post-encephalitic syndromes. Post-concussional syndrome is reported with

> **F07.81** Post-concussional syndrome
> Post-contusional syndrome (encephalopathy)
> Posttraumatic brain syndrome, nonpsychotic
> **Use additional code** to identify associated posttraumatic headache, if applicable **(G44.3-)**
> **Excludes 1:** current concussion (brain) **(S06.0-)**
> post-encephalitic syndrome **(F07.89)**

Note the instruction to use an additional code to identify associated posttraumatic headache, if applicable. Also notable is the excludes 1 note that prohibits reporting of current concussion **(S06.0-).** This instruction needs some further review. Category **S06** includes the following instructions:

> **S06** Intracranial injury
> **Includes:** traumatic brain injury
> **Code also** any associated open wound of head **(S01.-)**
> skull fracture **(S02.-)**
> **Excludes 1:** head injury NOS **(S09.90)**
> The appropriate seventh character is to be added to each code from category **S06**
> **A**–initial encounter
> **D**–subsequent encounter
> **S**–sequela

Note that there is a seventh character choice of **S** for sequela. This allows for reporting of codes in category **S06** when the condition is not current but the underlying cause of a sequela. In other words, the instruction at code **F07.81** excluding current concussion would not prohibit reporting of a code from category **S06** that represents a late effect or sequela of a concussion after the acute phase of an illness.

> From the guidelines: Section IB10—A sequela is the residual effect (condition produced) after the acute phase of an illness or injury has terminated. There is no time limit on when a sequela code can be used. The residual may be apparent early, such as in cerebral infarction, or it may occur months or years later, such as that due to a previous injury. Coding of sequela generally requires 2 codes sequenced in the following order: the condition or nature of the sequela is sequenced first; the sequela code is sequenced second.

The following example illustrates the reporting of post-concussional syndrome in a patient who sustained a concussion with brief loss of consciousness 6 months ago when he ran his all-terrain vehicle into a tree. He has had frequent headaches since the accident though he had no history of headaches prior to the accident. His parents have noted increased irritability and excitability as well. His short-term memory has returned to normal and he is generally doing well in school despite the ongoing symptoms.

F07.81 Post-concussional syndrome
G44.319 Acute posttraumatic headache, not intractable
S06.0X1S Concussion with loss of consciousness of 30 minutes or less

Note that code **G44.319** is reported as per the instruction at code **F07.81** to use an additional code to report posttraumatic headache. Irritability is not separately reported as the instructions for reporting irritability with code **R45.4** include the following excludes 1 note at the block level excluding irritability as part of a condition reported with codes **F01-F99**.

Symptoms and signs involving cognition, perception, emotional state, and behavior (R40-R46)
Excludes 1: symptoms and signs constituting part of a pattern of mental disorder **(F01-F99)**

The **S06.0X1S** code indicates that the condition is a sequela of a concussion with loss of consciousness of 30 minutes or less.

The other code in this subcategory, **F07.89** (other personality and behavioral disorders due to known physiological condition), is used to report conditions such as post-encephalitic syndrome.

Mental and Behavioral Disorders Due to Psychoactive Substance Use

The guidelines for *ICD-10-CM* provide instructions for reporting of codes related to psychoactive substance use. A primary guideline is regarding when to report substance use.

As with all other diagnoses, the codes for psychoactive substance use **(F10.9-, F11.9-, F12.9-, F13.9-, F14.9-, F15.9-, F16.9-)** should only be assigned based on provider documentation and when they meet the definition of a reportable diagnosis (see Section III, Reporting Additional Diagnoses). **The codes are to be used only when the psychoactive substance use is associated with a mental or behavioral disorder, and such a relationship is documented by the provider.** (Emphasis added.)

The codes included in the parentheses above are used to report use of alcohol, opioids, cannabis, sedatives, hypnotics or anxiolytics, cocaine, other stimulants, and hallucinogens. Not included are inhalant use **(F18.9-)** and other psychoactive substance use **(F19.9-)**. Indiscriminate or polysubstance drug use is reported with codes from category **F19**.

The reference above to Section III, Reporting Additional Diagnoses refers to guidelines for reporting additional diagnoses in an inpatient setting. The guidelines instruct that other reportable diagnoses are those that affect patient care in terms of requiring

- Clinical evaluation
- Therapeutic treatment
- Diagnostic procedures
- Extended length of hospital stay
- Increased nursing care and/or monitoring

In the outpatient setting, the guidelines instruct similarly, "Code all documented conditions that coexist at the time of the encounter/visit, and require or affect patient care treatment or management. Do not code conditions that were previously treated and no longer exist. However, history codes (categories **Z80-Z87**) may be used as secondary codes if the historical condition or family history has an impact on current care or influences treatment."

More briefly, if a patient's use of a psychoactive substance has bearing on the management and treatment of the condition for which they have sought care, it should be reported. An encounter with a 15-year-old for gastrointestinal complaints who admits to skipping school and drinking liquor the day before the encounter would indicate that the alcohol use or abuse likely influenced the management or treatment of the patient and is thus reportable. An encounter for a pre-college physical and immunization verification in a 17-year-old whose social history includes having experimented once with cannabis, which he describes as something he does not want to do again, would not likely meet the standard of affecting management or treatment.

These categories include subcategories that indicate use, abuse, and dependence of various psychoactive substances. These categories do not include abuse of non-psychoactive substances such as antacids, laxatives, or steroids that are reported with category **F55**. Each subcategory offers a spectrum of use, abuse, and dependence with extended information such as with intoxication, with withdrawal, with delusions, etc.

> Check it out: To further review the subcategories of use, abuse, and dependence, look at category **F16** (hallucinogen use) in the tabular list. Note the various subcategories and the total of 38 codes that further define the type of use and associated conditions, such as hallucinogen-induced anxiety disorder.

The guidelines also instruct on reporting use, abuse, and dependence of the same substance.

Only one code should be assigned to identify the pattern of use based on the following hierarchy:

- If both use and abuse are documented, assign only the code for abuse.
- If both abuse and dependence are documented, assign only the code for dependence.
- If use, abuse, and dependence are all documented, assign only the code for dependence.
- If both use and dependence are documented, assign only the code for dependence.

This block of codes also includes codes for dependence, in remission. The guidelines instruct that selection of codes for "in remission" (categories **F10-F19** with **-.21**) requires the provider's clinical judgment. The appropriate codes for "in remission" are assigned only on the basis of provider documentation.

Category **F10** (alcohol-related disorders) includes an instruction to use an additional code for blood alcohol level, if applicable **(Y90.-)**. Codes in category **Y90** are based on documented laboratory results.

Y90 Evidence of alcohol involvement determined by blood alcohol level
Code first any associated alcohol-related disorders **(F10)**
Y90.0	Blood alcohol level of less than 20 mg/100 mL
Y90.1	Blood alcohol level of 20–39 mg/100 mL
Y90.2	Blood alcohol level of 40–59 mg/100 mL
Y90.3	Blood alcohol level of 60–79 mg/100 mL
Y90.4	Blood alcohol level of 80–99 mg/100 mL
Y90.5	Blood alcohol level of 100–119 mg/100 mL
Y90.6	Blood alcohol level of 120–199 mg/100 mL
Y90.7	Blood alcohol level of 200–239 mg/100 mL
Y90.8	Blood alcohol level of 240 mg/100 mL or more
Y90.9	Presence of alcohol in blood, level not specified

Category **F17** provides codes for reporting nicotine dependence. This category does not include tobacco use without nicotine dependence **(Z72.0)** or history of tobacco dependence **(Z87.891)**. This category is not used to report tobacco use (smoking) during pregnancy, childbirth, and the puerperium **(O99.33-)** or toxic effect of nicotine **(T65.2-)**, but codes from this category may be reported in addition to these conditions when applicable. Counseling regarding tobacco abuse is reported with code **Z71.6**. This code has an instruction to use an additional code to report nicotine dependence **(F17.-)**.

Schizophrenia, Schizotypal, Delusional, and Other Non-Mood Psychotic Disorders

Within this block of codes **(F20-F29)**, the key coding guidance is that the categories and codes found here are not used to report mood disorders with psychotic symptoms, which are reported with codes in categories **F30-F33**.

Anxiety, Dissociative, Stress-Related, Somatoform, and Other Nonpsychotic Mental Disorders

The categories in this block include phobias, including social anxiety disorder of childhood **(F40.1-)**, phobic anxiety of childhood **(F40.8)**, panic disorders with agoraphobia **(F40.01)** and without agoraphobia **(F41.0)**, and obsessive compulsive disorder **(F42)**. Also included in this block are codes in subcategory **F43.2-** (adjustment disorders). The codes in subcategory **F43.2-** may be used to report conditions such as a grief reaction in children. An excludes 2 note at this subcategory advises that separation anxiety **(F93.0)** is not reported with these codes but may be reported in addition to codes in the subcategory when indicated.

Somatoform Disorders

Somatoform disorders reported with codes in category **F45** include somatization disorder, hypochondriacal disorders, and other somatoform disorders. Notable in this category are the codes **F45.41** and **F45.42**.

F45.4		Pain disorders related to psychological factors
Excludes 1:		pain NOS **(R52)**
F45.41		Pain disorder exclusively related to psychological factors
		Somatoform pain disorder (persistent)
F45.42		Pain disorder with related psychological factors
Code also associated acute or chronic pain **(G89.-)**		

The instruction to code also associated acute or chronic pain **(G89.-)** is also reflected in Section IC5a of the guidelines for *ICD-10-CM*. Category **G89.-** contains codes for central pain syndrome; acute pain due to trauma, post-thoracotomy, or post-procedural; chronic pain due to trauma, post-thoracotomy, or post-procedural; neoplasm-related pain; and chronic pain syndrome. The following note at category **G89.-** provides further clarification of reporting codes from this category in conjunction with code **F45.42**.

> **G89** Pain, not elsewhere classified
> **Code also** related psychological factors associated with pain **(F45.42)**
> **Excludes 1:** generalized pain NOS **(R52)**
> pain disorders exclusively related to psychological factors **(F45.41)**
> pain NOS **(R52)**

It is notable that each category has a code also note directing to the other because this gives no clear indication for sequencing of the codes. The chapter-specific guidelines for Chapter 6 of the tabular list include guidance on when a code from category

G89.- may be the principal or first-listed diagnosis. Report a code from category **G89.-** first when the encounter is for pain control or management or for insertion of a neurostimulator for pain control. When the reason for encounter is to treat an underlying condition, report first the code for that condition.

> From the guidelines: Section IC5a—Assign code **F45.41** for pain that is exclusively related to psychological disorders. As indicated by the excludes 1 note under category **G89**, a code from category **G89** should not be assigned with code **F45.41**.
>
> Code **F45.42** (pain disorders with related psychological factors) should be used with a code from category **G89** (pain, not elsewhere classified) if there is documentation of a psychological component for a patient with acute or chronic pain.

Behavioral Syndromes Associated With Physiological Disturbances and Physical Factors

The next block in Chapter 5 **(F50-F59)** includes codes for reporting eating disorders, including anorexia nervosa and bulimia nervosa, but not feeding disorders in infancy or childhood **(F98.2-)** or pica of infancy and childhood **(F98.3)**.

The block also includes sleep disorders not due to drugs or a known physiological condition, including insomnia, hypersomnia, sleep walking, and night terrors. Note that behavioral insomnia of childhood is reported with codes from Chapter 20 of the tabular list as follows:

Z73.810	Behavioral insomnia of childhood, sleep-onset association type
Z73.811	Behavioral insomnia of childhood, limit setting type
Z73.812	Behavioral insomnia of childhood, combined type
Z73.819	Behavioral insomnia of childhood, unspecified type

Postpartum depression **(F53)** is also included in this block.

Intellectual Disabilities

The block of codes **F70-F79** is used to report mild to profound intellectual disabilities. This block of codes does not include borderline intellectual functioning—IQ above 70 to 84 **(R41.83)**. When reporting codes **F70-F79**, first code any associated physical or developmental disorders. The example below demonstrates reporting of intellectual disabilities in a child with Down syndrome with developmental dysphasia. As per the code first note found at code **F70**, the physical or developmental disorders are reported before the intellectual disabilities.

Example
	Q90.0	Trisomy 21, non-mosaicism (meiotic nondisjunction)
	F80.1	Expressive language disorder
	F70	Mild intellectual disabilities

This example also aligns with an instruction at category **Q90** to use additional codes to identify any associated physical conditions and degree of intellectual disabilities **(F70-F79)**.

Pervasive and Specific Developmental Disorders

Along with expressive language disorder, the block of codes **F80-F89** includes other codes for reporting developmental disorders of speech and language, scholastic skills, and motor function. Category **F84** provides codes for reporting pervasive development disorders such as autistic disorder **(F84.0)**, Rett syndrome **(F84.2)**, and Asperger syndrome **(F84.5)**. When reporting these conditions, use additional codes to identify any associated medical condition and intellectual disabilities.

Behavioral and Emotional Disorders With Onset Usually Occurring in Childhood and Adolescence

There is a note at the beginning of this block that instructs that codes in this block are reported for the conditions with childhood and adolescent onset regardless of the age of the patient at the current encounter. It is noted that these disorders generally have onset within the childhood or adolescent years, but may continue throughout life or not be diagnosed until adulthood.

Attention deficit with hyperactivity is reported with codes from category **F90** based on the type of disorder: predominantly inattentive **(F90.0)**, predominantly hyperactive **(F90.1)**, combined **(F90.2)**, or other **(F90.8)**. In *ICD-10-CM*, report monitoring of pharmacotherapy for attention-deficit disorders with code **Z79.899** (other long-term [current] drug therapy).

Conduct disorders are also classified in this block. Category **F91** includes codes for conduct disorder confined to the family context, oppositional defiant disorder, and childhood or adolescent onset conduct disorder. This category does not include antisocial behavior **(Z72.81-)** or antisocial personality disorder (**F60.2**—an adult diagnosis).

Separation anxiety disorder of childhood is reported with code **F93.0**. Other disorders, such as mood (affective) disorders **(F30-F39)**, nonpsychotic mental disorders **(F40-F48)**, phobic anxiety disorder of childhood **(F40.8)**, or social phobia **(F40.1)** may be reported in addition to code **F93.0** when indicated. Code **F93.8** (other childhood emotional disorders) includes identity disorder but not gender identity disorder of childhood **(F64.2)**.

Disorders of Social Functioning With Onset Specific to Childhood and Adolescence

This block of codes includes selective mutism, reactive attachment disorder of childhood, and disinhibited attachment disorder of childhood (eg, institutionalism). It is important to read the notes for each of these codes as each has specific exclusions. When reporting reactive attachment disorder of childhood, also report any associated failure to thrive or growth retardation.

Other Behavioral and Emotional Disorders With Onset Usually Occurring in Childhood and Adolescence

The **F98** block includes codes for enuresis not due to physiological condition **(F98.0)**. An excludes 1 note at this code advises that enuresis NOS **(R32)** is not reported with this code. Coders should also be sure to separately identify nocturnal enuresis as **N39.44**.

Coding Scenarios

The mother of an 8-year-old child brings her to visit the pediatrician with concerns that she has begun complaining of abdominal pain and headaches on school mornings. The child reports no pain at this time, and examination of the child shows no abnormal findings. Interview of the mother indicates that the child's father is in the military and away on deployment for 1 year. This is his second deployment in 4 years. The physician talks with the child about school, which she says she likes, especially music. He acknowledges her father's deployment and asks if she worries about anything, to which she admits that she worries her father will not come home or that something will happen to her mother. The physician discusses with the mother the child's diagnosis of separation anxiety and recommends counseling at the nearby military base facility.

F93.0 Separation anxiety disorder of childhood

Though the abdominal pain and headaches prompted the visit, these were symptoms of the separation anxiety and do not meet the criteria for a separately reportable condition.

> From the guidelines: Section IB5&6—Signs and symptoms that are associated routinely with a disease process should not be assigned as additional codes unless otherwise instructed by the classification. Additional signs and symptoms that may not be associated routinely with a disease process should be coded when present.

An adolescent girl with diagnosed type 1 diabetes has been hospitalized for ketoacidosis for the second time in 3 months. In counseling the girl, the physician learns that she considers herself overweight since beginning insulin and is skipping insulin doses and decreasing the amount of insulin she takes with each injection in attempts to lose weight. She is diagnosed with an atypical eating disorder complicating type 1 diabetes mellitus.

E10.10 Type 1 diabetes mellitus with ketoacidosis without coma
F50.9 Eating disorder, unspecified
T38.3X6A Underdosing of insulin and oral hypoglycemic [antidiabetic] drugs
Z91.128 Patient's intentional underdosing of medication regimen for other reason

> From the guidelines: Section IB19e5c—Codes for underdosing should never be assigned as principal or first-listed codes. If a patient has a relapse or exacerbation of the medical condition for which the drug is prescribed because of the reduction in dose, then the medical condition itself should be coded.
>
> Noncompliance **(Z91.12-, Z91.13-)** or complication of care **(Y63.8-Y63.9)** codes are to be used with an underdosing code to indicate intent, if known.

A 17-year-old male is seen in the emergency department for a laceration to the scalp, which resulted from striking his head on the edge of a metal cabinet during what is described as "horsing around and I got shoved into the cabinet." Inquiry about alcohol or drug use determines that the patient and several other young men had been drinking beer for several hours while working on cars in the garage where the accident occurred. The patient estimates that he drank 2 beers over several hours along with eating pizza. He does not appear intoxicated on presentation to the emergency department, and brief screening does not indicate abuse or dependence. Diagnosis is laceration of scalp requiring staples.

S01.01XA Laceration without foreign body of scalp

> From the guidelines: Section IB5b3—As with all other diagnoses, the codes for psychoactive substance use **(F10.9-, F11.9-, F12.9-, F13.9-, F14.9-, F15.9-, F16.9-)** should only be assigned based on provider documentation and when they meet the definition of a reportable diagnosis (see Section III, Reporting Additional Diagnoses). The codes are to be used only when the psychoactive substance use is associated with a mental or behavioral disorder, and such a relationship is documented by the provider.

A 17-year-old patient is admitted for inpatient treatment for drug abuse after being found delirious with the drug known as bath salts and drug paraphernalia in her possession. She has a history of abuse of marijuana. She has been in foster care for the last year as her mother asked the state to take custody of her after an assault on her siblings. She admits to use of marijuana on a regular basis for several years, adding that bath salts were new to her. She tried the bath salts because she was told they would not show up if she was tested for drugs. She continued to have hallucinations periodically after admission. The patient's initial diagnosis is abuse of hallucinogenics with hallucination, and cannabis abuse with dependency.

F16.151 Hallucinogen abuse with hallucinogen-induced psychotic disorder with hallucinations

F12.20 Cannabis dependence, uncomplicated

≡ MENTAL, BEHAVIORAL, AND NEURODEVELOPMENTAL DISORDERS (F01-F09) ≡ 63

> From the guidelines: Section IB5b2—When the provider documentation refers to use, abuse, and dependence of the same substance (eg, alcohol, opioid, cannabis, etc), only one code should be assigned to identify the pattern of use based on the following hierarchy:
> - If both use and abuse are documented, assign only the code for abuse.
> - If both abuse and dependence are documented, assign only the code for dependence.
> - If use, abuse, and dependence are all documented, assign only the code for dependence.
> - If both use and dependence are documented, assign only the code for dependence.

Review What You Have Learned

6.1 A teenaged female patient has been referred for mental and behavioral health assessment for chronic bouts of abdominal pain for which extensive workup has shown no physical etiology. Her diagnosis is somatoform pain disorder. What code(s) should be reported?
   A. **F45.41**   Pain disorder exclusively related to psychological factors
   B. **G89.4**   Chronic pain syndrome
      F45.41   Pain disorder exclusively related to psychological factors
   C. **F45.42**   Pain disorder with related psychological factors
   D. **F45.42**   Pain disorder with related psychological factors
      G89.29   Other chronic pain
   E. None of the above

6.2 Codes in category **F60.3** (borderline personality disorder) would not be reported for the pediatric population.
   A. True
   B. False

6.3 Codes in the block **F90-F98** (behavioral and emotional disorders with onset usually occurring in childhood and adolescence) are reported only for pediatric patients.
   A. True
   B. False

6.4 A child has had generalized abdominal pain for 3 days with associated anorexia. The patient will be sent for additional workup, including computed tomography. At the end of this encounter, no further diagnosis is noted. The physician would report codes **R10.84** and **F50.8**.
   A. True
   B. False

6.5 A 17-year-old is seen in the emergency department for injuries incurred when he ran his car off the road and into a wooden fence. His injuries are minor but his blood alcohol level is 95 mg/100 mL and he admits to drinking heavily prior to the accident. Brief intervention and recommendations for further counseling regarding alcohol abuse are provided. The physician should report a code for alcohol use in addition to the codes for injuries incurred in the accident.
A. True
B. False

6.6 Using the case from question 6.5 above, the physician would report a code from category **Y90** to specify blood alcohol level.
A. True
B. False

≡ CHAPTER 7 ≡

Diseases of the Nervous System (G00-G99)

Diseases of the nervous system are captured with codes in Chapter 6 of the *International Classification of Diseases, Tenth Revision, Clinical Modification* (ICD-10-CM) tabular list. This chapter includes blocks **G00-G99** as follows:

Inflammatory diseases of the central nervous system **(G00-G09)**
Systemic atrophies primarily affecting the central nervous system **(G10-G14)**
Extrapyramidal and movement disorders **(G20-G26)**
Other degenerative diseases of the nervous system **(G30-G32)**
Demyelinating diseases of the central nervous system **(G35-G37)**
Episodic and paroxysmal disorders **(G40-G47)**
Nerve, nerve root, and plexus disorders **(G50-G59)**
Polyneuropathies and other disorders of the peripheral nervous system **(G60-G65)**
Diseases of myoneural junction and muscle **(G70-G73)**
Cerebral palsy and other paralytic syndromes **(G80-G83)**
Other disorders of the nervous system **(G89-G99)**

Inflammatory Diseases of the Central Nervous System

Included in this block are codes for bacterial meningitis, encephalitis, myelitis and encephalomyelitis, intracranial and intraspinal abscess and granuloma, and sequela of inflammatory diseases of the central nervous system.

Subcategory **G00** (bacterial meningitis, not elsewhere classified) includes codes for bacterial meningitis due to specific organisms, such as

G00.0	Hemophilus meningitis
G00.1	Pneumococcal meningitis
G00.2	Streptococcal meningitis
G00.3	Staphylococcal meningitis

Subcategories **G00.2** and **G00.3** require reporting of an additional code to further identify the infectious agent. A code from category **B95** (*Streptococcus, Staphylococcus,* and *Enterococcus* as the cause of diseases classified elsewhere) should be reported in addition to codes **G00.2** and **G00.3**. A code from category **B96** (other bacterial agents as the cause of diseases classified elsewhere) must be reported in addition to code **G00.8** (other bacterial meningitis), which is used to report conditions such as meningitis due to *Escherichia coli*.

Example: A 6-week-old infant is hospitalized for streptococcal meningitis identified as due to *Streptococcus pneumoniae.*

G00.2 Streptococcal meningitis

B95.3 *Streptococcus pneumoniae* as the cause of diseases classified elsewhere

The addition of code **B95.3** differentiates the underlying bacteria from other streptococci.

It is important to note that meningitis due to causes other than bacteria is often categorized in Chapter 1 of the tabular list as in **A87.0** (enteroviral meningitis). Be sure to start with the alphabetic index listing for meningitis to arrive at the correct category of codes.

Acute disseminated encephalitis and encephalomyelitis (ADEM) is reported with codes from category **G04.** Coders should query the provider if uncertain of the supporting documentation for the code selection in category **G04** to correctly assign codes for post-infectious, noninfectious, post-immunization, or unspecified ADEM. When ADEM is documented as post-immunization, codes from subcategories **T50.A-, T50.B-,** or **T50.Z-** should be reported in addition to code **G04.02.** These subcategories and instructions regarding a post-immunization condition also apply to codes in subcategory **G04.3** (acute necrotizing hemorrhagic encephalopathy).

> **Check it out:** To further review coding of post-immunization ADEM, look at categories **T50.A-, T50.B-,** and **T50.Z-** in the tabular list. Note the subcategories of poisoning, adverse effects, and underdosing of bacterial and viral vaccines and immunoglobulins.

Category **G05** (encephalitis, myelitis, and encephalomyelitis in diseases classified elsewhere) is reported for these conditions in underlying diseases such as HIV disease **(B20)** and suppurative otitis media **(H66.01-H66.4).** It is necessary, though, to carefully consult the alphabetic index when selecting a code for encephalitis, myelitis, and encephalomyelitis in diseases classified elsewhere as these conditions are often reported with codes from Chapter 1 of the tabular list, indicating these conditions are associated with infectious diseases (eg, adenoviral encephalitis, myelitis and encephalomyelitis, **A85.1**).

When reporting conditions in category **G06** (intracranial and intraspinal abscess and granuloma), use an additional code from categories **B95-B97** to identify an infectious agent.

Systemic Atrophies Primarily Affecting the Central Nervous System

This block includes codes in category **G12** for spinal muscular atrophies, including childhood types I **(G12.0)** and II **(G12.1)**. These conditions are included in the alphabetic index under the following main terms:

> Atrophy
> Disease
> Kugelberg-Welander Disease
> Syndrome
> Werdnig-Hoffmann Syndrome

Codes **G13.0** through **G13.8** provide for reporting of systemic atrophies associated with neoplastic disease and other underlying conditions. When reporting these conditions, code first the underlying neoplasm or condition.

Demyelinating Diseases of the Central Nervous System

This block of codes includes code **G35** for multiple sclerosis. Pediatric onset multiple sclerosis is not differentiated from adult-onset in *ICD-10-CM*. This block also includes codes for neuromyelitis optica **(G36.0),** which excludes optic neuritis not otherwise specified **(H46)**. Note that an excludes 1 note directs that code **G37.3** (acute transverse myelitis in demyelinating disease of central nervous system) does not include multiple sclerosis **(G35)** or neuromyelitis optica **(G36),** and these codes should not be reported in conjunction with code **G37.3**.

Epilepsy and Recurrent Seizures

Codes in category **G40** indicate the type of epilepsy as localization-related, generalized, absence, juvenile myoclonic, idiopathic, symptomatic, and other generalized epilepsy and epileptic syndromes. Codes are also provided for epilepsy related to external causes, including alcohol, drugs, hormonal changes, sleep deprivation, and stress. These codes also include the status of the condition as intractable or not intractable and with or without status epilepticus.

> **Terms to Know**
>
> **Localization-related**—involving one or more distinct parts of the brain
>
> **Generalized**—involving both sides of the brain at the same time
>
> **Idiopathic**—unknown cause
>
> **Status epilepticus**—an acute, prolonged epileptic crisis as determined by the treating physician

Both the alphabetic index and tabular list include the following note of instruction regarding assignment of intractable status when reporting epilepsy:

Note: The following terms are to be considered equivalent to intractable: pharmacoresistant (pharmacologically resistant), treatment resistant, refractory (medically), and poorly controlled.

When reporting generalized idiopathic epilepsy syndromes **(G40.3-)**, the tabular list instructs to code also for associated myoclonic epilepsy associated with ragged-red fibers **(E88.42).**

Category **G40.5** includes codes for reporting epilepsy due to external causes. This category includes the following notes:

Use additional code for adverse effect, if applicable, to identify drug (**T36-T50** with fifth or sixth character **5**)

Code also, if applicable, associated epilepsy and recurrent seizures **(G40.-)**

Example   A 15-year-old girl is seen in the office following increased episodes of seizures noted by her parents over the past 2 weeks. History reveals that the patient has been staying up at night to text a boy from school and estimates 5 to 6 hours of sleep nightly. Her physician explains the need for her to have adequate sleep due to adverse effects of inadequate sleep on juvenile myoclonic epilepsy. The girl agrees to resume longer sleep times. The diagnosis is epileptic seizures due to sleep deprivation in juvenile myoclonic epilepsy.

G40.509   Epileptic seizures related to external causes, not intractable, without status epilepticus

G40.B09   Juvenile myoclonic epilepsy, not intractable, without status epilepticus

> **Check it out:** To further review codes for reporting epilepsy, see the table of codes in Appendix B of this book. Note the various terms associated with each subcategory of codes.

Migraines and Headache Syndromes

As with epilepsy, migraines and headache syndromes are classified in *ICD-10-CM* as intractable or not intractable. Codes also indicate with or without status migrainosus. When migraines occur as an adverse effect of a drug or chemical, the tabular list instructs, "Use additional code for adverse effect, if applicable, to identify drug (**T36-T50** with fifth or sixth character **5**)."

The categories of migraine in *ICD-10-CM* include

	G43.0	Migraine without aura
	G43.1	Migraine with aura
	G43.4	Hemiplegic migraine
	G43.5	Persistent migraine aura without cerebral infarction
	G43.6	Persistent migraine aura with cerebral infarction
	G43.7	Chronic migraine without aura
	G43.A	Cyclical vomiting

G43.B	Ophthalmoplegic migraine
G43.C	Periodic headache syndromes in child or adult
G43.D	Abdominal migraine
G43.8	Other migraine
G43.9	Migraine, unspecified

Migraine with aura includes that preceded or accompanied by transient focal neurologic phenomena and may be referenced by such terms as classical migraine, migraine equivalents, and migraine-triggered seizures. When reporting migraine with aura, any associated seizure **(G40.-, R56.9)** should be reported in addition to the code for the migraine. Persistent migraine aura with cerebral infarction **(G43.6-)** is reported with an additional code to report the type of cerebral infarction **(I63.-)**.

Menstrual headaches are reported as menstrual migraines **(G43.8-)**. This subcategory includes conditions noted as menstrually related, premenstrual, and pure menstrual. Code also associated premenstrual tension syndrome **(N94.3)** when reporting a menstrual migraine.

A lower half migraine is reported as a cluster headache syndrome **(G44.00-)**. Category **G44.00-** is also used to report ciliary neuralgia.

Transient Cerebral Ischemic Attacks and Related Syndromes

Category **G45** includes codes for an unspecified transient cerebral ischemic attack **(G45.9)** and also better defined syndromes such as vertebra-basilar artery syndrome **(G45.0)** or carotid artery syndrome **(G45.1)**. The alphabetic index references these syndromes to "Insufficiency, arterial" as well as the main term, "Syndrome." Not included in this category are transient retinal artery occlusion **(H34.0)** and neonatal cerebral ischemia **(P91.0)**. This category does include codes for amaurosis fugax **(G45.3)** and transient global amnesia **(G45.4)**.

To report vascular syndromes of the brain in cerebrovascular diseases, see category **G46** and code the underlying cerebrovascular disease **(I60-I69)** first.

Sleep Disorders

Category **G47** includes codes for conditions such as insomnia, hypersomnia, and circadian rhythm disorders. It does not include nonorganic sleep disorders such as nightmares or night terrors (see category **F51**). This category also includes codes for sleep apnea but excludes sleep apnea of a newborn **(P28.3)**.

Sleep apnea is classified in subcategory **G47.3-** as obstructive, primary central, and central apnea in conditions classified elsewhere. A code also note applies to the entire subcategory **G47.3-**, indicating that an underlying condition should be reported in conjunction with codes for sleep apnea. However, sleep-related hypoventilation in conditions classified elsewhere and central sleep apnea in conditions classified elsewhere should be reported secondary to the underlying condition.

Examples

A child with Guillain-Barré syndrome is diagnosed with alveolar hypoventilation.

G61.0	Guillain-Barré syndrome

| G47.36 | Sleep related hypoventilation in conditions classified elsewhere |

A child with hypertrophic adenoids undergoes sleep testing and is diagnosed with obstructive sleep apnea with hypertrophy of adenoids.

| G47.33 | Obstructive sleep apnea (adult) (pediatric) |
| J35.2 | Hypertrophy of adenoids |

> From the guidelines: Section IA17—A code also note instructs that 2 codes may be required to fully describe a condition, but this note does not provide sequencing direction.

Nerve, Nerve Root, and Plexus Disorders

Categories **G50-G59** include codes for conditions such as trigeminal neuralgia **(G50.0)** and facial nerve disorders such as Bell's palsy **(G51.0)**. However, nerve disorders due to birth injuries are reported with codes from category **P11** or **P14**. Cranial nerve disorders due to conditions classified elsewhere **(G53)** include conditions due to a neoplasm. When reporting code **G53**, first report the code for the neoplasm.

Category **G52** includes disorders of other cranial nerves, but there is an excludes 2 note directing to code **H93.3** for disorders of the acoustic (eighth) nerve, **H46** or **H47** for disorders of the optic (second) nerve, and **H49.0-H49.2** for paralytic strabismus due to nerve palsy.

Polyneuropathies and Other Disorders of the Peripheral Nervous System

Included in categories **G60-G65** are hereditary and idiopathic neuropathies such as Charcot-Marie-Tooth **(G60.0)**, inflammatory polyneuropathies such as Guillain-Barré syndrome **(G61.0)**, polyneuropathy in diseases classified elsewhere **(G63)**, and sequelae of inflammatory and toxic polyneuropathies such as that due to Guillain-Barré syndrome **(G65.0)**. When reporting sequela of inflammatory and toxic polyneuropathies, first code the condition resulting from inflammatory and toxic polyneuropathies. Polyneuropathy in diseases classified elsewhere does not include polyneuropathy in diabetes, which would be reported with codes from categories **E08-E13** with fourth and fifth characters **.42**.

Diseases of Myoneural Junction and Muscle

The first category in this block of codes is **G70** (myasthenia gravis and other myoneural disorders). This category does not include transient neonatal myasthenia gravis **(P94.0)** or myoneural disorders due to botulism, such as *Clostridium botulinum* **(A05.1)** or infantile botulism **(A48.51)**. Myoneural disorders due to a toxic agent are reported with the code for the associated toxic agent **(T51-T65)** followed by code **G70.1**. Myasthenic syndromes in other diseases classified elsewhere are reported with code

G73.3. The underlying disease, such as neoplasm **(C00-D49)** or thyrotoxicosis **(E05.-)**, is reported first.

Category **G71** provides codes for primary disorders of muscles, including muscular dystrophy **(G71.0)**, myotonic disorders **(G71.1-)**, and congenital or mitochondrial myopathies. An excludes 2 note applies to this category as follows:

Excludes 2

>arthrogryposis multiplex congenita **(Q74.3)**
>metabolic disorders **(E70-E88)**
>myositis **(M60.-)**

When these conditions are documented in addition to primary muscle disorders, codes for these conditions should be separately reported in addition to the code for the primary muscle disorder.

Code **G71.19** (other specified myotonic disorders) includes the following conditions:

>Myotonia fluctuans
>Myotonia permanens
>Neuromyotonia [Isaacs]
>Paramyotonia congenita (of von Eulenburg)
>Pseudomyotonia
>Symptomatic myotonia

It does not include periodic paralysis (familial or potassium sensitive). These conditions are reported with code **G72.3** (periodic paralysis).

Unspecified mitochondrial myopathy is reported with code **G71.3**. Mitochondrial-related conditions that are not represented by this code include Kearns-Sayre syndrome **(H49.81)**, Leber disease **(H47.21)**, Leigh encephalopathy **(G31.82)**, mitochondrial metabolism disorders **(E88.4.-)**, and Reye syndrome **(G93.7)**. Myopathy of critical illness is reported with code **G72.81**.

Cerebral palsy is reported based on type with codes in category **G80**. The types identified in this category are

G80.0	Spastic quadriplegic cerebral palsy
G80.1	Spastic diplegic cerebral palsy
G80.2	Spastic hemiplegic cerebral palsy
G80.3	Athetoid cerebral palsy—dyskinetic cerebral palsy
G80.4	Ataxic cerebral palsy
G80.8	Other cerebral palsy—mixed cerebral palsy syndromes
G80.9	Cerebral palsy, unspecified

Hereditary spastic hemiplegia is not reported with codes from category **G80**. See code **G11.4**.

Hemiplegia and Hemiparesis

The *ICD-10-CM* guidelines for Chapter 6 offer specific instructions for reporting the dominant or nondominant side affected by hemiplegia and hemiparesis **(G81.-)**, monoplegia of lower limb **(G83.1)**, monoplegia of upper limb **(G83.2)**, and monoplegia, unspecified **(G83.3)**. For these categories and subcategories, should the affected side be documented, but not specified as dominant or nondominant, and the classification system does not indicate a default, code selection is as follows:

- For ambidextrous patients, the default should be dominant.
- If the left side is affected, the default is nondominant.
- If the right side is affected, the default is dominant.

Note that these code categories do not include congenital cerebral palsy **(G80.-)**.

Category **G81** is used to report flaccid, spastic, or unspecified hemiplegia or hemiparesis. The tabular list instructs the following regarding this category:

> This category is to be used only when hemiplegia (complete) (incomplete) is reported without further specification, or is stated to be old or long-standing but of unspecified cause. The category is also for use in multiple coding to identify these types of hemiplegia resulting from any cause.

Though the word "only" is used in the first sentence of this instruction, it is notable that the second sentence allows for reporting of hemiplegia in addition to other conditions. This same instruction applies to reporting of paraplegia, quadriplegia, and other paralytic syndromes.

Examples

A patient with long-standing paraparesis related to a T7 thoracic spine injury is seen for follow-up examination of neurologic status.

G82.22 Paraplegia, incomplete
S24.103S Unspecified injury at T7 level of thoracic spinal cord

In the above example, the patient is seen for long-standing paraparesis that is known to be a late effect of an old spinal cord injury. The multiple coding portion of the instruction would apply, as do the general *ICD-10-CM* guidelines that the condition or nature of the sequela is sequenced first. The sequela of injury code is sequenced second.

A patient with lumbar spina bifida without hydrocephalus but with complete paraplegia receives rehabilitation services.

Q05.7 Lumbar spina bifida without hydrocephalus
G82.21 Paraplegia, complete

In the above example, the multiple coding rule again applies to allow further description of the nature of the presenting condition as lumbar spina bifida without hydrocephalus with resulting complete paraplegia.

From the tabular list: Instructions for category **Q05** state, "Use additional code for any associated paraplegia (paraparesis) **(G82.2-)**."

From the guidelines: Section IA13—"Code first" and "use additional code" notes are also used as sequencing rules in the classification for certain codes that are not part of an etiology/manifestation combination.

Excluded from category **G81** are hemiplegia and hemiparesis due to sequela of cerebrovascular disease (see category **I69**). To report paralytic calcification and ossification of muscle, see subcategory **M61.2-**.

Pain, Not Elsewhere Classified

In previous chapters, codes in the **G89** category (pain, not elsewhere classified) have been noted as appropriate for reporting admissions or encounters to manage acute or chronic pain not solely psychological and pain related to neoplasms. The codes in this category are subject to both excludes 1 and excludes 2 notes that provide indication of conditions not reported with these codes. Pain that is classified elsewhere, such as causalgia **(G56.4-, G57.7-)** or complex regional pain syndrome I **(G90.5-),** should not be reported with codes from the **G89** category (pain, not elsewhere classified). There is also extended guidance in Section IC5a of the guidelines for *ICD-10-CM* on the use and sequencing of codes from category **G89**.

The codes in category **G89** are not reported when

- The pain is *not specified* as acute or chronic, post-thoracotomy, post-procedural, or neoplasm-related.
- An admission or encounter is aimed at treating a known underlying condition.

The following sequencing rules apply:

- When an encounter is for pain control or pain management, report the appropriate **G89** code first and then the code for an underlying condition, if known.
- When a patient is admitted for the insertion of a neurostimulator for pain control, assign the appropriate pain code as the principal or first-listed diagnosis.
- When insertion of a neurostimulator for pain control is performed in addition to treatment of an underlying condition at the same encounter, first code the underlying condition and then the pain code.
- If the encounter is for pain control or pain management, assign the code from category **G89** followed by the code identifying the specific site of pain.
- If the encounter is for any other reason, and a related definitive diagnosis has not been confirmed, assign the code for the specific site of pain first, followed by the appropriate code from category **G89**.

General guidance

- To identify acute or chronic pain due to presence of the device, implant, or graft, report code **G89.18** or **G89.28** in addition to codes from Chapter 19 **(T82.84-T85.84)**. Be sure to read instructions for reporting additional codes in Chapter 19.
- Routine or expected postoperative pain immediately after surgery should not be coded.
- The default for post-thoracotomy and other postoperative pain not specified as acute or chronic is the code for the acute form.
- Chronic pain must be specified by the provider and does not have a specified duration in *ICD-10-CM*.
- Assign code **F45.41** for pain that is exclusively related to psychological disorders. As indicated by the excludes 1 note under category **G89**, a code from category **G89** should not be assigned with code **F45.41**.

- Code **F45.42** (pain disorders with related psychological factors) should be used with a code from category **G89** (pain, not elsewhere classified) if there is documentation of a psychological component for a patient with acute or chronic pain.

Autonomic Disorders

Category **G90** includes codes for reporting autonomic disorders other than dysfunction of the autonomic nervous system due to alcohol **(G31.2)**. This category does include peripheral autonomic disorders such as carotid sinus syncope **(G90.01)**, multisystem degeneration of the autonomic nervous system or Shy-Drager **(G90.3)**, and complex regional pain syndrome I **(G90.5-)**.

Hydrocephalus

Category **G91** includes codes for reporting acquired hydrocephalus. The excludes 1 note for this chapter includes the following:

> Arnold-Chiari syndrome with hydrocephalus **(Q07.-)**
> congenital hydrocephalus **(Q03.-)**
> spina bifida with hydrocephalus **(Q05.-)**

Code **G91.4** (hydrocephalus in diseases classified elsewhere) does not include hydrocephalus due to congenital toxoplasmosis **(P37.1)**. When reporting code **G91.4**, report first the underlying condition, such as congenital syphilis **(A50.4-)** or a neoplasm.

Other Conditions of the Brain and Nervous System

The remaining categories of this chapter include various conditions affecting the brain and nervous system, including conditions that are intraoperative or postoperative.

Specific codes for disorders of the brain exclude several conditions that may be congenital or acquired in the neonatal period.

G93.0	Cerebral cysts, does not include acquired periventricular cysts of newborn **(P91.1)** or congenital cerebral cysts **(Q04.6)**
G93.1	Anoxic brain damage, does not include neonatal anoxia **(P84)**
G93.5	Compression of the brain, does not include traumatic compression of the brain **(S06.2-** or **S06.3-)**
G93.6	Cerebral edema, does not include that due to birth injury **(P11.0)** or trauma **(S06.1-)**

Reye syndrome is reported with code **G93.7**. The tabular list instructs to first code **T39.0-** if the syndrome is salicylate-induced.

Cerebrospinal fluid leak **(G96.0)** is reported for a leak other than that due to spinal puncture **(G97.0)**. Likewise, a dural tear **(G96.11)** is reported for tears other than due to accidental puncture or laceration of dura during a procedure **(G97.41)**. Headache due to lumbar puncture is reported with code **G97.1** (other reaction to spinal and lumbar puncture). Most intraoperative and post-procedural complications and disorders of the nervous system are reported with codes from category **G97**. However, intraoperative and post-procedural cerebrovascular infarctions are reported with codes from subcategories **I97.81-** and **I97.82-**.

The final category in this chapter, **G99,** includes codes for other disorders of the nervous system in diseases classified elsewhere. The underlying condition is reported first in each of the subcategories. There are also excludes 1 notes, such as the one indicating that autonomic neuropathy in diabetes is not classified in subcategory **G99.0** as diabetic autonomic neuropathy would be reported with codes in categories **E08-E13** with fourth and fifth characters **.43.** Code **G99.2** (myelopathy in diseases classified elsewhere) is not reported for myelopathy in intervertebral disease **(M50.0-, M51.0-)** or spondylosis **(M47.0-, M47.1-).** Code **G99.8** (other specified disorders of nervous system in diseases classified elsewhere) does not include nervous system involvement in cysticercosis **(B69.0),** rubella **(B06.0-),** or syphilis **(A52.1-).**

Coding Scenarios

A child who has undergone adenoidectomy due to hypertrophy with obstructive sleep apnea is retested in the sleep laboratory and diagnosed with continued obstructive sleep apnea.

G47.33	Obstructive sleep apnea (adult) (pediatric)
Z87.09	Personal history of other diseases of the respiratory system
Z90.89	Acquired absence of other organs

The patient no longer has hypertrophic adenoids but the history of this condition and acquired absence of the hypertrophic adenoids are pertinent to the reason for retesting.

> From the guidelines: Section IVJ—Do not code conditions that were previously treated and no longer exist. However, history codes **(Z80-Z87)** may be used as secondary codes if the historical condition or family history has an impact on current care or influences treatment. Section IB21c4: Personal history codes may be used in conjunction with follow-up codes, and family history codes may be used in conjunction with screening codes to explain the need for a test or procedure.

A patient presents to the emergency department with paraparesis that gradually developed over the last 24 hours. The patient has not been ill prior to the onset of symptoms and has no significant medical history. Laboratory testing and magnetic resonance imaging are performed with results leading to admission with a diagnosis of acute transverse myelitis.

G37.3	Acute transverse myelitis in demyelinating disease of central nervous system

> From the guidelines: Section IA7—Parentheses are used in both the alphabetic index and tabular list to enclose supplementary words that may be present or absent in the statement of a disease or procedure without affecting the code number to which it is assigned. The terms within the parentheses are referred to as nonessential modifiers.
>
> The alphabetic index listing for myelitis includes the subterm transverse with the parenthetical "(in demyelinating diseases of central nervous system)" and directs to code **G37.3**. The tabular list provides inclusion terms for code **G37.3**, including acute transverse myelitis NOS and acute transverse myelopathy.

A child who has undergone a lumbar puncture has developed an associated post-procedural headache.

G97.1 Other reaction to spinal and lumbar puncture
R51 Headache

> From the guidelines: Section IA9a—Codes titled "other" or "other specified" are for use when the information in the medical record provides detail for which a specific code does not exist. Alphabetic index entries with NEC in the line designate "other" codes in the tabular list. These alphabetic index entries represent specific disease entities for which no specific code exists, so the term is included within an "other" code.
>
> Code **G97.1** may also represent syncope following lumbar puncture.

A 17-year-old girl with focal epilepsy with simple partial seizures and recent increase in reported seizures undergoes video electroencephalogram (EEG) testing and Childhood Somatization and Functional Disability Inventories. Video EEG indicates both epileptic and non-epileptic events. The girl's responses to the somatic and functional disability inventories along with further psychiatric evaluation lead to a diagnosis of psychogenic non-epileptic seizures complicating focal epilepsy.

F44.5 Conversion disorder with seizures or convulsions

> From the guidelines: Section IA12a–An excludes 1 note indicates that the code excluded should never be used at the same time as the code above the excludes 1 note. An excludes 1 note is used when 2 conditions cannot occur together, such as a congenital form versus an acquired form of the same condition.
>
> The tabular list entry for category **G40** includes an excludes 1 notes as follows:
>
> Excludes 1: conversion disorder with seizures **(F44.5)**
> This precludes reporting of the diagnosed epilepsy in conjunction with psychogenic non-epileptic seizures (classified as a conversion disorder). Coders should query the physician to determine which diagnosis should be assigned when mutually exclusive conditions are diagnosed.

A 15-year-old girl is seen in the office for follow-up of premenstrual migraines. She notes that she also has trouble concentrating and feels very tired as her menstrual period approaches, even when her medication and diet lessen her migraine symptoms. The physician diagnoses (1) premenstrual tension syndrome (2) menstrual headache.

N94.3 Premenstrual tension syndrome
G43.829 Menstrual migraine, not intractable, without status migrainosus

> Section IVG: List first the *ICD-10-CM* code for the diagnosis, condition, problem, or other reason for encounter/visit shown in the medical record to be chiefly responsible for the services provided. List additional codes that describe any coexisting conditions. In some cases the first-listed diagnosis may be a symptom when a diagnosis has not been established (confirmed) by the physician.
>
> Section IA17: A code also note instructs that 2 codes may be required to fully describe a condition, but this note does not provide sequencing direction.
>
> The codes in this example each have a code also note referring to the other. The physician's first-listed code should be sequenced first in the situation.

Review What You Have Learned

7.1 A child is seen in the office to rule out complex regional pain syndrome II of the right foot due to continued pain following a minor injury. What is the appropriate code?
   A. **G57.71** Causalgia of right lower limb
   B. **G57.81** Other specified mononeuropathies of right lower limb
   C. **G56.41** Causalgia of right upper limb
   D. **G90.521** Complex regional pain syndrome I of right lower limb
   E. **M79.604** Pain in right leg

7.2 A patient who had Guillain-Barré syndrome 2 years ago presents with continued lack of endurance with any repetitive tasks and feeling that she is tired all the time. She is diagnosed with chronic fatigue as a residual effect of Guillain-Barré syndrome. What code(s) is appropriate?
   A. **R53.82** Chronic fatigue, unspecified
   B. **G61.0** Guillain-Barré syndrome
   C. **R53.82** Chronic fatigue, unspecified
      G61.000S Guillain-Barré syndrome
   D. **R53.82** Chronic fatigue, unspecified
      G65.0 Sequelae of Guillain-Barré syndrome
   E. None of the above

7.3 Polyneuropathy in type 1 diabetes is reported with the code for diabetes sequenced prior to the code for polyneuropathy.
   A. True
   B. False

7.4 A child has had recurrent abdominal pain for several months. The patient has had a thorough workup resulting in no findings of organic cause. The purpose of this encounter is to discuss pain management with a diagnosis of chronic abdominal pain. Code **G89.29** should be reported first, followed by a code indicating the abdominal pain.
   A. True
   B. False

7.5 A 17-year-old with juvenile myoclonic epilepsy is seen in the emergency department for seizures that lasted for more than 5 minutes. The physician evaluates the patient and documents the diagnosis as intractable juvenile myoclonic epilepsy. A code that includes status epilepticus should be reported.
   A. True
   B. False

7.6 A child with childhood absence epilepsy is seen for reevaluation following increased seizure activity. The physician documents the diagnosis as pharmacoresistant childhood absence epilepsy. The correct code for this diagnosis is **G40.A09.**
   A. True
   B. False

≡ CHAPTER 8 ≡

Diseases of the Eye and Adnexa (H00-H59)

Diseases of the eye and adnexa are captured with codes in Chapter 7 of the *International Classification of Diseases, Tenth Revision, Clinical Modification* (ICD-10-CM) tabular list. This chapter includes blocks **H00-H59**.

This chapter begins with a note reminding that an external cause code should be reported in addition to the code for a condition of the eye when applicable. The chapter includes codes for disorders of the eye but not injuries to the eye and orbit **(S05.-)**. Also excluded are conditions that are related to

- Diabetes or other endocrine, metabolic, or nutritional disorders
- Conditions originating in the perinatal period that are represented in Chapter 16
- Congenital conditions represented by codes in Chapter 17
- Infectious diseases represented by codes in Chapter 1
- Neoplasms represented in Chapter 2

Congenital conditions of the eye and adnexa are reported with codes from categories **Q10-Q15**. Injuries to the eye and orbit are reported with codes in category **S05**.

Disorders of the Eyelid

Up to now, most code categories discussed in this book have not included laterality of the site of a condition. As will be the case for most conditions that can occur unilaterally or bilaterally, codes for disorders of the eye and adnexa include laterality. Tables 8-1 and 8-2 illustrate that while final characters remain constant for categories **H00-H02.23,** codes in category **H02.3** are complete with fifth characters **0-6,** creating a different pattern for specifying site.

Likewise, codes in category **H02.4** (ptosis [mechanical, myogenic, paralytic, or unspecified]) include sixth character choices of **1** (right), **2** (left), **3** (bilateral), or **9** (unspecified). This reinforces the guidance to always select the code from the tabular list where complete codes are displayed.

Table 8-1. Laterality Characters H00-H02.23

Categories H00-H02.23 (Certain Disorders of the Eyelid)	
Final Character	Site
1	Right upper eyelid
2	Right lower eyelid
3	Right eye, unspecified eyelid
4	Left upper eyelid
5	Left lower eyelid
6	Left eye, unspecified eyelid
9	Unspecified eye, unspecified eyelid

Table 8-2. Laterality Characters H02.3

Category H02.3 Blepharochalasis	
Final Character	Site
0	Unspecified eye, unspecified eyelid
1	Right upper eyelid
2	Right lower eyelid
3	Right eye, unspecified eyelid
4	Left upper eyelid
5	Left lower eyelid
6	Left eye, unspecified eyelid

> From the guidelines: Section IB13—For bilateral sites, the final character of the codes in the *ICD-10-CM* indicates laterality. An unspecified side code is also provided should the side not be identified in the medical record. If no bilateral code is provided and the condition is bilateral, assign separate codes for both the left and right side.

Category **H00** provides codes for hordeolum externum and internum, abscess of the eyelid, and chalazion. Subcategory **H00.1** (chalazion) has an excludes 2 note indicating that an infected meibomian gland is reported with codes from subcategory **H00.02-,** indicating that while both conditions may be reported when both are present, an infected meibomian gland is not reported with codes in category **H00.1.**

On the other hand, subcategory **H01.0** (blepharitis) has an excludes 1 note indicating that blepharoconjunctivitis **(H10.5-)** is not coded here, and codes from these categories would not be reported together.

Subcategory **H02.5** provides codes for other disorders affecting eyelid function. An excludes 2 note for this subcategory indicates that blepharospasm **(G24.5)**, organic tic **(G25.69)**, and psychogenic tic **(F95.-)** are not reported with codes in subcategory **H02.5**.

When reporting a retained foreign body in the eyelid, subcategory **H02.81-** instructs to use an additional code to identify the type of retained foreign body **(Z18.-)**. Category **Z18** includes codes for reporting

Z18.0-	Retained radioactive fragments
Z18.1-	Retained metal fragments
Z18.2-	Retained plastic fragments
Z18.3-	Retained organic fragments
Z18.81	Retained glass fragments
Z18.83	Retained stone or crystalline fragments
Z18.89	Other specified retained foreign body fragments
Z18.9	Retained foreign body fragments, unspecified material

Codes from category **Z18.-** are also reported in addition to codes in subcategories **H05.5-** (retained [old] foreign body following penetrating wound of orbit), **H44.6-** (retained [old] intraocular foreign body, magnetic), and **H44.7-** (retained [old] intraocular foreign body, nonmagnetic).

An excludes 1 note indicates that codes from subcategory **H02.81-** do not represent a laceration of the eyelid with foreign body **(S01.12-)**, retained intraocular foreign body **(H44.6-, H44.7-)**, or superficial foreign body of the eyelid and periocular area **(S00.25-)**.

Disorders of the Lacrimal System

Category **H04.2-** provides codes for reporting epiphora due to excess lacrimation **(H04.21-)**, due to insufficient drainage **(H04.22-)**, or of unspecified cause **(H04.20-)**.

Code **H04.3** (acute and unspecified inflammation of lacrimal passages) includes codes for reporting of dacryocystitis specified as phlegmonous, acute, or unspecified and acute lacrimal canaliculitis. This subcategory does not include neonatal dacryocystitis **(P39.1)**. Chronic inflammation of the lacrimal passages is reported with codes in subcategory **H04.4**.

Subcategory **H04.53-** (neonatal obstruction of nasolacrimal duct) excludes congenital stenosis and stricture of the lacrimal duct **(Q10.5)**.

Conjunctivitis

Codes that may be commonly reported for conjunctivitis include those in subcategory **H10.01-** (acute follicular conjunctivitis), category **H10.1-** (acute atopic conjunctivitis), and **H10.41-** (chronic giant papillary conjunctivitis). Not included here are neonatal conjunctivitis and dacryocystitis, which are reported with code **P39.1**. Code **P39.1** includes neonatal chlamydial conjunctivitis but does not include gonococcal conjunctivitis **(A54.31)**.

Although category **H10** provides multiple subcategories of codes for conjunctivitis, it is important to note that codes for viral and bacterial conjunctivitis are also found in Chapter 1 of the tabular list.

Codes for viral conjunctivitis include

B00.53	Herpesviral conjunctivitis
B02.31	Zoster conjunctivitis
B30.1	Conjunctivitis due to adenovirus
B30.2	Viral pharyngoconjunctivitis
B30.3	Acute epidemic hemorrhagic conjunctivitis (enteroviral)
B30.8	Other viral conjunctivitis
B30.9	Viral conjunctivitis, unspecified

The alphabetic index for the main term "Conjunctivitis, NOS" includes staphylococcal and streptococcal as nonessential modifiers and directs to code **H10.9** (unspecified conjunctivitis). There is no subterm for bacterial under the term "conjunctivitis" in the alphabetic list. However, certain specific bacterial causes of conjunctivitis are listed. These include

A36.86	Diphtheritic conjunctivitis
A39.89	Other meningococcal infections
A52.71	Late syphilitic oculopathy
A54.31	Gonococcal conjunctivitis
A74.0	Chlamydial conjunctivitis
A71.0	Initial stage of trachoma
A71.1	Active stage of trachoma
B94.0	Sequelae of trachoma

Koch-Weeks conjunctivitis *(Haemophilus influenzae, Haemophilus aegyptius)* is reported with codes from subcategory **H10.02** (other mucopurulent conjunctivitis). Parinaud conjunctivitis or Parinaud oculoglandular syndrome is reported with code **H10.89**. Also reported with code **H10.89** are conjunctival ulcer and traumatic conjunctivitis.

Superficial keratitis with conjunctivitis is reported with codes in subcategory **H16.20** (unspecified keratoconjunctivitis). Keratoconjunctivitis due to adenovirus is reported with code **B30.0**. Other keratoconjunctivitis is reported with codes in category **H16.2-**. Codes in subcategory **H16.26-** are used to report vernal keratoconjunctivitis with limbal and corneal involvement. An excludes 1 note indicates that vernal conjunctivitis without limbal and corneal involvement is reported with code **H10.44**.

Serous conjunctivitis that is not noted to be viral or chemical is reported with codes from subcategory **H10.23-**.

Chemical conjunctivitis is reported with codes from subcategory **H10.21-**. This subcategory does not include codes for reporting burn and corrosion of eye and adnexa **(T26.-)**. When reporting chemical conjunctivitis, first code **(T51-T65)** to identify chemical and intent.

Example   A child who swam earlier in the day at an indoor swimming pool has had burning sensation and redness of the eyes for several hours despite flushing with cool water. Several other swimmers complained of eye or respiratory irritation. The pool area was noted to have a strong odor of chlorine, and per the parents, a door was opened to the outdoors to provide more ventilation after the initial complaints. The diagnosis is chemical conjunctivitis due to chloramine exposure.

T57.8X1A Toxic effect of other specified inorganic substances, accidental (unintentional)
H10.213 Acute toxic conjunctivitis, bilateral
Y92.34 Swimming pool (public) as the place of occurrence of the external cause
Y93.11 Activity, swimming
Y99.8 Other external cause status

> Note that the alphabetic index for *ICD-10-CM* directs to code **B30.1** for conjunctivitis, swimming pool. Code **B30.1** indicates conjunctivitis due to adenovirus and would not be reported when documentation indicates chemical conjunctivitis due to exposure to chemicals used in a swimming pool.

Corneal Disorders

Changes in the corneal membranes are reported with codes in category **H18.3**. Folds and rupture in the Bowman membrane are reported with codes in subcategory **H18.31-**. These conditions affecting the Descemet membrane are separated into subcategories for folds **(H18.32-)** and ruptures **(H18.33-)**.

ICD-10-CM categorizes keratoconus as unspecified **(H18.60-)**, stable **(H18.61-)**, or unstable **(H18.62-)**. Codes further specify right, left, or bilateral eye involvement.

Corneal edema secondary to contact lens is reported with codes in subcategory **H18.21-**. Other corneal disorders secondary to contact lens are reported with codes in subcategory **H18.82**.

Complications of a corneal transplant are reported with codes in category **T86.84-** for rejection, failure, or infection, and in category **T85.3-** for mechanical breakdown, displacement, mechanical obstruction, perforation, or protrusion. The appropriate seventh character is to be added to each code from category **T85** to identify the encounter as initial **(A)**, subsequent **(D)**, or sequela **(S)**.

Iridocyclitis

Category **H20** includes codes for iridocyclitis, including iritis and uveitis. Keratouveitis is cross-referenced to iridocyclitis in the alphabetic index. This category has a list of underlying conditions that are not reported here, including iridocyclitis, iritis, and uveitis in diabetes mellitus **(E08-E13** with **.39)** and in infectious diseases. Iridocyclitis in ankylosing spondylitis is reported with a code for ankylosing spondylitis **(M45)** (adult). There is no alphabetic index or tabular list instruction regarding the reporting of iridocyclitis in juvenile ankylosing spondylitis **(M08.1)**.

Subcategory **H20.0** includes acute and subacute iridocyclitis with codes specifying primary, recurrent, secondary infectious, secondary noninfectious, and hypopyon. Chronic iridocyclitis **(H20.1-)** is reported first with an additional code for any associated cataract **(H26.21-)**.

Juvenile Cataracts

Infantile and juvenile cataracts (other than congenital cataract **[Q12.0]** or traumatic cataract **[H26.1-]**) are reported with codes in subcategory **H26.0**. The codes are based on type of cataract and involvement of one or both eyes as shown in Table 8-3.

Table 8-3. *ICD-10-CM* **Codes for Juvenile Cataracts**

Type	Right Eye	Left Eye	Bilateral	Unspecified
Cortical, lamellar, or zonular	H26.011	H26.012	H26.013	H26.019
Nuclear cataract	H26.031	H26.032	H26.033	H26.039
Anterior subcapsular polar	H26.041	H26.042	H26.043	H26.049
Posterior subcapsular polar	H26.051	H26.052	H26.053	H26.059
Combined forms	H26.061	H26.062	H26.063	H26.069

Cataracts that are secondary to ocular disorders (degenerative) (inflammatory) are reported with codes in subcategory **H26.22-** with a second code reported to indicate the associated ocular disorder. Cataracts due to diabetes are reported with codes in categories **E08-E13** with fourth and fifth characters **.33**. Cataracts in diseases classified elsewhere, such as hypoparathyroidism **(E20.-)**, are reported with the code for the underlying condition followed by code **H28** (cataract in diseases classified elsewhere).

Traumatic cataracts **(H26.1-)** are classified as localized, partially resolved, or total. An additional code from Chapter 20 is used to identify the external cause of the trauma.

Disorders of the Lens

Category **H27** includes codes for aphakia **(H27.0-)** and for subluxation, anterior dislocation, or posterior dislocation of the lens **(H27.1-)**. To report pseudophakia, see code **Z96.1** (presence of intraocular lens). Complications of the intraocular lens are reported with codes in category **T85** as follows:

- **T85.21-** Breakdown (mechanical) of intraocular lens
- **T85.22-** Displacement of intraocular lens
- **T85.29-** Other mechanical complication of intraocular lens (eg, mechanical obstruction, perforation, or protrusion)
- **T85.79-** Infection and inflammatory reaction
- **T85.81-** Embolism
- **T85.82-** Fibrosis
- **T85.83-** Hemorrhage
- **T85.84-** Pain
- **T85.85-** Stenosis
- **T85.86-** Thrombosis

The appropriate seventh character is to be added to each code from category **T85** to identify the encounter as initial **(A)**, subsequent **(D)**, or sequela **(S)**.

Disorders of the Choroid and Retina

Retinopathy of prematurity is reported with codes in subcategory **H35.1-**. Codes in this subcategory allow for reporting of severity stages 0–5 (as it is in *ICD-9-CM*) with identification of either the right, left, or both eyes. Subcategory **H35.17** is used to report retrolental fibroplasia. Code **H36** (retinal disorders in diseases classified elsewhere) is reported secondarily to the code for the underlying condition, such as sickle cell disease. Code **H36** is not used to report diabetic retinopathy, which is reported with a code in categories **E08-E13.**

Glaucoma

Newborn or childhood cases of glaucoma may often be reported with code **Q15.0** (congenital glaucoma), but there are exceptions. Traumatic glaucoma due to birth injury is reported with code **P15.3** (birth injury to eye).

Glaucoma in diseases classified elsewhere is reported with code **H42**. First code the underlying condition.

> Amyloidosis **(E85-)**
> Aniridia **(Q13.1)**
> Lowe syndrome **(E72.03)**
> Reiger anomaly **(Q13.81)**
> Specified metabolic disorder **(E70-E88)**

This excludes glaucoma in diabetes mellitus (**E08-E13** with fourth and fifth digits **.39**) or in certain infectious diseases.

Glaucoma secondary to eye trauma is reported with codes in category **H40.3-**, with any associated underlying condition also reported. One of the following seventh characters is to be assigned to each code in subcategories **H40.3** (and several other categories for reporting glaucoma) to designate the stage of glaucoma.

> **0**–stage unspecified
> **1**–mild stage
> **2**–moderate stage
> **3**–severe stage
> **4**–indeterminate stage

This instruction also applies to subcategories **H40.4-** (glaucoma secondary to eye inflammation) and **H40.5-** (glaucoma secondary to other eye disorders). Glaucoma secondary to drugs is reported with codes from subcategory **H40.6-**, including a seventh character for stage and an additional code for adverse effect, if applicable, to identify the related drug (**T36-T50** with fifth or sixth character **5**).

Codes for complications of treatment include **H59.4-** (inflammation [infection] of post-procedural bleb). A filtering (vitreous) bleb after glaucoma surgery status is reported with code **Z98.83.**

Disorders of the Optic Nerve and Visual Pathways

When reporting disorders of the optic chiasm **(H47.4-)** and other visual pathways **(H47.5-),** also report the code for the underlying condition. The codes in these subcategories specify the disorder as in or due to inflammatory disorders, neoplasm, or vascular disorders. Code **H47.49** is used to report disorders of the optic chiasm in or due to disorders other than inflammatory disorders, neoplasm, or vascular disorders.

Disorders of Visual Cortex

The underlying condition is also reported with codes in subcategory **H47.6** (disorders of visual cortex). Injury to visual cortex **(S04.04)** is not included here. Codes for cortical blindness **(H47.61-)** specify the side of the brain involved as right, left, or unspecified. This is also true for disorders of the visual cortex in or due to inflammation **(H47.62-)**, neoplasm **(H47.63-)**, or vascular disorders **(H47.64-)**.

Disorders of Ocular Muscles, Binocular Movement, Accommodation, and Refraction

Category **H49** includes codes for paralytic strabismus with subcategories for third **(H49.0-)**, fourth **(H49.1-)**, and sixth nerve palsy **(H49.2-)** and for total ophthalmoplegia **(H49.3-)**, progressive external ophthalmoplegia **(H49.4-)**, and other paralytic strabismus **(49.8-)**. Each subcategory includes codes to specify right, left, or bilateral eyes.

Codes for esotropia **(H50.0-)** and exotropia **(H50.1-)** are categorized according to monocular or alternating and with an A or V pattern or other noncomitancies.

Blindness and Low Vision

When reporting blindness or low vision, first report the code for any associated underlying cause of the blindness. Codes for blindness and low vision are classified according to recommendations of the WHO Study Group on the Prevention of Blindness, Geneva, 6–10 November 1972 (table is included in *ICD-10-CM*). Codes in category **H54** indicate whether blindness or low vision affects one or both eyes and identify laterality. Code **H54.8** is used to report legal blindness, as defined in the United States.

Intraoperative and Post-Procedural Complications and Disorders

This category includes codes for intraoperative and post-procedural complications and disorders with the following subcategories:

H59.01-	Keratopathy (bullous aphakic) following cataract surgery
H59.02-	Cataract (lens) fragments in eye following cataract surgery
H59.03-	Cystoid macular edema following cataract surgery
H59.09-	Other disorders of the eye following cataract surgery
H59.11-	Intraoperative hemorrhage and hematoma of eye and adnexa complicating an ophthalmic procedure
H59.12-	Intraoperative hemorrhage and hematoma of eye and adnexa complicating other procedure
H59.21-	Accidental puncture and laceration of eye and adnexa during an ophthalmic procedure
H59.22-	Accidental puncture and laceration of eye and adnexa during other procedure

H59.31- Post-procedural hemorrhage and hematoma of eye and adnexa following an ophthalmic procedure
H59.32- Post-procedural hemorrhage and hematoma of eye and adnexa following other procedure
H59.4- Inflammation (infection) of post-procedural bleb
H59.81- Chorioretinal scars after surgery for detachment

Laterality is specified in each of these subcategories except **H59.4-**, which specifies the stage of inflammation and infection. Other intraoperative complications of eye and adnexa are reported with code **H59.88**. This category does not include codes for mechanical breakdown, displacement, or other mechanical complication of a prosthetic orbit **(T85.3-)**; mechanical complication of intraocular lens **(T85.2)**; or secondary cataracts **(H26.4-)**.

Family History of Eye Disorders

While some codes from other chapters have already been included here, the family history codes related to eye disorders found in Chapter 21 of the tabular list have not, but they may add information to support medically necessary encounters and testing. These include

Z83.511 Family history of glaucoma (other than blindness and visual loss)
Z83.518 Family history of other specified eye disorder
Z82.1 Family history of blindness and visual loss

Coding Scenarios

A teenager who began wearing extended wear contact lenses last year has developed ocular itching and contact lens intolerance. He is diagnosed with chronic giant papillary conjunctivitis of the right eye.

H10.411 Chronic giant papillary conjunctivitis, right eye

The same teenager returns 6 weeks later for reevaluation. He reports less itching and discomfort. Physical examination also shows improvement. The diagnosis is chronic giant papillary conjunctivitis of the right eye.

H10.411 Chronic giant papillary conjunctivitis, right eye

> **From the guidelines: Section IV—Chronic diseases treated on an ongoing basis may be coded and reported as many times as the patient receives treatment and care for the condition(s).**

A patient with diabetes mellitus type 1 presents to the clinic with a complaint of itching, watering, and redness of both eyes. The patient is diagnosed with allergic conjunctivitis.

H10.13 Acute atopic conjunctivitis, bilateral

> From the guidelines: Section IVJ—Code all documented conditions that coexist at the time of the encounter/visit and require or affect patient care treatment or management.
>
> In this scenario there is no indication that the patient's diabetes required or affected patient care, treatment, or management. The sole diagnosis given is allergic conjunctivitis that is categorized as acute atopic conjunctivitis in the alphabetic index.

A child is diagnosed with monocular esotropia of the right eye with amblyopia.

H53.031 Strabismic amblyopia, right eye

> From the guidelines: Section IB9—Assign only the combination code when that code fully identifies the diagnostic conditions involved or when the alphabetic index so directs. Multiple coding should not be used when the classification provides a combination code that clearly identifies all of the elements documented in the diagnosis.
>
> An excludes 1 note at category **H53** indicates that strabismus **(H50.-)** is not reported at the same time as strabismic amblyopia.

A first-grade boy is seen by his physician after a vision screening in his school indicated color blindness. The physician evaluates the child and diagnoses incomplete deuteranopia.

H53.53 Deuteranomaly

> Parentheses are used in both the alphabetic index and tabular list to enclose supplementary words that may be present or absent in the statement of a disease or procedure without affecting the code number to which it is assigned. The terms within the parentheses are referred to as nonessential modifiers.
>
> "Incomplete" is a nonessential modifier to the term "deuteranopia" in the alphabetic index.
>
> From the guidelines: Section I11—List of terms is included under some codes. These terms are the conditions for which that code is to be used. The terms may be synonyms of the code title or, in the case of "other specified" codes, the terms are a list of the various conditions assigned to that code. The inclusion terms are not necessarily exhaustive. Additional terms found only in the alphabetic index may also be assigned to a code.
>
> "Deuteranopia" is an inclusion term found listed under code **H53.53** (deuteranomaly) in the tabular list.

A 15-year-old girl is seen in consultation for chronic iridocyclitis associated with pauciarticular juvenile rheumatoid arthritis affecting the right ankle and left shoulder. She is diagnosed with mild-stage glaucoma secondary to the chronic iridocyclitis.

H40.41X1	Glaucoma secondary to eye inflammation, right eye
H20.11	Chronic iridocyclitis, right eye
M08.471	Pauciarticular juvenile rheumatoid arthritis, right ankle and foot
M08.412	Pauciarticular juvenile rheumatoid arthritis, left shoulder

> A code also note instructs that 2 codes may be required to fully describe a condition but does not provide sequencing direction.
>
> Subcategory **H40.4** instructs to code also the underlying condition, which in this scenario is chronic iridocyclitis (an underlying condition associated with pauciarticular juvenile rheumatoid arthritis). The physician's documentation lists the mild-stage glaucoma first, so it is sequenced first.

Review What You Have Learned

8.1 A child with chronic iridocyclitis has developed a cataract as a complication of the iridocyclitis. What subterm would help you find the code for this cataract in the alphabetic index for cataract?
   A. - in
   B. - complicated
   C. - due to
   D. - secondary
   E. All of the above

8.2 A child is diagnosed with superior oblique muscle paralysis of the right eye. What is the code for this diagnosis?
   A. **G52.9** Cranial nerve disorder, unspecified
   B. **H49.11** Fourth [trochlear] nerve palsy, right eye
   C. **H50.21** Vertical strabismus, right eye
   D. **H50.60** Mechanical strabismus, unspecified
   E. None of the above

8.3 A 4-month-old child is diagnosed with esotropia of the right eye. The seventh character of the code for this condition designates laterality.
   A. True
   B. False

8.4 The code for neonatal obstruction of the nasolacrimal duct is found in the tabular list in Chapter 16, Certain Conditions Originating in the Perinatal Period.
   A. True
   B. False

8.5 A 5-year-old is diagnosed with myopia. What code should be reported for this diagnosis?
   A. **H52.13** Myopia, bilateral
   B. **H52.10** Myopia, unspecified eye
   C. **H52.19** Myopia, unspecified eye
   D. **H52.4** Presbyopia
   E. None of the above

8.6 The code for a congenital cataract is included in the tabular list in Chapter 7, Diseases of the Eye and Adnexa.
   A. True
   B. False

≡ CHAPTER 9 ≡

Diseases of the Ear and Mastoid Process (H60-H95)

Diseases of the ear and mastoid process are captured with codes in Chapter 8 of the *International Classification of Diseases, Tenth Revision, Clinical Modification (ICD-10-CM)* tabular list. This chapter includes blocks **H60-H95** as follows:

Diseases of external ear **(H60-H62)**
Diseases of middle ear and mastoid **(H65-H75)**
Diseases of inner ear **(H80-H83)**
Other disorders of ear **(H90-H94)**
Intraoperative and post-procedural complications and disorders of ear and mastoid process, not elsewhere classified **(H95)**

This chapter begins with a note reminding that an external cause code should be reported in addition to the code for a condition of the ear when applicable. The chapter includes codes for disorders of the ear but not injuries to the ear **(S00.4-)**.

Disorders of the External Ear

This block includes codes for abscess or cellulitis of the external ear, otitis externa including swimmer's ear **(H60.33-)**, cholesteatoma **(H60.4-)**, and chondritis and perichondritis of the external ear. Codes include laterality.

The alphabetic index references and the instructions at subcategory **H62.4-** are necessary to determine the correct code(s) for reporting otomycosis. Certain fungal infections of the external ear are reported with a combination code such as **B37.84** (candidal otitis externa). Otomycosis without identification of the fungal organism is reported with code **B36.9** (superficial mycosis, unspecified) followed by a code for otitis externa in other diseases classified elsewhere **(H62.4-)**. Subcategory **H62.4-** is also used to report otitis externa in diseases such as impetigo **(L01.0, H62.4-)**.

Also included in this block are the codes for impacted cerumen

H61.20	Impacted cerumen, unspecified ear
H61.21	Impacted cerumen, right ear
H61.22	Impacted cerumen, left ear
H61.23	Impacted cerumen, bilateral

Diseases of the Middle Ear and Mastoid

This block begins with codes for otitis media and an instruction to report any associated tobacco use or exposure. The following codes are to be reported with many conditions that are affected by tobacco use or exposure:

>Exposure to environmental tobacco smoke **(Z77.22)**
>Exposure to tobacco smoke in the perinatal period **(P96.81)**
>History of tobacco use **(Z87.891)**
>Occupational exposure to environmental tobacco smoke **(Z57.31)**
>Tobacco dependence **(F17.-)**
>Tobacco use **(Z72.0)**

When otitis media is a manifestation of another condition it may be reported with codes from category **H67** (otitis media in diseases classified elsewhere). However, otitis media in certain conditions such as influenza may be reported with a combination code for that condition rather than a code from Chapter 8. There is an excludes 1 note at category **H67** identifying some conditions for which combination codes include otitis media.

>*Example:* A child is diagnosed with an influenza B virus complicated by otitis media.
>
>>**J10.83** Influenza due to other identified influenza virus with otitis media
>>**B97.89** Other viral agents as the cause of diseases classified elsewhere

Code **J10.83** is a combination code identifying the otitis media as a complication or manifestation of influenza. Type B influenza is not specified by **J10.83** and, although the tabular list entry for category **J10** instructs that an additional code from category **B97** should be reported to identify the virus, code **B97.89** is the most specific code for type B influenza.

When applicable, a perforated tympanic membrane is also reported in conjunction with otitis media using a code from category **H72.-**. It is not necessary to report a code from category **H72.-** for perforation when reporting acute suppurative otitis media with rupture of the tympanic membrane **(H66.01-)**. Codes for otitis media are categorized as acute or chronic and non-suppurative or suppurative as in the Table 9-1 and 9-2 (excludes codes for unspecified).

These tables include only the codes that represent specific types of otitis media with laterality specified. There are codes for unspecified types of acute and chronic, suppurative and non-suppurative otitis media and for each of the conditions in unspecified ears, but these codes should only be reported when the more specific information is unobtainable. Note that otitis media not specified as acute, subacute, or chronic is reported with an unspecified code **(H65.9, H66.4, or H66.9)**.

Mastoiditis and related conditions such as subperiosteal abscess, petrositis, and postauricular fistula are reported with codes in category **H70**. These conditions are classified as acute or chronic and location (laterality). Mastoiditis in infectious and parasitic disease classified elsewhere is reported with codes in category **H75**.

Table 9-1. ICD-10-CM Non-Suppurative Otitis Media

Type of Non-Suppurative Otitis Media	Right Ear	Left Ear	Bilateral
Serous, acute (secretory)	H65.01	H65.02	H65.03
Serous, recurrent acute	H65.04	H65.05	H65.06
Serous, chronic	H65.21	H65.22	H65.23
Allergic, acute & subacute	H65.111	H65.112	H65.113
Allergic, recurrent acute & subacute	H65.114	H65.115	H65.116
Allergic, chronic	H65.411	H65.412	H65.413
Other non-suppurative, acute (mucoid, sanguinous, seromucinous)	H65.191	H65.192	H65.193
Other non-suppurative, acute recurrent	H65.194	H65.195	H65.196
Other non-suppurative, chronic	H65.491	H65.492	H65.493
Chronic mucoid—excludes adhesive middle ear disease (H74.1)	H65.31	H65.32	H65.33

Table 9-2. ICD-10-CM Suppurative Otitis Media

Type of Suppurative Otitis Media	Right Ear	Left Ear	Bilateral
Suppurative otitis media, acute *without* spontaneous rupture of eardrum	H66.001	H66.002	H66.003
Suppurative otitis media, acute *without* spontaneous rupture of eardrum, recurrent	H66.004	H66.005	H66.006
Suppurative otitis media *with* spontaneous rupture of eardrum, acute	H66.011	H66.012	H66.013
Suppurative otitis media *with* spontaneous rupture of eardrum, acute, recurrent	H66.014	H66.015	H66.016
Chronic tubotympanic suppurative otitis media	H66.11	H66.12	H66.13
Chronic atticoantral suppurative otitis media	H66.21	H66.22	H66.23
Other chronic suppurative otitis media	H66.3X1	H66.3X2	H66.3X3

Cholesteatomas of the middle ear are reported with codes in category **H71** with distinction of site and laterality. Codes include cholesteatoma of the attic, tympanum, mastoid, or diffuse cholesteatoma. This category does not include cholesteatoma of the external ear **(H60.4-)**. Recurrent cholesteatoma of a post-mastoidectomy cavity is reported with codes **H95.00-H95.03**. Category **H95** also includes codes for other post-mastoidectomy complications such as granulation, mucosal cyst, or chronic inflammation.

Category **H72** includes codes for persistent posttraumatic perforation of the eardrum as well as post-inflammatory perforation. Not included is a current traumatic rupture of the eardrum **(S09.2-)**. Codes capture the extent and site of perforation, including central, attic, other marginal, multiple perforations, or total perforation.

Acute myringitis, not associated with otitis media, is reported with codes in category **H73**. Codes in category **H73** are not reported in addition to codes for otitis media **(H65, H66)**.

Loss of Hearing

Conductive, sensorineural, and mixed hearing loss are categorized in *ICD-10-CM* with specificity of bilateral conditions or unilateral with unrestricted hearing on the contralateral side. These conditions are reported with codes in category **H90** as shown in Table 9-3.

Table 9-3. *ICD-10-CM* Hearing Loss

Type of Hearing Loss	Bilateral	Right Ear (with unrestricted hearing left ear)	Left Ear (with unrestricted hearing right ear)
Conductive	H90.0	H90.11	H90.12
Sensorineural	H90.3	H90.41	H90.42
Mixed	H90.6	H90.71	H90.72

Noise-induced hearing loss is reported with codes **H83.3X1–H83.3X9**, which include noise effects on the inner ear. Hearing loss due to impacted cerumen is reported with a code for impacted cerumen **(H61.2-)**. Sudden idiopathic hearing loss is reported with codes in subcategory **H91.2-**. Code **H91.3** is used to report deaf, nonspeaking not otherwise specified.

Ototoxic hearing loss due to poisoning or adverse effect of a drug or toxin is reported with subcategory **H91.0-**. If the hearing loss is due to poisoning, a code from categories **T36–T50** with fifth or sixth character **1–4** or **6** (indicating poisoning by a specific drug or toxin and intent) is reported first, followed by the code from subcategory **H91.0-**. When hearing loss is due to an adverse effect of a drug, the **H91.0-** code is reported first, followed by a code from categories **T36–T50** with fifth or sixth character **5** to indicate the drug.

Otorrhagia

When reporting otorrhagia, codes in category **H92.2** are used only when the cause is not trauma. For otorrhagia due to trauma or fracture, see the appropriate injury codes, such as puncture of the ear canal **(S01.33-)** or eardrum **(S09.2-)**.

Complications of Procedures

Intraoperative and post-procedural complications of procedures to the ear and mastoid process are reported with codes in category **H95**. As noted previously, these include complications of mastoidectomy. Also included in this category are codes for intraoperative hemorrhage and hematoma, accidental puncture and laceration, and post-procedural hemorrhage or hematoma. Codes in subcategory **H95.81-** are specific to post-procedural stenosis of the ear canal.

Coding Scenarios

A 2-year-old child is diagnosed with acute recurrent otitis media with effusion of the right ear.

H65.194   Other acute non-suppurative otitis media, recurrent, right ear

> From the guidelines: Section I16—The "see" instruction following a main term in the alphabetic index indicates that another term should be referenced. It is necessary to go to the main term referenced with the "see" note to locate the correct code.
>
> The alphabetic index provides a "see" instruction for otitis, media, with effusion (non-purulent) directing to "see Otitis, media, non-suppurative, acute."

A 2-year-old child is diagnosed with acute recurrent otitis media with effusion of the right ear. The child's parents indicate that they smoke at home and in the car, exposing the child to secondhand cigarette smoke.

H65.194   Other acute non-suppurative otitis media, recurrent, right ear
Z77.22   Contact with and (suspected) exposure to environmental tobacco smoke

> From the guidelines: Section IB7—"Use additional code" notes are found in the tabular list at codes that are not part of an etiology/manifestation pair where a secondary code is useful to fully describe a condition. The sequencing rule is the same as the etiology/manifestation pair, "use additional code" indicates that a secondary code should be added.
>
> The tabular list instruction for category **H65** includes "Use an additional code" to identify exposure to environmental tobacco smoke **(Z77.22)** in addition to other codes that describe tobacco exposure, use, or history of use and dependence.

A 6-year-old boy is reevaluated for hearing loss following completion of chemotherapy with cisplatin. Results indicate that the child has significant loss of hearing in both ears in comparison to results of evaluations previously conducted. Diagnosis is ototoxic hearing loss as a late effect of chemotherapy.

H91.03   Ototoxic hearing loss, bilateral
T45.1X5S Adverse effect of antineoplastic and immunosuppressive drugs

> From the guidelines: Section IC19E5—When coding an adverse effect of a drug that has been correctly prescribed and properly administered, assign the appropriate code for the nature of the adverse effect followed by the appropriate code for the adverse effect of the drug **(T36-T50)**. The code for the drug should have a fifth or sixth character 5 (eg, **T36.0X5-**).

Review What You Have Learned

9.1 A child with left ear pain and tinnitus is diagnosed with acute fungal otitis externa of the left ear.
   A. **H60.92** Unspecified otitis externa, left ear
   B. **H60.8X2** Other otitis externa, left ear
   C. **H60.392** Other infective otitis externa, left ear
   D. **H60.312** Diffuse otitis externa, left ear
   E. **B36.9** Superficial mycosis, unspecified
   H62.42 Otitis externa in other diseases classified elsewhere, left ear

9.2 A teenager complains of loss of hearing in his left ear. The diagnosis is loss of hearing in the left ear due to cerumen impaction. What is the code for this diagnosis?
   A. **H91** Other and unspecified hearing loss
   B. **H91.22** Sudden idiopathic hearing loss, left ear
   C. **H91.8X2** Other specified hearing loss, left ear
   D. **H61.22** Impacted cerumen, left ear
   E. None of the above

9.3 A code indicating exposure to environmental tobacco smoke should be reported in addition to codes for otitis media when documentation indicates exposure.
   A. True
   B. False

9.4 What code or codes are reported for acute bilateral purulent otitis media with spontaneous rupture of the right tympanic membrane and intact left membrane?
   A. **H65.113** Acute and subacute allergic otitis media, bilateral
   H72.91 Unspecified perforation of tympanic membrane, right
   B. **H66.011** Acute suppurative otitis media with spontaneous rupture of eardrum, right ear
   H66.002 Acute suppurative otitis media without spontaneous rupture of eardrum, left ear
   C. **H65.193** Other acute non-suppurative otitis media, bilateral
   H72.821 Total perforations of tympanic membrane, right
   D. **H66.013** Acute suppurative otitis media with spontaneous rupture of eardrum, bilateral
   E. None of the above

9.5 Code **H92.22** would be reported for the diagnosis of a child who sustained a blow to the left jaw and ear resulting in otorrhagia.
   A. True
   B. False

≡ CHAPTER 10 ≡

Diseases of the Circulatory System (I00-I99)

Diseases of the circulatory system are captured with codes in Chapter 9 of the *International Classification of Diseases, Tenth Revision, Clinical Modification (ICD-10-CM)* tabular list. This chapter includes blocks **I00-I99** as follows:

Acute rheumatic fever **I00-I02**
Chronic rheumatic heart diseases **I05-I09**
Hypertensive diseases **I10-I15**
Ischemic heart diseases **I20-I25**
Pulmonary heart disease and diseases of pulmonary circulation **I26-I28**
Other forms of heart disease **I30-I52**
Cerebrovascular diseases **I60-I69**
Diseases of arteries, arterioles, and capillaries **I70-I79**
Diseases of veins, lymphatic vessels, and lymph nodes, not elsewhere classified **I80-I89**
Other and unspecified disorders of the circulatory system **I95-I99**

The following codes are to be reported with many conditions of the circulatory system that are affected by tobacco use or exposure:

Exposure to environmental tobacco smoke **(Z77.22)**
History of tobacco use **(Z87.891)**
Occupational exposure to environmental tobacco smoke **(Z57.31)**
Tobacco dependence **(F17.-)**
Tobacco use **(Z72.0)**

Rheumatic Fever

This chapter begins with codes for acute rheumatic fever **(I00-I01.9)**. Codes distinguish between rheumatic fever without heart involvement and with rheumatic pericarditis, endocarditis, myocarditis, and other or multiple types of heart involvement. Chronic rheumatic heart diseases are reported with codes in categories **I05-I09**. These include rheumatic valve diseases, chronic rheumatic pericarditis, and rheumatic heart failure.

Non-rheumatic valve disorders are reported with codes in categories **I34-I39**.

Acute Non-Rheumatic Carditis and Cardiomyopathy

Like many other conditions that may occur in infectious disease, carditis and cardiomyopathy may be reported in a variety of categories in *ICD-10-CM*. It is important to check the alphabetic index for the term and subterm to select the correct category. For instance, when the condition is associated with an infectious disease, it may be reported with combination codes from Chapter 1 of the tabular list. Some examples of this are:

A38.1	Scarlet fever with myocarditis
A69.29	Other conditions associated with Lyme disease (myocarditis)
B33.21	Viral endocarditis
B33.22	Viral myocarditis
B33.23	Viral pericarditis
B33.24	Viral cardiomyopathy
B37.6	Candidal endocarditis
J10.82	Influenza due to other identified influenza virus with myocarditis

Other forms of infectious carditis are reported with a combination of codes from Chapter 9 and Chapter 1 of the tabular list. When reporting the following codes, an additional code is reported from categories **B95-B97** to identify the infectious agent:

I30.1	Infective pericarditis
I33.0	Acute and subacute infective endocarditis
I40.0	Infective myocarditis

The categories of codes for **B95-B97** include

B95.-	*Streptococcus, Staphylococcus,* and *Enterococcus* as the cause of diseases classified elsewhere
B96.-	Other bacterial agents as the cause of diseases classified elsewhere
B97.-	Viral agents as the cause of diseases classified elsewhere

Complete codes in categories **B95-B97** include 4 or 5 characters that add specificity about the infectious agent.

Codes from the following categories are reported in addition to a code for the underlying condition:

I32	Pericarditis in diseases classified elsewhere
I39	Endocarditis and heart valve disorders in diseases classified elsewhere
I41	Myocarditis in diseases classified elsewhere

This instruction also applies to code **I43** (cardiomyopathy in diseases classified elsewhere). An example of this would be a child with Pompe disease complicated by cardiomyopathy.

E74.02	Pompe disease
I43	Cardiomyopathy in diseases classified elsewhere

Acute or chronic pancarditis is reported with code **I51.89** (other ill-defined heart diseases).

When cardiomyopathy is due to a drug or external agent, code **I42.7** is reported in conjunction with a code to identify the drug or toxin and whether the condition is due to poisoning or adverse effect.

Example: A 14-year-old is seen in follow-up of cardiomyopathy that presented following chemotherapy with an anthracycline.

  I42.7 Cardiomyopathy due to drug and external agent
  T45.1X5S Adverse effect of antineoplastic and immunosuppressive drugs

In *ICD-10-CM,* primary and secondary cardiomyopathies, not otherwise specified, are reported with the unspecified code **I42.9.** Newborn cardiomyopathy is reported with code **I42.8** (other cardiomyopathies). Congenital cardiomyopathy is reported with code **I42.4** (endocardial fibroelastosis). Other specific codes for reporting cardiomyopathy include

  I42.0 Dilated cardiomyopathy
  I42.1 Obstructive hypertrophic cardiomyopathy
  I42.2 Other hypertrophic cardiomyopathy
  I42.5 Other restrictive cardiomyopathy

Other Diseases of the Pericardium

Chronic pericarditis and other non-rheumatic diseases of the pericardium are included in category **I31.** This category includes code **I31.3** (pericardial effusion [non-inflammatory]), which does not include acute pericardial effusion **(I30.9).** Also included here is code **I31.4** (cardiac tamponade). When reporting cardiac tamponade, the code for the underlying cause is reported first.

Conduction Disorders

Wolff-Parkinson-White syndrome is reported with code **I45.6** (pre-excitation syndrome). Long QT syndrome is reported with code **I45.81.** Atrioventricular reentrant tachycardia (AVRT) and AV nodal reentrant tachycardia (AVNRT) are reported with code **I47.1** (supraventricular tachycardia).

Cardiac arrest is specified as due to an underlying cardiac condition **(I46.2),** due to other underlying condition **(I46.8),** or cause unspecified **(I46.9).** Cardiac arrest in a newborn is reported with code **P29.81.**

Not included in this chapter are newborn tachycardia **(P29.11)** and newborn bradycardia **(P29.12),** psychogenic tachycardia **(F45.8),** palpitations **(R00.2),** sinus tachycardia **(R00.0),** and sinus bradycardia **(R00.1).**

Presence of a cardiac pacemaker may be reported with code **Z95.0.** Category **Z95** also includes codes to indicate presence of an automatic cardiac defibrillator **(Z95.810)** and codes for indicating the patient has other cardiac implants and grafts. Encounters to adjust a pacemaker or other cardiac device may be reported with codes in category **Z45.**

Hypertensive Heart Diseases

This block includes codes for essential hypertension **(I10),** hypertensive heart disease, and hypertensive kidney disease. When reporting codes in this block, tobacco use or exposure should be reported in addition to the code for the hypertensive condition. Secondary hypertension is reported with code **I15** and a code for the underlying condition. Note that neonatal hypertension is reported with code **P29.2** and not included in this chapter. Primary pulmonary hypertension is reported with code **I27.0**. **Persistent pulmonary hypertension in a newborn is reported with code P29.3.**

When reporting hypertensive heart disease with heart failure **(I11.0)**, an additional code identifying the type of heart failure is reported **(I50.-)**. Hypertensive chronic kidney disease is reported with codes **I12.0** (stage 5) and **I12.9** (stages 1–4) with an additional code from category **N18** to distinguish the stage of chronic kidney disease. Codes from categories **I50** and **N18** are also reported in addition to codes in category **I13** to report hypertensive heart and chronic kidney disease.

Post-procedural hypertension is reported with code **I97.3**. Post-procedural heart failure is reported with code **I97.130** when the procedure was a cardiac surgery and with code **I97.131** when the procedure was another surgery. An additional code from category **I50** is reported to identify the heart failure when reporting codes **I97.130** and **I97.131**.

Acute Myocardial Infarction

Coronary artery spasm or spasm-induced angina is reported with code **I20.1**. An additional code should be reported for presence of hypertension **(I10-I15)** or for tobacco use or exposure.

Current acute myocardial infarction (AMI) is reported with codes in categories **I21** and **I22**. *ICD-10-CM* instructs that a current myocardial infarction is one that is 4 weeks (28 days) old or less and still requires continued care. Codes in category **I21** are used to report an initial AMI. Codes in category **I22** are used to report a second AMI within the 4 weeks following the initial AMI. Codes in both categories differentiate ST elevation (STEMI) myocardial infarction from Non-ST elevation (NSTEMI) or non-transmural myocardial infarction and identify the site of the STEMI infarction. When the site of a non-transmural or subendocardial infarction is documented, the appropriate NSTEMI code is still reported. If NSTEMI evolves to STEMI, the STEMI code is reported. If STEMI converts to NSTEMI due to thrombolytic therapy, it is still coded as STEMI. Codes for an initial AMI also indicate the involved artery.

Code **I21.3** (STEMI of unspecified site) is the default for unspecified AMI. If only STEMI or transmural myocardial infarction without the site is documented, assign code **I21.3**.

> From the guidelines: Section IC9e4—A code from category **I22** must be used in conjunction with a code from category **I21**. The sequencing of the **I22** and **I21** codes depends on the circumstances of the encounter.

Category **I23** provides codes for reporting complications within the 28-day period following an AMI. These codes are reported in addition to codes from categories **I21** and **I22** with sequencing based on the reason for encounter.

Cerebrovascular Disease

The block of codes for cerebrovascular disease includes categories **I60-I69**. Instructions for this block are to use additional codes to report tobacco use or exposure, alcohol abuse and dependence **(F10.-)**, or hypertension **(I10-I15)**. This block begins with codes for non-traumatic subarachnoid hemorrhage **(I60.-)**. The codes in this category specify the site of the hemorrhage (artery) and laterality where applicable. A ruptured congenital berry or cerebral aneurysm is reported with code **I60.7**. Other non-traumatic subarachnoid hemorrhages such as meningeal hemorrhage or rupture of cerebral arteriovenous malformation are reported with code **I60.8**.

Non-traumatic intracerebral hemorrhage is reported according to site with codes in category **I61**. Codes in category **I62** are used to report non-traumatic acute, subacute, or chronic subdural hemorrhage and non-traumatic extradural hemorrhage.

Intracranial non-traumatic hemorrhage in a newborn is reported with codes in category **P52**.

Cerebral infarction is reported with codes in category **I63**. These codes specify infarct due to thrombus, embolism, unspecified occlusion or stenosis, and the artery involved. Cerebral infarction due to nonpyogenic cerebral venous thrombosis is reported with code **I63.6**. Intraoperative and postoperative infarctions are reported based on cardiac or noncardiac surgery with codes in category **I97**.

Neurologic deficits or sequela of cerebrovascular disease are reported with codes in category **I69**. These codes apply only to sequela of non-traumatic hemorrhage as reported with codes in categories **I60-I67**.

> From the guidelines: Section IC9d3—Assign code **Z86.73** (personal history of transient ischemic attack and cerebral infarction without residual deficits), and not a code from category **I69**, as an additional code for history of cerebrovascular disease when no neurologic deficits are present.

Other Vascular Diseases

Acrocyanosis is reported with code **I73.8** except in newborns **(P28.2)**. Transient blue hands and feet in a newborn are not reported. The alphabetic index instructs to omit reporting of acrocyanosis in a newborn, meaning transient blue hands and feet.

Venous embolism and thrombosis are reported with codes in category **I82**. Embolism and thrombosis of renal vein are reported with code **I82.3**.

Compression of a vein including the vena cava is reported with code **I87.1**. Compression of the pulmonary vein is reported with code **I28.8**.

Disorders of Lymph Nodes

Included in this chapter are codes in category **I88** for mesenteric (acute or chronic) and other chronic lymphadenitis. Not included are codes for acute lymphadenitis other than mesenteric, which is reported with codes in category **L04**. Also not included here is the code for enlarged lymph node, not otherwise specified **(R59)**.

Hypotension

Category **I95** includes codes for idiopathic **(I95.0)**, orthostatic **(I95.1)**, post-procedural **(I95.81)**, and chronic hypotension. Code **I95.1** is not used to report neurogenic orthostatic hypotension **(G90.3)**. Hypotension due to drugs is reported with code **I95.2** and an additional code to identify the drug causing the adverse effect, when applicable. Hypotension of hemodialysis is reported with code **I95.3**.

Gangrene

Code **I96** is used to report gangrene that is not elsewhere classified. This does not include the following:

> Gangrene in atherosclerosis of native arteries of the extremities **(I70.26)**
> Gangrene in diabetes mellitus **(E08-E13)**
> Gangrene in hernia **(K40.1, K40.4, K41.1, K41.4, K42.1, K43.1-, K44.1, K45.1, and K46.1)**
> Gangrene in other peripheral vascular diseases **(I73.-)**
> Gangrene of certain specified sites—see alphabetic index
> Gas gangrene **(A48.0)**
> Pyoderma gangrenosum **(L88)**

The conditions listed above are not a complete list of gangrenous conditions listed elsewhere. See the alphabetic index listing for gangrene to determine the correct code. The index advises to see also the term "Necrosis."

> From the guidelines: Section IA16—A see also instruction following a main term in the alphabetic index instructs that there is another main term that may also be referenced that may provide additional alphabetic index entries that may be useful. It is not necessary to follow the see also note when the original main term provides the necessary code.

Intraoperative and Post-Procedural Complications

Categories **I97** and **I98** include codes for complications during or after procedures. Not included here is post-procedural shock **(T81.1-)**. Codes differentiate between complications of cardiac surgery and complications of other surgery.

Signs, Symptoms, and History

Symptoms and findings related to the circulatory system may be reported when a definitive diagnosis has not been established. These are reported with codes from Chapter 18 of the tabular list, as are abnormal results of clinical or other investigative procedures and ill-defined conditions for which no definitive diagnosis has been documented. Some codes for symptoms have been included earlier in this chapter. The following are examples of codes for other cardiovascular symptoms and findings.

R01.0	Benign and innocent (functional) cardiac murmurs
R01.1	Cardiac murmur, unspecified (bruit)
R01.2	Other cardiac sounds
R07.1	Chest pain on breathing
R07.2	Precordial pain
R55	Syncope and collapse
R57.0	Cardiogenic shock
R93.1	Abnormal findings on diagnostic imaging of heart and coronary circulation
R94.31	Abnormal electrocardiogram [ECG] [EKG]

Codes from Chapter 21 of the tabular list are useful for reporting factors that influence a person's health status but are not a current illness or injury. Codes here are used to identify an encounter for screening, patient status, and personal and family history.

Z13.6	Encounter for screening for cardiovascular disorders
Z82.41	Family history of sudden cardiac death
Z82.49	Family history of ischemic heart disease/other diseases of the circulatory system
Z86.74	Personal history of sudden cardiac arrest
Z86.79	Personal history of other diseases of the circulatory system

Code Scenarios

A newborn is diagnosed with aseptic myocarditis caused by coxsackievirus.

B33.22	Viral myocarditis

> From the guidelines: Section IB9—Combination codes are identified by referring to subterm entries in the alphabetic index and by reading the inclusion and exclusion notes in the tabular list. Assign only the combination code when that code fully identifies the diagnostic conditions involved or when the alphabetic index so directs.

A child is diagnosed with subacute infective endocarditis due to group A streptococcal infection complicated by glomerulonephritis.

I33.0	Acute and subacute infective endocarditis
N08	Glomerular disorders in diseases classified elsewhere
B95.0	Streptococcus, group A, as the cause of diseases classified elsewhere

> From the guidelines: Section IA13—Certain conditions have both an underlying etiology and multiple body system manifestations due to the underlying etiology. For such conditions, the *ICD-10-CM* has a coding convention that requires the underlying condition be sequenced first followed by the manifestation.
>
> In the alphabetic index both conditions are listed together with the etiology code first, followed by the manifestation codes in brackets. The code in brackets is always to be sequenced second.

A child with a history of rheumatic fever with chorea 1 month ago is seen for follow-up. She continues to have some episodes of twitching but has returned to school and otherwise has no complaints. The diagnosis is rheumatic heart disease with chorea.

> From the tabular list: An excludes 1 note at category **I01** excludes "chronic diseases of rheumatic origin **(I05–I09)** unless rheumatic fever is also present or there is evidence of reactivation or activity of the rheumatic process." Until the activity associated with the rheumatic process has ceased, codes in category **I01** are appropriately reported.

I02.9 Rheumatic chorea without heart involvement

Review What You Have Learned

10.1 A teenager with a family history of ischemic heart disease is diagnosed with essential hypertension. The teenager does not smoke but his mother smokes in their home. What code(s) is reported for this encounter?
   A. **I11.9**   Hypertensive heart disease without heart failure
   B. **I10**   Essential (primary) hypertension
   C. **Z77.22**   Exposure to environmental tobacco smoke
       I15.9   Secondary hypertension, unspecified
   D. **I10**   Essential (primary) hypertension
       Z77.22   Exposure to environmental tobacco smoke
       Z82.49   Family history of ischemic heart disease
   E. None of the above

10.2 Code **I45.6** (pre-excitation syndrome) includes which of the following diagnoses?
   A. Accelerated atrioventricular conduction
   B. Wolff-Parkinson-White syndrome
   C. Accessory atrioventricular conduction
   D. Pre-excitation atrioventricular conduction
   E. All of the above

10.3 A diagnosis of myocarditis due to scarlet fever is reported with code **I01.2** (acute rheumatic myocarditis).
   A. True
   B. False

10.4 What code or codes are reported for complete heart block as a complication following surgical repair of a ventricular septal defect?
   A. **I97.190**   Other post-procedural cardiac functional disturbances following cardiac surgery
      I44.2   Atrioventricular block, complete
   B. **I97.190**   Other post-procedural cardiac functional disturbances following cardiac surgery
   C. **I97.190**   Other post-procedural cardiac functional disturbances following cardiac surgery
      I45.3   Trifascicular block I
   D. **I44.2**   Atrioventricular block, complete
   E. None of the above

10.5 Acrocyanosis in a newborn is reported with code **I73.8.**
   A. True
   B. False

≡ CHAPTER 11 ≡

Diseases of the Respiratory System (J00-J99)

Diseases of the respiratory system are captured with codes in Chapter 10 of the *International Classification of Diseases, Tenth Revision, Clinical Modification (ICD-10-CM)* tabular list. This chapter includes blocks **J00-J99** as follows:

Acute upper respiratory infections **J00-J06**
Influenza and pneumonia **J09-J18**
Other acute lower respiratory infections **J20-J22**
Other diseases of upper respiratory tract **J30-J39**
Chronic lower respiratory diseases **J40-J47**
Lung diseases due to external agents **J60-J70**
Other respiratory diseases principally affecting the interstitium **J80-J84**
Suppurative and necrotic conditions of the lower respiratory tract **J85-J86**
Other diseases of the pleura **J90-J94**
Intraoperative and post-procedural complications and disorders of respiratory system, not elsewhere classified **J95**
Other diseases of the respiratory system **J96-J99**

The following codes are to be reported with any conditions of the respiratory system where applicable:

Exposure to environmental tobacco smoke **(Z77.22)**
Exposure to tobacco smoke in the perinatal period **(P96.81)**
History of tobacco use **(Z87.891)**
Occupational exposure to environmental tobacco smoke **(Z57.31)**
Tobacco dependence **(F17.-)**
Tobacco use **(Z72.0)**

When a respiratory condition is described as occurring in more than one site and is not specifically indexed, the code for the lower anatomical site should be reported (eg, tracheobronchitis to bronchitis in **J40**).

Acute Upper Respiratory Infections

This chapter begins with codes for acute upper respiratory infections **(J00-J06)**. An excludes 1 note for this block advises that chronic obstructive pulmonary disease with an acute lower respiratory infection is reported with code **J44.0,** and that respiratory manifestations of the influenza virus are reported with code **J09.X2, J10.1,** or **J11.1.**

Code **J00** is used to report acute nasopharyngitis including acute rhinitis and infective nasopharyngitis not otherwise specified. This code is not reported for acute pharyngitis, pharyngitis not otherwise specified, or rhinitis not otherwise specified **(J31.0)**. Code **J00** may be reported in addition to codes for allergic rhinitis, chronic pharyngitis, chronic rhinitis, chronic sore throat, chronic nasopharyngitis, and vasomotor rhinitis when a patient has multiple conditions at the same time.

When reporting acute sinusitis (codes in category **J01**), an additional code from categories **B95-B97** is reported to identify the infectious agent.

The categories of codes for **B95-B97** include

- **B95.-** *Streptococcus, Staphylococcus,* and *Enterococcus* as the cause of diseases classified elsewhere
- **B96.-** Other bacterial agents as the cause of diseases classified elsewhere
- **B97.-** Viral agents as the cause of diseases classified elsewhere

Complete codes in categories **B95-B97** include 4 or 5 characters that add specificity about the infectious agent.

Note that sinusitis not specified as acute or chronic is reported with code **J32.9**. Category **J01** includes codes that identify acute sinusitis as maxillary, frontal, ethmoidal, sphenoidal, pansinusitis, and other acute sinusitis. The codes for other acute sinusitis include conditions involving more than one sinus but not pansinusitis **(J01.4-)**. Codes also specify whether each type of acute sinusitis is recurrent or unspecified.

Example **J01.00** Acute maxillary sinusitis, unspecified
J01.01 Acute recurrent maxillary sinusitis

Codes to report unspecified acute sinusitis include **J01.90** (acute sinusitis, unspecified) and **J01.91** (acute recurrent sinusitis, unspecified).

Acute pharyngitis is reported with codes in category **J02**. This category includes streptococcal pharyngitis code **J02.0**. Code **J02.0** does not include scarlet fever **(A38.-)**, but both conditions may be reported when applicable. Code **J02.8** is reported for acute pharyngitis due to other specified organisms with an additional code from categories **B95-B97** required to indicate the type of organism.

Acute pharyngitis due to the following organisms is reported with combination codes from Chapter 1 of the tabular list:

Acute pharyngitis due to coxsackievirus **(B08.5)**
Acute pharyngitis due to gonococcus **(A54.5)**
Acute pharyngitis due to herpes [simplex] virus **(B00.2)**
Acute pharyngitis due to infectious mononucleosis **(B27.-)**
Enteroviral vesicular pharyngitis **(B08.5)**

Unspecified acute pharyngitis is reported with code **J02.9,** which includes acute forms of gangrenous, infectious, or ulcerative pharyngitis, not otherwise specified.

Category **J03** includes codes for acute streptococcal tonsillitis, acute tonsillitis due to other specified organisms, and unspecified acute tonsillitis. Codes designate the infection as unspecified or recurrent. This category does not include codes for hypertrophy of the tonsils **(J35.1)** or peritonsillar abscess **(J36)**. Chronic tonsillitis is reported with code **J35.0** and may be reported in addition to acute tonsillitis when both conditions are present.

Acute laryngitis and tracheitis other than acute obstructive laryngitis **(J05.0)** are reported with codes in category **J04**. Laryngismus **(J38.5)** may be reported in addition to codes for acute laryngitis and tracheitis when present. Codes for tracheitis specify whether the condition is with obstruction **(J04.11)** or without obstruction **(J04.10)**. Codes for supraglottitis also specify with obstruction **(J04.31)** or without obstruction **(J04.30)**. A single code **(J04.2)** is used to report acute laryngotracheitis. Acute obstructive laryngitis or croup is reported is with code **J05.0**. Acute epiglottitis is reported with code **J05.10** when without obstruction and code **J05.11** when with obstruction.

The final category in this block **(J06)** provides codes for acute upper respiratory infections of multiple and unspecified sites. This includes **J06.0** for acute laryngopharyngitis and **J06.9** for acute upper respiratory infection, unspecified.

Influenza and Pneumonia

This block includes codes for influenza and pneumonia due to identified and unidentified organisms. It does not include aspiration pneumonia **(J69.0)** or other forms of pneumonia associated with external causes. Combination codes are provided for influenza with pneumonia caused by the same influenza virus and influenza with an unspecified type of pneumonia.

Codes for influenza are categorized according to the type of influenza virus identified.

- **J09** Influenza due to certain identified influenza virus
- **J10** Influenza due to other identified influenza virus
- **J11** Influenza due to unidentified influenza virus

Category **J09** includes codes for avian, bird, A/H5N1, swine, and other influenza of animal origin when the physician has documented the influenza as one of these types. Laboratory confirmation is not required, but codes in category **J09** are not reported for suspected cases of avian or other novel influenza A virus. Codes in category **J10** are used to report other identified influenzas, such as A/H1N1.

Codes for influenza with pneumonia include

J09.X1	Influenza due to identified novel influenza A virus with pneumonia
J10.00	Influenza due to other identified influenza virus with unspecified type of pneumonia
J10.01	Influenza due to other identified influenza virus with the same other identified influenza virus pneumonia
J10.08	Influenza due to other identified influenza virus with other specified pneumonia
J11.00	Influenza due to unidentified influenza virus with unspecified type of pneumonia
J11.08	Influenza due to unidentified influenza virus with specified pneumonia

Each code for influenza with pneumonia includes instruction to also code a lung abscess, if applicable **(J85.1)**. When reporting influenza with a specified type of pneumonia other than that due to the same influenza virus, also code the specified type of pneumonia.

Example

J10.08	Influenza due to other identified influenza virus with other specified pneumonia
J13	Pneumonia due to *Streptococcus pneumoniae*

Combination codes are also used to report influenza with other respiratory manifestations, such as laryngitis and pharyngitis. An additional code is reported for manifestations of pleural effusion **(J91.8)** or sinusitis **(J01.-)** in influenza.

When intestinal influenza is documented, meaning viral gastroenteritis, see codes in category **A08**. However, combination codes are provided in categories **J09, J10,** and **J11** for influenza with gastrointestinal manifestations.

Otitis media, encephalopathy, and myocarditis as manifestations of influenza are also reported with combination codes.

Example

J10.83	Influenza due to other identified influenza virus with otitis media
	Use additional code for any associated perforated tympanic membrane **(H72.-)**

All other manifestations are reported with a code for influenza with other manifestations followed by a code describing the manifestation.

ICD-10-CM includes specific codes for the most common viral and bacterial pneumonias in categories **J12-J18**. Other pneumonia due to infectious organisms may be reported with a combination code from categories in Chapter 1 of the tabular list, such as whooping cough with pneumonia (**A37** with fifth character **1**). Category **J17** (pneumonia in diseases classified elsewhere) has an excludes 1 note that lists many of these conditions. As with most conditions occurring in the perinatal period, see codes in Chapter 16 of the tabular list for pneumonia in the neonate (eg, **P23.0** [congenital pneumonia]).

Lobar pneumonia is separately categorized only when the infecting organism is unspecified. Code **J18.1** is used to report lobar pneumonia due to unspecified organism. See the codes for specified bacterial or viral pneumonia for other lobar pneumonia. Hypostatic or passive pneumonia is reported with code **J18.2**.

When bacterial or viral pneumonia occurs as a post-procedural complication, first report code **J95.89** (other post-procedural complications and disorders of respiratory system, not else classified). Use an additional code to specify the type of pneumonia.

Acute Bronchitis and Bronchiolitis

Categories **J20-J21** include codes for acute and subacute bronchitis and bronchiolitis due to infectious organisms. Bronchitis with tracheitis in children younger than 15 years is reported with codes in category **J20**. Category **J40** (bronchitis not specified as acute or chronic) is used for patients 15 years and older.

Category **J20** includes acute and subacute bronchitis with bronchospasm, tracheitis, or acute tracheobronchitis as well as acute and subacute membranous, purulent, or septic bronchitis. Codes in this category specify the infectious organism except codes **J20.8** (acute bronchitis due to other specified organisms) and **J20.9** (unspecified acute bronchitis). An excludes 2 note at this category directs that bronchitis due to chemicals, fumes, and vapors **(J68.0)** and chronic forms of bronchitis may be additionally reported when present.

> From the guidelines: Section IB8—If the same condition is described as both acute (subacute) and chronic, and separate subentries exist in the alphabetic index at the same indentation level, code both and sequence the acute (subacute) code first.

Acute bronchiolitis codes also indicate the infectious organism and include acute bronchiolitis with bronchospasm.

Code **J22** is reported for an unspecified lower respiratory infection **(J22)**. Report code **J22** for a lower respiratory infection not specified as acute or chronic.

Vasomotor and Allergic Rhinitis

Category **J30** includes vasomotor rhinitis **(J30.0)**, allergic rhinitis due to pollen **(J30.1)**, other seasonal allergic rhinitis **(J30.2)**, allergic rhinitis due to animal hair and dander **(J30.81)**, other allergic rhinitis **(J30.89)**, and unspecified allergic rhinitis **(J30.9)**. These codes do not include allergic rhinitis with asthma (codes in category **J45**).

Chronic Upper Respiratory Conditions

Categories **J31** and **J32** include codes for chronic forms of rhinitis, nasopharyngitis, pharyngitis, and sinusitis. An additional code to indicate tobacco use or exposure should be reported with codes in these categories.

Codes for chronic nasopharyngitis **(J31.1)** and chronic pharyngitis **(J31.2)** have excludes 2 notes indicating that the acute forms of these conditions may also be reported when both acute and chronic conditions are diagnosed.

Codes in category **J32** indicate the affected sinus in chronic sinusitis but, unlike the codes for acute sinusitis, recurrence is not separately identified. This category includes abscess, empyema, infection, and suppuration of the sinuses. Acute sinusitis may be additionally reported when present, and tobacco use or exposure should also be reported.

Nasal polyps are reported with category **J33**. Code **J33.0** is used to report a polyp of the nasal cavity. Polypoid sinus degeneration or Woake syndrome is reported with code **J33.1**. Other polyps of the sinus, including accessory polyp, ethmoidal, maxillary, and sphenoidal polyps, are reported with code **J33.8**.

Category **J34** includes codes for abscess, carbuncle, and furuncle of the nose **(J34.0)** and for cyst and mucocele of the nose and nasal sinus **(J34.1)**. This category also includes codes for deviated nasal septum **(J34.2)** and hypertrophy of the nasal turbinates **(J34.3)**. However, congenital deviated nasal septum is reported with code **Q67.4**.

Nasal mucositis is reported with code **J34.81** and a code identifying the type of associated therapy, such as effects of chemotherapy or radiotherapy:

T45.1X- Poisoning by, adverse effect of, and underdosing of antineoplastic and immunosuppressive drugs

Y84.2 Radiological procedure and radiotherapy as the cause of abnormal reaction of the patient, or of later complication, without mention of misadventure at the time of the procedure

Code **J34.89** (other specified disorders of the nose and nasal sinuses) includes conditions such as perforation of the nasal septum (other than congenital or syphilitic) and rhinolith.

Chronic tonsillitis and adenoiditis are reported with codes in category **J35**. This category instructs to also report tobacco use or exposure codes when applicable. Codes for chronic tonsillitis and adenitis are as follows:

J35.01 Chronic tonsillitis
J35.02 Chronic adenoiditis
J35.03 Chronic tonsillitis and adenoiditis

The **J35.0-** codes include hypertrophy of the tonsils and adenoids when both conditions are present. For hypertrophy without chronic tonsillitis or adenoiditis, see codes **J35.1-J35.3**. Code **J35.8** includes other chronic diseases of tonsils and adenoids, such as adenoid vegetations, calculus of the tonsil, cicatrix of tonsil and adenoid, and ulcer of the tonsil. Peritonsillar abscess is reported with code **J36** and an additional code to identify the infectious agent **(B95-B97)**. Retropharyngeal and parapharyngeal abscess, other than peritonsillar abscess, are reported with code **J39.0**. For nasopharyngeal abscess, code **J39.1** is reported.

Chronic Lower Respiratory Diseases

This block of codes includes conditions such as chronic bronchitis, emphysema including unilateral pulmonary emphysema or Swyer-James syndrome **(J43.0)**, other chronic obstructive pulmonary disease **(J44)**, asthma **(J45.-)**, and bronchiectasis **(J47.-)**. Emphysema in a newborn is reported with code **P25.0**. Code **J44** (other chronic obstructive pulmonary disease) includes chronic obstructive asthma and chronic obstructive bronchitis.

Codes for asthma are categorized according to severity classifications of mild intermittent, mild persistent, moderate persistent, and severe persistent. As shown in Table 11-1, codes further specify the conditions as uncomplicated, with acute exacerbation, or with status asthmaticus.

> From the guidelines: Section IC10a—The codes in categories **J44** and **J45** distinguish between uncomplicated cases and those in acute exacerbation. An acute exacerbation is a worsening or a decompensation of a chronic condition. An acute exacerbation is not equivalent to an infection superimposed on a chronic condition, though an exacerbation may be triggered by an infection.

Table 11-1. Asthma Codes in *ICD-10-CM*

Asthma Type	Uncomplicated	Acute Exacerbation	Status Asthmaticus
Mild intermittent	J45.20	J45.21	J45.22
Mild persistent	J45.30	J45.31	J45.32
Moderate persistent	J45.40	J45.41	J45.42
Severe persistent	J45.50	J45.51	J45.52
Unspecified asthma	J45.909	J45.901	J45.902

Category **J45** also includes codes for exercise-induced bronchospasm **(J45.990)**, cough variant asthma **(J45.991)**, and other asthma **(J45.998)**. Not included in category **J45** are codes for asthma due to external agents, wheezing **(R06.2)**, or eosinophilic asthma **(J82)**.

Lung Diseases Due to External Agents

The block of codes **J60-J70** includes codes for pulmonary conditions related to environmental exposures, pneumonitis due to inhaled solids and liquids, respiratory conditions due to radiation, drug-induced lung disorders, and smoke inhalation. Additional codes are reported to identify external causes such as inhaled substances **(T61-T65)**, foreign body in the respiratory tract **(T17.-)**, or drug **(T36-T50)** when reporting codes in categories **J68-J70**.

Aspiration pneumonia is reported with codes in category **J69** based on the substance inhaled. This category does not include neonatal aspiration syndromes **(P24.-)** or post-procedural pneumonitis **(J95.4)**. Report a code from category **J69** in addition to code **J95.89** (other post-procedural complications and disorders of respiratory system, not elsewhere classified) when aspiration pneumonia is a postoperative complication.

Interstitial Respiratory Disease

Code **J80** is used to report acute respiratory distress syndrome in an adult or a child other than a newborn **(P22.0)**.

Category **J84** includes other interstitial pulmonary diseases, including alveolar and parieto-alveolar conditions such as idiopathic pulmonary hemosiderosis **(J84.03)**. When reporting idiopathic pulmonary hemosiderosis, first code the underlying disease, such as disorders of iron metabolism **(E83.1-)**. Code **J84.03** does not include acute idiopathic pulmonary hemorrhage in infants **(R04.81)**, and the codes are not reported together.

Surfactant mutations of the lung are reported with code **J84.83**. Subcategory **J84.84** includes the following other interstitial lung diseases of childhood:

- **J84.841** Neuroendocrine cell hyperplasia of infancy
- **J84.842** Pulmonary interstitial glycogenosis
- **J84.843** Alveolar capillary dysplasia with vein misalignment
- **J84.848** Other interstitial lung diseases of childhood

Pleural Diseases

Codes in the block **J90-J94** include conditions such as pleural effusion and pneumothorax. Pleural effusion is reported with code **J90** when not elsewhere classified. This code does not include pleurisy without effusion **(R09.1)**, tuberculous pleural effusion **(A15.6)**, malignant pleural effusion **(J91.0)**, or pleural effusion in conditions classified elsewhere **(J91.8)**. When reporting malignant pleural effusion, first report the code for the underlying neoplasm, such as lymphoma. Likewise, first report a code for the underlying condition, such as influenza, when pleural effusion is diagnosed in conditions classified elsewhere.

Category **J93** includes codes for spontaneous tension pneumothorax **(J93.0)** and for primary **(J93.11)** and secondary **(J93.12)** spontaneous pneumothorax. Congenital and perinatal pneumothorax are reported with code **P25.1**. A traumatic pneumothorax is reported with codes from subcategory **S27.0XX-** with a seventh character to indicate the encounter is initial **(A)**, subsequent **(D)**, or addressing a sequela **(S)**.

Intraoperative and Post-Procedural Complications

Category **J95** includes codes for complications during or after procedures and disorders of the respiratory system not elsewhere classified. Tracheostomy complications are reported with codes in subcategory **J95.0**. Hemorrhage from the tracheostomy stoma is reported with code **J95.01**. Code **J95.02** is used to report an infection of the stoma. A code indicating the type of infection should be reported in addition to code **J95.02**. Mechanical complication, obstruction, and tracheal stenosis are reported with code **J95.03**. A tracheoesophageal fistula following tracheostomy is reported with code **J95.04**.

Acute pulmonary insufficiency following a procedure is classified according to whether the surgery was thoracic **(J95.1)** or non-thoracic **(J95.2)**. Chronic pulmonary insufficiency following surgery is reported with code **J95.3**. Functional disturbances following cardiac surgery **(I97.0, I97.1-)** may be reported in addition to codes for pulmonary insufficiency following surgery when applicable.

Codes for reporting intraoperative hemorrhage and hematoma of a respiratory system organ or structure **(J95.6-)** and accidental puncture and laceration of a respiratory system organ or structure **(J95.7-)** also indicate whether the procedure was a respiratory system procedure or other procedure. Post-procedural hemorrhage or hematoma of a respiratory system organ or structure is reported with code **J95.830** following a respiratory procedure or **J95.831** following another type of procedure.

This category also includes ventilator-associated pneumonia **(J95.851)**. An additional code from categories **B95-B97** should be reported to indicate the infecting organism. Do not assign an additional code from categories **J12-J18** to identify the type of pneumonia. However, if a patient with one type of pneumonia subsequently develops ventilator-associated pneumonia, both a code from categories **J12-J18** and code **J95.851** may be reported for encounters addressing both conditions.

> From the guidelines: Section IC10d—Code **J95.851** (ventilator-associated pneumonia) should be assigned only when the provider has documented ventilator-associated pneumonia. Code **J95.851** should not be assigned for cases where the patient has pneumonia and is on a mechanical ventilator and the provider has not specifically stated that the pneumonia is ventilator-associated pneumonia.
>
> Coders should confirm with the physician if documentation is unclear regarding the association between pneumonia and ventilator use.

Respiratory Failure

Acute and chronic respiratory failures are reported with codes in category **J96**. Codes describe acute, chronic, or acute and chronic respiratory failure with further designations of "with hypoxia," "with hypercapnia," or "unspecified whether with hypoxia or hypercapnia." This category does not include newborn respiratory failure **(P28.5)**, cardiorespiratory failure **(R09.2)**, or post-procedural respiratory failure **(J95.82-)**.

Respiratory Disorders in Diseases Classified Elsewhere

Code **J99** is used to report respiratory disorders in certain diseases classified elsewhere. There is an excludes 1 note for this code listing many conditions to which this code is not applicable. However, a code first note provides indications of conditions for which this code is applicable.

Code first underlying disease, such as

- Amyloidosis **(E85-)**
- Ankylosing spondylitis **(M45)**
- Congenital syphilis **(A50.5)**
- Cryoglobulinemia **(D89.1)**
- Early congenital syphilis **(A50.0)**
- Schistosomiasis **(B65.0-B65.9)**

Signs, Symptoms, and History

Symptoms and findings related to the respiratory system may be reported when a definitive diagnosis has not been established. These are reported with codes from Chapter 18 of the tabular list, as are abnormal results of clinical or other investigative procedures and ill-defined conditions for which no definitive diagnosis has been documented. Some codes for symptoms have been included earlier in this chapter. The following are examples of codes for other respiratory symptoms and findings.

R05	Cough
R06.00	Dyspnea, unspecified
R06.01	Orthopnea
R06.02	Shortness of breath
R06.09	Other forms of dyspnea
R06.1	Stridor
R06.2	Wheezing (excludes asthma)

R06.83	Snoring	
R07.1	Chest pain on breathing	
R09.81	Nasal congestion	
R09.82	Postnasal drip	

Codes from Chapter 21 of the tabular list are useful for reporting factors that influence a person's health status but are not a current illness or injury.

Examples

Z77.120	Contact with and (suspected) exposure to mold (toxic)
Z77.121	Contact with and (suspected) exposure to harmful algae and algae toxins
Z82.5	Family history of asthma and other chronic lower respiratory diseases
Z86.11	Personal history of tuberculosis
Z94.2	Lung transplant status
Z94.3	Heart and lungs transplant status
Z99.11	Dependence on respirator [ventilator] status

Code Scenarios

A 15-year-old patient is seen for complaint of sore throat and fever. Following examination and in-office laboratory testing, the physician diagnoses pharyngitis in infectious mononucleosis due to Epstein-Barr virus.

B27.00   Gammaherpesviral mononucleosis without complication

> From the guidelines: Section IB5—Signs and symptoms that are associated routinely with a disease process should not be assigned as additional codes, unless otherwise instructed by the classification.

A child reports to the emergency department in significant distress due to exacerbation of moderate persistent asthma. Symptoms are not relieved with initial treatment, but improvement is seen after continued treatment. The child is admitted to observation for continued treatment and monitoring with a diagnosis of moderate persistent asthma with status asthmaticus.

J45.42   Moderate persistent asthma with status asthmaticus

> From the guidelines: Section IC10a—The codes in categories **J44** and **J45** distinguish between uncomplicated cases and those in acute exacerbation. An acute exacerbation is a worsening or a decompensation of a chronic condition. An acute exacerbation is not equivalent to an infection superimposed on a chronic condition, though an exacerbation may be triggered by an infection.

A child recently diagnosed with mild intermittent asthma is seen in her pediatrician's office with coughing and dyspnea not relieved by use of her inhaler. The mother notes that the child has had increased symptoms and inhaler use since starting to stay before school with her grandfather who smokes a pipe. The child receives treatment in the office with improvement and is able to return to school. The physician diagnoses mild intermittent asthma with acute exacerbation and exposure to tobacco smoke.

    J45.21   Mild intermittent asthma with (acute) exacerbation
    Z77.22   Exposure to environmental tobacco smoke

> From the tabular list: The instructions for category **J45** include the following:
>
> Use additional code to identify exposure to environmental tobacco smoke **(Z77.22)**

Review What You Have Learned

11.1 A child presents to the pediatric clinic with symptoms of fever, runny nose, and cough. A rapid influenza test is performed with a result positive for influenza B. Physical examination reveals serous otitis media of the right ear without rupture of the tympanic membrane. The physician diagnoses influenza type B and serous otitis media of the right ear. What code(s) should be reported for this encounter?
    A. **J10**   Influenza due to other identified influenza virus
    B. **J10.83**   Influenza due to other identified influenza virus with otitis media
    C. **J11.83**   Influenza due to unidentified influenza virus with otitis media
    D. **J10.83**   Influenza due to other identified influenza virus with otitis media
        B97.89   Other viral agents as the cause of diseases classified elsewhere
    E. None of the above

11.2 A child is diagnosed with hypertrophy of the tonsils and adenoids with chronic tonsillitis and adenoiditis. What code(s) is reported?
    A. **J35.01**   Chronic tonsillitis
        J35.02   Chronic adenoiditis
        J35.3   Hypertrophy of tonsils with hypertrophy of adenoids
    B. **J35.3**   Hypertrophy of tonsils with hypertrophy of adenoids
    C. **J35.03**   Chronic tonsillitis and adenoiditis
    D. **J35.8**   Other chronic diseases of tonsils and adenoids
    E. None of the above

11.3 Codes for chronic sinusitis specify whether the condition is recurrent.
    A. True
    B. False

11.4 What is the code(s) for croup?
- A. **J04.2**   Acute laryngotracheitis
- B. **J04.11**   Acute tracheitis with obstruction
- C. **J04.31**   Supraglottitis, unspecified, with obstruction
- D. **J05.0**   Acute obstructive laryngitis
- E. None of the above

11.5 Codes for acute sinusitis and chronic sinusitis may be reported for the same encounter.
- A. True
- B. False

11.6 Acute streptococcal pharyngitis is reported with which code(s)?
- A. **J02.8**   Acute pharyngitis due to other specified organisms
  B95.1   *Streptococcus,* group B, as the cause of diseases classified elsewhere
- B. **J02.8**   Acute pharyngitis due to other specified organisms
  B95.0   *Streptococcus,* group A, as the cause of diseases classified elsewhere
- C. **J02.8**   Acute pharyngitis due to other specified organisms
  B95.3   *Streptococcus pneumoniae* as the cause of diseases classified elsewhere
- D. **J02.0**   Streptococcal pharyngitis
- E. **A38.8**   Scarlet fever with other complications

≡ CHAPTER 12 ≡

Diseases of the Digestive System (K00-K95)

Diseases of the digestive system are captured with codes in Chapter 11 of the *International Classification of Diseases, Tenth Revision, Clinical Modification (ICD-10-CM)* tabular list. This chapter includes blocks **K00-K95** as follows:

Diseases of oral cavity and salivary glands **K00-K14**
Diseases of esophagus, stomach and duodenum **K20-K31**
Diseases of appendix **K35-K38**
Hernia **K40-K46**
Non-infective enteritis and colitis **K50-K52**
Other diseases of intestines **K55-K64**
Diseases of peritoneum and retroperitoneum **K65-K68**
Diseases of liver **K70-K77**
Disorders of gallbladder, biliary tract and pancreas **K80-K87**
Other diseases of the digestive system **K90-K95**

Disorders of Tooth Development and Eruption

Category **K00** includes specific codes for certain disorders of tooth development, such as teething syndrome **(K00.7)**. Other codes in this category are less specific and include multiple disorders. Code **K00.6** (disturbances of tooth eruption) is reported for both premature shedding of a primary tooth and for a retained primary tooth. A distinction is made between supernumerary teeth **(K00.1)** and supernumerary roots **(K00.2)**, but both codes may be reported when present. Code **K00.4** (disturbances in tooth formation) does not include mottled teeth **(K00.3)**.

Category **K08** (other disorders of teeth and supporting structures) does not include dentofacial anomalies or malocclusion or disorders of the jaw. This category does include codes to specify exfoliation of teeth due to systemic causes **(K08.0)** and complete loss of teeth. When reporting exfoliation of teeth due to systemic causes, the code for the underlying systemic condition should also be reported. Codes for complete loss of teeth are based on the amount of compromise to the mandibular bone height, maxillomandibular relationship, residual ridge morphology of the maxilla, and muscle attachments. There are 4 classes of compromise: (1) ideal or minimal, (2) moderate, (3) substantial, and (4) severe.

These classes are represented by the sixth character of each of the codes in subcategory **K08.1**. For example, complete loss of teeth of unspecified cause with severe compromise of structures is reported with code **K08.104**. The classes are also represented by the sixth character in subcategory **K08.4** (partial loss of teeth). The fifth character in each subcategory represents the cause of the loss as trauma, periodontal disease, caries, or other specified cause.

Stomatitis and Related Lesions

This block of codes begins with the code for recurrent oral aphthae or canker sores **(K12.0)**. Code **K12.2** (cellulitis and abscess of the mouth) includes abscess of the floor of the mouth and submandibular abscess, but not abscess of the salivary gland **(K11.3)** or tongue **(K14.0)**.

Subcategory **K12.3** is used to report oral mucositis with fifth characters, indicating the cause of the oral mucositis as unspecified; due to antineoplastic therapy **(K12.31)**; due to other drugs **(K12.32)**; due to radiation **(K12.33)**; or due to other cause, such as viral mucositis **(K12.39)**.

Additional codes should be reported with codes **K12.31-K12.33** as shown by the instructions below each code.

> **K12.31 Oral mucositis (ulcerative) due to antineoplastic therapy**
> Use additional code for adverse effect, if applicable, to identify antineoplastic and immunosuppressive drugs **(T45.1X5)**
> Use additional code for other antineoplastic therapy, such as
> Radiological procedure and radiotherapy **(Y84.2)**
>
> **K12.32 Oral mucositis (ulcerative) due to other drugs**
> Use additional code for adverse effect, if applicable, to identify drug **(T36-T50** with fifth or sixth character **5)**
>
> **K12.33 Oral mucositis (ulcerative) due to radiation**
> Use additional external cause code **(W88-W90, X39.0-)** to identify cause

Diseases of the Esophagus

Category **K20** includes codes for eosinophilic esophagitis **(K20.0)**, other esophagitis **(K20.8)**, and unspecified esophagitis **(K20.9)**. Not included here are esophagitis with gastroesophageal reflux disease **(K21.0)** or ulcerative esophagitis **(K22.1-)**. When eosinophilic gastritis or gastroenteritis **(K52.81)** is also present, this code may be reported in addition to codes in category **K20**.

Codes in category **K21** identify gastroesophageal reflux disease as that with esophagitis **(K21.0)** and without esophagitis **(K21.9)**. Esophagitis without gastroesophageal reflux is reported with code **K20**. Newborn esophageal reflux is reported with code **P78.83**.

Ulcer or erosion of the esophagus is reported with code **K22.1**. When ulceration is due to poisoning or the adverse effect of a drug, additional codes from categories **T36-T65** should be reported. For poisoning, report a code from categories **T36-T65** with fifth or sixth characters that indicate the intent as accidental, intentional self-harm, assault, or undetermined.

Other codes in this subcategory include **K22.2** for esophageal obstruction, which includes compression, constriction, stenosis, and stricture of the esophagus. Nontraumatic perforation of the esophagus is reported with code **K22.3**. Dyskinesia of the esophagus is reported with code **K22.4,** but this does not include cardiospasm

(K22.0). Gastroesophageal laceration-hemorrhage syndrome or Mallory-Weiss syndrome is reported with code **K22.6.**

Stomach and Duodenal Disorders

Categories **K25-K28** include codes for gastric, duodenal, peptic, and gastrojejunal ulcers with specification of acute or chronic and whether each is with hemorrhage, with perforation, with both hemorrhage and perforation, or without hemorrhage or perforation. Each category includes an instruction to use an additional code to identify alcohol abuse and dependence when present.

Category **K29** includes codes for gastritis and duodenitis. Codes in this category specify the type of gastritis or duodenitis with or without bleeding.

Examples

K29.00	Acute gastritis without bleeding
K29.01	Acute gastritis with bleeding
K29.20	Alcoholic gastritis without bleeding
K29.21	Alcoholic gastritis with bleeding
K29.30	Chronic superficial gastritis without bleeding
K29.31	Chronic superficial gastritis with bleeding

> From the tabular list: Instructions for subcategories **K29.0** and **K29.2**—An additional code from category **F10** should be reported when alcohol abuse and dependence are diagnosed in addition to acute or alcoholic gastritis.

Besides the examples shown above, this category also includes codes for chronic atrophic gastritis, unspecified chronic gastritis (includes chronic antral gastritis), other gastritis (includes granulomatous), duodenitis, and unspecified gastroduodenitis. Not included here is eosinophilic gastritis or gastroenteritis **(K52.81).**

Code **K30** is reported for functional dyspepsia. This does not include dyspepsia not otherwise specified **(R10.13),** heartburn **(R12),** or psychogenic dyspepsia **(F45.8).**

Codes for other stomach and duodenal disorders in category **K31** include acute dilatation of the stomach **(K31.0),** pylorospasm not elsewhere classified **(K31.3),** gastric diverticulum **(K31.4),** and obstruction of the duodenum **(K31.5).** These codes do not include the congenital or infantile forms of these conditions found in categories **Q40** and **Q41.**

Appendicitis and Other Diseases of the Appendix

Categories **K35-K37** include codes for appendicitis. Codes in category **K35** are used to report acute appendicitis. Code **K35.2** is used to report acute appendicitis with generalized peritonitis and includes perforated or ruptured appendix not otherwise specified. Code **K35.3** is used to report acute appendicitis with localized peritonitis with or without rupture of the appendix. Fecalith and other appendicular concretions are reported with code **K38.1.**

Hernias

The block of codes **K40-K46** are used to report various types of hernias, including congenital hernias other than congenital diaphragmatic **(Q79.0)** or hiatal hernia **(Q40.1)**.

> Key point: When a hernia is both obstructed and gangrenous, it is classified as a hernia with gangrene.

Category **K40** includes codes for bilateral and unilateral inguinal hernias. The codes in this category specify hernia with obstruction but without gangrene, with gangrene, without obstruction or gangrene, and also whether or not the hernia is recurrent. Right or left laterality is not specified in the codes for unilateral hernia.

Example

K40.00	Bilateral inguinal hernia, with obstruction, without gangrene, not specified as recurrent
K40.01	Bilateral inguinal hernia, with obstruction, without gangrene, recurrent
K40.10	Bilateral inguinal hernia, with gangrene, not specified as recurrent
K40.11	Bilateral inguinal hernia, with gangrene, recurrent
K40.20	Bilateral inguinal hernia, without obstruction or gangrene, not specified as recurrent
K40.21	Bilateral inguinal hernia, without obstruction or gangrene, recurrent

Unilateral inguinal hernias are structured in the same way with codes **K40.30-K40.91**. Category **K41** (femoral hernia) is structured in the same manner as category **K40**.

Categories **K42-K46** include codes for umbilical, ventral, diaphragmatic, other abdominal, and unspecified abdominal hernia. Each category includes codes to specify with obstruction but without gangrene, with gangrene, and without obstruction or gangrene. Umbilical hernia does not include omphacele **(Q79.2)**. Category **K43** (ventral hernia) includes incisional and parastomal hernia. Epigastric, hypogastric, midline, spigelian, and subxiphoid hernia are classified as other and unspecified ventral hernia in subcategories **K43.6-K43.9**. Category **K46** (unspecified abdominal hernia) includes enterocele, epiplocele, and interstitial, intestinal, and intra-abdominal hernia.

Noninfective Enteritis and Colitis

The block of codes **K50-K52** includes codes for Crohn disease, ulcerative colitis, inflammatory polyps of the colon, and gastroenteritis and colitis due to causes such as radiation, toxic agent, allergic and dietetic, and eosinophilic disorder.

In *ICD-10-CM*, Crohn disease is the main term used for regional enteritis (the opposite of *ICD-9-CM*). Codes for Crohn disease are specific to sites of small, large, or small and large intestine and either without complications or with specified complications.

Example

K50.80	Crohn disease of both small and large intestine without complications
K50.811	Crohn disease of both small and large intestine with rectal bleeding
K50.812	Crohn disease of both small and large intestine with intestinal obstruction
K50.813	Crohn disease of both small and large intestine with fistula
K50.814	Crohn disease of both small and large intestine with abscess
K50.818	Crohn disease of both small and large intestine with other complication
K50.819	Crohn disease of both small and large intestine with unspecified complications

An additional code to identify manifestations such pyoderma gangrenosum **(L88)** should be reported with codes in category **K50** when applicable.

Ulcerative colitis is reported with codes in category **K51**, which specify site and complications. Subcategories include

K51.0	Ulcerative (chronic) pancolitis
K51.2	Ulcerative (chronic) proctitis
K51.3	Ulcerative (chronic) rectosigmoiditis
K51.4	Inflammatory polyps of colon
K51.5	Left sided colitis

In each of the above subcategories, codes are specific to the absence of complications or with complications, including rectal bleeding, intestinal obstruction, fistula, or abscess.

Other Diseases of Intestines

Vascular disorders of the intestines are reported with codes in category **K55** with the exception of necrotizing enterocolitis of the newborn.

Category **K56** (paralytic ileus and intestinal obstruction without hernia) excludes many conditions in the neonatal period and those that are congenital. Exclusions include congenital stricture or stenosis of the intestine **(Q41-Q42)**; meconium ileus, not otherwise specified **(P76.0)**; and neonatal intestinal obstructions classifiable to category **P76**. The following codes are included in category **P76**:

P76.0   Meconium plug syndrome

Excludes 1: meconium ileus in cystic fibrosis **(E84.11)**

P76.1   Transitory ileus of newborn

Excludes 1: Hirschsprung disease **(Q43.1)**

P76.2   Intestinal obstruction due to inspissated milk

P76.8   Other specified intestinal obstruction of newborn

Excludes 1: intestinal obstruction classifiable to **K56.-**

P76.9   Intestinal obstruction of newborn, unspecified

Note that code **P76.8** (other specified intestinal obstruction of newborn) has an excludes 1 note indicating that intestinal obstruction classified to category **K56** is not coded here. Based on the exclusion notes at categories **K56** and **P76,** codes in category **K56** would be reported for newborn obstruction when no code for the specified obstruction is found in category **P76.** Applicable codes from category **K56** include

K56.0	Paralytic ileus
K56.1	Intussusception
K56.2	Volvulus
K56.3	Gallstone ileus
K56.41	Fecal impaction
K56.49	Other impaction of intestine
K56.5	Intestinal adhesions [bands] with obstruction
K56.60	Unspecified intestinal obstruction
K56.7	Ileus, unspecified

Diverticular disease of the intestine is classified with codes in category **K57** based on small, large, or small and large intestine involvement, with or without perforation and abscess, and with or without bleeding.

Category **K58** includes codes for irritable bowel syndrome with or without diarrhea. Category **K59** includes codes for unspecified constipation, slow transit constipation, outlet dysfunction constipation, other constipation, functional diarrhea, neurogenic bowel not elsewhere classified, megacolon that is neither infectious nor congenital, anal spasm, and other specified functional intestinal disorders.

Fissure and fistula of anal and rectal regions are classified in category **K60.** This category excludes fissure and fistula of the anal and rectal regions with abscess or cellulitis, as codes in category **K61** are used to report those. It also excludes old healed non-traumatic anal tears **(K62.81),** congenital anal fissure **(Q43.8),** and congenital fistulas **(Q42.-, Q43.-).**

Peritonitis

Generalized acute peritonitis; peritoneal abscess; and spontaneous bacterial peritonitis, choleperitonitis, and sclerosing mesenteritis are specific types of peritonitis included in category **K65.** However, there is a long list of codes for peritonitis in infectious and other conditions such as diverticulitis for which combination codes from other categories describe the condition.

Example from alphabetic index

Diverticulitis
– intestine **K57.92**
– – with
– – – abscess, perforation or peritonitis **K57.80**

Because code **K57.80** includes diverticulitis of the intestine with abscess, perforation, or peritonitis, a code from category **K65** is unnecessary.

Other Disorders of the Peritoneum and Retroperitoneum

Peritoneal adhesions other than female pelvic adhesions **(N73.6)** and peritoneal adhesions with intestinal obstruction **(K56.5)** are reported with code **K66.0**. Ascites **(R18.-)** or peritoneal effusion **(R18.8)** may be reported in addition to codes in category **K66** when appropriate.

Non-traumatic hemoperitoneum is reported with code **K66.1**. Traumatic hemoperitoneum should be reported with a code from category **S36**.

Retroperitoneal abscess is specified as post-procedural **(K68.11)**, psoas muscle abscess **(K68.12)**, or other abscess **(K68.19)**.

Diseases of the Liver

Toxic liver disease due to poisoning is reported with a code for the drug or toxin **(T36-T65)** followed by a code from category **K71**. Codes in category **K71** specify the condition caused by the toxin, such as toxic liver disease with hepatic necrosis with coma **(K71.11)** or with hepatic necrosis without coma **(K71.10)**.

When toxic liver disease is due to the adverse effect of a drug, an additional code from categories **T36-T50** should be reported to identify the drug.

Hepatic failure not elsewhere classified is reported with codes in category **K72**. Included in this category are conditions such as acute hepatitis with hepatic failure and fulminant hepatitis with hepatic failure. Alcoholic hepatic failure is reported with codes in category **K70**. Category **K73** provides codes for chronic hepatitis not elsewhere classified.

Disorders of the Gallbladder

Cholelithiasis and cholecystitis are reported with codes in categories **K80** and **K81**. Code descriptors for cholelithiasis and choledocholithiasis do not include these terms. Instead, *ICD-10-CM* refers to each as calculus of the gallbladder and calculus of the bile duct. Category **K80** includes codes to specify calculus of the gallbladder or bile duct or the gallbladder and bile duct.

Table 12-1 illustrates the codes for calculus of the gallbladder, calculus of the bile duct, and calculus of the gallbladder and bile duct according to presentations with or without obstruction and with or without associated cholecystitis or cholangitis.

Not included in this table are codes for other cholelithiasis without obstruction **(K80.80)** and with obstruction **(K80.81)** and for obstruction of the gallbladder or cystic duct without cholelithiasis **(K82.0)**.

Codes for cholecystitis without cholelithiasis are not included in the Table 12-1. These conditions are reported with codes in category **K81,** which specify the condition as acute, chronic, acute and chronic, or unspecified. Cholangitis without choledocholithiasis is reported with code **K83.0**.

Table 12-1. ICD-10-CM Codes for Calculus of Gallbladder and/or Bile Duct

Calculus of Gallbladder Without Obstruction	Calculus of Gallbladder With Obstruction	Calculus of Bile Duct Without Obstruction	Calculus of Bile Duct With Obstruction	Calculus of Gallbladder and Bile Duct Without Obstruction	Calculus of Gallbladder and Bile Duct With Obstruction
K80.00 With acute cholecystitis	K80.01 With acute cholecystitis	K80.30 With cholangitis, unspecified	K80.31 With cholangitis, unspecified	K80.60 With cholecystitis, unspecified	K80.61 With cholecystitis, unspecified
K80.10 With chronic cholecystitis	K80.11 With chronic cholecystitis	K80.32 With acute cholangitis	K80.33 With acute cholangitis	K80.62 With acute cholecystitis	K80.63 With acute cholecystitis
K80.12 With acute and chronic cholecystitis	K80.13 With acute and chronic cholecystitis	K80.34 With chronic cholangitis	K80.35 With chronic cholangitis	K80.64 With chronic cholecystitis	K80.65 With chronic cholecystitis
K80.18 With other cholecystitis	K80.19 With other cholecystitis	K80.36 With acute and chronic cholangitis	K80.37 With acute and chronic cholangitis	K80.66 With acute and chronic cholecystitis	K80.67 With acute and chronic cholecystitis
K80.20 Without cholecystitis	K80.21 Without cholecystitis	K80.40 With cholecystitis, unspecified	K80.41 With cholecystitis, unspecified	K80.70 Without cholecystitis	K80.71 Without cholecystitis
		K80.42 With acute cholecystitis	K80.43 With acute cholecystitis		
		K80.44 With chronic cholecystitis	K80.45 With chronic cholecystitis		
		K80.46 With acute and chronic cholecystitis	K80.47 With acute and chronic cholecystitis		
		K80.50 Without cholangitis or cholecystitis	K80.51 Without cholangitis or cholecystitis		

Intestinal Malabsorption

Codes in category **K90** include conditions such as celiac disease **(K90.0)**, blind loop syndrome **(K90.2,** excludes congenital blind loop **Q43.8**), and malabsorption due to intolerance, not elsewhere classified **(K90.4)**. Code **K90.4** may be reported in addition to codes **K90.0** (celiac disease) and codes in category **E73** for lactose intolerance.

Intraoperative and Post-Procedural Complications

Category **K91** includes codes for complications during or after procedures and disorders of the gastrointestinal system not elsewhere classified. This includes codes for vomiting following gastrointestinal surgery **(K91.0)** and post-procedural intestinal obstruction **(K91.3)**.

Codes for reporting intraoperative hemorrhage and hematoma of a digestive system organ or structure **(K91.6-)** and accidental puncture and laceration of a digestive system organ or structure **(K91.7-)** also indicate whether the procedure was a digestive system procedure or other procedure. Post-procedural hemorrhage or hematoma of a digestive system organ or structure is reported with code **K91.840** following a digestive system procedure or **K91.841** following another type of procedure. Subcategory **K91.85** includes codes for complications of an intestinal pouch.

Complications of bariatric procedures are reported with codes in category **K95**.

Other Gastrointestinal Diseases

When the cause of gastrointestinal hemorrhage is not specified, code **K92.2** (gastrointestinal hemorrhage, unspecified) may be reported. This code should not be reported for hemorrhage in conditions such as diverticular disease with hemorrhage **(K57.-0)** or gastritis and duodenitis with hemorrhage **(K29.-)**. Hemorrhage of the anus and rectum is reported with code **K62.5**.

As with oral mucositis, gastrointestinal mucositis **(K92.81)** is reported with additional codes to specify the type of associated therapy. See codes in subcategory **T45.1X** to report associated therapy with antineoplastic and immunosuppressive drugs or code **Y84.2** for radiological procedure and radiotherapy.

Complications of Artificial Openings of the Digestive System

Complications of colostomy, enterostomy, gastrostomy, and esophagostomy are reported with codes in category **K94** based on the type of complication.

Example

K94.20	Gastrostomy complication, unspecified
K94.21	Gastrostomy hemorrhage
K94.22	Gastrostomy infection
K94.23	Gastrostomy malfunction
K94.29	Other complications of gastrostomy

When reporting an infection of the ostomy site, an additional code is required to identify the infection. For colostomy, enterostomy, or gastrostomy infection, additional codes for cellulitis of abdominal wall **(L03.311)** or sepsis **(A40.-, A41.-)** may be reported in addition to codes for infection.

Signs, Symptoms, and History

Symptoms and findings related to the digestive system may be reported when a definitive diagnosis has not been established. These are reported with codes from Chapter 18 of the tabular list, as are abnormal results of clinical or other investigative procedures and ill-defined conditions for which no definitive diagnosis has been documented. Some codes for symptoms have been included earlier in this chapter. The following are examples of codes for other digestive symptoms and findings:

R11.0	Nausea (without vomiting)
R11.11	Vomiting without nausea
R11.12	Projectile vomiting
R11.2	Nausea with vomiting, unspecified
R13.0	Aphagia
R14.0	Abdominal distension (gaseous)
R19.12	Hyperactive bowel sounds
R19.7	Diarrhea, unspecified
R62.51	Failure to thrive (child)
R63.0	Anorexia
R63.3	Feeding difficulties

ICD-10-CM provides different categories of codes for abdominal pain, abdominal tenderness, and rebound abdominal tenderness. Each category includes codes specifying the site of pain or tenderness and for generalized pain or tenderness.

Examples

R10.0	Acute abdomen
R10.11	Right upper quadrant pain
R10.12	Left upper quadrant pain
R10.13	Epigastric pain
R10.31	Right lower quadrant pain
R10.32	Left lower quadrant pain
R10.33	Periumbilical pain
R10.84	Generalized abdominal pain
R10.827	Generalized rebound abdominal tenderness

Codes from Chapter 21 of the tabular list are useful for reporting factors that influence a person's health status but are not a current illness or injury.

Examples

Z83.71	Family history of colonic polyps
Z93.0	Tracheostomy status
Z93.1	Gastrostomy status
Z93.2	Ileostomy status
Z93.3	Colostomy status
Z93.4	Other artificial openings of gastrointestinal tract status

Code Scenarios

An infant is diagnosed with a congenital right inguinal hernia without obstruction. The code reported is **K40.90**.

> From the tabular list instructions for block **K40-K46** (hernia): An includes note at the beginning of this block states a congenital hernia except diaphragmatic or hiatus hernia is included in this block.

A 15-year-old patient is admitted after taking an overdose of acetaminophen in an attempted suicide because she was upset over trouble fitting in at her new school and loss of contact with old friends. Her mother states that the girl has recently been diagnosed with adjustment disorder with anxiety. The patient is admitted and, after developing liver failure, is transferred to another facility for further treatment. The discharge diagnoses are toxic liver disease with hepatic necrosis without coma due to attempted suicide by acetaminophen overdose and adjustment disorder with anxiety.

T39.1X2A Poisoning by 4-Aminophenol derivatives, intentional self-harm
K71.10 Toxic liver disease with hepatic necrosis, without coma
F43.22 Adjustment disorder with anxiety

> From the guidelines: Section IC19e5b—When coding a poisoning or reaction to the improper use of a medication (eg, overdose, wrong substance given or taken in error, wrong route of administration), first assign the appropriate code from categories **T36-T50**. The poisoning codes have an associated intent as their fifth or sixth character (accidental, intentional self-harm, assault, and undetermined). Use additional code(s) for all manifestations of poisonings.

A patient presents with an acute gastric ulcer that is diagnosed as acute gastric ulcer due to *Helicobacter pylori*.

K25.3 Acute gastric ulcer without hemorrhage or perforation
B96.81 *Helicobacter pylori* as the cause of disease classified elsewhere

> From the guidelines: Section IC1b—Certain infections are classified in chapters other than Chapter 1, and no organism is identified as part of the infection code. In these instances, it is necessary to use an additional code from Chapter 1 to identify the organism. A code from category **B95** (*Streptococcus, Staphylococcus,* and *Enterococcus*) as the cause of diseases classified to other chapters, **B96** (other bacterial agents as the cause of diseases classified to other chapters), or **B97** (viral agents as the cause of diseases classified to other chapters) is to be used as an additional code to identify the organism.
>
> Though no instructional note is included in the tabular list to direct coding of *H pylori* in addition to codes for acute gastric ulcer, it is correct to include the code when supported by documentation because *H pylori* is not an integral part of the disease process of an acute gastric ulcer.

Review What You Have Learned

12.1 A child is diagnosed with acute ruptured appendicitis with peritoneal abscess. What code(s) is reported?
   A. **K35.80**   Unspecified acute appendicitis
   B. **K35.80**   Unspecified acute appendicitis
      K65.1   Peritoneal abscess
   C. **K35.3**   Acute appendicitis with localized peritonitis
   D. **K36**   Other appendicitis
   E. None of the above

12.2 A child is diagnosed with eosinophilic esophagitis. What code(s) is reported?
   A. **K22.8**   Other specified diseases of esophagus
   B. **D72.1**   Eosinophilia
      K23   Disorders of esophagus in diseases classified elsewhere
   C. **K20.0**   Eosinophilic esophagitis
   D. **K20.9**   Esophagitis, unspecified
   E. None of the above

12.3 A child is diagnosed with a paraumbilical hernia without gangrene or obstruction. Code **K42.9** (umbilical hernia without obstruction or gangrene) is reported.
   A. True
   B. False

12.4 Code **K00.6** (disturbances of tooth eruption) is reported for both premature shedding of a primary tooth and for a retained primary tooth.
   A. True
   B. False

12.5 The codes for diverticulitis of the intestines specify the segment of colon affected (eg, rectosigmoiditis) and whether or not there are associated complications.
   A. True
   B. False

12.6 A child who has had a colostomy for 6 months is diagnosed with an uncomplicated small parastomal hernia. What code is reported for the parastomal hernia?
   A. **K94.00**   Colostomy complication, unspecified
   B. **K94.09**   Other complications of colostomy
   C. **K43.5**   Parastomal hernia without obstruction or gangrene
   D. **K43.6**   Other and unspecified ventral hernia with obstruction, without gangrene
   E. None of the above

≡ CHAPTER 13 ≡

Diseases of the Skin and Subcutaneous Tissue (L00-L99)

Diseases of the skin and subcutaneous tissue are captured with codes in Chapter 12 of the *International Classification of Diseases, Tenth Revision, Clinical Modification (ICD-10-CM)* tabular list. This chapter includes blocks **L00-L99** as follows:

Infections of the skin and subcutaneous tissue **L00-L08**
Bullous disorders **L10-L14**
Dermatitis and eczema **L20-L30**
Papulosquamous disorders **L40-L45**
Urticaria and erythema **L49-L54**
Radiation-related disorders of the skin and subcutaneous tissue **L55-L59**
Disorders of skin appendages **L60-L75**
Intraoperative and post-procedural complications of skin and subcutaneous tissue **L76**
Other disorders of the skin and subcutaneous tissue **L80-L99**

Infections of the Skin and Subcutaneous Tissue

The block of codes **L00-L08** provides codes for reporting infections of the skin and subcutaneous tissue. An instruction to use an additional code to identify the infectious agent applies to this block of codes.

Certain infectious conditions of the skin will not be found in this chapter of *ICD-10-CM*, such as local infections of the skin classified to Chapter 1, including viral warts, mycosis, or candidiasis of the skin.

Code **L00** is used to report staphylococcal scalded skin syndrome. This code is not used to report bullous impetigo **(L01.03)** or toxic epidermal necrolysis **(L51.2)**, and these codes would not be reported with code **L00**. An additional code from category **L49** is used to identify the percentage of skin exfoliation in staphylococcal scalded skin syndrome.

L49.0 Exfoliation due to erythematous condition involving less than 10 percent of body surface
L49.1 Exfoliation due to erythematous condition involving 10–19 percent of body surface
L49.2 Exfoliation due to erythematous condition involving 20–29 percent of body surface

L49.3		Exfoliation due to erythematous condition involving 30–39 percent of body surface
L49.4		Exfoliation due to erythematous condition involving 40–49 percent of body surface
L49.5		Exfoliation due to erythematous condition involving 50–59 percent of body surface
L49.6		Exfoliation due to erythematous condition involving 60–69 percent of body surface
L49.7		Exfoliation due to erythematous condition involving 70–79 percent of body surface
L49.8		Exfoliation due to erythematous condition involving 80–89 percent of body surface
L49.9		Exfoliation due to erythematous condition involving 90 or more percent of body surface

Report impetigo that is not otherwise specified with code **L01.00**. Non-bullous impetigo is reported with code **L01.01**. Bockhart impetigo (**L01.02**) includes impetigo follicularis and superficial pustular perifolliculitis. Code **L01.1** is used to report impetiginization of other dermatoses.

Category **L02** provides codes for reporting cutaneous abscess, furuncle, and carbuncle by site. This category has an excludes 2 note indicating that conditions such as abscess of the anal and rectal region and abscess of female or male genital organs are not reported with codes from this category but may be reported in addition to conditions reported here.

> **Terms to Know**
>
> **Abscess**–an enclosed collection of liquefied tissue (pus) in any part of the body
>
> **Furuncle**–also called a boil, a deep infection of a hair follicle (folliculitis) involving subcutaneous tissue
>
> **Carbuncle**–a single inflammatory mass formed from multiple inflamed follicles

Abscess, furuncle, and carbuncle are separately reported. Codes for each condition are specific to site.

Example

L02.01	Cutaneous abscess of face
L02.02	Furuncle of face
L02.03	Carbuncle of face

When these conditions affect the trunk, codes are specific to abdominal wall, back other than buttock, chest wall, groin, perineum, and umbilicus. These codes are found in subcategory **L02.2-**. Note that omphalitis is not included here but is reported with code **L08.82** for non-newborn omphalitis or a code from category **P38** for omphalitis of a newborn. An abscess of the breast is reported with code **N61**.

Laterality is not included in codes for abscess, furuncle, or carbuncle of the buttock **(L02.3-)**, but laterality is specified by use of a sixth character for these conditions affecting the limbs.

Example

L02.32	Furuncle of buttock
L02.421	Furuncle of right axilla
L02.422	Furuncle of left axilla
L02.423	Furuncle of right upper limb
L02.424	Furuncle of left upper limb
L02.425	Furuncle of right lower limb
L02.426	Furuncle of left lower limb
L02.429	Furuncle of limb, unspecified

Category **L03** includes codes for cellulitis and acute lymphangitis. These conditions in sites such as the anal and rectal region, external auditory canal, eyelid, and external genital organs are classified elsewhere. Infections of the nail are included here. The alphabetic index listing for the term "Hangnail" directs to cellulitis of a digit (onychia) or lymphangitis of a digit (paronychia). Thus hangnail of a finger without lymphangitis would be reported as cellulitis subcategory **L03.01-** with a sixth character identifying laterality of the finger as right, left, or unspecified.

Acute lymphadenitis is classified in category **L04**. This category does not include mesenteric lymphadenitis **(I88.0)** or HIV disease resulting in generalized lymphadenopathy **(B20)**. Codes in category **L04** are specific to the site of the lymphadenitis but are not specific to sites of lymphadenitis of the trunk **(L04.1)**. For chronic or subacute lymphadenitis, see code **I88.1**.

> **Terms to Know**
>
> **Cellulitis**—a skin infection caused by bacteria commonly presenting as non-necrotizing inflammation of the skin and subcutaneous tissues
>
> **Lymphangitis**—an inflammation of the lymph channels from an infection beginning distal to the channel
>
> **Lymphadenitis**—inflammation or enlargement of a lymph node or nodes often in response to local or generalized viral infection

Pilonidal cyst and sinus are reported with codes in category **L05** based on the presence or absence of abscess. Separate codes identify cyst or sinus with or without abscess.

Bullous Disorders

This block of codes for bullous (blistering) disorders begins with codes for pemphigus in category **L10**. This category does not include benign familial pemphigus **(Q82.8)** or pemphigus neonatorum **(L01.03)**. Code **L12.2** is used to report chronic bullous disease of childhood or juvenile dermatitis herpetiformis. Code **L14** is reported for bullous disorders in conditions classified elsewhere.

Dermatitis and Eczema

In the block of codes **L20-L30,** the terms dermatitis and eczema are used synonymously and interchangeably. This block includes codes for common conditions such as seborrhea capitis (cradle cap) **(L21.0),** seborrheic infantile dermatitis **(L21.1),** and diaper dermatitis **(L22).** Acute or chronic infantile eczema is reported with code **L20.83.**

Category **L23** includes codes for allergic contact dermatitis, including contact to skin with metals, adhesives, cosmetics, drugs (not ingested), dyes and other chemical products, food (not ingested), plants (except food), and animal dander.

Irritant contact dermatitis is reported with codes in category **L24.** These codes include irritants such as detergents, oils and greases, solvents, cosmetics, drugs (not ingested), food (not ingested), plants, and metals.

When contact dermatitis is not specified as allergic or irritant, codes from category **L25** are reported. Codes in category **L25** include the substance associated with the dermatitis similar to those in categories **L23** and **L24.** Dermatitis due to substances taken internally is reported with codes in category **L27** based on the type of substance ingested (drugs and medicaments, food, or other substances). When ingested drugs or medicaments are indicated as the cause of dermatitis, the codes specify whether the skin eruption is generalized or localized.

Papulosquamous Disorders

Categories **L40-L45** include codes for disorders such as psoriasis. Codes in category **L40** are used to identify the type of psoriasis, such as guttate psoriasis **(L40.4).** This category includes code **L40.54** (psoriatic juvenile arthropathy). Code **L40.8** (other psoriasis) is used to report flexural psoriasis.

Also included in this block is code **L44.4** (infantile papular acrodermatitis or Gianotti-Crosti).

Urticaria and Erythema

Codes for urticaria or hives are found in category **L50** and include the type of urticaria.

L50.0	Allergic urticaria
L50.1	Idiopathic urticaria
L50.2	Urticaria due to cold and heat
L50.3	Dermatographic urticaria
L50.4	Vibratory urticaria
L50.5	Cholinergic urticaria
L50.6	Contact urticaria
L50.8	Other urticaria (includes chronic and recurrent periodic urticaria)
L50.9	Urticaria, unspecified

This category does not include giant urticaria or angioneurotic edema **(T78.3),** urticaria neonatorum **(P83.8),** or solar urticaria **(L56.3).**

> **Terms to Know**
>
> **Erythema multiforme**—an acute, self-limited, and often recurring skin disorder with red patches with purple-gray centers (sometimes called target or iris lesions) due to a hypersensitivity reaction to infections, such as herpes simplex virus, or to drugs (ICD-10-CM does not differentiate minor or major.)
>
> **Toxic epidermal necrolysis**—an erythematous life-threatening condition (commonly drug induced) causing blistering of the mucous membranes and significant skin sloughing involving more than 30% of the body surface area (also referred to as Lyell syndrome)
>
> **Stevens-Johnson syndrome**—a lesser form of toxic epidermal necrolysis involving skin sloughing of less than 10% of the body surface area
>
> **Stevens-Johnson syndrome–toxic epidermal overlap syndrome**—a form of toxic epidermal necrolysis overlapping Stevens-Johnson syndrome involving 10% to 30% of the body surface area

Category **L51** (erythema multiforme) includes codes for non-bullous erythema multiforme, Stevens-Johnson syndrome, toxic epidermal necrolysis, and Stevens-Johnson syndrome–toxic epidermal necrolysis overlap syndrome. These syndromes may require reporting of multiple codes, including a code from category **L49** to identify the percentage of skin exfoliation. When the adverse effect of a drug is documented, an additional code to identify the drug (**T36-T50** with fifth or sixth character **5**) should be reported. Associated manifestations, such as arthropathy with dermatologic disorders **(M14.8-)**, should also be reported in addition to codes in category **L51**.

Radiation-Related Disorders of the Skin and Subcutaneous Tissue

The block of codes **L55-L59** includes codes for skin changes due to sun exposure; nonionizing radiation such as a welding arc, tanning beds, or infrared radiation; and radiodermatitis due to exposure to x-rays, radioactive isotopes, or other ionizing radiation.

Sunburn is the condition reported with codes in category **L55**. The codes are specific to the degree of sunburn (first, second, third, or unspecified).

Conditions included in category **L56** are those involving acute skin changes due to ultraviolet radiation. Each of the conditions identified by codes in **L56** will require both a code from category **L56** and additional codes to identify the source of ultraviolet radiation and, if applicable, to identify a drug associated with an adverse effect.

Codes to identify the source of ultraviolet radiation include

- **W89.0XX-** Exposure to welding light (arc)
- **W89.1XX-** Exposure to tanning bed
- **W89.8XX-** Exposure to other man-made visible and ultraviolet light
- **W89.9XX-** Exposure to unspecified man-made visible and ultraviolet light
- **X32.XXX-** Exposure to sunlight

Each of the above codes is completed with a seventh character indicating initial encounter **(A)**, subsequent encounter **(D)**, or sequela **(S)**. These codes are also used to identify the source of nonionizing radiation in conjunction with codes in category **L57**.

> **Terms to Know**
>
> **Phototoxic response**—changes to cell membranes due to damaging effects of light-activated compounds, similar to an exaggerated sunburn of the exposed areas and occurring soon after exposure
>
> **Photoallergic response**—immune response to a light-activated change in a drug or other chemical, similar to allergic contact dermatitis; severe or prolonged reactions may spread beyond exposed skin; reaction occurs 1 to 3 days after exposure
>
> **Photocontact dermatitis**—allergic reaction caused by sun exposure following exposure to a photosensitizing agent (eg, citrus juice, certain perfumes)

Codes **L56.0** and **L56.1** are used to report phototoxic and photoallergic response to a drug. With each of these codes, a code from categories **T36-T50** should be reported to identify the drug associated with the adverse effect in addition to a code to identify the source of ultraviolet radiation.

Category **L57** includes codes for skin changes due to chronic exposure to nonionizing radiation (exposures represented by **W89** and **X32** categories).

Category **L58** includes codes for acute, chronic, or unspecified radiodermatitis. X-ray alopecia is reported with code **L58.1** (chronic radiodermatitis). An additional code from categories **W88** or **W90** is required to identify the source of the radiation when reporting codes from category **L58**.

W88.0XX- Exposure to x-rays
W88.1XX- Exposure to radioactive isotopes
W88.8XX- Exposure to other ionizing radiation
W90.0XX- Exposure to radiofrequency
W90.1XX- Exposure to infrared radiation
W90.2XX- Exposure to laser radiation
W90.8XX- Exposure to other nonionizing radiation

A seventh character is required to complete each of the above codes specifying initial encounter **(A)**, subsequent encounter **(D)**, or sequela **(S)**.

Disorders of Skin Appendages

This block of codes includes codes for conditions affecting the nails, hair, hair follicles, and sebaceous glands. Not included here are congenital malformations of the integument **(Q84.-)**.

Nail disorders are reported with codes in category **L60** with the exception of clubbing of the nails **(R68.3)** or infectious conditions such as onychomycosis **(B35.1)**, onychia, or paronychia **(L03.-)**.

Onychocryptosis or ingrowing nail is reported with code **L60.0**. Onycholysis or separation of the nail from the nail bed is reported with code **L60.1**. Koilonychia (spoon nail) and onychogryphosis (ram's horn nail) are reported with code **L60.3** except when congenital **(Q84.6)**. **L60.4** is used to report Beau lines. Code **L60.8** includes disorders such as leukonychia other than congenital **(Q84.4)** and onychomadesis (nail shedding). Code **L62** (nail disorders in diseases classified elsewhere) is used in addition to a code for an underlying disease.

Codes in categories **L63-L65** are used to identify various forms of alopecia areata, androgenic alopecia, and other non-scarring hair loss. Specific alopecia areata other than alopecia totalis, alopecia universalis, and ophiasis is reported with code **L63.8** (other alopecia areata). Drug-induced hair loss should be reported with a code from categories **T36-T50** in addition to a code for drug-induced androgenic alopecia **(L64.0)** or a code from category **L65**.

Codes in category **L65** include

L65.0	Telogen effluvium
L65.1	Anagen effluvium
L65.2	Alopecia mucinosa
L65.8	Other specified non-scarring hair loss
L65.9	Non-scarring hair loss, unspecified

> **Terms to Know**
> **Telogen effluvium**—acute onset loss of hair in the resting phase of the growth cycle caused by metabolic or hormonal stress (eg, childbirth or surgery) or by medications
> **Anagen effluvium**—a reversible loss of growth phase hairs often associated with chemotherapy
> **Alopecia mucinosa**—also called follicular mucinosa, caused by accumulation of mucinous material in hair follicles and sebaceous glands that leads to hair loss

Other disorders of the hair and hair follicles include those for excess hair such as hirsutism **(L68.0)** and localized hypertrichosis **(L68.2)**.

Acne is reported with codes in category **L70**, which includes acne vulgaris **(L70.0)**, infantile acne **(L70.4)**, and acné excoriée de jeune filles (picker acne, **L70.5**). Acne keloid is reported with code **L73.0**.

Follicular cysts are reported based on type, including epidermal **(L72.0)**, pilar **(L72.11)**, trichodermal (trichilemmal, **L72.12**), and sebaceous **(L72.3)**.

Eccrine sweat disorders are reported with codes in category **L74**. This does not include generalized hyperhidrosis **(R61)**. **L74** does include codes for miliaria rubra **(L74.0)**, anhidrosis **(L74.4)**, and focal hyperhidrosis **(L74.5-)**. Focal hyperhidrosis is specified as primary by site or as secondary as follows:

L74.510	Primary focal hyperhidrosis, axilla
L74.511	Primary focal hyperhidrosis, face
L74.512	Primary focal hyperhidrosis, palms
L74.513	Primary focal hyperhidrosis, soles

L74.519	Primary focal hyperhidrosis, unspecified	
L74.52	Secondary focal hyperhidrosis	

Intraoperative and Post-Procedural Complications

Category **L76** includes codes for complications during or after procedures and disorders of the skin and subcutaneous tissue during or after procedures. Codes for reporting intraoperative hemorrhage and hematoma of skin and subcutaneous tissue **(L76.0-)** and accidental puncture and laceration of skin and subcutaneous tissue **(L76.1-)** also indicate whether the procedure was dermatologic or other. Postprocedural hemorrhage or hematoma of skin and subcutaneous tissue is reported with code **L76.21** following a dermatologic procedure or **L76.22** following another type of procedure. Other intraoperative complications are reported with code **L76.81** and other postoperative complications are reported with code **L76.82**.

Other Disorders of Skin and Subcutaneous Tissue

Disorders of pigmentation are included in categories **L80-L81**. Vitiligo **(L80)** includes sites other than the eyelids **(H02.73-)** and vulva **(N90.89)**. Café au lait spots are reported with code **L81.3**.

Acanthosis nigricans is reported with code **L83**. Corns and callosities are reported with code **L84**. Scar conditions and fibrosis of skin are reported with code **L90.5**. A hypertrophic scar or keloid other than an acne keloid is reported with code **L91.0**. Other hypertrophic disorders of the skin are reported with code **L91.8**. This appears to be the most specific code for skin tags other than congenital accessory skin tags that are reported with code **Q82.8** (other specific congenital malformations of the skin). However, the *ICD-9-CM to ICD-10-CM General Equivalency Mappings* map the code for unspecified hypertrophic and atrophic conditions of the skin **(701.9)** to atrophic disorder of skin **(L90.9)** and hypertrophic disorder of the skin, unspecified **(L91.9)**.

Foreign body granuloma of the skin and subcutaneous tissue is reported with code **L92.3** and an additional code to identify the type of retained foreign body **(Z18.-)**. Pyogenic granuloma, including that of the umbilical cord, is reported with code **L98.0**.

Skin Ulcers

Pyoderma gangrenosa is reported with code **L88**. Pressure ulcers are reported by site and stage. The example below includes codes for a pressure ulcer of the right elbow with a definition of each stage following each code descriptor.

Example

L89.010	Pressure ulcer of right elbow, unstageable—Documentation states stage cannot be clinically determined	
L89.011	Pressure ulcer of right elbow, stage 1—Skin changes limited to persistent focal edema	
L89.012	Pressure ulcer of right elbow, stage 2—Pressure ulcer with abrasion, blister, partial thickness skin loss involving epidermis and/or dermis	
L89.013	Pressure ulcer of right elbow, stage 3—Pressure ulcer with full thickness skin loss involving damage or necrosis of subcutaneous tissue	

L89.014 Pressure ulcer of right elbow, stage 4—Pressure ulcer with necrosis of soft tissues through to underlying muscle, tendon, or bone

L89.019 Pressure ulcer of right elbow, unspecified stage—documentation does not provide descriptive terms necessary to identify stage

A healed pressure ulcer is not reported. In hospitalized patients, a pressure ulcer that is at one stage on admission but progresses to a higher stage during the stay is reported at the highest stage documented for that site.

> From the guidelines: Section IC12a2—Assignment of the code for unstageable pressure ulcer **(L89.--0)** should be based on the clinical documentation. These codes are used for pressure ulcers whose stage cannot be clinically determined (eg, the ulcer is covered by eschar or has been treated with a skin or muscle graft) and pressure ulcers that are documented as deep tissue injury but not documented as due to trauma. This code should not be confused with the codes for unspecified stage **(L89.--9)**. When there is no documentation regarding the stage of the pressure ulcer, assign the appropriate code for unspecified stage **(L89.--9)**.

When reporting pressure ulcers, any associated gangrene **(I96)** is coded first. When a patient has pressure ulcers of multiple sites, a code for each site is assigned. An excludes 2 note for category **L89** indicates that diabetic ulcers (**E08-E13** with **.621** or **.622**), non-pressure chronic skin ulcers **(L97.-),** and skin infections **(L00-L08)** are not included here but may be reported in addition to codes for pressure ulcers when both conditions are present.

Non-pressure chronic ulcers of the lower limb are reported with codes in category **L97** according to site and severity. Underlying conditions such as diabetes (**E08-E13** with **.621** or **.622**) are reported first, as is gangrene **(I96)**. Pressure ulcers and infections may be additionally reported when applicable.

Sites specified by codes in category **L97** are thigh, calf, ankle, heel and midfoot, other part of foot, and other part of lower leg. Each of these sites is further identified as unspecified, right, or left. Note that toes are included as other part of foot.

Severity is identified as shown in the following example:

L97.321 Non-pressure chronic ulcer of left ankle limited to breakdown of skin

L97.322 Non-pressure chronic ulcer of left ankle with fat layer exposed

L97.323 Non-pressure chronic ulcer of left ankle with necrosis of muscle

L97.324 Non-pressure chronic ulcer of left ankle with necrosis of bone

L97.329 Non-pressure chronic ulcer of left ankle with unspecified severity

Non-pressure chronic ulcers of the skin of other sites are reported with codes in subcategory **L98.4** according to site and the same severity levels used in reporting non-pressure ulcers of the lower limbs. This category includes codes for the buttock (laterality not specified), back, and skin of other sites.

When multiple non-pressure ulcers are diagnosed, include codes for each by site and severity.

Signs, Symptoms, and History

Symptoms and findings related to the integumentary system may be reported when a definitive diagnosis has not been established. These are reported with codes from Chapter 18 of the tabular list as are abnormal results of clinical or other investigative procedures and ill-defined conditions for which no definitive diagnosis has been documented. Some codes for symptoms have been included earlier in this chapter. The following are examples of codes for other integumentary symptoms and findings.

R21	Rash and other nonspecific skin eruption
R23.0	Cyanosis
R23.1	Pallor
R23.2	Flushing
R23.3	Spontaneous ecchymosis

Common skin infections and other skin-related conditions will be found in other chapters of the tabular list. Melanocytic nevi are classified to category **D22** with codes specific to the site of the nevus. Some examples from other chapters include

F98.8	Nail-biting, thumb-sucking, nose-picking
B07.0	Plantar wart
B07.8	Other viral warts (common, flat, verruca plana)
B08.1	Molluscum contagiosum
D18.01	Hemangioma of skin and subcutaneous tissue
Q82.5	Congenital non-neoplastic nevus

Code Scenarios

A type I diabetic patient is seen for a non-healing sore on his left small toe that was caused by stubbing his toe on a chair leg. He is quite concerned that the ulcer may not heal. The patient is diagnosed with an ulcer of the left small toe limited to breakdown of the skin and instructed on care of the wound and avoidance of pressure or further injury.

E10.621	Type 1 diabetes mellitus with foot ulcer
L97.521	Non-pressure chronic ulcer of other part of left foot limited to breakdown of skin

> From the guidelines: Section IB9—When the combination code lacks necessary specificity in describing the manifestation or complication, an additional code should be used as a secondary code.

A 15-year-old patient who is wheelchair dependent is seen for an injury to her right buttock caused by pressure from sitting on a worn seat cushion. She is diagnosed with a 2-cm pressure ulcer of the right buttock.

L89.319	Pressure ulcer of right buttock, unspecified stage

> From the guidelines: Section IC12a2—When there is no documentation regarding the stage of the pressure ulcer, assign the appropriate code for unspecified stage (L89.--9).

Review What You Have Learned

13.1 A teenager undergoes excision of a foreign body granuloma from the subcutaneous tissue of the right foot caused by a fragment of glass that was retained from stepping on something a year ago. The patient had felt he had something in his foot but could not see it. What code(s) is reported?
  A. **T81.509** Unspecified complication of foreign body accidentally left in body following unspecified procedure
  B. **S91.341S** Puncture wound with foreign body, right foot
  C. **S91.321S** Laceration with foreign body, right foot
  D. **L92.3** Foreign body granuloma of the skin and subcutaneous tissue
   Z18.81 Retained glass fragments
  E. None of the above

13.2 A child reports with an itching rash that began on the last day of a camping trip. He is diagnosed with allergic reaction to contact with poison ivy. What code(s) is reported?
  A. **L24.7** Irritant contact dermatitis due to plants, except food
  B. **T62.2X4** Toxic effect of other ingested (parts of) plant(s), undetermined
  C. **L23.7** Allergic contact dermatitis due to plants, except food
  D. **Y92.833** Campsite as the place of occurrence of the external cause
  E. None of the above

13.3 Diaper dermatitis is reported with code **B37.2** (candidiasis of skin and nail).
  A. True
  B. False

13.4 Allergic contact dermatitis of the eyelid is reported with code **L23.7.**
  A. True
  B. False

13.5 Infantile acne is reported with a code from category **P83.**
  A. True
  B. False

13.6 What code is reported for chronic infantile eczema?
  A. **L21.1** Seborrheic infantile dermatitis
  B. **L20.83** Infantile eczema
  C. **L20.89** Other atopic dermatitis
  D. **L21.0** Seborrhea capitis
  E. None of the above

≡ CHAPTER 14 ≡

Diseases of the Musculoskeletal System and Connective Tissue (M00-M99)

Diseases of the musculoskeletal system and connective tissue are captured with codes in Chapter 13 of the *International Classification of Diseases, Tenth Revision, Clinical Modification (ICD-10-CM)* tabular list. This chapter includes blocks **M00-M99**. An instruction that applies to this chapter is to use an additional code, if applicable, to identify the cause of a musculoskeletal condition.

> **Terms to Know**
>
> **Polyarthritis**—arthritis affecting 5 or more joints (American College of Rheumatology definition)
>
> **Pauciarticular**—also called oligoarticular; involves fewer than 5 joints; often associated with iritis or uveitis
>
> **Ankylosing spondylitis**—a chronic, multisystem inflammatory disorder primarily involving the spine and sacroiliac joints and where ligaments and muscles attach to bones (enthesitis)

Infectious Arthropathy

Categories **M00-M02** include codes for reporting infectious arthropathy. The following instruction from the tabular list applies to these categories:

> This block comprises arthropathies due to microbiological agents. Distinction is made between the following types of etiological relationship:
> a) direct infection of joint, where organisms invade synovial tissue and microbial antigen is present in the joint;
> b) indirect infection, which may be of two types: a reactive arthropathy, where microbial infection of the body is established but neither organisms nor antigens can be identified in the joint, and a post-infective arthropathy, where microbial antigen is present but recovery of an organism is inconstant and evidence of local multiplication is lacking.

Pyogenic arthritis **(M00)** is reported with codes indicating the infecting agent and the infected joint. Subcategories include

M00.0	Staphylococcal arthritis and polyarthritis **(B95.61-B95.8)**
M00.1	Pneumococcal arthritis and polyarthritis
M00.2	Other streptococcal arthritis and polyarthritis **(B95.0-B95.2, B95.4-B95.5)**
M00.8	Arthritis and polyarthritis due to other bacteria **(B96)**
M00.9	Pyogenic arthritis, unspecified

Codes include laterality where applicable and sites specified as shoulder, elbow, wrist, hand, hip, knee, ankle and foot, and vertebrae. Each subcategory also includes a code for polyarthritis.

When direct infection is due to an infectious and parasitic disease classified elsewhere, codes from category **M01** are reported in addition to the code for the underlying condition. Underlying conditions include conditions such as mycoses **(B35-B49)**. Many conditions, such as arthritis in Lyme disease **(A69.23)**, do not require a code from category **M01**. See the alphabetic index listing for arthritis and the excludes 1 note in the tabular list for category **M01** to determine when these codes are reported.

Category **M01** includes one subcategory **M01.X** (direct infection of joint in infectious and parasitic diseases classified elsewhere). This subcategory also includes codes for infection by site. Code **M01.X9** is used to report direct infection of multiple joints in infectious and parasitic diseases classified elsewhere.

Post-infective and reactive arthropathies are reported with codes in category **M02** in addition to a code for the underlying condition, such as infective endocarditis **(I33.0)**. However an excludes 1 note indicates conditions with which the **M02** codes are not reported, such as rheumatic fever **(I00)**. Subcategories include

M02.0	Arthropathy following intestinal bypass
M02.1	Post-dysenteric arthropathy
M02.2	Post-immunization arthropathy
M02.3	Reiter disease (reactive)
M02.8	Other reactive arthropathies

As with other categories in this block, codes include the site of the infection.

Inflammatory Polyarthropathies

The block of codes **M05-M14** includes category **M08** (juvenile arthritis). Also code Crohn disease **(K50.-)** or ulcerative colitis **(K51.-)** when either is an underlying disease in juvenile arthritis. This category does not include juvenile dermatomyositis **(M33.0-)** or psoriatic juvenile arthropathy **(L40.54)**.

M08.0	Unspecified juvenile rheumatoid arthritis
M08.1	Juvenile ankylosing spondylitis
M08.2	Juvenile rheumatoid arthritis with systemic onset (Still disease)
M08.3	Juvenile rheumatoid polyarthritis (seronegative)
M08.4	Pauciarticular juvenile rheumatoid arthritis
M08.8	Other juvenile arthritis

≡ DISEASES OF THE MUSCULOSKELETAL SYSTEM AND CONNECTIVE TISSUE ≡ 147

Codes in subcategories **M08.0, M08.2, M08.4,** and **M08.8** include laterality where applicable and sites specified as shoulder, elbow, wrist, hand, hip, knee, ankle and foot, and vertebrae. Codes are also included to report conditions affecting multiple sites. Categories **M08.1** and **M08.3** include only one code each as further specification of site is unnecessary in these conditions.

Subcategory **M14.8** is used to report arthropathies in other specified diseases classified elsewhere, including arthropathy in sickle cell disorders, hyperparathyroidism, and hypothyroidism. The code for the underlying condition is reported first with an additional code from subcategory **M14.8** identifying the site of the arthropathy.

Other Joint Disorders

Categories **M20-M25** include codes for joint deformities other than spinal joints. Conditions such as hallux valgus (bunion) and genu valgum (knock-knee) are included here, but it is important to differentiate between congenital (eg, congenital genu valgum, **Q74.1**) and acquired conditions (eg, adolescent idiopathic genu valgum, **M21.06-**).

Unequal limb length is reported with codes from subcategory **M21.7** with the site corresponding to the shorter limb.

> *Example:* A child is seen for unequal length of her legs. Her right femur is 2 inches longer than her left femur.
> **M21.752** Unequal limb length (acquired), left femur

Category **M22** includes codes for recurrent dislocation or subluxation of the patella. This does not include traumatic dislocation of the patella **(S83.0-)** or pathological dislocation of the knee **(M24.36-)**. Internal derangement of the knee is reported with codes in category **M23.** This category does not include current injury **(S80-S89)** or osteochondritis dissecans **(M93.2-).** Subcategories include cystic meniscus **(M23.0),** derangement of meniscus due to old tear or injury **(M23.2),** and other meniscus derangements **(M23.3).** Codes in these subcategories include laterality and site of the meniscal damage (eg, anterior horn of medial meniscus). Subcategory **M23.6** includes codes for other spontaneous disruption of ligaments of the knee, such as disruption of the anterior cruciate ligament with specification of laterality. Subcategory **M23.4** includes codes for loose body in the knee. For loose body in another joint, see subcategory **M24.0.**

Ligamentous laxity and instability due to an old ligament injury are reported with codes in subcategory **M24.2** specifying the joint affected. This category has an excludes 1 note for familial ligamentous laxity **(M35.7)** and an excludes 2 note for internal derangement of the knee **(M23.5-M23.89).**

Subcategory **M25.5** is used to report pain in a joint. Code **M25.50** is used to report pain in an unspecified joint. This category is specific to joint pain and should not be reported for pain in other body areas, such as hand or fingers **(M79.64-).** Table 14-1 illustrates codes for joint pain.

Table 14-1. *ICD-10-CM* **Joint Pain**

Joint	Right	Left	Unspecified
Shoulder	M25.511	M25.512	M25.519
Elbow	M25.521	M25.522	M25.529
Wrist	M25.531	M25.532	M25.539
Hip	M25.551	M25.552	M25.559
Knee	M25.561	M25.562	M25.569
Ankle or toe	M25.571	M25.572	M25.579

Systemic Connective Tissue Disorders

This block of codes **(M30-M36)** includes autoimmune, collagen, systemic autoimmune, and systemic collagen disease but excludes autoimmune disease of a single organ or single cell type. Included here are conditions such as juvenile polyarteritis **(M30.2)**, mucocutaneous lymph node or Kawasaki syndrome **(M30.3)**, and systemic lupus erythematosus **(M32.-)**. Codes for systemic lupus erythematosus include manifestations such as endocarditis **(M32.11)** and glomerular disease **(M32.14)**. Likewise, category **M33** (dermatopolymyositis) includes codes for juvenile dermatopolymyositis with respiratory involvement **(M33.01)**, myopathy **(M33.02)**, or other organ involvement **(M33.09)**. Category **M36** includes codes for systemic disorders of connective tissue in diseases classified elsewhere, including dermatopolymyositis in neoplastic disease **(M36.0)**, arthropathy in neoplastic disease **(M36.1)**, and hemophilic arthropathy **(M36.2)**. The underlying condition, such as leukemia **(C91-C95)** or hemophilia **(D66-D68.1)**, is reported first with codes in category **M36** reported as additional codes.

Dorsopathies

Categories **M40-M54** include codes for these conditions of the spine. Blocks of codes include deforming dorsopathies **(M40-M43)**, spondylopathies **(M45-M49)**, and other dorsopathies **(M50-M54)**.

> **Terms to Know**
>
> **Kyphosis**–an excessive forward curvature of the spine
>
> **Juvenile osteochondrosis of the spine**–also known as Scheuermann or Calvé disease; kyphosis deformity of the lumbar or thoracolumbar spine
>
> **Lordosis**–excessive curvature of the lumbar spine
>
> **Scoliosis**–abnormal sideways curvature of the spine usually idiopathic but may be congenital or neuromuscular
>
> **Spondylolysis**–a defect or stress fracture of the pars interarticularis of the vertebra
>
> **Spondylolisthesis**–a vertebra shifts forward, often due to the spondylolysis

Category **M40** includes codes for kyphosis and lordosis. This does not include congenital kyphosis or lordosis **(Q76.4)** or post-procedural kyphosis and lordosis **(M96.-)**. Included are codes for postural kyphosis; other secondary kyphosis; other and unspecified kyphosis; flatback syndrome; postural lordosis; and lordosis, unspecified. Each subcategory includes codes to identify the affected region of the spine. Juvenile osteochondrosis of the spine is reported by spinal region with codes in subcategory **M42.0-**.

Scoliosis is reported with codes in category **M41** with subcategories for infantile idiopathic scoliosis **(M41.0-)**, juvenile idiopathic scoliosis **(M41.11-)**, adolescent idiopathic scoliosis **(M41.12-)**, other idiopathic scoliosis **(M41.2-)**, thoracogenic scoliosis **(M41.3-)**, neuromuscular scoliosis **(M41.4-)**, other secondary scoliosis **(M41.5-)**, and other forms of scoliosis **(M41.8-)**. Each subcategory includes codes specifying the spinal region affected. When reporting neuromuscular scoliosis, report first the code for the underlying condition, such as cerebral palsy.

Codes in subcategory **M43.0** are used to report spondylolysis by spinal region. An excludes 1 note indicates that this category is not reported for patients with a diagnosis of spondylolisthesis **(M43.1-)**. Subcategory **M43.1** also has an excludes 1 note indicating that acute trauma of the lumbar region **(S33.1)** or other vertebrae is not included here. Also excluded is congenital spondylolisthesis **(Q76.2)**.

Code **M43.6** (torticollis) does not include congenital torticollis **(Q68.0)**, psychogenic torticollis **(F45.8)**, spasmodic torticollis **(G24.3)**, or torticollis due to birth injury **(P15.2)**.

Disorders of Muscles

Category **M60** includes codes for infective myositis **(M60.0-)**, interstitial myositis **(M60.1)**, and foreign body granuloma of soft tissue **(M60.2)**. When reporting infective myositis, an additional code from categories **B95-B97** should be reported to identify the infectious agent. Codes in this subcategory are specific to the shoulder, upper arm, forearm, hand, fingers, thigh, lower leg, ankle, foot, toes, and other or multiple sites, including laterality. Subcategory **M60.2** does not include foreign body granuloma of the skin and subcutaneous tissue **(L92.3)**. Use an additional code from category **Z18.-** to identify the type of retained foreign body when reporting codes for foreign body granuloma of the soft tissue. Category **M60.8** is used to report other myositis.

Immobility syndrome is reported with code **M62.3**. Contracture of muscle is reported with codes in subcategory **M62.4**. Muscle wasting and atrophy, not elsewhere classified, is reported with codes in subcategory **M62.5**. This category excludes neuralgic amyotrophy **(G54.5)** and progressive muscular atrophy **(G12.29)**. Generalized muscle weakness is reported with code **M62.81**. Non-traumatic rhabdomyolysis is reported with code **M62.82**. Traumatic rhabdomyolysis is reported with code **T79.6**.

Disorders of Synovium and Tendon

Categories **M65-M67** include codes for synovitis and tenosynovitis, spontaneous rupture of synovium and tendons, and other conditions affecting the synovium and tendons except current injury and soft tissue disorders related to use, overuse, and pressure **(M70.-)**.

Synovitis and tenosynovitis are reported with codes in category **M65.** When reporting an abscess of a tendon sheath **(M65.0-),** use an additional code to identify the bacterial agent **(B95-B96).** Transient synovitis is reported with codes in subcategory **M67.3.**

Trigger thumb or trigger finger is reported with a code from subcategory **M65.3** specifying the thumb or finger involved by right or left thumb, or index, middle, ring, or little finger. To report a ganglion of a joint or tendon, see subcategory **M67.4.**

Category **M70** includes codes for acute or chronic crepitant synovitis of the hand and wrist and for bursitis. When reporting these conditions, an external cause code from category **Y93** is also reported to identify the activity causing the disorder.

Rotator cuff tear or rupture that is not specified as traumatic is reported with codes in subcategory **M75.1.** For traumatic rotator cuff tear, see **S46.01-.**

Category **M76** includes codes for enthesopathies of the lower limb, excluding the foot, and includes codes for Achilles tendinitis **(M76.6-).** An acquired short Achilles tendon is reported with codes in subcategory **M67.0.**

Other and unspecified soft tissue disorders in category **M79** include myalgia **(M79.1);** unspecified neuralgia and neuritis **(M79.2);** residual foreign body in soft tissue **(M79.5);** and codes for pain in limb, hand, foot, fingers, and toes **(M79.6-).** Subcategory **M79.6** includes 31 codes for specifying pain in the right or left arm, leg, upper arm, forearm, hand, fingers, thigh, lower leg, foot, or toes. Codes identify both nonspecific pain in a limb and more specific sites such as upper arm and forearm.

Disorders of Bone Density and Structure

Categories **M80-M85** include codes for osteoporosis, adult osteomalacia, pathological and stress fractures, other disorders of continuity of bone, and disorders of bone density and structure.

Stress fractures are reported with codes in subcategory **M84.3** with the exception of stress fractures of vertebrae **(M48.4-).** Pathological fractures are not included here and are reported with codes in category **M80** or subcategories **M84.4-M84.6.** Codes for these fractures require a seventh character to identify the type of encounter and healing status. The applicable characters for this subcategory are

- **A** Initial encounter for fracture
- **D** Subsequent encounter for fracture with routine healing
- **G** Subsequent encounter for fracture with delayed healing
- **K** Subsequent encounter for fracture with nonunion
- **P** Subsequent encounter for fracture with malunion
- **S** Sequela

Codes in subcategory **M84.3-** specify the site of the stress fracture with some bones specifically reported (eg, **M84.351** [stress fracture, right femur]) and others reported by body area (eg, **M84.344** [stress fracture, right finger]). Report a personal history of a healed stress fracture with code **Z87.312.**

Pathological fractures are categorized according to cause.

- Pathological fracture in neoplastic disease **(M84.5-)**
- Pathological fracture in osteoporosis **(M80.-)**
- Pathological fracture in other disease **(M84.6-)**
- Pathological fracture, not elsewhere classified **(M84.4)**

When a pathological fracture occurs in neoplastic disease, the code for the condition that is the focus of treatment is reported first. This sequencing guidance also applies to pathological fracture in other disease **(M84.6-)**.

Solitary bone cysts are reported with codes in subcategory **M85.4-** except a solitary cyst of the jaw **(M27.4)**. Aneurysmal bone cysts are reported with codes in subcategory **M85.5**.

Other Osteopathies

This block of codes includes those for osteopathies such as osteomyelitis **(M86)**, osteonecrosis **(M87)**, osteitis deformans **(M88)**, physeal arrest **(M89.1-)**, other disorders of bone development and growth **(M89.2-)**, and osteitis deformans in neoplastic disease **(M90.6-)**.

Major osseous defect codes in subcategory **M89.7** are reported in addition to codes for several other conditions in this block of codes, including osteomyelitis and osteonecrosis.

Certain codes for osteomyelitis are reported with codes in Chapter 1 of the tabular index using combination codes that identify the infecting organism. These include osteomyelitis in echinococcus **(B67.2)**, gonococcus **(A54.43)**, or salmonella **(A02.24)**. Osteomyelitis of certain bones is classified elsewhere. These include the orbit **(H05.0-)**, petrous bone **(H70.2-)**, and vertebra **(M46.2-)**.

Osteomyelitis in category **M86** is classified according to type and site. Subcategories for osteomyelitis include

M86.0	Acute hematogenous osteomyelitis
M86.1	Other acute osteomyelitis
M86.2	Subacute osteomyelitis
M86.3	Chronic multifocal osteomyelitis
M86.4	Chronic osteomyelitis with draining sinus
M86.5	Other chronic hematogenous osteomyelitis
M86.6	Other chronic osteomyelitis
M86.8	Other osteomyelitis
M86.9	Osteomyelitis, unspecified

Osteonecrosis category **M87** does not include juvenile osteonecrosis **(M91-M92)** or osteochondropathies **(M90-M93)**. Osteonecrosis in hemoglobinopathy is reported with a code for the hemoglobinopathy followed by a code from subcategory **M90.5** (osteonecrosis in diseases classified elsewhere). Osteonecrosis due to drugs is reported with codes in subcategory **M87.1** with an additional code from categories **T36-T50** to identify the drug.

Osteitis deformans or Paget disease of bone, other than that due to neoplastic disease **(M90.6)**, is reported with codes in category **M88**.

Physeal arrest is reported with codes in subcategory **M89.1** with codes specifying complete or partial physeal arrest by site.

Chondropathies

Categories **M91-M94** include codes for juvenile osteochondrosis, coxa plana, pseudocoxalgia, coxa magna, non-traumatic slipped upper femoral epiphysis, osteochondritis dissecans, chondrocostal junction syndrome (Tietze), and chondromalacia.

Category **M91** (juvenile osteochondrosis of the hip and pelvis) has an excludes 1 note directing to subcategory **M93.0** to report non-traumatic slipped upper femoral epiphysis. Code **M91.0** is used to report juvenile osteochondrosis of the pelvis. Legg-Calvé-Perthes disorder or juvenile osteochondrosis of the head of the femur is reported with codes in subcategory **M91.1,** indicating laterality of the involved leg. To report juvenile osteochondrosis of the hip and pelvis after reduction of a congenital hip dislocation, see codes **M91.81** for the right leg and **M91.82** for the left leg. Juvenile osteochondrosis of other sites are reported with codes in category **M92**.

Codes in subcategory **M93.0** categorize non-traumatic slipped femoral epiphysis as unspecified, acute, chronic, and acute or chronic. Laterality is also specified. Chondrolysis of the hip **(M94.35-)** is reported in addition to codes for non-traumatic slipped femoral epiphysis when applicable.

Category **M94** includes code **M94.0** for reporting chondrocostal junction syndrome as well as codes for relapsing polychondritis and chondromalacia. Subcategory **M94.2** includes codes for chondromalacia that specify the involved joint. Not included here is the code for chondromalacia patellae **(M22.4)**.

Other Acquired Deformities of the Musculoskeletal System and Connective Tissue

Category **M95** includes codes for reporting acquired deformities not classified elsewhere. This excludes acquired absence of limbs **(Z89-Z90)**, acquired deformity of limbs **(M20-M21)**, deforming dorsopathies **(M40-M43)**, and post-procedural musculoskeletal disorders **(M96.-)**. An acquired deformity of the nose **(M95.0)** is included here with the exception of deviated nasal septum **(J34.2)**. Cauliflower ear is reported with codes **M95.11** (right) and **M95.12** (left).

Intraoperative and Post-Procedural Complications and Disorders of Musculoskeletal System

Category **M96** includes codes for intraoperative and post-procedural complications and disorders but does not include complications of internal orthopedic devices, implants, and grafts **(T84.-)**. Post-procedural conditions include post-radiation kyphosis **(M96.2)** and scoliosis **(M96.5)** and other conditions following spine surgery. Fracture of a bone following or during insertion of orthopedic implant, joint prosthesis, or bone plate is reported with codes in subcategory **M96.6** based on the bone fractured. Post-procedural hemorrhage or hematoma of a musculoskeletal structure is reported with codes indicating whether the complication follows a musculoskeletal procedure **(M96.830)** or other procedure **(M96.831)**. The type of procedure is also included in codes for intraoperative hemorrhage or hematoma of a musculoskeletal structure **(M96.81-)** and accidental puncture or laceration of a musculoskeletal structure **(M96.82-)**. Code **M96.89** (other intraoperative and post-procedural complications and disorders of the musculoskeletal system) includes instability of a joint secondary to removal of a joint prosthesis. An additional code should be reported to further specify the disorder when applicable.

Biomechanical Lesions

Category **M99** includes codes for biomechanical lesions not elsewhere classified, and codes in this category should not be reported when the condition is classified elsewhere. Conditions included here are segmental and somatic dysfunction, vertebral subluxation complex, and certain conditions affecting the neural canal or intervertebral foramina.

Signs, Symptoms, and History

Symptoms and findings related to the musculoskeletal system may be reported when a definitive diagnosis has not been established. These are reported with codes from Chapter 18 of the tabular list, as are abnormal results of clinical or other investigative procedures and ill-defined conditions for which no definitive diagnosis has been documented. Some codes for symptoms have been included earlier in this chapter. The following are examples of codes for other musculoskeletal symptoms and findings:

R29.3	Abnormal posture
R29.4	Clicking hip
R29.6	Repeated falls
R62.52	Short stature
R68.3	Clubbing of fingers
R68.84	Jaw pain

Related codes for personal history and for surveillance or screening include

Z00.2	Encounter for examination for period of rapid growth in childhood
Z00.70	Encounter for examination for period of delayed growth in childhood without abnormal findings
Z00.71	Encounter for examination for period of delayed growth in childhood with abnormal findings
Z13.828	Encounter for screening for other musculoskeletal disorder
Z85.6	Personal history of leukemia
Z85.72	Personal history of non-Hodgkin lymphomas
Z85.830	Personal history of malignant neoplasm of bone
Z85.831	Personal history of malignant neoplasm of soft tissue
Z87.76	Personal history of (corrected) congenital malformations of integument, limbs, and musculoskeletal system
Z87.81	Personal history of (healed) traumatic fracture

Code Scenarios

A child is diagnosed with septic arthritis involving the right knee due to methicillin-susceptible staphylococcal infection.

M00.061	Staphylococcal arthritis, right knee
B95.61	Methicillin-susceptible *Staphylococcus aureus* infection as the cause of diseases classified elsewhere

> From the guidelines: Section IC1b—Certain infections are classified in chapters other than Chapter 1, and no organism is identified as part of the infection code. In these instances, it is necessary to use an additional code from Chapter 1 to identify the organism.

A 14-year-old patient has a diagnosis of muscular dystrophy with neuromuscular kyphoscoliosis of the thoracic region. The main focus of the visit is the kyphoscoliosis.

M41.44 Neuromuscular scoliosis, thoracic region
G71.0 Muscular dystrophy

> From the guidelines: Section IA17—A code also note instructs that 2 codes may be required to fully describe a condition, but this note does not provide sequencing direction.

A teenager is seen for pain in the wrist and says there is a crackling sound sometimes on moving her fingers. She has been playing a golf game on her Wii system quite often for the last month as well as other games. She is diagnosed with crepitant synovitis of the left wrist.

M70.032 Crepitant synovitis (acute) (chronic), left wrist
Y93.C2 Activity, handheld interactive electronic device
Y92.019 Unspecified place in single-family (private) house as the place of occurrence of the external cause
Y99.8 Other external cause status

> From the tabular list: An includes note at category **M70** instructs, "Use additional external cause code to identify activity causing disorder **(Y93.-)**." An introductory note to category **Y93** states, "These codes are appropriate for use for both acute injuries, such as those from Chapter 19, and conditions that are due to the long-term, cumulative effects of an activity, such as those from Chapter 13. They are also appropriate for use with external cause codes for cause and intent if identifying the activity provides additional information on the event. These codes should be used in conjunction with codes for external cause status **(Y99)** and place of occurrence **(Y92)**."
>
> From the guidelines: Section IC20a8—No external cause code from Chapter 20 is needed if the external cause and intent are included in a code from another chapter (eg, **T36.0X1-** [poisoning by penicillins, accidental (unintentional)]).
>
> Because the diagnosis of crepitant synovitis describes an overuse injury, no further description of the cause or intent is needed. Code **Y93C2** indicates the activity related to the overuse, and codes **Y92.019** and **Y99.8** indicate that the condition is not work-related or likely the liability of another party.

Review What You Have Learned

14.1 A child who is treated for regional enteritis of the ileum is also diagnosed with Still disease with involvement of multiple joints. What code(s) is reported?
   A. **M08.29** Juvenile rheumatoid arthritis with systemic onset, multiple sites
   B. **M02.352** Reiter disease, left hip
   C. **K50.018** Crohn disease of small intestine with other complication
   D. **K50.018** Crohn disease of small intestine with other complication
   M08.29 Juvenile rheumatoid arthritis with systemic onset, multiple sites
   E. None of the above

14.2 A teenager is diagnosed with gouty arthropathy of the right ankle and foot in sickle cell disease. What code(s) is reported?
   A. **D57.1** Sickle-cell disease without crisis
   B. **D57.1** Sickle-cell disease without crisis
   M14.871 Arthropathies in other specified diseases classified elsewhere, right ankle and foot
   C. **M14.8** Arthropathies in other specified diseases classified elsewhere
   D. **M36.3** Arthropathy in other blood disorders
   E. None of the above

14.3 Juvenile osteonecrosis is reported with codes in category **M87** (osteonecrosis).
   A. True
   B. False

14.4 Chondromalacia patellae is reported with code **M22.4** not code **M94.269.**
   A. True
   B. False

14.5 Code **M79.601** is the most specific code for diagnosis of pain in the right axilla.
   A. True
   B. False

14.6 What code(s) is reported for acute hematogenous osteomyelitis of the left tibia with major osseous defect?
   A. **M87.062** Idiopathic aseptic necrosis of left tibia
   B. **M86.062** Acute hematogenous osteomyelitis, left tibia and fibula
   M89.761 Major osseous defect, right lower leg
   C. **M86.062** Acute hematogenous osteomyelitis, left tibia and fibula
   M89.762 Major osseous defect, left lower leg
   D. **M86.062** Acute hematogenous osteomyelitis, left tibia and fibula
   E. None of the above

≡ CHAPTER 15 ≡

Diseases of the Genitourinary System (N00-N99)

Diseases of the genitourinary system are classified in Chapter 14 of the tabular list for *International Classification of Diseases, Tenth Revision, Clinical Modification (ICD-10-CM)*. Codes **N00-N99** describe conditions of the urinary system and the male and female genital organs. The blocks of codes for this chapter are

>Glomerular diseases **N00-N08**
>Renal tubulointerstitial diseases **N10-N16**
>Acute kidney failure and chronic kidney disease **N17-N19**
>Urolithiasis **N20-N23**
>Other disorders of kidney and ureter **N25-N29**
>Other diseases of the urinary system **N30-N39**
>Diseases of male genital organs **N40-N53**
>Disorders of breast **N60-N65**
>Inflammatory diseases of female pelvic organs **N70-N77**
>Non-inflammatory disorders of female genital tract **N80-N98**
>Intraoperative and post-procedural complications and disorders of genitourinary system, not elsewhere classified **N99**

Glomerular Diseases

The first block in this chapter includes codes for nephritic and nephrotic syndromes in glomerular disease. (Tubulointerstitial nephritis is separately classified.) Two instructions apply to the full block of codes.
1. Hypertensive chronic kidney disease **(I12.-)** is not reported with these codes.
2. Code also any associated kidney failure **(N17-19).**

Kidney failure is classified as acute, chronic, or unspecified. Codes for acute kidney failure differentiate failure with tubular necrosis **(N17.0),** failure with acute cortical necrosis **(N17.1),** and failure with acute medullary necrosis **(N17.2).** Chronic kidney disease is classified by stage.

>| | |
>|---|---|
>| **N18.1** | Chronic kidney disease, stage 1 |
>| **N18.2** | Chronic kidney disease, stage 2 (mild) |
>| **N18.3** | Chronic kidney disease, stage 3 (moderate) |
>| **N18.4** | Chronic kidney disease, stage 4 (severe) |
>| **N18.5** | Chronic kidney disease, stage 5 (not requiring chronic dialysis) |
>| **N18.6** | End-stage renal disease (requiring dialysis) |

Chronic kidney disease codes are reported in addition to codes for associated conditions such as diabetes or hypertensive chronic kidney disease. When reporting end-stage renal disease, code **Z99.2** is also reported to identify dialysis status. When applicable, report code **Z94.0** to identify transplant status.

> **Terms to Know**
>
> **Nephritic syndrome**–disorder characterized by hematuria and red blood cell casts due to inflammation of the glomeruli due to trapped antigens
>
> **Nephrotic syndrome**–kidney disease with proteinuria, hypoalbuminemia, and edema due to damage caused by a glomerular disorder

With the exception of category **N08** (glomerular disorders in diseases classified elsewhere), each of the code categories for glomerular disease in *ICD-10-CM* start with the 3-character code category and are completed with fourth characters that identify the clinical presentation. The categories include

- **N00** Acute nephritic syndrome
- **N01** Rapidly progressive nephritic syndrome
- **N02** Recurrent and persistent hematuria
- **N03** Chronic nephritic syndrome
- **N04** Nephrotic syndrome (includes congenital nephritic syndrome)
- **N05** Unspecified nephritic syndrome
- **N06** Isolated proteinuria with specified morphological lesion
- **N07** Hereditary nephropathy, not elsewhere classified

The fourth characters that complete codes of the above categories are

- 0 With minor glomerular abnormality
- 1 With focal and segmental glomerular lesions
- 2 With diffuse membranous glomerulonephritis
- 3 With diffuse mesangial proliferative glomerulonephritis
- 4 With diffuse endocapillary proliferative glomerulonephritis
- 5 With diffuse mesangiocapillary glomerulonephritis
- 6 With dense deposit disease
- 7 With diffuse crescentic glomerulonephritis
- 8 With other morphologic lesions
- 9 With unspecified morphologic lesions

Example

    N03.1   Chronic nephritic syndrome with focal and segmental glomerular lesions

Category **N02** (recurrent and persistent hematuria) does not include acute cystitis with hematuria **(N30.01)**, hematuria NOS **(R31.9)**, or hematuria not associated with specified morphologic lesions **(R31.-)**.

Unspecified nephrotic syndrome **(N05)** does not include nephropathy, not otherwise specified, with no stated morphological lesion **(N28.9)**.

Hereditary nephropathy, not elsewhere classified **(N07)** does not include Alport syndrome **(Q87.81-)**, hereditary amyloid nephropathy, nail patella syndrome **(Q87.2)**, or non-neuropathic heredofamilial amyloidosis **(E85.-)**.

Code **N08** is used to report glomerular disorders in conditions such as sickle cell disease. However, an excludes 1 note for this category lists many conditions that are not reported with this code. These include diabetes with diabetic nephropathy, systemic lupus erythematosus, and antiglomerular basement membrane disease **(M31.0)**.

Renal Tubulointerstitial Diseases

The block of codes **N10-N16** includes codes for acute tubulonephritis, chronic tubulonephritis with and without obstruction, obstructive and reflux uropathy, and drug- and heavy metal–induced tubulointerstitial and tubular conditions. Pyeloureteritis cystica **(N28.85)** is not included here.

> **Terms to Know**
>
> **Tubulointerstitial disease**—disease involving the structures in the kidney outside the glomerulus, including the tubules and interstitium of the kidney
>
> **Vesicoureteral reflux**—backward flow of urine from the bladder to the kidneys

When reporting acute or chronic tubulointerstitial disease, also report a code for the infectious agent **(B95-B97)**. Category **N11** includes codes for chronic tubulointerstitial nephritis specified as non-obstructive reflux-associated **(N11.0)**, obstructive **(N11.1)**, other non-obstructive **(N11.8)**, and unspecified **(N11.9)**. When tubulointerstitial nephritis is not specified as acute or chronic, report unspecified code **N12**.

Obstructive and reflux uropathy is reported with codes in category **N13**. An excludes 2 note for this category indicates the following conditions are not classified here but may be reported in addition to codes in **N13** when indicated.

> Calculus of kidney and ureter without hydronephrosis **(N20.-)**
> Congenital obstructive defects of renal pelvis and ureter **(Q62.0-Q62.3)**
> Hydronephrosis with ureteropelvic junction obstruction **(Q62.1)**
> Obstructive pyelonephritis **(N11.1)**

Code **N13.6** (pyonephrosis) includes the conditions represented by code **N13.1-N13.5** with infection. Codes from categories **B95-B97** are reported in addition to code **N13.6** to identify the infecting organism. Codes **N13.1-N13.5** are

N13.1	Hydronephrosis with ureteral stricture, not elsewhere classified
N13.2	Hydronephrosis with renal and ureteral calculous obstruction
N13.30	Unspecified hydronephrosis
N13.39	Other hydronephrosis
N13.4	Hydroureter
N13.5	Crossing vessel and stricture of ureter without hydronephrosis

Subcategory **N13.7** includes codes for vesicoureteral reflux with or without reflux nephropathy and with or without hydroureter. Reflux-associated pyelonephritis **(N11.0)** is not included here.

Code **N13.8** (other obstructive and reflux uropathy) includes urinary obstruction due to a specified cause. A code first note instructs that any causal condition should be reported first, with code **N13.8** reported as an additional diagnosis.

Codes in category **N14** are used to report drug-induced or heavy metal–induced tubulointerstitial and tubular conditions. Poisoning due to a drug or toxin is reported first with codes from categories **T36-T65** when applicable. An adverse effect of a drug causing tubulointerstitial and tubular conditions is reported with a code from subcategory **N14** followed by a code from categories **T36-T50** with fifth or sixth character **5**.

Example

A child is seen in follow-up for a recently diagnosed acute pyelonephritis due to a hypersensitivity reaction to penicillin.

N14.1 Nephropathy induced by other drugs, medicaments, and biological substances

T36.0X5D Adverse effect of penicillins (subsequent encounter)

Acute or chronic kidney failure would be reported in addition to codes in category **N14** when applicable.

Code **N16** is used to report tubulointerstitial disorders in diseases classified elsewhere. Codes for underlying conditions such as leukemia **(C91-C95)**, lymphoma **(C81.0-C85.9, C96.-)**, or sepsis **(A40.0-A41.9)** are reported first. Excluded from this category are tubulointerstitial nephritis in diabetes and infectious diseases for which combination codes identify both conditions.

Acute Kidney Failure and Chronic Kidney Disease

A brief discussion of these conditions was presented in relation to the instruction to report acute or chronic kidney failure with codes for glomerular disease when applicable. Also notable is the excludes 2 note instructing that conditions such as congenital renal failure may be reported in addition to codes in this block when both conditions are diagnosed.

When reporting acute kidney failure **(N17.-)**, also code the underlying condition. This category does not include posttraumatic renal failure **(T79.5)** as instructed by an excludes 1 note.

Urolithiasis

The block of codes **N20-N23** includes codes for calculus of the kidney **(N20.0)**, ureter **(N20.1)**, kidney and ureter **(N20.2)**, bladder **(N21.0)**, urethra **(N21.1)**, other lower urinary tract **(N21.8)**, and calculus of the urinary tract in disease classified elsewhere, such as gout or schistosomiasis. Not reported with these codes are nephrocalcinosis **(E83.5)** and calculus of the kidney and ureter with hydronephrosis **(N13.2)**.

Other Disorders of Kidney and Ureter (N25-N29)

Disorders resulting from impaired renal tubular function are reported with codes in category **N25**. This includes renal osteodystrophy **(N25.0)**, nephrogenic diabetes insipidus **(N25.1)**, and secondary hyperparathyroidism of renal origin **(N25.81)**.

Also included here are codes **N27.0** (unilateral small kidney) and **N27.1** (bilateral small kidney).

Category **N28** includes codes for ischemia and infarction of a kidney **(N28.0)**, an acquired cyst of the kidney **(N28.1)**, hypertrophy of kidney **(N28.81)**, and megaloureter **(N28.82)** among others.

Cystitis and Bladder Disorders

Category **N30** includes codes for cystitis and trigonitis. Cystitis is classified as acute, chronic interstitial, other chronic, irradiation, or other cystitis with separate codes indicating with or without hematuria for each type of cystitis. Trigonitis **(N30.3-)** is also specified as with or without hematuria. An additional code from categories **B95-B97** should be reported to indicate the infectious agent in cystitis.

Category **N31** includes codes for neuropathic bladder specified as uninhibited **(N31.0)**, reflex **(N31.1)**, flaccid **(N31.2)**, or other **(N31.8)**. Report an additional code for associated urinary incontinence **(N39.3-, N39.4-)** when reporting these conditions.

Conditions such as bladder-neck obstruction **(N32.0)** and diverticulum of the bladder **(N32.3)** do not include congenital conditions **(Q64.-)**.

Code **N32.81** (overactive bladder) is not used when reporting frequent urination due to a specified bladder condition that is elsewhere classified.

Disorders of Male Genital Organs

Categories **N40-N53** include codes for disorders of the male genital organs.

Category **N43** includes codes for hydrocele of the spermatic cord, testis, or tunica vaginalis. Congenital hydrocele is reported with code **P83.5**. An encysted hydrocele is reported with code **N43.0**. An infected hydrocele is reported with code **N43.1** followed by a code from categories **B95-B97** to identify the infectious agent.

A single spermatocele of the epididymis is reported with code **N43.41**. Multiple spermatoceles are reported with code **N43.42**.

Codes for torsion of the testis are as follows:

N44.00	Torsion of testis, unspecified
N44.01	Extravaginal torsion of spermatic cord
N44.02	Intravaginal torsion of spermatic cord
N44.03	Torsion of appendix testis
N44.04	Torsion of appendix epididymis

Orchitis **(N45.2)** and epididymitis **(N45.1)** are reported with codes in category **N45** with an additional code from categories **B95-B97** to identify the infectious agent. Epididymo-orchitis is reported with code **N45.3**.

Category **N47** includes codes for disorders of the prepuce. Adherent prepuce of a newborn is reported with code **N47.0**. Phimosis **(N47.1)** and paraphimosis **(N47.2)** are also included here. Balanoposthitis is reported with code **N47.6** and an additional code to identify the infectious agent **(B95-B97)**. Balanitis code **N48.1** excludes balanitis xerotica obliterans (leukoplakia) and conditions specified by combination codes such as candidal balanitis **(B37.42)**.

Codes for priapism **(N48.3-)** are reported in addition to a code for the underlying cause.

Example

A child with sickle cell Hb-SD disease presents with priapism.
D57.819 Other sickle cell disorders with crisis, unspecified
N48.32 Priapism due to disease classified elsewhere

Disorders of the Breast

Disorders of the breast are classified in categories **N60-N65**. Mastitis and other inflammatory disorders of the breast are reported with code **N61**. However, this excludes that following childbirth **(O91.-)** and neonatal infective mastitis **(P39.0),** and that associated with carcinoma of the breast.

Gynecomastia or hypertrophy of the breast is reported with code **N62**. Breast engorgement of a newborn is reported with code **P83.4**.

Category **N64** includes codes for other specified disorders of the breast, including galactorrhea not associated with childbirth **(N64.3)** and mastodynia **(N64.4).**

Inflammatory Disease of the Female Pelvic Organs

Categories **N70-N77** include codes for inflammatory conditions of the female pelvic organs. For sexually transmitted chlamydial infections, see category **A56**. Trichomonal infections are reported with codes in category **A59**.

Inflammatory disease of the cervix uteri **(N72)** includes cervicitis, endocervicitis, and exocervicitis with or without erosion or ectropion. Category **N73** includes codes for conditions such as acute or chronic parametritis and pelvic cellulitis; acute and chronic pelvic peritonitis; female post-infective peritoneal adhesions; and pelvic inflammatory disease, unspecified **(N73.9)**. An additional code from categories **B95-B97** is required to identify the infectious agent when reporting condition in categories **N72** and **N73**.

This block also includes codes for cyst **(N75.0)** or abscess **(N75.1)** of the Bartholin gland.

Category **N76** includes codes for vaginitis, vulvovaginitis, and vulvitis. Candidal vaginitis is reported with code **B37.3**. This category also includes code **N76.81** (mucositis of the vagina and vulva). A code for the related therapy should be reported in addition to code **N76.81**. For mucositis due to antineoplastic and immunosuppressive drugs, see subcategory **T45.1X**. Code **Y84.2** is used to report associated radiological procedure and radiotherapy.

Noninflammatory Disorders of the Female Pelvic Organs

Noninflammatory disorders of the female pelvic organs are reported with codes in categories **N80-N98**.

Ovarian cysts are reported with codes in category **N83**. A follicular cyst of the ovary is reported with code **N83.0**. Report a corpus luteum cyst with code **N83.1**. Unspecified ovarian cysts are reported with code **N83.20**. Polycystic ovarian syndrome is reported with code **E28.2**.

Category **N87** (dysplasia of the cervix uteri) includes codes for mild cervical dysplasia (cervical intraepithelial neoplasia [CIN] I, **N87.0**) and moderate cervical dysplasia (CIN II, **N87.1**). Cervical intraepithelial neoplasia (CIN III) is reported with codes in category **D06**. Vaginal dysplasia is reported with codes in category **N89** with codes for mild vaginal intraepithelial neoplasia (VAIN) grade I **(N89.0)** and moderate VAIN grade II **(N89.1)**. VAIN grade III is reported with code **D07.2**. Likewise, codes **N90.0** and **N90.1** are used to report mild and moderate vulvar dysplasia (vulval intraepithelial neoplasia [VIN]). Code **D07.1** is used to report VIN III.

Absent, scanty, and rare menstruation are reported with codes in category **N91**. This category does not include ovarian dysfunction **(E28.-)**. Amenorrhea is classified as primary **(N91.0)** or secondary **(N91.1)**. This is also true for primary oligomenorrhea **(N91.3)** and secondary oligomenorrhea **(N91.4)**.

Excessive, frequent, and irregular menstruation are reported with codes in category **N92**. This does exclude precocious puberty **(E30.1)**. Excessive and frequent menstruation is reported with regular cycle **(N92.0)** or irregular cycle **(N92.1)**. Excessive menstruation at puberty is reported with code **N92.2**.

Painful conditions of the female genital organs and menstrual cycle are reported with codes in category **N94**. These include Mittelschmerz **(N94.0)**, vaginismus **(N94.2)**, premenstrual tension syndrome **(N94.3)**, and primary **(N94.4)** and secondary **(N94.5)** dysmenorrhea. When reporting premenstrual syndrome, associated menstrual migraine is also reported with codes in subcategory **G43.8**.

Intraoperative and Post-Procedural Complications and Disorders of Genitourinary System, Not Elsewhere Classified

Category **N99** includes codes for complications in the intraoperative and post-procedural periods. Code **N99.0** is reported for post-procedural kidney failure with an additional code to report the type of kidney disease.

Complications of cystostomy and other external stoma of the urinary tract are reported with codes in subcategory **N99.5**. Conditions reported here include hemorrhage; infection; malfunction; or other complication of cystostomy, other external stoma, or other stoma of the urinary tract.

As in other system-specific chapters, the final subcategories in this chapter are used to report intraoperative hemorrhage or hematoma, accidental puncture or laceration, and post-procedural hemorrhage and hematoma either relative to a genitourinary system procedure or another procedure. Code **N99.81** is used to report a not otherwise specified intraoperative complication of the genitourinary system.

Signs, Symptoms, and History

Symptoms and findings related to the genitourinary system may be reported when a definitive diagnosis has not been established. These are reported with codes from Chapter 18 of the tabular list, as are abnormal results of clinical or other investigative procedures and ill-defined conditions for which no definitive diagnosis has been documented. Some codes for symptoms have been included earlier in this chapter. The following are examples of codes for other symptoms and findings:

R30.0	Dysuria
R30.9	Painful micturition, unspecified
R31.0	Gross hematuria
R31.1	Benign essential microscopic hematuria
R31.2	Other microscopic hematuria

R34	Anuria and oliguria
R35.0	Frequency of micturition
R35.1	Nocturia
R79.89	Other specified abnormal findings of blood chemistry (azotemia)
R80.1	Persistent proteinuria, unspecified
R80.9	Proteinuria, unspecified
R82.4	Acetonuria
R82.5	Elevated urine levels of drugs, medicaments and biological substances
R82.7	Abnormal findings on microbiological examination of urine

Code **R33.0** is used to report drug-induced retention of urine. Use an additional code from categories **T36-T50** to identify the drug when reporting this condition. Other retention of urine is reported with code **R33.8** with any causal condition reported first.

Related codes for personal history and for surveillance or screening include

Z48.22	Encounter for aftercare following kidney transplant
Z87.440	Personal history of urinary (tract) infections
Z87.441	Personal history of nephrotic syndrome
Z87.442	Personal history of urinary calculi
Z87.710	Personal history of (corrected) hypospadias
Z87.448	Personal history of other diseases of urinary system
Z87.718	Personal history of other specified (corrected) congenital malformations of genitourinary system
Z90.5	Acquired absence of kidney
Z93.6	Other artificial openings of urinary tract status
Z94.0	Kidney transplant status
Z84.1	Family history of disorders of kidney and ureter
Z01.411	Encounter for gynecological examination (general) (routine) with abnormal findings (also report abnormal finding)
Z01.419	Encounter for gynecological examination (general) (routine) without abnormal findings

Code **Z04.42** is reported for an encounter for examination and observation for suspected child sexual abuse or rape that is ruled out. Suspected child sexual abuse is reported with code **T76.22-**. Child sexual abuse, confirmed, is reported with code **T74.22-**.

Code Scenarios

A child is diagnosed with acute renal failure due to acute nephritis with segmental glomerular sclerosis.

N17.9	Acute kidney failure, unspecified
N00.1	Acute nephritic syndrome with focal and segmental glomerular lesions

> From the guidelines: Section IA17—A code also note instructs that 2 codes may be required to fully describe a condition, but this note does not provide sequencing direction.

A child is seen for frequent and painful urination. Diagnosis is acute cystitis with hematuria due to *Escherichia coli*.

N30.01 Acute cystitis with hematuria
B96.20 Unspecified *Escherichia coli [E coli]* as the cause of diseases classified elsewhere

> From the guidelines: Section IC1b—Certain infections are classified in chapters other than Chapter 1, and no organism is identified as part of the infection code. In these instances, it is necessary to use an additional code from Chapter 1 to identify the organism.

Review What You Have Learned

15.1 A child is diagnosed with pyelonephritis with vesicoureteral reflux. What code(s) is reported?
   A. **N11.0** Non-obstructive reflux-associated chronic pyelonephritis
   B. **N11.8** Other chronic tubulointerstitial nephritis
   C. **N13.71** Vesicoureteral reflux without reflux nephropathy
   D. **N13.8** Other obstructive and reflux uropathy
   E. None of the above

15.2 A 13-year-old boy is diagnosed and treated for intravaginal torsion of the left testicle. What code(s) is reported?
   A. **N44.00** Torsion of the testis, unspecified
   B. **N44.02** Intravaginal torsion of spermatic cord
   C. **N44.8** Other non-inflammatory disorders of the testis
   D. **N44.0** Torsion of the testis
   E. None of the above

15.3 Code **N48.1** is reported for candidal balanitis.
   A. True
   B. False

15.4 Code **N13.6** (pyonephrosis) is reported for conditions in subcategories **N13.1**-**N13.5** with infection.
   A. True
   B. False

15.5 Codes **N13.70** and **N13.4** are appropriately reported for vesicoureteral reflux with hydroureter.
- A. True
- B. False

15.6 What code(s) is reported for diagnosis of painful ovulation?
- A. **R10.2** Pelvic and perineal pain
- B. **N94.6** Dysmenorrhea, unspecified
- C. **N94.89** Other specified conditions associated with female genital organs and menstrual cycle
- D. **N94.0** Mittelschmerz
- E. None of the above

≡ CHAPTER 16 ≡

Pregnancy, Childbirth, and the Puerperium (O00-O9A)

This chapter will give an overview of the codes for conditions related to pregnancy, childbirth, and the puerperium. These codes are found in Chapter 15 of the tabular list. Codes in this chapter are never used on newborn records. These codes apply only to the maternal record. If you provide or assign codes for maternity care, it is recommended that you become familiar with the *International Classification of Diseases, Tenth Revision, Clinical Modification (ICD-10-CM)* guidelines for Chapter 15. Some key points

- Chapter 15 codes have sequencing priority over codes from other chapters.
- Most codes in Chapter 15 have a final character indicating the trimester of pregnancy. The provider's documentation of the number of weeks may be used to assign the appropriate code identifying the trimester.
- Where applicable, a seventh character is to be assigned for certain categories (**O31, O32, O33.3 - O33.6, O35, O36, O40, O41, O60.1, O60.2, O64,** and **O69**) to identify the fetus for which the complication code applies. A zero is assigned for single gestation or an unspecified fetus in multiple gestations.
- For routine prenatal outpatient visits for patients with high-risk pregnancies, a code from category **O09** (supervision of high-risk pregnancy) should be used as the first-listed diagnosis.
- In episodes when no delivery occurs, the principal diagnosis should correspond to the principal complication of the pregnancy that necessitated the encounter.
- If the patient was admitted with a condition that resulted in the performance of a cesarean procedure, that condition should be selected as the principal diagnosis.
- When assigning codes from Chapter 15, it is important to assess if a condition was preexisting prior to pregnancy or developed during or due to the pregnancy in order to assign the correct code.
- Codes from categories **O35** (maternal care for known or suspected fetal abnormality and damage) and **O36** (maternal care for other fetal problems) are assigned only when the fetal condition is actually responsible for modifying the management of the mother.
- No code from Chapter 16, the perinatal codes, should be used on the mother's record to identify fetal conditions. Surgery performed in utero on a fetus is still to be coded as an obstetric encounter.

The codes for conditions related to pregnancy, childbirth, and the puerperium are substantially different from those in *ICD-9-CM,* where the episode of care (antepartum, delivered, postpartum) was an axis around which codes were selected. *ICD-10-CM* codes in Chapter 15 identify the trimester of the current encounter where this concept applies. Certain codes also specify "in childbirth" or "during delivery."

Pregnancy Diagnosis and Prevention

The most commonly reported diagnoses related to pregnancy are likely the codes for pregnancy testing and contraceptive counseling, initiation, and monitoring. In *ICD-10-CM,* these are typically Z codes from Chapter 21.

Tests for pregnancy are reported based on the result.

Z32.01	Encounter for pregnancy test, result positive
Z32.02	Encounter for pregnancy test, result negative

When the result of a pregnancy test is positive, it may be necessary to counsel the patient regarding an unwanted pregnancy. Code **Z64.0** (problems related to unwanted pregnancy) may be used to report the reason for these services. When results are negative or when a patient seeks to prevent pregnancy through contraception, counseling regarding those choices may be necessary. Prescription of emergency contraception is reported with diagnosis code **Z30.012**. Other contraceptive services, including counseling, initiation, and surveillance, are reported with codes in category **Z30**.

When counseling is provided without prescription or initiation of contraceptives, the following codes may be reported:

Z30.02	Counseling and instruction in natural family planning to avoid pregnancy
Z30.09	Encounter for other general counseling and advice on contraception

Prescription of contraceptives and associated counseling in the same encounter are reported based on whether the encounter is for the initial prescription, an insertion procedure, or surveillance. The codes listed below are grouped by type of contraceptive.

Contraceptive pills

Z30.011	Encounter for initial prescription of contraceptive pills
Z30.41	Encounter for surveillance of contraceptive pills

Injectable contraceptive

Z30.013	Encounter for initial prescription of injectable contraceptive
Z30.42	Encounter for surveillance of injectable contraceptive

Intrauterine contraceptive device

Z30.014	Encounter for initial prescription of intrauterine contraceptive device
Z30.430	Encounter for insertion of intrauterine contraceptive device
Z30.431	Encounter for routine checking of intrauterine contraceptive device
Z30.432	Encounter for removal of intrauterine contraceptive device
Z30.433	Encounter for removal and reinsertion of intrauterine contraceptive device

Other

Z30.018	Encounter for initial prescription of other contraceptives
Z30.019	Encounter for initial prescription of contraceptives, unspecified
Z30.49	Encounter for surveillance of other contraceptives

Caring for the Pregnant Patient

When providing care unrelated to pregnancy and not affecting the pregnancy, the codes for the conditions being managed should be reported followed by code **Z33.1** (pregnant state, incidental).

> From the guidelines: Section IC15a1—Should the provider document that the pregnancy is incidental to the encounter, then code **Z33.1** (pregnant state, incidental) should be used in place of any Chapter 15 codes. It is the provider's responsibility to state that the condition being treated is not affecting the pregnancy.

Codes in category **Z34** are reported for supervision of normal pregnancy, but these codes apply only to patients who will be 16 years old or older on the expected delivery date and are experiencing no complications. Codes from Chapter 15 **(O00-O99)** will be applicable for supervision of patients who will be 15 years old or younger on the expected delivery date even if no other complication or high-risk condition is applicable.

Supervision of High-Risk Pregnancy

Category **O09** provides codes for supervision of high-risk pregnancy. Other codes in Chapter 15 may be used in conjunction with these codes to report other conditions affecting the management of the patient. When a pregnant patient will be younger than 16 years on the expected delivery date, codes from subcategory **O09.6** are used to report supervision of the high-risk pregnancy. Codes from category **Z3A** are also reported to identify the weeks of gestation.

O09.611	Supervision of young primigravida, first trimester
O09.612	Supervision of young primigravida, second trimester
O09.613	Supervision of young primigravida, third trimester
O09.621	Supervision of young multigravida, first trimester
O09.622	Supervision of young multigravida, second trimester
O09.623	Supervision of young multigravida, third trimester

> From the tabular list: Trimesters are counted from the first day of the last menstrual period. They are defined as follows:
>
> First trimester—less than 14 weeks 0 days
>
> Second trimester—14 weeks 0 days to less than 28 weeks 0 days
>
> Third trimester—28 weeks 0 days until delivery

As previously noted, codes from category **Z3A** are reported in addition to codes in Chapter 15 to specify the weeks of pregnancy. The codes identify pregnancy of less than 8 weeks and then each week from week 8 through week 40 or greater. Fifth characters for subcategories **Z3A.1** to **Z3A.4** are numbers **0** to **9**.

Z3A.00	Weeks of gestation of pregnancy not specified
Z3A.01	Less than 8 weeks' gestation of pregnancy
Z3A.08	8 weeks' gestation of pregnancy
Z3A.09	9 weeks' gestation of pregnancy
Z3A.1-	Weeks of gestation of pregnancy, weeks 10–19
Z3A.2-	Weeks of gestation of pregnancy, weeks 20–29
Z3A.3-	Weeks of gestation of pregnancy, weeks 30–39
Z3A.4-	Weeks of gestation of pregnancy, weeks 40 or greater

Example

A 14-year-old is seen for supervision of her first pregnancy. She is now 22 weeks into the pregnancy. She is progressing well without complaints. Diagnosis is young primigravida at 22 weeks' gestation.

O09.612	Supervision of young primigravida, second trimester
Z3A.22	22 weeks of gestation of pregnancy

Were the patient experiencing any complications, other codes from Chapter 15 would be used to describe the complication and would be reported as the primary diagnosis. It is notable that medical, mental, and social complications are represented by codes in this chapter. Some of the conditions included are maternal care for known or suspected fetal abnormality; alcohol, drug, or tobacco use during pregnancy, childbirth, and the puerperium; bariatric surgery status complicating pregnancy; and physical, sexual, or psychological abuse during pregnancy, childbirth, or the puerperium. Suspected or confirmed cases of abuse of a pregnant patient is reported with codes from subcategories **O9A.3-O9A.5** followed by codes to identify any associated injury due to physical abuse, sexual abuse, or the perpetrator of abuse **(Y07.-)**. External cause codes for assault **(X92-Y08)** may also be reported to describe the external cause of injury (eg, assault by unarmed brawl or fight, **Y04.0-**).

When reporting maternal care for fetal problems (eg, maternal care for suspected chromosomal abnormality), seventh characters identifying the affected fetus will often apply. It is important to reference category instructions in the tabular list when selecting codes to identify where these seventh characters apply. Codes in category **O35** (maternal care for known or suspected fetal abnormality and damage) are reported when surgery is performed on a fetus. No code for a perinatal condition would apply because surgery performed in utero is an obstetric encounter.

> **Check it out:** To further review the coding of maternal care for fetal problems, read the instructions for category **O35**. Look for the includes, code also, and excludes 1 notes.

Encounter for Delivery

A code from category **Z37** (outcome of delivery) should be included on every maternal record when a delivery has occurred. These codes are not to be used on subsequent records or on the newborn record. These codes describe single and multiple births with specificity of live births and stillbirths. Codes from Chapter 15 are reported first to identify the delivery without complications or the type of complication(s) affecting the delivery, with codes from category **Z37** identifying that delivery occurred and the outcome.

A full-term uncomplicated delivery is reported with codes **O80** and **Z37.0** (single liveborn infant). This includes delivery requiring no or minimal assistance, with or without episiotomy, without fetal manipulation or instrumentation of a spontaneous, cephalic, vaginal, full-term single, live-born infant. Code **O80** is always the principal diagnosis and is not used if any code for a complication is applicable.

Code **O82** is used to report a cesarean delivery without indication.

If a mother delivers outside the hospital setting but is admitted for care and examination immediately afterward and no complications occur, code **Z39.0** is reported.

Pregnancy With Abortive Outcome

Ectopic pregnancy is reported with codes in category **O00**, including abdominal pregnancy **(O00.0)**, tubal pregnancy **(O00.1)**, ovarian pregnancy **(O00.2)**, and other ectopic pregnancy **(O00.8)**. Category **O08** provides codes for reporting complications following ectopic pregnancy that are used with codes in categories **O00-O02**.

Code **O02.1** is reported for a missed abortion defined as early fetal death, before completion of 20 weeks of gestation, with retention of the fetus. Conditions not included here are failed induced abortion **(O07.-)**, missed abortion with blighted ovum **(O02.0)**, missed abortion with hydatidiform mole **(O01.-)**, or missed abortion with other abnormal products of conception **(O02.8-)**.

Category **O03.0** is used to report incomplete or complete spontaneous abortion and associated complications. Table 16-1 shows the codes for incomplete and complete spontaneous abortion in the second and third columns aligned with the complication each reports listed in the first column of the same row.

The same fourth and fifth characters used to specify complications of complete spontaneous abortion **(O03.5-O03.9)** are applied to category **O04** describing complications following induced termination of pregnancy. An exception is fourth character **.9,** which does not apply because an uncomplicated elective termination of pregnancy is reported with code **Z33.2** (encounter for elective termination of pregnancy).

Category **O07** includes codes for failed attempted termination of pregnancy with complications specified with the same fourth and fifth characters assigned to codes for incomplete spontaneous abortion (eg, **O07.37** [sepsis following failed attempted termination of pregnancy]). The guidelines provide instruction for reporting live birth following attempted termination; assign code **Z33.2** (encounter for elective termination of pregnancy) and a code from category **Z37** (outcome of delivery).

Complications following ectopic or molar pregnancy are reported with codes in category **O08**. Again the associated complications are specified by the fourth and fifth characters, but these codes do not follow either of the patterns in Table 16-1. Codes in

Table 16-1. Complications of Spontaneous Abortion

Type of Complication	Following Incomplete Spontaneous Abortion	Following Complete Spontaneous Abortion
Genital tract and pelvic infection	O03.0	O03.5
Delayed or excessive hemorrhage	O03.1	O03.6
Embolism	O03.2	O03.7
Unspecified complication	O03.30	O03.80
Shock (not due to infection)	O03.31	O03.81
Renal failure	O03.32	O03.82
Metabolic disorder	O03.33	O03.83
Damage to pelvic organs	O03.34	O03.84
Other venous complications	O03.35	O03.85
Cardiac arrest	O03.36	O03.86
Sepsis (code also **B95-B97** and if applicable severe sepsis **R65.2-**)	O03.37	O03.87
Urinary tract infection	O03.38	O03.88
Other complications	O03.39	O03.89
Without complication	O03.4	O03.9

this category represent the same complications seen in categories **O03-O07,** but only subcategory **O08.8** includes fifth characters.

> Check it out: To further review codes for complications of ectopic or molar pregnancy, find the codes for cardiac arrest following ectopic and molar pregnancy and for an unspecified complication following an ectopic and molar pregnancy.

Conditions in the Puerperium

The peripartum period is defined as the last month of pregnancy to 5 months postpartum. A postpartum complication is one that occurs in the period immediately after delivery through 6 weeks following delivery. Even though a condition occurs after the peripartum or postpartum period, a code from Chapter 15 may be reported if the physician or provider documents that it is pregnancy-related.

If after the postpartum period a sequela of a complication of pregnancy develops, report code **O94** (sequela of complication of pregnancy, childbirth, and the puerperium) in addition to the code describing the sequelae of the complication.

Routine postpartum follow-up encounters are reported with diagnosis code **Z39.2.**

Other Encounters Related to Pregnancy, Childbirth, and the Puerperium

Many encounters related to pregnancy, childbirth, and the puerperium that may not involve a confirmed complication or routine supervision are included in Chapter 21.

Z01.83	Encounter for blood typing (Rh typing)
Z03.71	Encounter for suspected problem with amniotic cavity and membrane ruled out
Z03.72	Encounter for suspected placental problem ruled out
Z03.73	Encounter for suspected fetal anomaly ruled out
Z03.74	Encounter for suspected problem with fetal growth ruled out
Z03.75	Encounter for suspected cervical shortening ruled out
Z03.79	Encounter for other suspected maternal and fetal conditions ruled out
Z31.62	Encounter for fertility preservation counseling
Z31.82	Encounter for Rh incompatibility status
Z39.1	Encounter for care and examination of lactating mother

Code Scenarios

A 15-year-old girl comes into the walk-in clinic seeking advice because she had unprotected sex with her boyfriend the night before and is afraid of an unwanted pregnancy. After counseling the patient, a prescription for an emergency contraceptive is provided along with a referral to a gynecologist for further management. The diagnosis is need for emergency contraceptive with provision of prescription for the same.

Z30.012	Encounter for prescription of emergency contraception

> From the guidelines: Section IC21c10—Counseling Z codes are used when a patient or family member receives assistance in the aftermath of an illness or injury, or when support is required in coping with family or social problems. They are not used in conjunction with a diagnosis code when the counseling component of care is considered integral to standard treatment.

A 17-year-old seen 1 week ago with a positive pregnancy test returns to ask for assistance to quit smoking. She has smoked 5 to 10 cigarettes a day for 2 years. She has tried to abstain since learning she is pregnant but has withdrawal symptoms. Diagnosis is pregnancy of 8 weeks' gestation complicated by smoking and nicotine dependence with withdrawal.

O99.331	Smoking (tobacco) complicating pregnancy, first trimester
F17.213	Nicotine dependence, cigarettes, with withdrawal
Z3A.08	8 weeks' gestation of pregnancy

> From the guidelines: Section IC15l2—Codes under subcategory **O99.33** (smoking [tobacco] complicating pregnancy, childbirth, and the puerperium) should be assigned for any pregnancy case when a mother uses any type of tobacco product during the pregnancy or postpartum. A secondary code from category **F17** (nicotine dependence) should also be assigned to identify the type of nicotine dependence.

Review What You Have Learned

16.1 A pregnant 15-year-old is expected to deliver 6 weeks before her 16th birthday. What code(s) is reported for routine supervision of this pregnancy?
   A. **Z33.1** Pregnant state, incidental
   B. Codes in category **Z34** (encounter for supervision of normal pregnancy)
   C. Codes in categories **Z34** (encounter for supervision of normal pregnancy) and **Z3A** (weeks of gestation)
   D. Codes in categories **O09.6** (supervision of young primigravida) and **Z3A** (weeks of gestation)
   E. None of the above

16.2 A 17-year-old girl who is pregnant is seen for concerns regarding a mole on her right shoulder. The diagnosis is nevus right shoulder with incidental pregnancy. What code(s) is reported?
   A. **D23.61** Other benign neoplasm of skin of right upper limb, including shoulder
      Z34.00 Encounter for supervision of normal first pregnancy, unspecified trimester
   B. **D23.61** Other benign neoplasm of skin of right upper limb, including shoulder
      Z03.79 Encounter for other suspected maternal and fetal conditions ruled out
   C. **D23.61** Other benign neoplasm of skin of right upper limb, including shoulder
      Z33.1 Pregnant state, incidental
   D. **Z33.1** Pregnant state, incidental
   E. None of the above

16.3 Pregnancy in a 16-year-old is always reported with codes in category **O09** as a high-risk pregnancy.
   A. True
   B. False

16.4 Surgery is performed on a fetus to close a spinal defect. Code **O35.0XX0** (maternal care for [suspected] central nervous system malformation in fetus) should be used on the mother's record.
   A. True
   B. False

16.5 Only one code from Chapter 15 may be reported for each encounter.
   A. True
   B. False

16.6 When a patient is admitted and delivers a liveborn infant with or without complication, what code category signifies the delivery and outcome on the mother's record?
   A. Category **O80** (encounter for full-term uncomplicated delivery)
   B. Category **Z38** (liveborn infants according to place of birth and type of delivery)
   C. Complications of labor and delivery **(O60-O77)**
   D. Category **Z37** (outcome of delivery)
   E. All of the above

≡ CHAPTER 17 ≡

Certain Conditions Originating in the Perinatal Period (P00-P96)

This chapter reviews the coding guidelines for reporting certain conditions that originate in the perinatal period. Codes for these conditions are found in Chapter 16 of the *International Classification of Diseases, Tenth Revision, Clinical Modification (ICD-10-CM)* tabular list. For coding and reporting purposes the perinatal period is defined as before birth through the 28th day following birth.

Should a condition originate in the perinatal period and continue throughout the life of the patient, the perinatal code should continue to be used regardless of the patient's age.

An excludes 2 note for this chapter indicates that codes in the chapter are not used to report

- Congenital malformations, deformations, and chromosomal abnormalities **(Q00-Q99)**
- Endocrine, nutritional, and metabolic diseases **(E00-E88)**
- Neoplasms **(C00-D49)**
- Tetanus neonatorum **(A33)**

However, conditions included above may be reported in conjunction with codes for conditions in Chapter 16 when present. If the reason for the encounter is a perinatal condition, the code for the perinatal condition should be sequenced first.

Conditions that are included in Chapter 16 are

> Newborn affected by maternal factors and by complications of pregnancy, labor, and delivery **(P00-P04)**
> Disorders of newborn related to length of gestation and fetal growth **(P05-P08)**
> Abnormal findings on neonatal screening **(P09)**
> Birth trauma **(P10-P15)**
> Respiratory and cardiovascular disorders specific to the perinatal period **(P19-P29)**
> Infections specific to the perinatal period **(P35-P39)**
> Hemorrhagic and hematological disorders of newborn **(P50-P61)**
> Transitory endocrine and metabolic disorders specific to newborn **(P70-P74)**
> Digestive system disorders of newborn **(P76-P78)**
> Conditions involving the integument and temperature regulation of newborn **(P80-P83)**
> Other problems with newborn **(P84)**
> Other disorders originating in the perinatal period **(P90-P96)**

All clinically significant conditions noted in a newborn examination should be reported. For conditions in the newborn period, the definition of "clinically significant" is expanded to include those conditions that have implications for future health care needs. Conditions specified as having implications for future health care needs are not reported for adult patients.

> From the guidelines: Section III—For reporting purposes the definition for "other diagnoses" is interpreted as additional conditions that affect patient care in terms of requiring
>
> Clinical evaluation, or
>
> Therapeutic treatment, or
>
> Diagnostic procedures, or
>
> Extended length of hospital stay, or
>
> Increased nursing care and/or monitoring

Some conditions may either be due to the birth process or community acquired. If documentation does not specify a condition as either due to birth process or community acquired, report the condition as due to birth process with codes in Chapter 16. Conditions documented as community acquired are not reported with codes in Chapter 16.

Principal Diagnosis for the Birth Record

The principal code assigned to a newborn's birth record will not be from Chapter 16. Codes in category **Z38** are used on the newborn's birth record (never the mother's record) to identify place of birth and type of delivery for liveborn infants. These codes are reported only once and only at the facility where the initial newborn care is provided. If an infant is transferred to another facility, the receiving facility does not report a code from category **Z38.**

Codes in category **Z38** are

Z38.00	Single liveborn infant, delivered vaginally
Z38.01	Single liveborn infant, delivered by cesarean
Z38.1	Single liveborn infant, born outside hospital
Z38.2	Single liveborn infant, unspecified as to place of birth
Z38.30	Twin liveborn infant, delivered vaginally
Z38.31	Twin liveborn infant, delivered by cesarean
Z38.4	Twin liveborn infant, born outside hospital
Z38.5	Twin liveborn infant, unspecified as to place of birth
Z38.61	Triplet liveborn infant, delivered vaginally
Z38.62	Triplet liveborn infant, delivered by cesarean
Z38.63	Quadruplet liveborn infant, delivered vaginally
Z38.64	Quadruplet liveborn infant, delivered by cesarean
Z38.65	Quintuplet liveborn infant, delivered vaginally

Z38.66	Quintuplet liveborn infant, delivered by cesarean
Z38.68	Other multiple liveborn infant, delivered vaginally
Z38.69	Other multiple liveborn infant, delivered by cesarean
Z38.7	Other multiple liveborn infant, born outside hospital
Z38.8	Other multiple liveborn infant, unspecified as to place of birth

For those facilities that create separate records for the stillborn, code **P95** is the code for stillbirth. For reporting of stillbirth on the mother's record, see codes for outcome of delivery, stillbirth (**Z37.1, Z37.3, Z37.4,** and **Z37.7**).

Maternal Factors and Complications Affecting the Newborn

Codes in categories **P00-P04** are used to report maternal conditions specified as the cause of confirmed or potential morbidity originating in the perinatal period. In another circumstance where the *ICD-10-CM* guidelines differ from those of *ICD-9-CM*, codes in these categories may be reported when evaluation and/or treatment is begun for newborns who are suspected of having an abnormal condition resulting from exposure from the mother or the birth process, which after examination and study do not exist.

> From the tabular list: Codes from these categories are also for use for newborns who are suspected of having an abnormal condition resulting from exposure from the mother or the birth process, but without signs or symptoms, and, which after examination and observation, is found not to exist. These codes may be used even if treatment is begun for a suspected condition that is ruled out.

The categories in this block of codes are

- **P00** Newborn (suspected to be) affected by maternal conditions that may be unrelated to present pregnancy
- **P01** Newborn (suspected to be) affected by maternal complications of pregnancy
- **P02** Newborn (suspected to be) affected by complications of placenta, cord, and membranes
- **P03** Newborn (suspected to be) affected by other complications of labor and delivery
- **P04** Newborn (suspected to be) affected by noxious substances transmitted via placenta or breast milk

Codes in these categories are sequenced after codes for current conditions in the newborn. Inclusion terms following each code provide information on the types of maternal conditions included. Several codes in this block are followed by excludes 1 and/or excludes 2 notes that guide correct reporting.

Example   **P00.2** Newborn (suspected to be) affected by maternal infectious and parasitic diseases
Newborn (suspected to be) affected by maternal infectious disease classifiable to **A00-B99, J09,** and **J10**
Excludes 1
infections specific to the perinatal period **(P35-P39)**
maternal genital tract or other localized infections **(P00.8)**

The inclusion term following code **P00.2** indicates that this code may be used to report confirmed or suspected conditions in a newborn due to maternal infectious disease classifiable to **A00-B99** or **J09-J10**. The excludes 1 note directs to codes **P35-P39** for infections specific to the perinatal period and to code **P00.8** for a confirmed or suspected condition in a newborn due to maternal genital tract or other localized infections. Code **P00.2** would not be reported when a code in categories **P35-P39** or code **P00.8** is reported.

Abnormal findings on neonatal screening may be reported with code **P09**. Codes to identify signs, symptoms, and conditions associated with the screening may also be reported. An excludes 2 note for this code instructs that nonspecific serologic evidence of HIV is not included here but may be additionally reported with code **R75** when appropriate.

Gestational Age and Fetal Growth Disorders

Categories **P05-P08** include codes for disorders related to the length of gestation and fetal growth. Category **P05** includes codes for low birth weight due to slow fetal growth and fetal malnutrition. Codes indicate light for gestational age **(P05.0-)** or small for gestational age (**P05.1-,** includes small and light for dates) based on the newborn's weight in grams. Also included here is code **P05.2** (newborn affected by fetal [intrauterine] malnutrition not light or small for gestational age). This code is used to report signs of fetal malnutrition such as dry, peeling skin and loss of subcutaneous tissue in an infant who is not light or small for gestational age.

Codes in category **P05** are not reported in conjunction with most codes in category **P07** (disorders of newborn related to short gestation and low birth weight, not elsewhere classified).

> **Terms to Know**
>
> **Light for gestational age**—usually refers to weight below the 10th percentile with height above the 10th percentile
>
> **Small for gestational age**—usually refers to weight and height below the 10th percentile

Category **P07** includes codes indicating birth weight and codes indicating the gestational age. When both weight and gestational age are documented, report both with weight sequenced before gestational age.

Extremely low birth weight and low birth weight are reported with codes in subcategories **P07.0** and **P07.1** based on the newborn's weight in grams.

Extreme immaturity, less than 28 completed weeks of gestation, is reported with codes in subcategory **P07.2** based on the number of completed weeks of gestation.

Example

A neonate's gestational age is 23 weeks, 6 days.

P07.22 Extreme immaturity of newborn, gestational age 23 completed weeks

In this example, the appropriate code is that for 23 completed weeks of gestation because gestational age is not rounded up or down. Only complete weeks are included.

Codes in subcategory **P07.3** are used to report the completed weeks of gestation in preterm newborns. Preterm refers to newborns with 28 or more completed weeks of gestation but less than 37 weeks. Gestational age of less than 28 completed weeks is classified as extreme immaturity as noted above.

Codes for large and exceptionally large newborns and late newborns that are not heavy for gestational age are found in subcategory **P08**. These codes are not used to report syndromes of infants of a diabetic mother **(P70.1)** or a mother with gestational diabetes **(P70.0)**. A diagnosis of exceptionally large newborn usually implies a birth weight of 4,500 g or more. Newborns weighing 4,000 to 4,499 g may be diagnosed as heavy for gestational age.

Post-term newborns are those with a gestational period of more than 40 completed weeks to 42 completed weeks. Prolonged gestation of a newborn refers to a gestational period of more than 42 completed weeks in a newborn that is not heavy or large for dates.

Birth Trauma

Birth trauma is reported with codes in categories **P10-P15** indicating the types or site of each injury. This block of codes does not include codes for non-traumatic injuries such as non-traumatic intracranial hemorrhage of the newborn **(P52.-)**. The alphabetic index includes references to these codes, such as those found under the term "fracture."

Example

Fracture
- bone NEC **T14.8**
-- birth injury **P13.9**
- due to
-- birth injury—*see* Birth, injury, fracture

This example includes only 2 of the references to the birth injury codes under the term "fracture." Other birth injuries are referenced under terms such as "hematoma," "hemorrhage," and "injury."

Bruising of the scalp **(P12.3)** and cephalhematoma **(P12.0)** are included in this block of codes, but other neonatal cutaneous hemorrhage is reported with code **P54.5**.

Respiratory and Cardiovascular Disorders Specific to the Perinatal Period

The block of codes **P19-P29** includes codes for both respiratory and cardiovascular conditions originating in the perinatal period. Congenital malformations of the respiratory and cardiovascular systems are not included here.

> **Terms to Know**
>
> **Metabolic acidosis**—a pH imbalance in which the body has accumulated too much acid and does not have enough bicarbonate to neutralize the effects of the acid; symptoms include tachypnea or hyperpnea
>
> **Meconium**—the first intestinal discharge from newborns, a sterile dark-green substance composed of water, epithelial cells, lanugo, mucus, and intestinal secretions like bile; meconium passage in utero results in meconium-stained amniotic fluid that may be aspirated before or during birth

Metabolic acidosis of the newborn first noted before onset of labor, during labor, or at birth is reported with codes in category **P19**. Late metabolic acidosis of a newborn is reported with code **P74.0**.

Category **P22** includes codes for respiratory distress of the newborn. This does not include neonatal respiratory arrest **(P28.81)** or respiratory failure **(P28.5)**. Category **P23** (congenital pneumonia) includes infective pneumonia acquired in utero or during birth but excludes neonatal pneumonia resulting from aspiration **(P24.-)**. An additional code from category **B97** is reported to identify the infectious agent when reporting congenital viral pneumonia **(P23.0)**. Code **P23.0** does not include congenital rubella pneumonitis **(P35.0)**. An additional code from categories **B95-B96** are reported in addition to code **P23.6** (congenital pneumonia due to other bacterial agents).

Codes in category **P24** (neonatal aspiration) specify the type of substance aspirated and the presence or absence of associated respiratory symptoms.

Example

P24.00	Meconium aspiration without respiratory symptoms
P24.01	Meconium aspiration with respiratory symptoms

When neonatal aspiration with respiratory symptoms is reported, report also **I27.2** for secondary pulmonary hypertension, if applicable.

Infections Specific to the Perinatal Period

Codes in categories **P35-P39** are used to report infections acquired in utero, during birth via the umbilicus, or during the first 28 days after birth. An excludes 2 note for this block of codes indicates infectious conditions that are not reported with codes in this block but may be additionally reported when applicable (eg, asymptomatic HIV infection status, **Z21**).

Bacterial sepsis of a newborn is assumed to be congenital **(P36.-)** when not specified as congenital or community acquired. Codes from category **B96** should be additionally reported to identify the infectious organism when reporting code **P36.8** (other bacterial sepsis of the newborn). Additional codes to identify the infectious organism are not necessary with codes in category **P36** that include identification of the organism (eg, **P36.4,** newborn sepsis due to *Escherichia coli*). When severe sepsis **(R65.2-)** and associated organ dysfunction are documented, use additional codes to identify these conditions.

Infectious neonatal diarrhea is not included in this block of codes. These conditions are reported with codes **A00-A09**. Noninfectious neonatal diarrhea is reported with code **P78.3**.

Code **P39.4** is used to report neonatal skin infection other than pemphigus neonatorum **(L00)**. Use an additional code to identify the organism or specific infection when reporting codes in category **P39**.

Hemorrhagic and Hematological Disorders of the Newborn

The block of codes **P50-P61** includes codes for hemorrhagic and hematological disorders of the newborn with exclusion of conditions such as Crigler-Najjar syndrome **(E80.5)**, Dubin-Johnson syndrome **(E80.6)**, and Gilbert syndrome **(E80.4)**. Also not included here are hemolytic anemias **(D55-D58)** and congenital stenosis and stricture of bile ducts **(Q44.3)**.

This category does include codes for the newborn affected by intrauterine blood loss specifying the type of hemorrhage. Congenital anemia from intrauterine blood loss is reported with code **P61.3**. Umbilical hemorrhages of the newborn are classified as massive **(P51.0),** omphalitis with mild hemorrhage **(P38.1),** umbilical hemorrhage from cut end of co-twins cord **(P50.5),** and other umbilical hemorrhages **(P51.8)**.

Intracranial hemorrhage due to anoxia or hypoxia is reported with codes in category **P52**. This does not include traumatic hemorrhage due to birth injury **(P10.-)** or other injury **(S06.-)**.

Neonatal hematemesis and melena are reported with codes **P54.0** and **P54.1** except when these conditions are due to swallowed maternal blood **(P78.2)**.

Jaundice due to isoimmunization is reported with codes in categories **P55-P57** to specify hemolytic disease of the newborn, hydrops fetalis due to hemolytic disease of the newborn, or kernicterus. Neonatal jaundice due to other excessive hemolysis is reported with codes in category **P58**. When neonatal jaundice is due to drugs or toxins transmitted from the mother or given to the newborn, codes **P58.41-P58.42** are reported in conjunction with codes to identify poisoning **(T36-T65)** or adverse effect **(T36-T50)**. Jaundice due to inborn errors of metabolism is reported with codes in categories **E70-E88**. Neonatal jaundice due to preterm delivery or hyperbilirubinemia of prematurity is reported with code **P59.0**.

Transitory Endocrine and Metabolic Disorders Specific to the Newborn

Neonatal diabetes mellitus **(P70.2)** and other transitory endocrine and metabolic disorders of the newborn are reported with codes in categories **P70-P74**.

Transitory congenital goiter with normal functioning is reported with code **P72.0** (neonatal goiter, not elsewhere classified). Congenital hypothyroidism with or without goiter is reported with codes **E03.0-E03.1**. For dyshormogenetic goiter, see code **E07.1**.

Digestive System Disorders of the Newborn

Codes in categories **P76-P78** are used to report intestinal obstructions, necrotizing enterocolitis, and other perinatal digestive system disorders. These conditions associated with cystic fibrosis are not reported here but are included in categories **E84.0-E84.9**. Also not included in categories **P76-P78** are conditions classified in category **K56,** such as paralytic ileus, intussusception, volvulus, or fecal impaction. Transitory ileus of the newborn is reported with code **P76.1**. This does not include Hirschsprung disease **(Q43.1)**.

Necrotizing enterocolitis is reported with codes in category **P77** based on the stage of the condition.

P77.1	Stage 1 necrotizing enterocolitis in newborn Necrotizing enterocolitis without pneumatosis, without perforation
P77.2	Stage 2 necrotizing enterocolitis in newborn Necrotizing enterocolitis with pneumatosis, without perforation
P77.3	Stage 3 necrotizing enterocolitis in newborn Necrotizing enterocolitis with perforation Necrotizing enterocolitis with pneumatosis and perforation

Codes in category **P78** are used to report other perinatal gastrointestinal disorders such as perinatal intestinal perforation **(P78.0)**, congenital cirrhosis of the liver **(P78.81)**, peptic ulcer of the newborn **(P78.82)**, and newborn esophageal reflux **(P78.83)**.

Conditions Involving the Integument and Temperature Regulation of the Newborn

Category **P80** includes codes for reporting hypothermia including cold injury syndrome **(P80.0)** and other hyperthermia of the newborn **(P80.8)**. Hyperthermia of the newborn is reported with codes in category **P81**. This includes **P81.9** (disturbance of temperature regulation of the newborn), which is reported for fever of the newborn, not otherwise specified.

Other conditions of the integument specific to the newborn are included in category **P83**. An excludes 1 note for this category excludes congenital malformation of the skin and integument **(Q80-Q84)**, hydrops fetalis due to hemolytic disease **(P56.-)**, neonatal skin infection **(P39.4)**, and staphylococcal scalded skin syndrome **(L00)**. This category also has an excludes 2 note indicating that cradle cap **(L21.0)** and diaper dermatitis **(L22)** are not included here but may be additionally reported when applicable. A variety of other conditions are included in category **P83** as follows

P83.0	Sclerema neonatorum
P83.1	Neonatal erythema toxicum
P83.2	Hydrops fetalis not due to hemolytic disease
P83.30	Unspecified edema specific to newborn
P83.39	Other edema specific to newborn
P83.4	Breast engorgement of newborn (noninfective mastitis of newborn)
P83.5	Congenital hydrocele
P83.6	Umbilical polyp of newborn

Code **P84** is reported for other problems with the newborn not specified elsewhere, including acidemia, acidosis, anoxia, asphyxia, hypercapnia, hypoxemia, hypoxia, and mixed metabolic and respiratory acidosis.

Other Disorders Originating in the Perinatal Period

Codes in categories **P90-P96** include conditions affecting cerebral status, feeding problems, disorders of muscle tone, congenital renal failure, neonatal withdrawal symptoms, complications to the newborn due to intrauterine procedure **(P96.5),** and others. Convulsions of the newborn **(P90)** does not include benign myoclonic epilepsy in infancy **(G40.3-).**

Codes for reporting feeding problems in the neonate include

P92.01	Bilious vomiting of newborn
P92.09	Other vomiting of newborn
P92.1	Regurgitation and rumination of newborn
P92.2	Slow feeding of newborn
P92.3	Underfeeding of newborn
P92.4	Overfeeding of newborn
P92.5	Neonatal difficulty in feeding at breast
P92.6	Failure to thrive in newborn

It is important to note that these conditions in children older than 28 days after birth are reported elsewhere, including the codes for signs and symptoms found in Chapter 18 of the tabular list.

Codes **P96.1** and **P96.2** include withdrawal symptoms in a newborn from maternal use of drugs of addiction and from therapeutic use of drugs in a newborn. Exposure to parental and environmental tobacco smoke in the perinatal period is reported with code **P96.81**. Environmental exposure to tobacco smoke after the 28-day perinatal period is reported with code **Z77.22**.

Other Care in the Perinatal Period

Health examinations in the neonatal period, such as an office encounter within 8 days following hospital discharge of the newborn, are reported with codes in subcategory **Z00.11.**

Z00.110	Health examination for newborn under 8 days old
Z00.111	Health examination for newborn 8 to 28 days old

Any abnormal findings should be reported in addition to codes **Z00.110** and **Z00.111.**

An encounter to provide child care instruction to the parent or other caregiver is reported with code **Z32.3**. Code **Z39.1** is reported for an encounter for care and examination of a lactating mother, including supervision of lactation. For disorders of lactation, see category **O92.**

When a congenital malformation has been corrected and does not still require medical treatment, codes in subcategory **Z87.7** are used to indicate the personal history of corrected congenital malformation. For congenital malformations that still require medical care, see codes in Chapter 17 of the tabular list **(Q00-Q89).**

Code Scenarios

A neonate is delivered vaginally at a gestational age of 26 weeks 3 days' gestation weighing 1,129 g and is transferred to the neonatal intensive care unit in the same facility. The infant is diagnosed with respiratory distress syndrome.

    Z38.00   Single liveborn infant, delivered vaginally
    P07.14   Other low birth weight newborn, 1,000–1,249 g
    P07.25   Extreme immaturity of newborn, gestational age 26 completed weeks
    P22.0   Respiratory distress syndrome of newborn

> From the guidelines: Section IC16–
>
> a2. When coding the birth episode in a newborn record, assign a code from category **Z38** (liveborn infants according to place of birth and type of delivery) as the principal diagnosis.
>
> d. When both birth weight and gestational age are available, 2 codes from category **P07** should be assigned, with the code for birth weight sequenced before the code for gestational age.

A 15-day-old infant is readmitted with a diagnosis of sepsis due to streptococcus group B.

    P36.0   Sepsis of newborn due to streptococcus, group B

> From the guidelines: Section IC16–
>
> f. Category **P36** (bacterial sepsis of newborn) includes congenital sepsis. If a perinate is documented as having sepsis without documentation of congenital or community acquired, the default is congenital and a code from category **P36** should be assigned. If the **P36** code includes the causal organism, an additional code from category **B95** (*Streptococcus, Staphylococcus,* and *Enterococcus*) as the cause of diseases classified elsewhere, or **B96** (other bacterial agents as the cause of diseases classified elsewhere) should not be assigned.
>
> 2. A code from category **Z38** is assigned only once, to a newborn at the time of birth.

A 2,721-g neonate is delivered vaginally at 36 weeks 2 days' gestation to a mother who had a fever during labor and delivery. The pediatrician is alerted that maternal chorioamnionitis is suspected. The neonate is closely monitored and diagnosed with congenital pneumonia due to *E coli*.

    Z38.00   Single liveborn infant, delivered vaginally
    P07.39   Preterm newborn, gestational age 36 completed weeks
    P23.4   Congenital pneumonia due to *Escherichia coli*
    P02.7   Newborn (suspected to be) affected by chorioamnionitis

> From the tabular list: Instructions for block **P00-P04** are provided in a note at the beginning of the block as follows.
>
> Note: These codes are for use when the listed maternal conditions are specified as the cause of confirmed morbidity or potential morbidity, which have their origin in the perinatal period (before birth through the first 28 days after birth). Codes from these categories are also for use for newborns who are suspected of having an abnormal condition resulting from exposure from the mother or the birth process, but without signs or symptoms and which, after examination and observation, is found not to exist. These codes may be used even if treatment is begun for a suspected condition that is ruled out.

Review What You Have Learned

17.1 A neonate is started on intravenous antibiotics due to suspected infection transferred during birth due to a localized infection in the mother. Infection in the neonate is ruled out following stabilization and negative culture results. What code(s), if any, is reported for the suspected neonatal infection?
   A. **P00.2** Newborn (suspected to be) affected by maternal infectious and parasitic diseases
   B. **P00.89** Newborn (suspected to be) affected by other maternal conditions
   C. **P37.9** Congenital infectious or parasitic disease, unspecified
   D. The suspected condition is not reported
   E. None of the above

17.2 A neonate is diagnosed with pneumonia due to aspiration of meconium-stained amniotic fluid. What diagnosis code(s) is reported for this condition?
   A. **P24.11** Neonatal aspiration of (clear) amniotic fluid and mucus with respiratory symptoms
   B. **P96.83** Meconium staining
   C. **P24.01** Meconium aspiration with respiratory symptoms
   D. **P23.9** Congenital pneumonia, unspecified
   E. None of the above

17.3 Codes in Chapter 16 are never reported with codes from other chapters in *ICD-10-CM*.
   A. True
   B. False

17.4 Codes identifying birth weight and gestational age are reported only in the neonatal period.
   A. True
   B. False

17.5 Guidelines for reporting conditions originating in the perinatal period are identical to those for other conditions.
   A. True
   B. False

17.6 Projectile vomiting in a 28-day-old infant is reported with which code(s)?
    A. **R11.10**   Vomiting, unspecified
    B. **P92.09**   Other vomiting of newborn
    C. **R11.12**   Projectile vomiting
    D. **P92.1**   Regurgitation and rumination of newborn
    E. None of the above

≡ CHAPTER 18 ≡

Congenital Malformations, Deformations, and Chromosomal Abnormalities (Q00-Q99)

Congenital malformations and deformations and chromosomal abnormalities are reported with codes **Q00-Q99** from Chapter 17 of the *International Classification of Diseases, Tenth Revision, Clinical Modification (ICD-10-CM)* tabular list. Codes in this chapter may be the principal or secondary diagnosis.

Manifestations of congenital malformation/deformation or chromosomal abnormality that are an inherent component of the anomaly are not separately reported when a specific code describes the anomaly. When no code specifically describes an anomaly or there are manifestations that are not routinely associated with an anomaly, additional codes for the manifestations should be reported.

The blocks in Chapter 17 are

    Congenital malformations of the nervous system **(Q00-Q07)**
    Congenital malformations of eye, ear, face, and neck **(Q10-Q18)**
    Congenital malformations of the circulatory system **(Q20-Q28)**
    Congenital malformations of the respiratory system **(Q30-Q34)**
    Cleft lip and cleft palate **(Q35-Q37)**
    Other congenital malformations of the digestive system **(Q38-Q45)**
    Congenital malformations of genital organs **(Q50-Q56)**
    Congenital malformations of the urinary system **(Q60-Q64)**
    Congenital malformations and deformations of the musculoskeletal system **(Q65-Q79)**
    Other congenital malformations **(Q80-Q89)**
    Chromosomal abnormalities, not elsewhere classified **(Q90-Q99)**

Conditions of the neonate described by codes **Q00-Q99** are not reported on the maternal or fetal records. Corrected congenital malformations and deformations that no longer require medical treatment are reported with codes from subcategory **Z87.7** in Chapter 21 of the tabular list.

    Z87.710   Personal history of (corrected) hypospadias
    Z87.718   Personal history of other specified (corrected) congenital malformations of genitourinary system
    Z87.720   Personal history of (corrected) congenital malformations of eye
    Z87.721   Personal history of (corrected) congenital malformations of ear
    Z87.728   Personal history of other specified (corrected) congenital malformations of nervous system and sense organs

Z87.730	Personal history of (corrected) cleft lip and palate	
Z87.738	Personal history of other specified (corrected) congenital malformations of digestive system	
Z87.74	Personal history of (corrected) congenital malformations of heart and circulatory system	
Z87.75	Personal history of (corrected) congenital malformations of respiratory system	
Z87.76	Personal history of (corrected) congenital malformations of integument, limbs, and musculoskeletal system	
Z87.790	Personal history of (corrected) congenital malformations of face and neck	
Z87.798	Personal history of other (corrected) congenital malformations	

Codes indicating post-procedural status; presence of grafts, implants, or devices; or transplanted organs or tissues should be additionally reported with codes for corrected congenital malformations. Congenital malformations that have been partially corrected or repaired but still require medical treatment are reported with a code for that condition.

Congenital Malformations of the Nervous System

Codes in categories **Q00-Q07** are used to report congenital conditions such as anencephaly, encephalocele, microcephaly other than that in Meckel-Gruber syndrome **(Q61.9)**, hydrocephalus, malformations of the brain, spina bifida, and other malformations of the spinal cord.

> **Terms to Know**
>
> **Hydrocephalus**—accumulation of excess cerebrospinal fluid in the ventricles of the brain
>
> **Spina bifida**—congenital condition due to incomplete closure of the embryonic neural tube, meningocele, or myelomeningocele are associated except in mild cases (spina bifida occulta)
>
> **Chiari and Arnold-Chiari syndromes**—four types of brain malformations that may be referenced by multiple terms, each involves abnormalities of the posterior portion of the brain
>
> >Type I—most common, least severe, often not discovered until adulthood, reported in *ICD-10-CM* as compression of the brain **(G93.5)**
> >
> > Type II—displacement of the lower brain stem that may occur with or without spina bifida or hydrocephalus, category **Q07** in *ICD-10-CM*
> >
> > Type III—rare, causes severe neurologic defects, referenced as encephalocele **(Q01.-)** in *ICD-10-CM*, an occipital encephalocele is often associated **(Q01.2)**
> >
> > Type IV—extremely rare, characterized by lack of cerebral development, classified to other congenital malformations of the brain in *ICD-10-CM* **(Q04.8)**

Spina bifida is classified in category **Q05** with codes specifying the portion of the spine affected and the presence or absence of hydrocephalus. An excludes 1 note for this category directs to codes in subcategory **Q07.0** for spina bifida in Arnold-Chiari syndrome type II and to code **Q76.0** for spina bifida occulta. Codes in subcategory **Q07.0** specify Arnold-Chiari syndrome type II, with or without spina bifida and hydrocephalus.

Congenital Malformations of Eye, Ear, Face, and Neck

This block of codes includes malformations of the eye, ear, face, and neck but not of the lips or palate, cervical spine, larynx, thyroid gland, parathyroid gland, or nose. When malformations of the excluded sites are documented, codes for these are reported in addition to codes for malformations of the eye, ear, face, or neck.

Code **Q11.2** includes microphthalmos and cryptophthalmos, not otherwise specified but excludes Fraser or cryptophthalmos syndrome **(Q87.0)**. Macrophthalmos is reported with code **Q11.3** except when found in congenital glaucoma **(Q15.0)**. When reporting a congenital absence of the iris, use an additional code for associated glaucoma **(H42)**. Associated glaucoma is also reported with Rieger anomaly **(Q13.81)**.

Congenital nystagmus is reported with code **H55.01**. Other conditions of the eye not included in Chapter 17 are ocular albinism **(E70.31)**, optic nerve hypoplasia **(H47.03-)**, and retinitis pigmentosa **(H35.52)**.

Category **Q16** includes codes for malformations of the ear causing impaired hearing but does not include congenital deafness **(H90-)**. Misshapen or misplaced ear(s) is reported with codes in category **Q17**.

Congenital Malformations of the Circulatory System

Category **Q20** includes codes for congenital malformations of the cardiac chambers and connections such as common arterial trunk **(Q20.0)**. It does not include mirror-image atrial arrangement with situs inversus **(Q89.3)**. It also does not include congenital malformations of the cardiac septa **(Q21.-)**.

Ventricular septal defect or Roger disease is reported with code **Q21.0**, but a ventricular septal defect described as Eisenmenger defect is reported with code **Q21.8**. For Eisenmenger syndrome, see code **I27.8**. Code **Q21.8** is also the code for reporting pentalogy of Fallot. Tetralogy of Fallot is reported with code **Q21.3**.

Congenital stenosis of the aortic valve is reported with code **Q23.0**, but this code excludes congenital stenosis of the aortic valve in hypoplastic left heart syndrome **(Q23.4)**, congenital subaortic stenosis **(Q24.4)**, and supravalvular aortic stenosis **(Q25.3)**.

Certain conditions of the circulatory system are not included in this block. Congenital retinal aneurysm is reported with code **Q14.1**. A ruptured cerebral arteriovenous malformation is reported with code **I60.8**. A ruptured malformation of precerebral vessels is reported with code **I72.0**.

Congenital Malformations of the Respiratory System

Codes in category **Q30** are used to report congenital malformations of the nose but exclude congenital deviation of the nasal septum **(Q67.4)**.

Category **Q31** includes codes for malformations of the larynx. An excludes 1 note directs to code **P28.89** for congenital laryngeal stridor.

Codes for malformations of the trachea and bronchus are found in category **Q32** with the exception of congenital bronchiectasis **(Q33.4)**, which is included in category **Q33** for malformations of the lung. Category **Q33** does not include cystic fibrosis **(E84.0)** or cystic lung disease, acquired or unspecified **(J98.4)**. Code **Q33.6** is used to report congenital hypoplasia and dysplasia of the lung but does not include pulmonary hypoplasia associated with short gestation **(P28.0)**. Congenital central alveolar hypoventilation syndrome is reported with code **G47.35**.

Cleft Lip and Cleft Palate

Categories **Q35-Q37** include codes for cleft palate and cleft lip. When reporting codes in these categories, use an additional code to identify any associated malformation of the nose **(Q30.2)**. These categories do not include Robin syndrome **(Q87.0)**. Codes for cleft palate specify cleft hard palate **(Q35.1)**, cleft soft palate **(Q35.2)**, cleft hard and soft palates **(Q35.5)**, and cleft uvula **(Q35.7)**. Cleft palate with cleft lip is reported with codes in category **Q37**. Codes in this category specify cleft hard, soft, or hard and soft palates with unilateral or bilateral cleft lip. Other malformations of the palate, such as congenital absence of the uvula and high-arched palate, are reported with code **Q38.5**.

Cleft lip without cleft palate is reported with codes in category **Q36** with codes for bilateral **(Q36.0)**, median **(Q36.1)**, and unilateral **(Q36.9)**. Other congenital malformations of the lips are reported with code **Q38.0**.

Other Congenital Malformations of the Digestive System

Codes in categories **Q38-Q45** are used to report congenital malformations of the digestive system that are not elsewhere classified. Dentofacial anomalies are classified in category **M26**.

Congenital hiatal hernia **(Q40.1)** does not include congenital diaphragmatic hernia **(Q79.0)**. Category **Q41** includes codes for reporting congenital obstruction, occlusion, or stricture of the small intestine or intestine not otherwise specified. This does not include meconium ileus without cystic fibrosis **(P76.0)** or cystic fibrosis with intestinal manifestation **(E84.11)**. Other congenital malformations of the intestines are reported in categories **Q42** (large intestine) and **Q43**, which includes Meckel diverticulum **(Q43.0)** and Hirschsprung disease **(Q43.1)**.

Congenital malformations of the pancreas are included in codes in category **Q45**. Congenital diabetes mellitus **(E10.-)**, cystic fibrosis **(E84.-)**, and neonatal diabetes mellitus **(P70.2)** are not included here.

Congenital Malformations of Genital Organs

Categories **Q50-Q56** include codes for malformations of the genital organs. An excludes 1 note directs to codes in subcategory **E34.5** for reporting androgen insensitivity syndrome and to codes **Q90-Q99** for syndromes associated with anomalies in the number and form of chromosomes. For example, congenital absence of unilateral or bilateral ovaries **(Q50.01-Q50.02)** would not be reported when reporting Turner syndrome **(Q96.-)**.

Doubling of the uterus is reported with codes in subcategories **Q51.1-Q51.2**. Doubling of the uterus with doubling of the cervix and vagina without obstruction is reported with code **Q51.10**. The same condition with obstruction is reported with code **Q51.11**. Other doubling of the uterus is reported with code **Q51.2**. Cervical duplication without doubling of the uterus and vagina is reported with code **Q51.820**. Doubling of the vagina without doubling of the uterus and cervix is reported with code **Q52.10**.

Hypospadias is reported with codes in category **Q54**. For epispadias, see code **Q64.0**. Hypospadias codes specify balanic **(Q54.0)**, penile **(Q54.1)**, penoscrotal **(Q54.2)**, perineal **(Q54.3)**, or other hypospadias **(Q54.8)**. Congenital chordee without hypospadias is reported with code **Q54.4**. Lateral curvature of the penis is reported with code **Q55.61**.

A code first note directs to report any associated cystic fibrosis **(E84.-)** first when reporting atresia of the vas deferens **(Q55.3)**.

Codes in category **Q56** include indeterminate sex and pseudohermaphroditism. True hermaphrodite and pseudohermaphrodite with specified chromosomal anomaly are reported with codes in categories **Q96-Q99**.

Congenital Malformations of the Urinary System

The block of codes **Q60-Q64** includes codes for renal agenesis and reduction defects of the kidneys **(Q60.-)**, cystic kidney disease **(Q61.-)**, congenital obstructive defects of the renal pelvis and malformation of the ureter **(Q62.-)**, congenital malformations of the kidney **(Q63.-)**, and other congenital malformations of the urinary system **(Q64.-)**. Congenital nephrotic syndrome **(N04.-)** is not included here.

Potter syndrome is reported with code **Q60.6**. Congenital renal cysts are reported with **Q61.01** for a single renal cyst, **Q61.02** for multiple renal cysts, and **Q61.00** for unspecified renal cyst. Infantile type polycystic kidney is reported with code **Q61.11** when reporting cystic dilatation of collecting ducts and **Q61.29** when reporting other infantile polycystic kidney. Renal dysplasia is reported with code **Q61.4**.

Subcategory **Q64.7** includes code **Q64.70** for unspecified malformation of the bladder and urethra, but this does not include congenital prolapse of the bladder **(Q79.4)**.

Congenital Malformations and Deformations of the Musculoskeletal System

Codes in categories **Q65-Q79** include codes for congenital malformations and deformations of the musculoskeletal system, with some codes specifying laterality or bilateral conditions where applicable. Laterality is not specified for all conditions that might be unilateral or bilateral.

In category **Q65,** codes for congenital deformities of the hip include dislocation **(Q65.0-Q65.2)** and partial dislocation **(Q65.3-Q65.5)**. Also included in this category are congenital unstable hip **(Q65.6)**, congenital coxa valga **(Q65.81),** and congenital coxa vara **(Q65.82)**. Not included here is clicking hip **(R29.4)**.

Category **Q67** includes congenital malformations of the head, face, spine, and chest. This includes code **Q67.4** (other congenital deformities of the skull, face, and jaw), which includes congenital depressions in the skull, congenital hemifacial atrophy or hypertrophy, congenital deviation of the nasal septum, and congenital squashed or bent nose. Code **Q67.5** (congenital deformity of the spine) includes postural scoliosis but does not include infantile idiopathic scoliosis **(M41.0)** or scoliosis due to congenital bony malformation **(Q76.3)**.

Category **Q76** includes codes for congenital malformations of the spine and bony thorax. Spina bifida occulta **(Q76.0),** Klippel-Feil syndrome **(Q76.1),** and congenital spondylolisthesis **(Q76.2)** are included here. Also included in this category are codes for congenital kyphosis and lordosis with codes specifying the spinal region affected.

Category **Q71** (reduction defects of upper limb) includes codes for complete absence of the right, left, or bilateral upper limbs; absence of upper arm and forearm with hand present; absence of forearm and hand; absence of hand and finger; longitudinal reduction defect of the radius or ulna; lobster-claw hand; and other congenital reduction defects of the upper limb. Category **Q72** includes similarly structured codes for reduction defects of the lower limb.

> **Terms to Know**
>
> **Osteochondrodysplasia**–a variety of conditions involving abnormal bone and cartilage growth leading to skeletal maldevelopment
>
> **Congenital myotonic chondrodystrophy**–also called Schwartz-Jampel syndrome, genetic disorder characterized by muscle weakness/stiffness, bone dysplasia, joint contractures, and/or growth delays resulting in abnormally short stature
>
> **Mucopolysaccharidosis**–a group of lysosomal storage diseases that includes bone and skeletal abnormalities in addition to other clinical features of varying severities depending on the type of mucopolysaccharidosis

Osteochondrodysplasias are classified to categories **Q77** and **Q78**. Category **Q77** includes osteochondrodysplasias with defects of growth of tubular bones and spine. Category **Q78** includes codes for other osteochondrodysplasias. Mucopolysaccharidosis **(E76-E76.3)** is not included in these categories. Congenital myotonic chondrodystrophy **(G71.13)** is not included here but may be reported in addition to codes in categories **Q77** and **Q78** when applicable. An excludes 1 note in the *ICD-10-CM* 2013 tabular listing for code **Q77.3** directs to code **E71.43** for the reporting of rhizomelic chondrodysplasia punctata. However, this may be an error, as both the alphabetic index and tabular list for rhizomelic chondrodysplasia punctata provide code **E71.540** for this condition.

Category **Q79** includes codes for congenital malformations of the musculoskeletal system not elsewhere classified, including exomphalos **(Q79.2)** and congenital hernia of the bladder **(Q79.51)**. Umbilical hernia **(K42.-)** is not included here.

Other Congenital Malformations

The block of codes **Q80-Q89** includes codes for other congenital malformations of the skin, breast, hair, nails, phakomatoses (neurocutaneous syndromes), due to exogenous causes, and affecting multiple systems. Category **Q89** includes various congenital malformations not included elsewhere.

Category **Q80** includes codes for ichthyosis, with code **Q80.0** used to report ichthyosis vulgaris. Epidermolysis bullosa is reported with codes in category **Q81**. Category **Q82** includes codes for other congenital malformations of skin including hereditary lymphedema **(Q82.0)**, xeroderma pigmentosa **(Q82.1)**, and congenital non-neoplastic nevus **(Q82.5)**.

Category **Q83** includes codes for congenital absence of breast and nipple **(Q83.0)**, accessory breast **(Q83.1)**, absent nipple **(Q83.2)**, and accessory nipple **(Q83.3)**. Category **Q84** includes congenital alopecia **(Q84.0)**, anonychia **(Q84.3)** excluding nail patella syndrome **(Q87.2)**, congenital leukonychia **(Q84.4)**, and enlarged and hypertrophic nails **(Q84.5)**.

Category **Q85** includes neurofibromatosis type 1 **(Q85.01)**, neurofibromatosis type 2 **(Q85.02)**, and schwannomatosis **(Q85.03)**.

Category **Q86** is used to report congenital malformations due to known exogenous cause. Iodine deficiency–related hypothyroidism **(E00-E02)** and non-teratogenic effects of substances transmitted via placenta and breast milk **(P04.-)** may be reported in addition to codes in category **Q86** when applicable. Codes include **Q86.0** (fetal alcohol syndrome), **Q86.1** (fetal hydantoin syndrome), and **Q86.2** (dysmorphism due to warfarin).

Category **Q87** includes codes for malformation syndromes affecting multiple systems. Box 18-1 lists some of the syndromes represented by codes in this category.

Box 18-1. *ICD-10-CM* Malformation Syndromes

Q87.0 Predominantly affecting facial appearance	Q87.1 Predominantly associated with short stature	Q87.2 Predominantly involving limbs	Q87.3 Involving early overgrowth
Acrocephalopolysyndactyly Acrocephalosyndactyly [Apert] Cryptophthalmos syndrome Cyclopia Goldenhar syndrome Moebius syndrome Oro-facial-digital syndrome Robin syndrome Whistling face	Aarskog syndrome Cockayne syndrome De Lange syndrome Dubowitz syndrome Noonan syndrome Prader-Willi syndrome Robinow-Silverman-Smith syndrome Russell-Silver syndrome Seckel syndrome	Holt-Oram syndrome Klippel-Trenaunay-Weber syndrome Nail patella syndrome Rubinstein-Taybi syndrome Sirenomelia syndrome Thrombocytopenia with absent radius [TAR] syndrome VATER syndrome	Beckwith-Wiedemann syndrome Sotos syndrome Weaver syndrome

Other conditions included in category **Q87** are Marfan syndrome with aortic dilation **(Q87.410)**, with other cardiovascular manifestations **(Q87.418)**, with ocular manifestations **(Q87.42)**, and with skeletal manifestations **(Q87.43)**. Alport syndrome is reported with code **Q87.81** and an additional code to identify stage of chronic kidney disease **(N18.1-N18.6)**.

Category **Q89** includes congenital malformations of the adrenal gland **(Q89.1)** but does not include adrenogenital disorders **(E25.-)** or congenital adrenal hyperplasia **(E25.0)**.

Conjoined twins are reported with code **Q89.4**.

Chromosomal Abnormalities, Not Elsewhere Classified

Categories **Q90-Q99** include codes for chromosomal abnormalities not including mitochondrial metabolic disorders **(E88.4-)** that may be additionally reported when applicable. Codes for Down syndrome or trisomy 21 are specified as non-mosaicism or meiotic nondisjunction **(Q90.0)**, mosaicism or mitotic nondisjunction **(Q90.1)**, or translocation **(Q90.2)**. Physical conditions and intellectual disabilities associated with Down syndrome are additionally reported when applicable. Trisomy 18 **(Q91.0-Q91.2)** and trisomy 13 **(Q91.4-Q91.6)** are also classified as non-mosaicism, mosaicism, or translocation. Whole chromosome trisomy is classified as non-mosaicism **(Q92.0)** or mosaicism **(Q92.1)**.

Turner syndrome and other sex chromosome abnormalities are reported with codes in categories **Q96-Q99**.

Code Scenarios

A child is diagnosed with clefts of the hard and soft palates with unilateral cleft lip.

Q37.5 Cleft hard and soft palate with unilateral cleft lip

> From the guidelines: Section IB9—Assign only the combination code when that code fully identifies the diagnostic conditions involved or when the alphabetic index so directs. Multiple coding should not be used when the classification provides a combination code that clearly identifies all of the elements documented in the diagnosis. When the combination code lacks necessary specificity in describing the manifestation or complication, an additional code should be used as a secondary code.

A neonate is diagnosed with aniridic glaucoma.

Q13.1 Absence of iris
H42 Glaucoma in diseases classified elsewhere

> From the guidelines: Section IB7—Code first notes are also under certain codes that are not specifically manifestation codes but may be due to an underlying cause. When there is a code first note and an underlying condition is present, the underlying condition should be sequenced first.

Review What You Have Learned

18.1 An infant is diagnosed with congenial goiter. What diagnosis code is reported?
- A. **Q89.2** Congenital malformations of other endocrine glands
- B. **P00.89** Newborn (suspected to be) affected by other maternal conditions
- C. **P72.0** Neonatal goiter, not elsewhere classified
- D. **E03.0** Congenital hypothyroidism with diffuse goiter
- E. None of the above

18.2 A child is diagnosed with rhizomelic chondrodysplasia punctata. What diagnosis code(s) is reported for this condition?
- A. **Q77.3** Chondrodysplasia punctata
- B. **E71.43** Iatrogenic carnitine deficiency
- C. **E71.540** Rhizomelic chondrodysplasia punctata
- D. **Q78.9** Osteochondrodysplasia, unspecified
- E. None of the above

18.3 All codes for congenital conditions are found in Chapter 17 of the tabular list.
- A. True
- B. False

18.4 A pediatrician is present at a cesarean delivery of a fetus diagnosed with lumbar spina bifida based on ultrasound and alpha-fetoprotein results. On delivery the neonate is evaluated and diagnosed with spina bifida with lumbosacral meningocele without hydrocephalus. What will be the principal diagnosis on this birth record?
- A. **Q07** Lumbar spina bifida without hydrocephalus
- B. **Q05.8** Sacral spina bifida without hydrocephalus
- C. **Q76.0** Spina bifida occulta
- D. **Z38.01** Single liveborn infant, delivered by cesarean
- E. All of the above

18.5 Additional codes to identify physical conditions and degree of intellectual disabilities may be reported with codes for Down syndrome.
- A. True
- B. False

18.6 Unilateral cleft lip status post-reconstruction would be assigned code **Z87.730.**
- A. True
- B. False

≡ CHAPTER 19 ≡

Symptoms, Signs, and Abnormal Clinical and Laboratory Findings Not Elsewhere Classified (R00-R99)

Chapter 18 of the *International Classification of Diseases, Tenth Revision, Clinical Modification (ICD-10-CM)* tabular list includes codes for symptoms, signs, abnormal clinical and laboratory findings, and ill-defined conditions that are not elsewhere classified. Certain signs and symptoms are classified to other chapters of the tabular list based on the likelihood that the sign or symptom is limited to a particular diagnostic category. Most signs, symptoms, and findings in Chapter 18 are those that may be found in multiple conditions.

The tabular list instructs that the conditions and signs or symptoms included in categories **R00-R94** consist of

a) Cases for which no more specific diagnosis can be made even after all the facts bearing on the case have been investigated
b) Signs or symptoms existing at the time of initial encounter that proved to be transient and whose causes could not be determined
c) Provisional diagnosis in a patient who failed to return for further investigation or care
d) Cases referred elsewhere for investigation or treatment before the diagnosis was made
e) Cases in which a more precise diagnosis was not available for any other reason
f) Certain symptoms, for which supplementary information is provided, that represent important problems in medical care in their own right

An excludes 2 note applies to this chapter, identifying conditions not included here but that may be reported in addition to codes in Chapter 18 when indicated. These conditions include abnormal findings on antenatal screening of mother **(O28.-)**, certain conditions originating in the perinatal period **(P04-P96)**, signs and symptoms classified in other body system chapters, and signs and symptoms of breast **(N63,N64.5).**

The blocks in Chapter 18 are

> Symptoms and signs involving the circulatory and respiratory systems **R00-R09**
> Symptoms and signs involving the digestive system and abdomen **R10-R19**
> Symptoms and signs involving the skin and subcutaneous tissue **R20-R23**

Symptoms and signs involving the nervous and musculoskeletal systems **R25-R29**

Symptoms and signs involving the genitourinary system **R30-R39**

Symptoms and signs involving cognition, perception, emotional state and behavior **R40-R46**

Symptoms and signs involving speech and voice **R47-R49**

General symptoms and signs **R50-R69**

Abnormal findings on examination of blood, without diagnosis **R70-R79**

Abnormal findings on examination of urine, without diagnosis **R80-R82**

Abnormal findings on examination of other body fluids, substances and tissues, without diagnosis **R83-R89**

Abnormal findings on diagnostic imaging and in function studies, without diagnosis **R90-R94**

Abnormal tumor markers **R97**

Ill-defined and unknown cause of mortality **R99**

Throughout Chapter 18, there are numerous excludes 1 notes indicating that certain signs, symptoms, or findings are classified elsewhere. Notes instructing to use additional codes and notes providing supplementary information regarding the intended use of a category are also provided.

Example

R03.0 Elevated blood-pressure reading, without diagnosis of hypertension

Note: This category is to be used to record an episode of elevated blood pressure in a patient in whom no formal diagnosis of hypertension has been made, or as an isolated incidental finding.

Signs and symptoms in the perinatal period are often excluded from codes in Chapter 18 as these signs and symptoms are included in Chapter 16 codes **P00-P96.**

> Check it out: This chapter references excludes 1 and excludes 2 notes and other *ICD-10-CM* conventions. To review these conventions, see section IA of the *ICD-10-CM* guidelines.

Guideline Instructions for Signs and Symptoms

The guidelines for reporting signs and symptoms were previously addressed, but review at this point seems appropriate.

- Report codes for signs and symptoms only when a definitive diagnosis has not been established or the signs and symptoms are not commonly associated with the conditions for which the patient was seen.
- Unless otherwise directed by *ICD-10-CM* instructions, signs and symptoms that are common to a condition are not separately reported.
- Signs and symptoms may be reported for conditions noted as impending or threatened when these subterms are not included in the alphabetic listing for the condition. (The subterms impending and threatened are currently applied to coronary

syndrome or myocardial infarction, delirium tremens, spontaneous abortion or miscarriage, labor, and job loss.)
- Certain combination codes identify both a diagnosis and common symptoms. When this is the case, do not separately report the symptom.

    Example: **P38.1**   Omphalitis with mild hemorrhage
    Hemorrhage would not be separately reported because the combination code identifies this.

It is especially important to follow the convention of consulting the alphabetic index first when reporting signs, symptoms, and findings. Though the notes provided in the tabular list for categories and codes offer direction toward codes included elsewhere, these are not exhaustive. For example, subcategory **R09.0** (asphyxia and hypoxemia) has an excludes 1 note indicating that asphyxia due to carbon monoxide, foreign body in the respiratory tract, birth, or that reported in category **T71** (asphyxiation) are not coded here. The note also excludes hypercapnia and hyperventilation. However, the alphabetic index listing for asphyxia also offers other code options, such as **S28.0** (crushed chest) and **T75.1** (unspecified effects of drowning and nonfatal submersion).

> Check it out: To review codes for signs, symptoms, and test results that may be commonly reported in pediatric practice, see Appendix C of this manual. Note the codes for signs and symptoms that do not come from Chapter 18 and those that have a code first note.

Coma

Codes in subcategory **R40.2** are used to identify the coma scale used in conjunction with traumatic brain injury codes, acute cerebrovascular disease, or sequelae of cerebrovascular diseases. Though the codes are primarily for use by trauma registries, they may be used in any setting where this information is collected. Codes in **R40.2** are sequenced after the code for the related diagnoses.

The scale provides codes for each of the 3 categories: eyes open **(R40.21-)**, best verbal response **(R40.22-)**, and best motor response **(R40.23-) with sixth characters specifying the status of each category.** A code from each category should be reported. The coma scale codes are completed with a seventh character indicating when the scale was recorded. These are applied to a code from each of the 3 categories.

    0   unspecified time
    1   in the field [EMT or ambulance]
    2   at arrival to emergency department
    3   at hospital admission
    4   24 hours or more after hospital admission

Codes in subcategory **R40.24** are used to report the Glasgow coma scale total score when individual scores are not documented.

Example

A patient arrives at the emergency department following an accident where his skull was fractured. There was loss of consciousness at the time of injury, but the initial scale by an emergency medical technician (EMT) in the field was documented as total score of 11 **(R40.2421)**. At arrival in the emergency department, nursing staff document each category with eyes open to sound **(R40.2132)**, best verbal response, confused conversation **(R40.2242)**, best motor response, and flexion withdrawal **(R40.2342)**.

The *ICD-10-CM* guidelines specify that the total score is reported only when the individual category scores were not documented. The facility may document the score from the EMT and/or scores captured in the facility. Facilities reporting to a trauma registry should at a minimum report the score at arrival. In this example, the total score from the field and the individual scores at arrival may be reported.

Repeated Falls and History of Falling

Codes **R29.6** (repeated falls) and **Z91.81** (history of falling) may be reported for the same patient encounter but do not have the same meaning. Report code **R29.6** when a patient has recently fallen and the cause of the fall is being investigated. Code **Z91.81** is reported when a patient has fallen in the past and is at risk to fall again.

Functional Quadriplegia

Functional quadriplegia **(R53.2)** is defined in *ICD-10-CM* as the lack of ability to use one's limbs or to ambulate due to extreme debility. It is not associated with neurologic deficit or injury, and code **R53.2** should not be used for neurologic quadriplegia. Documentation must specify functional quadriplegia for code **R53.2** to be assigned.

Systemic Inflammatory Response Syndrome

When systemic inflammatory response syndrome occurs as a result of noninfectious disease processes, such as trauma or malignant neoplasm, and no subsequent infection is documented, codes in category **R65** may be reported after the code for the underlying condition.

Codes in category **R65** are

R65.10	Systemic inflammatory response syndrome (SIRS) of noninfectious origin without acute organ dysfunction
R65.11	Systemic inflammatory response syndrome (SIRS) of noninfectious origin with acute organ dysfunction

When assigning code **R65.11,** additional codes should be assigned to identify the specific acute organ dysfunction, such as acute kidney failure **(N17-).**

Death, Not Otherwise Specified

Code **R99** (ill-defined and unknown cause of mortality) should only be reported when a patient arrives at a health care facility and is pronounced dead on arrival. It does not represent the discharge disposition of death. This code would be reported for crib death or sudden infant death syndrome.

≡ SYMPTOMS, SIGNS, ABNORMAL CLINICAL AND LABORATORY FINDINGS (R00-R99) ≡ 203

Coding Scenarios

A 10-year-old child who has no history of musculoskeletal disorders and is generally healthy is seen for complaints of leg pain at night. Diagnosis is growing pains.

    R29.898 Other symptoms and signs involving the musculoskeletal system

> From the alphabetic index: The code for reporting growing pains can be found under the term "growing pains, children."

A parent brings her 3-year-old to the office with concerns that his speech is still mostly unintelligible. The child follows simple commands and though much of his speech is unclear, verbalizes while playing and interacting socially and has some clear words. Diagnosis is late talker.

    R62.0   Delayed milestone in childhood

> From the tabular list: Signs and symptoms may be reported in cases for which no more specific diagnosis can be made even after all the facts bearing on the case have been investigated.

A newborn's result from HIV-testing is inconclusive.

    R75 Inconclusive laboratory evidence of human immunodeficiency virus (HIV)

> From the guidelines: Section IC1a2e—Patients with inconclusive HIV serology, but no definitive diagnosis or manifestations of the illness, may be assigned code **R75** (inconclusive laboratory evidence of human immunodeficiency virus [HIV]).

A child is seen for complaint of epigastric pain and referred to a pediatric gastrointestinal specialist for evaluation.

    R10.13   Epigastric pain

> From the tabular list: Signs and symptoms may be reported in cases referred elsewhere for investigation or treatment before the diagnosis was made.

Review What You Have Learned

19.1 Codes for joint pain are included in Chapter 18 of the tabular list.
 A. True
 B. False

19.2 A 24-month-old is diagnosed with salmonella bacteremia. What code(s) is reported for this condition?
 A. **R78.81** Bacteremia
 B. **R78.81** Bacteremia
  A02.9 Salmonella infection, unspecified
 C. **A02.1** Salmonella sepsis
 D. **A41.89** Other specified sepsis
 E. All of the above

19.3 Code **R09.01** (asphyxia) is reported for asphyxia due to carbon monoxide poisoning.
 A. True
 B. False

19.4 A 25-day-old child is diagnosed with respiratory arrest. Code **R09.2** is the appropriate code for reporting this condition.
 A. True
 B. False

19.5 A child with asthma is seen for wheezing. Code **R06.2** (wheezing) is not reported in addition to the code specifying the type of asthma.
 A. True
 B. False

19.6 A child undergoing treatment of acute lymphoblastic leukemia is diagnosed with a fever. What diagnosis code(s) is reported?
 A. **R50.9** Fever, unspecified
 B. **C91.00** Acute lymphoblastic leukemia not having achieved remission
  R50.81 Fever presenting with conditions classified elsewhere
 C. **R50.81** Fever presenting with conditions classified elsewhere
  C91.00 Acute lymphoblastic leukemia not having achieved remission
 D. **C91.00** Acute lymphoblastic leukemia not having achieved remission
 E. None of the above

≡ CHAPTER 20 ≡

Injury, Poisoning, and Certain Other Consequences of External Causes (S00-T88)

Chapter 19 of the *International Classification of Diseases, Tenth Revision, Clinical Modification (ICD-10-CM)* tabular list includes codes for injuries, poisoning and adverse effects of medicines and other substances, certain foreign bodies, burns, corrosions, frostbite, and early complications of trauma. Not included in this chapter are codes for birth trauma, obstetrical trauma, and fractures due to osteoporosis **(M80.-)**. The codes in the chapter span **S00-T88**. Codes **S00-S99** include codes for different types of injuries to single body regions starting at the head and progressing to the foot. Codes **T00-T88** specify injuries to unspecified body regions, poisoning, and certain other consequences of external causes.

This chapter has codes for unspecified multiple injuries **(T07)** and burn and corrosion of unspecified body region **(T30-T32).** However, these codes should not be used in an inpatient setting and rarely, if ever, in the outpatient setting. Multiple injuries, burns, or corrosions typically require multiple codes identifying the site of each.

Most codes in this chapter are reported with additional codes to specify the cause of injury. This does not apply to codes in the T section that include the external cause in the code descriptor. Codes **T36-T65** describe poisoning and adverse effects of medicines and non-medicinal substances. These codes do not require additional codes to specify cause of injury. This is also true for certain other codes in the T section.

Example

T71.111	Asphyxiation due to smothering under pillow, accidental
T71.112	Asphyxiation due to smothering under pillow, intentional self-harm
T71.113	Asphyxiation due to smothering under pillow, assault
T71.114	Asphyxiation due to smothering under pillow, undetermined

The codes for asphyxiation due to smothering under a pillow include the cause and intent in the code descriptors. No additional code to identify cause or intent is necessary.

Example

T68 Hypothermia
  Use additional code to identify source of exposure
  Exposure to excessive cold of man-made origin **(W93)**
  Exposure to excessive cold of natural origin **(X31)**

Instructions following code **T68** direct to code **W93** or code **X31** to identify the source of exposure leading to hypothermia.

Certain categories will also instruct to report a code from category **Y92** to identify the place of occurrence, though no other external cause code is needed. For instance, a code from categories **T51-T65** identify the chemical and intent related to a corrosion injury so no other external cause code is needed, but the tabular list instructions at the category of codes describing the body area and degree of corrosion instruct to report the place the event occurred.

In Chapter 21 we will provide more detail on reporting external causes, but some information will be included here because the external cause codes complete the reporting of injuries and other consequences of external causes. It is helpful to become familiar with the external cause codes as they relate to the different types of injury and other consequence codes.

Seventh Characters

Most codes in this chapter also require seventh characters to indicate the type of encounter. For many conditions, these are **A** (initial), **D** (subsequent), or **S** (sequela). The **A, D,** and **S** characters apply to codes for reporting most injuries and burns. When reporting burns, it is permissible to report both a sequela **(S)** of one burn and initial **(A)** or subsequent care **(D)** of another healing burn because burns do not heal at the same rate.

For traumatic fractures, the seventh characters **A, B,** and **C** identify initial encounters while the patient is receiving active treatment. Active treatment is defined as surgical treatment, emergency department encounter, and evaluation and treatment by a new physician. The initial encounter seventh characters also apply when a patient has delayed seeking treatment of a fracture or nonunion.

Subsequent encounters for fractures are those that take place after the patient has completed active treatment of the fracture and is receiving routine care during the recovery or healing phase. Services in these encounters include cast change or removal, removal of external or internal fixation devices, medication adjustment, and follow-up visits.

Certain complications of fractures such as malunion and non-union are also reported with seventh characters. Open fractures in categories **S52, S72,** and **S82** have seventh characters to include the Gustilo classification of the fracture. Table 20-1 provides an overview of the criteria for the classes of open fracture.

Certain subcategories include different seventh characters from what apply to the remainder of the category. It is important to look first at instructions for the subcategory and then refer to the instructions for category to determine what instructions apply for the condition documented.

Table 20-1. Gustilo Classification

Class	Criteria		
I	Low energy, wound less than 1 cm, clean wound, minimal comminution		
II	Wound greater than 1 cm with moderate soft tissue damage, moderate contamination, minimal comminution		
III High energy, velocity, or crushing		IIIA	Adequate soft tissue cover despite laceration or flaps or high-energy trauma
		IIIB	Inadequate soft tissue cover, bony exposure, contamination
		IIIC	Associated with major arterial injury

> Check it out: To further review seventh characters used in coding of fractures, see category **S52** (fracture of forearm). Note that seventh characters **A, B,** and **C** are used to report initial encounters while characters **D-R** identify subsequent encounters by fracture type with routine healing, delayed healing, non-union, or malunion. The character **S** is used to identify sequela. Also see subcategory **S52.01** for an example of seventh characters applied at the subcategory level.

Injuries

Codes in categories **S00-T14** are used to report traumatic injuries. These codes should not be used to report normal, healing surgical wounds or to identify complications of surgical wounds.

A separate code is reported for each injury unless a combination code is provided. Superficial injuries such as abrasions or contusions are not reported when associated with more severe injuries of the same site. The most serious injury as determined by the physician is sequenced first.

Types of superficial injuries included here are abrasions, non-thermal blisters, contusions, external constriction, superficial foreign body, insect bites, and other superficial bites. Categories for open wound include codes for lacerations, puncture wound, and open bite. Strain of a muscle is reported with codes for injury of muscle, fascia, and tendon by site. Sprains are reported with codes for dislocation and sprain of joints and ligaments by site. Codes distinguish between subluxation and dislocations. For dislocation with fracture, the alphabetic index directs to "see Fracture," inferring that the dislocation is not separately reported unless instructions in the tabular list (eg, excludes 2 note) direct to code also a dislocation.

> **Term to Know**
>
> **Subluxation**—incomplete or partial dislocation

Example

    S83.011   Lateral subluxation of right patella
    S83.014   Lateral dislocation of right patella

Category **S06** includes codes for concussion and other intracranial injuries with and without loss of consciousness. Codes for these injuries with loss of consciousness indicate the duration of lost consciousness. Codes for any associated open wound of the head **(S01.-)** or skull fracture **(S09.90)** should be reported in addition to codes in this category.

Minor injuries to peripheral nerves or blood vessels associated with a primary injury are reported in addition to the code for the primary injury. When the primary injury is to the nerves or blood vessels, that injury is sequenced first.

Fracture Care

The principles of multiple coding of injuries should be followed when reporting fractures. Codes for multiple fractures are sequenced according to severity. A fracture not indicated as open or closed should be coded to closed. A fracture not indicated whether displaced or not displaced should be coded to displaced.

Care for complications of surgical treatment during the healing or recovery phase should be coded with the appropriate complication codes, such as those in category **T84** (complications of internal orthopedic prosthetic devices, implants, and grafts).

Codes for fractures of specified sites are found in the following categories and subcategories:

S02	Fracture of skull and facial bones
S12	Fracture of cervical vertebra and other parts of neck
S22	Fracture of rib(s), sternum, and thoracic spine
S32	Fracture of lumbar spine and pelvis
S42	Fracture of shoulder and upper arm
S49.0-	Physeal fracture of upper end of humerus
S49.1-	Physeal fracture of lower end of humerus
S52	Fracture of forearm
S59.0-	Physeal fracture of lower end of ulna
S59.1-	Physeal fracture of upper end of radius
S59.2-	Physeal fracture of lower end of radius
S62	Fracture at wrist and hand level
S72	Fracture of femur
S79.0-	Physeal fracture of upper end of femur
S79.1-	Physeal fracture of lower end of femur
S82	Fracture of lower leg, including ankle
S89.0-	Physeal fracture of upper end of tibia

S89.1-	Physeal fracture of lower end of tibia
S89.2-	Physeal fracture of upper end of fibula
S89.3-	Physeal fracture of lower end of fibula
S92	Fracture of foot and toe, except ankle

Categories **S49, S59, S79,** and **S89** include subcategories of codes for physeal (growth plate) fractures with codes based on 4 levels of the Salter-Harris classification system for physeal fractures. The 4 levels classified are

I) Fracture through the growth plate separating the epiphysis from the diaphysis
II) Fracture through the growth plate and metaphysis or portion of the diaphysis (shaft) without a fracture of the epiphysis
III) Fracture through the growth plate and epiphysis with a complete break through the epiphysis, intra-articular; does not involve the metaphysis
IV) Fracture through the diaphysis (shaft), metaphysis, growth plate, and epiphysis

Example

A child is seen in the office for follow-up of a Salter-Harris type I fracture of the upper end of the humerus of her right arm. Delayed healing is documented (seventh character **G**).

S49.011G Salter-Harris type I physeal fracture of upper end of humerus, right arm

Reporting of sacral fractures is based on classification of the fracture as vertical, transverse, or both. Vertical fractures may be specified as zone I–III and non-displaced, minimally displaced, severely displaced, or unspecified displacement. The zones represent the Denis classification of vertical sacral fractures. The following are brief descriptions of the 3 zones:

V) Sacral alar fracture, lateral to the neural foramina
VI) Sacral foramina fracture not involving spinal canal
VII) Vertical sacral fracture involving the spinal canal

Instructions in the tabular list for subcategory **S32.1** instruct to code vertical fractures to the most medial fracture extension.

Transverse sacral fractures are classified as types 1–4 representing the Roy-Camille and Strange-Vognsen classifications. These classifications indicate the displacement associated with the fracture.

1. Transverse sacral fracture without displacement
2. Transverse sacral fracture with posterior displacement
3. Transverse sacral fracture with anterior displacement
4. Transverse segmental comminution of upper sacrum

When both vertical and transverse sacral fractures are present, codes for each are reported. Any associated pelvic ring fracture would also be reported.

Example

A teenager is involved in an automobile accident incurring injuries including a minimally displaced zone I fracture of the sacrum and a type 1 transverse flexion fracture of the sacrum. (External cause codes are not included here.)

S32.111A   Minimally displaced zone I fracture of sacrum
S32.14XA   Type 1 fracture of sacrum

Any associated spinal cord and spinal nerve injury **(S34-)** would be reported first when reporting fractures of the lumbar spine and pelvis.

Aftercare for fractures is reported with the code for the fracture with the appropriate seventh character. Do not report Z codes from Chapter 21 of the tabular list for aftercare related to fractures.

Care of Burns and Corrosions

ICD-10-CM uses separate codes to distinguish corrosions (ie, chemical burns) from thermal burns due to a heat source, electricity, or radiation. Sunburns are reported with codes in category **L55.** Codes are assigned for each burn site.

Current burns are classified by depth, extent, and agent (external cause X code). Codes indicating source, intent, and place of occurrence should also be reported. Depth is classified as

First degree—erythema
Second degree—blistering
Third degree—full-thickness involvement

Only the highest degree is reported when burns of multiple degrees affect a single site. Burns of the eye and internal organs are classified by site but not by degree. Codes for burns of multiple sites are sequenced with the code for the highest degree of burn reported first. When a patient has both internal and external burns and/or related complications, the circumstances of the admission or encounter determine the sequence of codes reported.

Categories **T31** and **T32** are used to report burns according to the extent of body surface involved. Codes in these categories may be reported when the site of the burn is not documented or when these codes provide additional information regarding burn mortality. The tabular list instructs that codes from categories **T31-T32** are reported in addition to codes in categories **T20-T25** (burns and corrosions of external body surface by site) to identify the extent of body surface involved.

The *ICD-10-CM* guidelines recommend reporting codes from category **T31** in addition to codes for the burn sites when there is documentation of third degree burn involving 20% or more of the body surface. Body surface is calculated using the rule of nines. As shown in the Table 20-2, the percentages may be changed to fit the patient, especially when reporting the extent of burns in children.

Table 20-2. Total Body Surface Area

Body Area	Adult	Child	Infant <10 kg
Head & neck	9%	18%	20%
Anterior trunk	18%	18%	16%
Posterior trunk	18%	18%	16%
Each arm	9%	9%	8%
Each leg	18%	13.5%	16%
Genitalia	1%	1%	1%

A non-healing burn is classified as an acute burn, as is necrosis of burned skin. An infection of a burn site is reported using the code for the site of the burn and an additional code to specify the infection.

Adverse Effects, Poisoning, Underdosing, and Toxic Effects

As previously reviewed in Chapter 1, the table of drugs and chemicals provides a list of codes or subcategories of codes by substance, with columns indicating accidental poisoning, intentional self-harm poisoning, poisoning by assault, undetermined poisoning, adverse effect, and underdosing. This table serves as an index directing to the correct code category or subcategory in the tabular list. Directions in the tabular list, including selection of seventh characters, must be referenced to select the appropriate, complete code.

> **Terms to Know**
>
> **Adverse effect**—effect of a drug that has been correctly prescribed and administered
>
> **Poisoning**—effect a wrong substance prescribed or administered, intentional overdose, interaction of a correctly prescribed and administered drug with a non-prescribed drug or medicinal agent, or the interaction of drugs and alcohol
>
> **Underdosing**—effects of a reduction in the prescribed dosage of a medication
>
> **Toxic effect**—the effect of ingestion or contact with a harmful substance

When reporting a relapse or exacerbation of the condition due to underdosing of a prescribed medication, the medical condition itself should be reported. If intent is known, codes for noncompliance **(Z91.12-, Z91.13-)** or complication of care **(Y63.6-Y63.9)** should be reported.

Adult and Child Abuse, Neglect, and Other Maltreatment

Included in this chapter are 2 categories of codes for reporting confirmed or suspected abuse, neglect, and other maltreatment.

T74 Adult and child abuse, neglect, and other maltreatment, confirmed
T76 Adult and child abuse, neglect, and other maltreatment, suspected

Codes in these categories are completed with seventh characters **A, D,** or **S** to identify the encounter. These codes are sequenced first and followed by codes to identify any associated current injury. For category **T74,** a code to identify the perpetrator **(Y07.-)** and external cause codes from the assault section **(X92-Y08)** should also be reported to identify the cause of injuries.

When suspected child abuse is ruled out during the course of an encounter, codes from category **T76** should not be reported. The following codes are reported instead:

Z04.72 Encounter for examination and observation following alleged child physical abuse, ruled out
Z04.42 Encounter for examination and observation following alleged child rape

Category **Z04** is to be used when a person without a diagnosis is suspected of having an abnormal condition, without signs or symptoms, which requires study, but after examination and observation, is ruled out. This category is also for use for administrative and legal observation status.

Early Complications of Trauma

Certain early complications of trauma are reported with codes in category **T79.** This category does not include complications of surgical and medical care. It does include the following conditions:

> Air embolism (traumatic)
> Fat embolism (traumatic)
> Traumatic secondary and recurrent hemorrhage and seroma
> Traumatic shock
> Traumatic anuria
> Traumatic ischemia of muscle
> Traumatic subcutaneous emphysema
> Traumatic compartment syndrome

Complications of Care

Certain codes for complications of care are also included in Chapter 19. These are found in categories **T80-T88.** Instructions for this block of codes are

- Use additional code for adverse effect, if applicable, to identify drug (**T36-T50** with fifth or sixth character **5**)
- Use additional code(s) to identify the specified condition resulting from the complication
- Use additional code to identify devices involved and details of circumstances (**Y62-Y82**)

The guidelines provide specific directions regarding certain codes in this block for pain due to medical devices and transplant complications. Code **G89.18** or code **G89.28** should be reported in addition to codes for pain due to specified medical devices and transplant complications to identify the acute or chronic pain due to the presence of the device, implant, or graft.

Example

A patient has pain due to an internal fixation device of the left tibia that was placed to repair a fracture due to a fall on the ice. She is seen for a subsequent evaluation.

T84.84XD	Pain due to internal orthopedic prosthetic devices, implants, and grafts
W00.0XXD	Fall on same level due to ice and snow
G89.18	Other acute post-procedural pain

Complications affecting the function of a transplanted organ are reported with a combination of a code from category **T86** describing the complication or rejection of a transplanted organ and a code that identifies the complication. Preexisting conditions or conditions that develop after a transplant are not coded as complications unless they affect the transplanted organ(s).

≡ INJURY, POISONING, OTHER CONSEQUENCES OF EXTERNAL CAUSES (S00-T88) ≡ 213

Chronic kidney disease (CKD) that remains after a transplant because kidney function was not fully restored is not reported with a code in category **T86** unless a transplant complication such as rejection or transplant failure is documented. Assign the appropriate **N18** code for the patient's stage of CKD and code **Z94.0** (kidney transplant status when no other transplant complication is documented). Other conditions affecting the function of a transplanted kidney would be assigned a code from category **T86** in addition to a code describing the complication.

Category **T88** provides codes for complications of surgical and medical care not classified elsewhere. This category includes complications following immunization (eg, rash).

Locating Codes in Chapter 19

When reporting injury, poisoning, and other consequences of external causes, the full alphabetic index, including the external cause of injuries index and the table of drugs and chemicals, should be consulted first and followed with verification of complete codes and code instructions in the tabular list. Coding from the index alone will often result in incomplete codes and other errors.

Example

A patient is seen in an urgent care clinic after he was burned by sulfuric acid when he and a friend attempted to jump-start his car battery in the high school parking lot. The battery exploded sending acid onto his left cheek and the palm of his left hand. He is diagnosed with first degree burns of his left cheek and left hand.

> **Term to Know**
> **Toxic effect**—when a harmful substance is ingested or comes in contact with a person

T54.2X1A Toxic effect of corrosive acids and acid-like substances, accidental (unintentional)
T20.56XA Corrosion of first degree of cheek
T23.552A Corrosion of first degree of left palm
Y92.213 High school as the place of occurrence of the external cause

To locate the correct codes for this scenario

1. Find the term "corrosion" in the alphabetic index and then the subterms "cheek, first degree" and "palm, left, first degree." This directs you to incomplete codes **T20.56** and **T23.552.**
2. In the tabular list entries for these code categories, you will find the instructions to complete these codes with **A, D,** or **S** as seventh characters. You will also find direction to report first a code identifying the chemical and intent **(T51-T65)** and an external cause code to indicate the place.
3. To find the chemical and intent, you must refer to the table of drugs and chemicals. For sulfuric acid, you must choose a code from one of the columns in the table identifying intent. In this case the intent was accidental, and this code is found in

the first column labeled poisoning, accidental, **T54.2X1**. The table does not include the term "toxic effect."

4. Going back to the tabular list, you are directed to complete code **T54.2X1** with an **A, D,** or **S** as the seventh character.
5. Finally, to find the code identifying the place where the accident occurred, you should consult the external cause of injuries index entry for place of occurrence and the subterms "school," "high school," **Y92.213**. There is also a subterm for parking lot, but "place of service school" includes the buildings and grounds.

> **Check it out:** To review use of the table of drugs and chemicals and the external cause of injuries index, follow the directions above to find the codes for this scenario or change some of the details of the scenario and find the codes for that scenario.

Coding Scenarios

A 3-year-old is examined for complaint of nosebleed, which the child reports may be due to a Lego piece she inserted in her nose and couldn't get out. The Lego piece is retrieved. Diagnosis is foreign body left nostril.

    T17.1XXA   Foreign body in nostril

> **From the external cause of injuries index:** The only listings for foreign bodies in this index are those entering through skin. However, there is a listing for "bean in nose" that directs to codes in category **T17**. The index also directs to codes in categories **T17** and **T18** for accidents involving choking on food.

An external fixation is removed from a child's femur following successful treatment of a displaced comminuted fracture of the shaft of her left femur that occurred when she was hit by a car while walking. The fracture was a Gustilo type IIIB due to a large open wound with contamination.

    S72.352F   Displaced comminuted fracture of shaft of left femur
    V03.10XD   Pedestrian on foot injured in collision with car, pickup truck, or van in traffic accident

> **From the guidelines:** Section IC19c1—Fractures are coded using the appropriate seventh character for subsequent care for encounters after the patient has completed active treatment of the fracture and is receiving routine care for the fracture during the healing or recovery phase. Examples of fracture aftercare are cast change or removal, removal of external or internal fixation device, medication adjustment, and follow-up visits following fracture treatment.

A 14-year-old girl was injured when she collided with another girl during a soccer match. She sustained a concussion without loss of consciousness but with posttraumatic amnesia of about 20 minutes' duration. She is reevaluated at her physician's office 6 months later. Her parents note that since the accident, she has had some lack of concentration and irritability. The patient has no physical complaints but admits to periodic difficulty concentrating. Diagnosis is follow-up of concussion without loss of consciousness with late effects of concentration deficit and irritability.

R45.4	Irritability and anger
R41.840	Attention and concentration deficit
S06.0X0S	Concussion without loss of consciousness
W03.XXXS	Other fall on same level due to collision with another person

> From the guidelines: Section IC19a—Seventh character **S** (sequela) is for use for complications or conditions that arise as a direct result of a condition, such as scar formation after a burn. The scars are sequelae of the burn. When using seventh character **S**, it is necessary to use both the injury code that precipitated the sequela and the code for the sequela itself. The **S** is added only to the injury code, not the sequela code.

A child is evaluated after falling from her bike while riding on her home's driveway. The parents are concerned that the child may have a serious injury to her wrist as she tried to catch herself when falling. After examination and x-ray, no fracture or dislocation is found. The child has abrasions on her right hand and right knee. Diagnoses are abrasions to right hand and knee.

S60.511A	Abrasion of right hand
S80.211A	Abrasion, right knee
V18.0XXA	Pedal cycle driver injured in non-collision transport accident in non-traffic accident
Y92.014	Private driveway to single-family (private) house as the place of occurrence of the external cause
Y99.8	Other external cause status (leisure activity)

> From the guidelines: Section 19a—When coding injuries, assign separate codes for each injury unless a combination code is provided, in which case the combination code is assigned.

Review What You Have Learned

20.1 Codes for pathological fracture are included in Chapter 19 of the tabular list.
   A. True
   B. False

20.2 A 24-month-old is diagnosed with second degree burns of her right thumb and first and second fingers. What is the diagnosis code(s) for the initial encounter for the burns (not including cause of injury codes)?
   A. **T23.221A** Burn of second degree of single right finger (nail) except thumb
   T23.211A Burn of second degree of right thumb (nail)
   B. **T23.241** Burn of second degree of multiple right fingers (nail), including thumb
   C. **T23.241A** Burn of second degree of multiple right fingers (nail), including thumb
   D. **X16.XXXA** Contact with hot heating appliances, radiators, and pipes
   E. All of the above

20.3 In what portion of the alphabetic index will you find reference to the code for accidental poisoning by brown recluse spider bite?
   A. External cause of injuries index
   B. Index to diseases and injuries
   C. Table of drugs and chemicals
   D. Tabular list
   E. All of the above

20.4 A minor injury to a peripheral nerve associated with a primary injury is not separately reported.
   A. True
   B. False

20.5 All codes in Chapter 19 include seventh characters.
   A. True
   B. False

20.6 A child has a hypertrophic scar on his nose that was caused by an open fracture of his nose. What diagnosis code(s) is reported?
   A. **L91.0** Hypertrophic scar
   B. **L91.0** Hypertrophic scar
   S02.2XXS Fracture of nasal bones
   C. **S00.31** Abrasion of nose
   D. **S01.20XS** Unspecified open wound of nose
   E. None of the above

≡ CHAPTER 21 ≡

External Causes of Morbidity (V00-Y99)

Chapter 20 of the *International Classification of Diseases, Tenth Revision, Clinical Modification* tabular list includes codes for reporting the external cause of morbidity. These codes are used in conjunction with codes for injuries and health conditions for which an external cause is identified. The codes capture the following information:

- Cause—how the injury or health condition happened
- Intent—accidental or intentional assault or self-harm
- Place of occurrence
- Activity of the patient at the time of the event
- Status of the patient—work activity, military activity, leisure activity, volunteer activity

The place of occurrence, activity, and status codes are reported only at the initial encounter for an event.

Though they are most applicable to injuries, external cause codes may also identify the source of an infection or the activity that may have contributed to a health event (eg, vehicle or type of motion causing motion sickness). Cause and intent codes are reported for each encounter for which the injury or condition is being treated. The seventh characters **A, D,** and **S** are used to indicate whether the encounter is the initial, subsequent, or to address a sequela. The seventh characters are not applicable to codes in categories **Y92** (place of occurrence) and **Y93** (activity), as these are reported only at the initial encounter for treatment.

External cause codes are always secondary to a principal diagnosis for an injury or condition. Multiple external cause codes may be reported when necessary to fully describe each cause.

Example

A patient fell from a bridge and was hit by an ice yacht while walking his dog. (Injuries would be reported first.)

W13.1XXA	Fall from, out of or through bridge
V98.2XXA	Accident to, on, or involving ice yacht
Y93.K1	Activity, walking an animal
Y92.89	Other specified places as the place of occurrence of the external cause

If limited in the number of cause codes that may be reported, report the code for the cause most related to the principal diagnosis. Cause and intent, including medical misadventures, should take precedence over place, activity, and status codes. Certain external cause codes take priority over others.

- External cause codes for child and adult abuse take priority over all other external cause codes.
- External cause codes for terrorism events take priority over all other external cause codes except child and adult abuse.
- External cause codes for cataclysmic events take priority over all other external cause codes except child and adult abuse and terrorism.
- External cause codes for transport accidents take priority over all other external cause codes except cataclysmic events, child and adult abuse, and terrorism.
- Activity and external cause status codes are assigned following all causal (intent) external cause codes.

Adult and child abuse, neglect, and maltreatment are classified as assault. Any code listed under the term "assault" in the external cause of injuries index may be used to report the cause of injury resulting from confirmed abuse. A code from category **Y07** is also reported to indicate the perpetrator of abuse.

Intent

The default for intent is accidental. If it is unknown whether the intent was assault, self-harm, or accident, report a code for accident. Assume accidental intent for all transport accidents. There is a classification of undetermined intent, but these codes are reported only when the documentation indicates that intent cannot be determined at the time of the encounter.

Terrorism is reported with codes in category **Y38**. The tabular list provides a definition of terrorism as defined by the US Federal Bureau of Investigation (FBI).

> "These codes are for use to identify injuries resulting from the unlawful use of force or violence against persons or property to intimidate or coerce a Government, the civilian population, or any segment thereof, in furtherance of political or social objective."

Only cases identified by the FBI as terrorism are reported with codes in category **Y38**. When terrorism is suspected but not confirmed, it is reported as assault. Multiple codes in category **Y38** may be reported when a confirmed act of terrorism is carried out by more than one mechanism. Secondary effects of terrorism are reported with code **Y38.9**. This code is used to report only injuries not due to the initial terrorist event but may be reported in addition to a code from category **Y38** identifying the initial event when injuries due to both the initial event and a subsequent result are treated.

Sequelae of a Previous Injury

Sequelae of an injury are reported with the seventh character **S** on both the cause of injury and injury code. The code for the condition that is a sequela of the injury is not appended with the seventh character **S**. Sequelae are only reported when a condition is documented as a sequela. If a patient encounter is a subsequent visit for follow-up care to assess healing or provide rehabilitation services and no sequela is documented, the encounter should not be reported with seventh character **S**. An external cause code is never appended with **S** for sequela in conjunction with reporting of a code for a current injury.

Place of Occurrence and Activity Codes

Place of occurrence and activity codes are reported at the initial encounter for an injury or other condition due to an external cause. These are always secondary codes reported after the code for the injury or condition and other external cause codes. Certain categories in the tabular list will instruct to report also the place of occurrence when cause and intent are identified by the other codes such as those for poisoning and adverse or toxic effects.

> *Example* **T20.4** Corrosion of unspecified degree of head, face, and neck
> **Code first (T51-T65)** to identify chemical and intent
> **Use additional** external cause code to identify place **(Y92)**

Activity codes in category **Y93** describe the activity of the person at the time of an accident. These codes are not applicable to poisoning, adverse effects, misadventures, or sequela. Activity codes are appropriate if identifying the activity provides additional information about the event. If the activity is not stated, do not assign an activity code. Code **Y93.9** (unspecified activity) is not reported if the activity is not stated.

The external cause of injuries index includes both place of occurrence and activity as main terms. The place of occurrence codes for certain locations are specific to rooms or areas of a building or home. For instance, the term "hospital" is followed by subterms "cafeteria," "corridor," "operating room," "patient bathroom," "patient room," and "specified place in hospital not elsewhere classified." An abandoned house **(Y92.89)** is differentiated from a house under construction **(Y92.61)** and a residence. Residences include both private and institutional settings, including separate categories such as apartment, boarding house, single family house, military base, prison, or nursing facility.

Activity codes include many forms of recreational activities, exercises, and some occupational activities. Activity codes combine with cause codes to identify conditions such as an auto accident that occurred while the driver was using a cellular phone or other electronic equipment **(Y93.C-)**.

External Cause Status

The status code indicates whether an injury or condition due to an external cause occurred during military activity, while a civilian was at work, while volunteering, or at leisure at the time of the causal event. These codes are reported only once at the initial encounter and only one status code is reported for an event. No status code is reported if no external cause code is reported to indicate cause or activity or if the patient's status is not stated. Status codes are not applicable to poisoning, adverse effects, misadventures, or late effects.

> Status of external cause **Y99.9**
> – child assisting in compensated work for family **Y99.8**
> – civilian activity done for financial or other compensation **Y99.0**

- civilian activity done for income or pay **Y99.0**
- family member assisting in compensated work for other family member **Y99.8**
- hobby not done for income **Y99.8**
- leisure activity **Y99.8**
- military activity **Y99.1**
- off-duty activity of military personnel **Y99.8**
- recreation or sport not for income or while a student **Y99.8**
- specified NEC **Y99.8**
- student activity **Y99.8**
- volunteer activity **Y99.2**

Transport Accidents

The V section of Chapter 20 is dedicated to transport accidents by type of vehicle and the patient's position as driver, animal rider, passenger, hanger-on, or boarding and alighting. The tabular list defines a transport accident as one in which the vehicle involved must be moving or running or in use for transport purposes at the time of the accident. If an accident occurs while an agriculture vehicle, automobile, or motor cycle is in stationary use or is undergoing maintenance, the type of related accident is coded. Assault by crashing of a motor vehicle is reported with codes in category **Y03**.

Additional codes are reported for the following when reporting a transport accident:

Airbag injury **(W22.1)**

Type of street or road **(Y92.4-)**

Use of cellular telephone and other electronic equipment at the time of the transport accident **(Y93.C-)**

Codes in categories **X34-X38** may be reported in addition to codes for transport accident when the accident occurs due to a cataclysm.

There are 12 blocks in the V section, with the first 2 characters in each code identifying the type of vehicle of which the patient was an occupant or that the patient was a pedestrian at the time of the accident.

V00-V09	Pedestrian injured in transport accident
V10-V19	Pedal cycle rider injured in transport accident
V20-V29	Motorcycle rider injured in transport accident
V30-V39	Occupant of 3-wheeled motor vehicle injured in transport accident
V40-V49	Car occupant injured in transport accident
V50-V59	Occupant of pickup truck or van injured in transport accident
V60-V69	Occupant of heavy transport vehicle injured in transport accident
V70-V79	Bus occupant injured in transport accident
V80-V89	Other land transport accidents
V90-V94	Water transport accidents
V95-V97	Air and space transport accidents
V98-V99	Other and unspecified transport accidents

Introductory text to the block of codes **V00-V99** provides 26 definitions of terms used in this block. These define traffic and non-traffic accidents, types of vehicles, and drivers or riders. Knowledge of these definitions is helpful to code selection.

> Check it out: To further review the definitions used in describing transport accidents, find the list of definitions at the beginning of the block of codes **V00-V99** and then find the terms used to describe a tricycle, a passenger in a sidecar of a motorcycle, and a minivan or SUV.

When using the external cause of injuries index to locate a code describing a patient injured in a transport accident, the subterm "transport" below the main term "accident" is followed by further subterms describing types of transport vehicles and occupants. If unsure of the terminology for a vehicle, the references under the subterm "occupant" are helpful. For instance, if you are seeking the code for a person injured in a transport accident while in a tractor, you could follow the subterms under accident, transport, and occupant to the subterm tractor, where you will be directed to see "accident, transport, agricultural vehicle occupant." At the listing for "accident, transport, agricultural vehicle occupant," you will find first "non-traffic driver," "hanger-on," and "passenger" references followed by "traffic," "driver," "hanger-on," and "passenger" and finally while "boarding or alighting."

The listing of subterms under the term "accident" is extensive and requires careful attention to the dashes that connect subterms. The following excerpt from the external cause of injuries index shows the path from the subterm "transport" (under the main term "accident") to the reference for driver of a tractor in a traffic accident.

- **transport** (involving injury to) **V99**
-- 18 wheeler—see Accident, transport, truck occupant
-- **agricultural vehicle occupant (non-traffic) V84.9**
--- driver **V84.5**
--- hanger-on **V84.7**
--- passenger **V84.6**
--- **traffic V84.3**
---- **driver V84.0**
---- hanger-on **V84.2**
---- passenger **V84.1**
--- while boarding or alighting **V84.4**

Once a reference is found in the external cause of injuries index, the tabular list for the code (in this case, **V84.0**) will provide further information regarding the inclusions and exclusions for the code category, and appropriate seventh characters.

Other External Causes of Injury

The block of codes **W00-X58** includes codes for certain non-transport accidents not associated with intentional self-harm, assault or undetermined intent, legal or military operations, terrorism, or medical care. Terms related to this category include bite or bitten by, bumping, butted by animal, caught, collision, constriction, contact (as in contact with a sharp object), crushed, discharge, diving, dropped, drowning, exposure, explosion, fall, forces of nature, foreign body entering through skin, ignition, inhalation, jumping from or into, kicking against, malfunction, powder burn, pushed, scratch, slipping, stepping on, striking against or struck by, stumbling, tackle, and tripping. Familiarity with the terms used in the index is helpful when seeking codes for cause of injury.

Locating the term for the cause of an injury requires definition of the factor most responsible for an injury and modifying factors. For instance, a person incurs a fractured ankle and head laceration when they slip and fall striking their head on a table. The underlying cause of both injuries was the fall due to slipping modified by striking against the table. Under the term "fall" in the external causes of injury index are the subterms "slipping" and "with subsequent striking against an object," which refers to code **W01.10**. In the tabular list, a review of codes in subcategory **W01.1** will lead to code **W01.190** (fall on same level from slipping, tripping, and stumbling with subsequent striking against furniture). This combination code includes all of the elements of the cause of injury: slipping, falling, and striking against furniture.

> **Check it out:** To further review the classification of external causes of injury, search the external cause of injury index for the entry describing a minor laceration to the skin caused by the edge of a piece of paper. (Hint: Skin is cut when it comes in contact with the paper, which is a foreign body.) For an extra challenge, find the entry for struck by a duck.

Categories **W32-W34** include codes for accidental discharge of handguns, rifles, shotguns, and larger firearms, and gas, air, or spring-operated guns. Also included here are injuries related to malfunctions such as explosion of a firearm, injury by a slide trigger mechanism, injury due to recoil, and powder burn. Accidents involving BB guns, pellet guns, and paintball guns are classified in category **W34**.

Code **X58** (exposure to other factors) includes numerous accidents and exposures not classified elsewhere, such as dehydration from lack of water, deprivation, desertion, infanticidal intent, poisoned by a thorn or plant, mental cruelty, and starvation.

Self-harm and Assault

Categories **X71-X83** are used to report purposely self-inflicted injuries and suicide attempts (so documented). If documentation is not clear regarding intent to self-inflict, unintentional or accidental is assumed. Codes are categorized according to cause, such as drowning or running before a moving motor vehicle.

Types of assault are classified in categories **X92-Y04** and **Y08**. Category **Y07** includes codes for identifying the perpetrator of assault, maltreatment, and neglect. Codes in this category are used only in cases of confirmed abuse **(T74.-)**. The code selection is based on the relationship between the perpetrator and victim. The relationships include spouse or partner, biological or adoptive parent, sibling, foster parent, stepparent, step-sibling, cousin, other family member, daycare provider, health care provider, teacher or instructor, and other nonfamily member perpetrator of maltreatment and neglect.

Categories **Y21-Y33** are used to report causes of injury that are documented as undetermined intent. These codes are reported only when there is documentation that intent is not yet determined, as in cases where an external agency will investigate suspected abuse or neglect.

Legal Intervention, Operations of War, Military Operations, and Terrorism

Codes in category **Y35** (legal intervention) apply to injuries sustained during an encounter with law enforcement officers (on duty or off) serving in any capacity and include injuries to the law enforcement officers, suspects, and bystanders.

Operations of war, including injuries to military personnel and civilians caused by war, civil insurrection, and peacekeeping missions, are classified to category **Y36.** Codes specify the type of action and whether the injured patient is military personnel or civilian. Injuries occurring in military peacetime operations are classified to category **Y37.**

Transport accidents involving military vehicles during peacetime are reported with the codes for transport accidents in categories **V09-V79.**

Medical and Surgical Misadventures

Codes in categories **Y62-Y69** are used to report causes of events due to failure, misadministration, and other misadventures during medical and surgical care. Accidental overdose of a drug or wrong drug given in error are not included here. Codes in categories **T36-T50** are used to specify those events.

Adverse events associated with medical devices are classified in categories **Y70-Y82** with codes categorized by the type of device (eg, anesthesiology devices or neurologic devices). Included here are breakdowns or malfunction of medical devices.

Abnormal reactions and complications of medical procedures that develop without mention of misadventure at the time of the procedure are reported with codes in categories **Y83-Y84.** Codes in these categories identify the type of medical procedure associated with the abnormal reaction or complication.

Supplementary Factors

Included in this section of Chapter 20 are codes for supplementary information, such as the **Y92** (place of occurrence) and **Y93** (activity) codes. Also included here are codes in category **Y90** that identify the blood alcohol level of a patient and may be coded in addition to codes identifying alcohol-related disorders **(F10).** The codes in category **Y90** identify the blood alcohol level in milligrams per 100 mL.

Code **Y95** is used to report nosocomial condition.

This chapter ends with the **Y99** (external cause) status codes to identify the status of the person at the time of an event.

Coding Scenarios

A child is examined for a new complaint of superficial wounds on her lower legs that she received while feeding the chickens in the chicken coup at her uncle's farm.

S80.811A Abrasion, right lower leg
S80.812A Abrasion, left lower leg
W61.33XA Pecked by chicken
Y92.72 Chicken coop as the place of occurrence of the external cause
Y93.K9 Activity, other involving animal care
Y99.8 Other external cause status

> From the guidelines: Section IC20a2—Assign the external cause code with the appropriate seventh character (initial encounter, subsequent encounter, or sequela) for each encounter for which the injury or condition is being treated.

A teenager who was the passenger on a bus filled with people being evacuated from a city during a hurricane was injured when high winds and heavy rain caused the bus to hit a guardrail on the highway. She is seen in follow-up for a diagnosis of whiplash.

S13.4XXD Sprain of ligaments of cervical spine, subsequent encounter
X37.0XXD Hurricane
V77.6XXD Passenger on bus injured in collision with fixed or stationary object in traffic accident
Y92.411 Interstate highway as the place of occurrence of the external cause

> From the guidelines: Section IC20a4—Assign as many external cause codes as necessary to fully explain each cause. If only one external code can be recorded, assign the code most related to the principal diagnosis.
> Section IC20f—External cause codes for cataclysmic events take priority over all other external cause codes except child and adult abuse and terrorism.

An 8-month-old boy is treated in the emergency department for fractured ribs. The mother states that the infant was crying when she picked him up from child care, and she found bruises on the child after she got home. Abuse is suspected and, after further interview, the mother admits her boyfriend shook the child. The diagnosis is fractures of multiple ribs bilateral due to child abuse by mother's partner.

T74.12XA Child physical abuse, confirmed
S22.43XA Multiple fractures of ribs, bilateral
Y04.8XXA Assault by other bodily force
Y07.432 Male friend of parent (co-residing in household), perpetrator of maltreatment and neglect

> From the guidelines: Section IC19f—For cases of confirmed abuse or neglect, an external cause code from the assault section **(X92-Y08)** should be added to identify the cause of any physical injuries. A perpetrator code **(Y07)** should be added when the perpetrator of the abuse is known. For suspected cases of abuse or neglect, do not report an external cause or perpetrator code.

Review What You Have Learned

21.1 External cause codes are reported only with codes from categories **S00-T88.**
   A. True
   B. False

21.2 What external cause code(s) is reported to identify the cause of injuries incurred by a child who rode his tricycle off the front porch of his house (subsequent visit)? (External cause codes only.)
   A. **V19.3XXA** Pedal cyclist (driver) (passenger) injured in unspecified non-traffic accident
   Y93.59XA Activity, other involving other sports and athletics played individually
   B. **V19.88XD** Pedal cyclist (driver) (passenger) injured in other specified transport accidents
   C. **V18.0XXD** Pedal cycle driver injured in non-collision transport accident in non-traffic accident
   D. All of the above
   E. None of the above

21.3 In what portion of the alphabetic index will you find reference to the code for reporting a nosocomial condition?
   A. External cause of injuries index
   B. Index to diseases and injuries
   C. Table of drugs and chemicals
   D. Tabular list
   E. All of the above

21.4 An injury that is caused by an accident on roller skates is classified as a pedestrian accident.
   A. True
   B. False

21.5 Any of the assault codes may be used to indicate the external cause of any injury resulting from suspected abuse.
   A. True
   B. False

21.6 A child is injured by debris in a tornado. Which external cause code(s) is reported first at the initial encounter?
   A. **X58.XXXA** Exposure to other specified factors
   B. **X37.1XXA** Tornado
   C. **T07** Unspecified multiple injuries
   D. **Y92.018** Other place in single-family (private) house as the place of occurrence of the external cause
   E. None of the above

≡ CHAPTER 22 ≡

Factors Influencing Health Status and Contact With Health Services (Z00-Z99)

Chapter 21 of *International Classification of Diseases, Tenth Revision, Clinical Modification (ICD-10-CM)* tabular list includes codes for reporting reasons for specified encounters and services, and factors that influence health status but are not a current condition or disease. These are the Z codes that have been mentioned in many previous chapters because these codes often provide supplemental information that helps identify the complexity of a patient's status or the need for services, such as preventive care or screening. The 14 blocks in this chapter include a variety of reasons for seeking health care and circumstances or problems that influence a person's health status. The blocks are

- Persons encountering health services for examinations **Z00-Z13**
- Genetic carrier and genetic susceptibility to disease **Z14-Z15**
- Resistance to antimicrobial drugs **Z16**
- Estrogen receptor status **Z17**
- Retained foreign body fragments **Z18**
- Persons with potential health hazards related to communicable diseases **Z20-Z28**
- Persons encountering health services in circumstances related to reproduction **Z30-Z39**
- Encounters for other specific health care **Z40-Z53**
- Persons with potential health hazards related to socioeconomic and psychosocial circumstances **Z55-Z65**
- Do not resuscitate status **Z66**
- Blood type **Z67**
- Body mass index (BMI) **Z68**
- Persons encountering health services in other circumstances **Z69-Z76**
- Persons with potential health hazards related to family and personal history and certain conditions influencing health status **Z77-Z99**

Z codes represent reasons for encounters and services but are not procedures. Procedure codes must be reported in conjunction with Z codes to prescribe the service rendered (eg, laboratory test to screen for lead). Z codes may be either the first-listed (principal for inpatient encounters and services) or secondary codes for an encounter depending on the circumstances, with the exception of certain Z codes that must always be the first-listed code.

The following are Z codes that may only be principal or first-listed diagnosis:

Z00	Encounter for general examination without complaint, suspected or reported diagnosis
Z01	Encounter for other special examination without complaint, suspected or reported diagnosis
Z02	Encounter for administrative examination
Z03	Encounter for medical observation for suspected diseases and conditions ruled out
Z04	Encounter for examination and observation for other reasons
Z33.2	Encounter for elective termination of pregnancy
Z31.81	Encounter for male factor infertility in female patient
Z31.82	Encounter for Rh incompatibility status
Z31.83	Encounter for assisted reproductive fertility procedure cycle
Z31.84	Encounter for fertility preservation procedure
Z34	Encounter for supervision of normal pregnancy
Z39	Encounter for maternal postpartum care and examination
Z38	Liveborn infants according to place of birth and type of delivery
Z42	Encounter for plastic and reconstructive surgery following medical procedure or healed injury
Z51.0	Encounter for antineoplastic radiation therapy
Z51.1-	Encounter for antineoplastic chemotherapy and immunotherapy
Z52	Donors of organs and tissues

Except: Z52.9 Donor of unspecified organ or tissue

Z76.1	Encounter for health supervision and care of foundling
Z76.2	Encounter for health supervision and care of other healthy infant and child
Z99.12	Encounter for respirator [ventilator] dependence during power failure

Health Services for Examinations

The first codes in Chapter 21 are those in category **Z00** used to report encounters for general examination without complaint or suspected or reported diagnosis. These codes are not used to report suspected conditions or encounters for treatment purposes. However, abnormal findings during the course of a routine health examination and preexisting and chronic conditions that are not the focus of the health examination may be reported in addition to codes in category **Z00**. This category does not include encounters solely for administrative purposes, such as school or sports physicals **(Z02.-)** and recruitment to armed forces **(Z02.3)**.

Codes for newborn health examinations are based on the newborn's age as follows:

Z00.110	Health examination for newborn under 8 days old
Z00.111	Health examination for newborn 8 to 28 days old

These codes are not reported for newborn observation for a suspected condition that is ruled out **(P00-P04)**.

Health examinations of children 29 days and older are reported with codes in subcategory **Z00.12** based on findings of the encounter.

Z00.121 Encounter for routine child health examination with abnormal findings

Use additional code to identify abnormal findings

Z00.129 Encounter for routine child health examination without abnormal findings

Code **Z00.121** is reported with additional codes describing abnormal findings, which include codes for abnormal laboratory, imaging, or other test results in categories **R70-R94**. Code **Z00.129** may be reported for examinations without abnormal findings and those for which test results are not back at the time of coding.

Related codes for specific health examinations include

Z00.2 Encounter for examination for period of rapid growth in childhood
Z00.3 Encounter for examination for adolescent development state
Z00.70 Encounter for examination for period of delayed growth in childhood without abnormal findings
Z00.71 Encounter for examination for period of delayed growth in childhood with abnormal findings

Use additional code to identify abnormal findings

Encounters for routine health examinations of specific systems, such as the eyes and ears, are reported with codes in category **Z01**. Routine gynecological examinations are reported with code **Z01.411** when abnormalities are documented and **Z01.419** when no abnormalities are documented. Additional codes may be assigned for abnormalities found, screening for human papillomavirus **(Z11.51)**, and screening vaginal Pap smear **(Z12.72)** when applicable. Screening for malignant neoplasm of the cervix (Pap smear) is not separately reported when reporting a general gynecological examination. This category also includes codes for pre-procedural examinations **(Z01.81-)**, allergy testing **(Z01.82)**, blood typing **(Z01.83)**, and antibody response and immunity status examination **(Z01.84)**.

Category **Z02** includes codes for encounters for administrative purposes that include not only school, sports, and armed services recruitment examinations, but also encounters for blood alcohol and blood drug test **(Z02.83** and code for findings when applicable). Code **Z02.89** (encounter for other administrative examinations) includes examinations for camp and immigration and naturalization.

An encounter for a child other than a newborn who is without symptoms or diagnosis but is suspected to have a condition that is ruled out after examination and observation is reported with codes in category **Z03**. This category includes an encounter for observation for suspected poisoning with no finding of poisoning **(Z03.6)**. It does not include encounters related to contact with and exposure to health hazards **(Z77.-)**.

Category **Z04** is used to report encounters that may combine examination and observation for a suspected condition and examination for administrative and legal observation status. Included here are codes for an encounter for examination and observation following a transport accident **(Z04.1)**, encounter for examination and observation following alleged child rape, ruled out **(Z04.42)**, encounter for psychiatric examination, requested by authority **(Z04.6)**, and an encounter for examination and observation following alleged child physical abuse, rule out **(Z04.72)**.

Medical surveillance following completed treatment is reported with codes in categories **Z08** and **Z09**. These codes are not used to report aftercare following medical care **(Z43-Z49, Z51)**, surveillance of contraception **(Z30.4-)**, or surveillance of prosthetic and other medical devices **(Z44-Z46)**. Codes for medical surveillance are classified to that after completed treatment for malignant neoplasm and that after completed treatment for conditions other than malignant neoplasm.

> **Z08** Encounter for follow-up examination after completed treatment for malignant neoplasm
> **Use additional code** to identify any acquired absence of organs **(Z90.-)**
> **Use additional code** to identify the personal history of malignant neoplasm **(Z85.-)**
> **Z09** Encounter for follow-up examination after completed treatment for conditions other than malignant neoplasm
> **Use additional code** to identify any applicable history of disease code **(Z86.-. Z87.-)**

Screening for infectious and parasitic disease or disease precursors in asymptomatic individuals is reported with codes in category **Z11**.

> **Z11.0**   Encounter for screening for intestinal infectious diseases
> **Z11.1**   Encounter for screening for respiratory tuberculosis
> **Z11.2**   Encounter for screening for other bacterial diseases
> **Z11.3**   Encounter for screening for infections with a predominantly sexual mode of transmission
> **Z11.4**   Encounter for screening for human immunodeficiency virus [HIV]
> **Z11.51**   Encounter for screening for human papillomavirus (HPV)
> **Z11.59**   Encounter for screening for other viral diseases

Code **Z11.8** (encounter for screening for other infectious and parasitic diseases) includes screening for chlamydia, rickettsial, spirochetal, and mycoses.

Screening for malignant neoplasm in asymptomatic patients is reported with codes in category **Z12** based on the site of potential malignancy (eg, cervix). Use an additional code to identify any family history of malignant neoplasm **(Z80.-)** when reporting screening. Code **Z12.4** is used to report screening for malignant neoplasm of the cervix except when screening is part of a general gynecological examination **(Z01.4)**.

Screening for other diseases and disorders in asymptomatic individuals is reported with codes in category **Z13**. This includes screening for the following conditions:

> **Z13.0**   Encounter for screening for diseases of the blood and blood-forming organs and certain disorders involving the immune mechanism
> **Z13.1**   Encounter for screening for diabetes mellitus
> **Z13.220**   Encounter for screening for lipoid disorders
> **Z13.228**   Encounter for screening for other metabolic disorders
> **Z13.29**   Encounter for screening for other suspected endocrine disorder
> **Z13.4**   Encounter for screening for certain developmental disorders in childhood

Z13.5	Encounter for screening for eye and ear disorders
Z13.6	Encounter for screening for cardiovascular disorders
Z13.71	Encounter for non-procreative screening for genetic disease carrier status
Z13.79	Encounter for other screening for genetic and chromosomal anomalies
Z13.810	Encounter for screening for upper gastrointestinal disorder
Z13.811	Encounter for screening for lower gastrointestinal disorder
Z13.818	Encounter for screening for other digestive system disorders
Z13.820	Encounter for screening for osteoporosis
Z13.828	Encounter for screening for other musculoskeletal disorder
Z13.83	Encounter for screening for respiratory disorder NEC
Z13.84	Encounter for screening for dental disorder
Z13.850	Encounter for screening for traumatic brain injury
Z13.858	Encounter for screening for other nervous system disorders
Z13.88	Encounter for screening for disorder due to exposure to contaminants
Z13.89	Encounter for screening for other disorder

Note the excludes 1 notes within this category, like that one following code **Z13.4** that excludes reporting of routine developmental testing of an infant or child **(Z00.1-)** in conjunction with code **Z13.4.**

Retained Foreign Body Fragments

Codes in category **Z18** identify different substances that are retained fragments of foreign bodies. These codes may be reported in addition to codes identifying conditions such as toxic effects **(T51-T65),** injuries, and foreign body granuloma **(M60.2-).** Codes in category **Z18** are not used to report artificial joint status **(Z96.6)** or other organ or tissue replaced by artificial means or transplant, foreign body accidentally left during a procedure **(T81.5-),** foreign body entering through orifice **(T15-T19),** superficial foreign body, or personal history of retained foreign body fully removed **(Z87.821).**

Potential Hazards Related to Communicable Diseases

Codes in category **Z20** are used to report contact with and suspected exposure to communicable disease. It does not include contact with and suspected exposure to health hazards **(Z77).** Codes specify contact with and suspected exposure to disease such as HIV, meningococcus, and varicella. This does not include asymptomatic HIV infection status **(Z21).**

Category **Z22** includes codes for carrier or suspected carrier status for specified diseases. These conditions may be documented as colonization.

> From the guidelines: Section IC21c3—Status codes indicate that a patient is either a carrier of a disease or has the sequelae or residual of a past disease or condition. This includes such things as the presence of prosthetic or mechanical devices resulting from past treatment. A status code is informative because the status may affect the course of treatment and its outcome. A status code is distinct from a history code. The history code indicates that the patient no longer has the condition.

An encounter for immunization is simplified in *ICD-10-CM* with only one code **(Z23)** used to identify an encounter for immunization. This recognized that individual diagnosis codes specifying the type of prophylactic immunization needed are unnecessary, as procedure codes provide that information. This code may be reported in addition to codes for routine child health examination when applicable.

Codes in category **Z28** are used to report underimmunization status and vaccination not carried out. Codes specify the reason a vaccination was not carried out, such as vaccination not carried out due to acute or chronic illness, immune compromised state, allergy, religious belief, and caregiver refusal **(Z28.82)**. Code **Z28.3** is used to report delinquent immunization status or lapsed immunization schedule.

Visits Related to Birth

The first code reported as a principal diagnosis on a newborn's birth record should be from category **Z38**. These codes were previously reviewed in Chapter 17. Codes specify birth in a facility or outside, single or multiple births, and delivery method. Visits with expectant parents including pre-adoption visits are reported with code **Z76.81** (expectant parent[s] pre-birth pediatrician visit). An encounter for care and examination of a lactating mother is reported with code **Z39.1** when no disorder of lactation is diagnosed **(O92.-)**.

Encounters for Attention and Aftercare

Codes in category **Z42** are used to report plastic and reconstructive surgery following a medical procedure or healed injury. Code **Z42.8** is reported for an encounter for plastic and reconstructive surgery following a medical procedure or injury other than a mastectomy **(Z42.1)**.

> From the guidelines: Section IC21a7—Aftercare visit codes cover situations when the initial treatment of a disease has been performed and the patient requires continued care during the healing or recovery phase, or for the long-term consequences of the disease.

Attention to artificial openings, category **Z43,** has an excludes 1 note advising that this category does not include artificial opening status only without need for care **(Z93.-)** or complications of external stoma **(J95.0-, K94.-,** and **N99.5-)**. Codes for fitting and adjustment of prosthetic and other devices **(Z44-Z46)** may be reported in addition to codes in category **Z43** when applicable. Codes in categories **Z44-Z46** are not used to report malfunction or other complications of external, implanted, or other devices or for status only without fitting, adjustment, removal, or replacement **(Z95-Z97)**.

Category **Z47** includes codes for reporting orthopedic aftercare not including aftercare for healing fractures, which are reported with fracture codes with seventh character **D**. Codes in this category include aftercare following joint replacement and joint prosthesis surgery, encounter for removal of internal fixation device **(Z47.2)**, and aftercare following scoliosis surgery **(Z47.82)**.

Other post-procedural aftercare is reported with codes in category **Z48,** including encounters for attention to dressings, sutures, and drains **(Z48.0-);** planned post-procedural wound closure **(Z48.1);** aftercare following organ transplant **(Z48.2-);** aftercare following surgery for neoplasm **(Z48.3** and additional code to identify neoplasm); and encounters for other specified post-procedural care by body system **(Z48.81-).**

Encounters for care related to dialysis are reported with the following codes from category **Z49:**

Z49.01	Encounter for fitting and adjustment of extracorporeal dialysis catheter
Z49.02	Encounter for fitting and adjustment of peritoneal dialysis catheter
Z49.31	Encounter for adequacy testing for hemodialysis
Z49.32	Encounter for adequacy testing for peritoneal dialysis

Category **Z51** includes codes for other aftercare, including antineoplastic therapies, palliative care, and therapeutic drug level monitoring. Unlike other aftercare codes, code **Z51.0** (encounter for antineoplastic radiation therapy) and codes from subcategory **Z51.1** (encounter for antineoplastic chemotherapy and immunotherapy) may be used when treatment is directed at current acute disease. These codes are to be first-listed, followed by the diagnosis code for the malignancy when a patient's encounter is solely to receive radiation therapy, chemotherapy, or immunotherapy for the treatment of a neoplasm. If the reason for the encounter is more than one type of antineoplastic therapy, code **Z51.0** and a code from subcategory **Z51.1** may be assigned together, in which case one of these codes would be reported as a secondary diagnosis. Codes in this category do not include chemotherapy or immunotherapy for non-neoplastic conditions, which are reported with a code for the condition being treated.

When reporting therapeutic drug level monitoring, code **Z51.81** is sequenced before a code from category **Z79.-** for any long-term drug therapy. Some of the drugs included in category **Z79** are

Z79.01	Long-term (current) use of anticoagulants
Z79.02	Long-term (current) use of anti-thrombotics/anti-platelets
Z79.1	Long-term (current) use of nonsteroidal anti-inflammatories (NSAIDs)
Z79.2	Long-term (current) use of antibiotics
Z79.3	Long-term (current) use of hormonal contraceptives
Z79.4	Long-term (current) use of insulin
Z79.51	Long-term (current) use of inhaled steroids
Z79.52	Long-term (current) use of systemic steroids

Health Hazards Related to Socioeconomic and Psychosocial Circumstances

Categories **Z55-Z65** include codes for socioeconomic and psychosocial problems. Category **Z55** includes codes for problems related to education and literacy, including failed school examinations **(Z55.2)**, underachievement in school **(Z55.3)**, and educational maladjustment and discord with teachers and classmates **(Z55.4)**. Disorders of psychological development **(F80-F89)** should not be reported with these codes.

Category **Z59** (problems related to housing and economic circumstances) includes codes for conditions such as homelessness **(Z59.0)**, inadequate housing **(Z59.1)**, problems related to living in a residential institution **(Z59.3)**, extreme poverty **(Z59.5)**, and low income **(Z59.6)**. Code **Z59.4** is reported for lack of adequate food and safe drinking water. An excludes 1 note advises that effects of hunger **(T73.0)**, inappropriate diet or eating habits **(Z72.4)**, and malnutrition **(E40-E46)** are not reported with code **Z59.4**.

Exclusion and rejection on the basis of personal characteristics, such as unusual physical appearance, illness, or behavior, are reported with code **Z60.4**. This is not reported in conjunction with code **Z60.5** (target of [perceived] adverse discrimination and persecution).

Category **Z62** (problems related to upbringing) includes codes for current and past negative life events in childhood and of a child related to upbringing. Included in this category are

Z62.0	Inadequate parental supervision and control
Z62.1	Parental overprotection
Z62.21	Child in welfare custody
Z62.22	Institutional upbringing
Z62.29	Other upbringing away from parents
Z62.3	Hostility towards and scapegoating of child
Z62.6	Inappropriate (excessive) parental pressure
Z62.810	Personal history of physical and sexual abuse in childhood
Z62.811	Personal history of psychological abuse in childhood
Z62.812	Personal history of neglect in childhood
Z62.819	Personal history of unspecified abuse in childhood
Z62.820	Parent-biological child conflict
Z62.821	Parent-adopted child conflict
Z62.822	Parent-foster child conflict
Z62.890	Parent-child estrangement NEC
Z62.891	Sibling rivalry
Z62.898	Other specified problems related to upbringing

This category does not include current abuse or neglect, and codes in category **Z62** would not be reported in conjunction with codes for current abuse or neglect.

Category **Z63** provides codes for reporting conditions regarding separation of family members, relationship problems, disappearance and death of a family member, and alcohol and drug abuse in the family. Health problems in the family and anxiety about a sick person in the family are reported with code **Z63.79**. Codes **Z63.31** and **Z63.71** are used to report absence of a family member due to military deployment and stress on a family due to return of a family member from military deployment.

Pediatric Body Mass Index

The body mass index (BMI) codes below are for use for patients aged 2 to 20 years. The percentiles are based on the growth charts published by the Centers for Disease Control and Prevention.

Z68.51 Body mass index (BMI) pediatric, less than 5th percentile for age
Z68.52 Body mass index (BMI) pediatric, 5th percentile to less than 85th percentile for age
Z68.53 Body mass index (BMI) pediatric, 85th percentile to less than 95th percentile for age
Z68.54 Body mass index (BMI) pediatric, greater than or equal to 95th percentile for age

Health Services in Other Circumstances

Categories **Z69-Z76** include codes for encounters for services related to mental, behavioral, and other health care needs that are not classified elsewhere. Included here are codes for mental health services to both victims and perpetrators of abuse **(Z69.-)**. Codes in this category are specific to types of abuse, such as victim of parental child abuse **(Z69.010)** and victim of non-parental child abuse **(Z69.020)**. Code **Z69.81** (encounter for mental health services for victim of other abuse) includes an encounter for counseling for a rape victim.

Category **Z71** includes code **Z71.1** (person encountering health services in whom no diagnosis is made), which may be reported for encounters in which the concern or problem was a normal state (worried well). Also included here are codes for dietary counseling and surveillance **(Z71.3)**, alcohol abuse counseling and surveillance **(Z71.4-)**, drug abuse counseling and surveillance **(Z71.5-)**, and tobacco abuse counseling **(Z71.6)**. Several codes in this category are followed by instructions to use additional codes to report related conditions, such as nicotine dependence **(F17.-)**.

Category **Z72** includes codes for problems related to lifestyle, such as tobacco use **(Z72.0)** and lack of physical exercise **(Z72.3)**. Code **Z72.4** (inappropriate diet and eating habits) has an excludes 1 note indicating this code is not used when reporting behavioral eating disorders of infancy and childhood **(F98.2-,F98.3)** or other conditions related to eating disorders, lack of adequate food, or malnutrition.

Code **Z72.810** is used to report antisocial behavior by a child or adolescent without manifest psychiatric disorder. This code may be used to report truancy, stealing in the company of others, or gang-related offenses.

Behavioral insomnia of childhood is reported with codes in subcategory **Z73.8** specifying sleep-onset association type, limit setting type, or combined type.

Categories **Z74** and **Z75** include codes for identifying dependency on caregivers and problems related to availability and accessibility of health care. This does not include awaiting organ transplant status **(Z76.82)**. Dependency on enabling machines and devices is classified to category **Z99,** including the following:

Z99.0 Dependence on aspirator
Z99.11 Dependence on respirator [ventilator] status
Z99.12 Encounter for respirator [ventilator] dependence during power failure

Z99.2	Dependence on renal dialysis	
Z99.3	Dependence on wheelchair (code first cause of dependence)	
Z99.81	Dependence on supplemental oxygen	
Z99.89	Dependence on other enabling machines and devices	

An encounter for issue of a repeat prescription is reported with code **Z76.0**. This does not include repeat prescription of contraceptives **(Z30.4-)** or issuance of medical certificates **(Z02.7)**. Also included in this category are codes for supervision and care of a foundling **(Z76.1)** and supervision and care of other healthy infant and child **(Z76.2)**.

Other Contact With and Exposures to Health Hazards

Category **Z77** includes codes for exposure to hazardous metals, aromatic compounds, chemicals, pollution and toxins, noise, and radon. It also includes exposure to potentially hazardous body fluids **(Z77.21)** and exposure to environmental tobacco smoke **(Z77.22)**.

Physical restraint status is reported with code **Z78.1**. This may be reported when documentation indicates that a patient was placed in restraints during an encounter. This code should not be reported for temporary restraining during a procedure.

Family History

Family history codes **(Z80-Z84)** are used to indicate that the family member of a patient has had a particular disease that increases the risk for the patient. These codes may be used with screening codes to indicate the need for screening and testing.

> From the guidelines: Section IC21c4—History codes are also acceptable on any medical record regardless of the reason for the visit. A history of an illness, even if no longer present, is important information that may alter the type of treatment ordered.

Category **Z85** is used to report personal history of malignant neoplasm. Codes in this category may be reported as additional codes when any follow-up examination after treatment of a malignant neoplasm is provided. Instructions for this category also direct to use an additional code to identify alcohol use and dependence **(F10.-)**; exposure to tobacco smoke, environment **(Z77.2)** or occupational **(Z57.31)**; tobacco dependence **(F17.-)**; and tobacco use **(Z72.0)**. Personal history of in situ neoplasm is reported with codes in subcategory **Z86.00-**. This subcategory also includes codes for personal history of colonic polyps **(Z86.010)**, benign neoplasm of the brain **(Z86.011)**, and benign carcinoid tumor **(Z86.012)**.

Subcategory **Z86.1** includes codes for reporting personal history of infectious and parasitic diseases, such as personal history of methicillin-resistant *Staphylococcus aureus* infection **(Z86.14)**. It does not include personal history of infectious diseases specific to a body system or sequelae of infectious and parasitic diseases **(B90-B94)**.

Category **Z87** includes codes for personal history of congenital malformations. Conditions classifiable to categories **Q00-Q89** that have been repaired or corrected are reported with codes in this category. This does not include congenital malformations that have been partially corrected or repaired but that still require medical treatment. Status codes such as presence of implants, grafts, or devices may be reported in conjunction with codes in category **Z87**. Transplanted organ and tissue status **(Z94.-)** may also be reported in conjunction with codes from category **Z87**.

Code **Z87.892** is used to report personal history of anaphylaxis. When reporting this code, report also the allergy status. Allergy status codes are found in categories **Z88** (allergy status to drugs, medicaments, and biological substances) and **Z91** (allergy status, other than to drugs and biological substances). Category **Z91** includes codes for allergies to peanuts **(Z91.010)**, milk products **(Z91.011)**, eggs **(Z91.012)**, seafood **(Z91.013)**, other foods and food additives, insects, latex **(Z91.040)**, and radiographic dye **(Z91.041)**.

Category **Z89** (acquired absence of limb) includes amputation status and procedural or posttraumatic loss of limb. It does not include acquired deformities of limbs **(M20-M21)** or congenital absence of limbs **(Q71-Q73)**. Acquired absence of organs is reported with codes in category **Z90**. This category does not include congenital absence, but codes in this category may be reported in conjunction with post-procedural absence of endocrine glands **(E89.-)**.

Personal history of medical treatment, category **Z92**, includes codes for reporting personal history of antineoplastic chemotherapy **(Z92.21)**, monoclonal drug therapy **(Z92.22)**, inhaled steroid therapy **(Z92.240)**, systemic steroid therapy **(Z92.241)**, and personal history of immunosuppression therapy **(Z92.25)**. Personal history of irradiation is reported with code **Z92.3**. This does not include exposure to radiation in the physical environment or occupation exposure to radiation.

Codes for reporting transplanted organ and tissue status are used to report organ or tissue replaced by heterogenous or homogenous transplant. Category **Z94** includes codes for reporting transplant status based on the type of transplant. An excludes 1 note directs that codes in category **Z94** are not reported when complications of transplanted organ or tissue are reported. Codes in category **Z95** are used to report the presence of cardiac and vascular implants and grafts. Presence of other functional implants is reported with codes in category **Z96**, such as cochlear implant status **(Z96.21)** or myringotomy tube(s) status **(Z96.22)**.

Coding Scenarios

A child who has a newly placed gastrostomy is seen in follow-up to ensure that caregivers understand care instructions. There are no complaints and the patient and family appear to be adapting well. Diagnosis is follow-up newly placed gastrostomy.

Z43.1   Encounter for attention to gastrostomy

> From the guidelines: Section IC21a7—Status Z codes may be used with aftercare Z codes to indicate the nature of the aftercare. For example, code **Z95.1** (presence of aortocoronary bypass graft) may be used with code **Z48.812** (encounter for surgical aftercare following surgery on the circulatory system) to indicate the surgery for which the aftercare is being performed. A status code should not be used when the aftercare code indicates the type of status, such as using **Z43.0** (encounter for attention to tracheostomy) with **Z93.0** (tracheostomy status).

A 4-year-old infant is seen for a well-child visit and receives immunizations to protect against diphtheria, tetanus, pertussis, polio, measles, mumps, rubella, varicella, influenza, and pneumococcus. No abnormalities or problems are noted. Diagnosis is well-child visit with immunization administration.

Z00.129 Encounter for routine child health examination without abnormal findings

Z23 Encounter for immunization

> From the guidelines: Section IC21c2—Code **Z23** is for encounters for inoculations and vaccinations. It indicates that a patient is being seen to receive a prophylactic inoculation against a disease. Procedure codes are required to identify the actual administration of the injection and the type(s) of immunizations given. Code **Z23** may be used as a secondary code if the inoculation is given as a routine part of preventive health care, such as a well-baby visit.

A mother brings her child in for examination after the child was exposed to another child who reportedly has chickenpox. The child appears healthy and the mother is reassured that her child has had appropriate immunization against the disease. Diagnosis is suspected exposure to varicella.

Z20.820 Contact with and (suspected) exposure to varicella

> From the guidelines: Section IC21c1—Category **Z20** indicates contact with, and suspected exposure to, communicable diseases. These codes are for patients who do not show any sign or symptom of a disease but are suspected to have been exposed to it by close personal contact with an infected individual or are in an area where a disease is epidemic.

Review What You Have Learned

22.1 Codes from Chapter 21 are not used to report aftercare during a healing phase of a fracture.
   A. True
   B. False

22.2 What code indicates that a patient has tested positive for HIV but has manifested no signs or symptoms of the disease?
   A. **Z21** Asymptomatic human immunodeficiency virus [HIV] infection status
   B. **Z20.6** Contact with and (suspected) exposure to human immunodeficiency virus [HIV]
   C. **B20** Human immunodeficiency virus [HIV] disease
   D. All of the above
   E. None of the above

22.3 Codes in category **Z79** (long-term [current] drug therapy) may be reported for which of the following?
   A. Long-term use of insulin
   B. Long-term use of a systemic steroid
   C. Antibiotics taken on long-term prophylactic basis
   D. None of the above
   E. All of the above (A–C)

22.4 A diagnosis of tobacco use is reported with code **Z71.6** (tobacco abuse counseling) and a code from category **F17** to identify the nicotine dependence.
   A. True
   B. False

22.5 Z codes are never the first-listed or principal diagnosis.
   A. True
   B. False

22.6 What type of code is sequenced first to indicate a patient encounter is for a fully treated condition that no longer exists but the patient has a personal history of the condition?
   A. Personal history code
   B. Family history code
   C. Aftercare code
   D. Follow-up code
   E. None of the above

≡ APPENDICES ≡

Appendix A: Answer Key for Review What You Have Learned

Chapter 1

1.1 All codes in *ICD-10-CM* are more than 3 characters long.

   B. False—Some codes are complete at the 3-character category level.

1.2 The external cause of injury index is used to find codes for reporting

   E. All of the above—These codes capture the cause, intent, place of occurrence, activity of the patient at the time of the event, and the patient status (eg, civilian, military).

1.3 Terms found at the same indentation level within the alphabetic index are never reported for the same encounter.

   B. False—If a condition is stated as both acute (subacute) and chronic and codes for acute and chronic are listed at the same indentation level in the alphabetic index, both codes may be reported for the same encounter. Other terms found at the same indentation levels may be reported when separate conditions or sites are represented.

1.4 The excludes 1 note at code **Q03** (congenital hydrocephalus) indicates that code **P37.1** (hydrocephalus due to congenital toxoplasmosis) may be reported in addition to **Q03.**

   B. False—An excludes 1 note means the conditions in the note are not coded here.

1.5 Code **M48.52A** is a correct code for reporting a collapsed vertebra, not elsewhere classified, cervical region, initial encounter.

   B. False—The placeholder X must be added to complete the code: **M48.52XA.**

1.6 What section of *ICD-10-CM* is the final resource used to select a complete diagnosis code for a neoplasm?

   D. The tabular list—The tabular list should then be referenced to verify that the correct code has been selected from the table of neoplasms and that a more specific site code does not exist.

1.7 Brackets are used in the alphabetic index to enclose synonyms, alternative wording, or explanatory phrases.

   B. False—Brackets are used in the alphabetic index to identify manifestation codes.

Chapter 2

2.1 When reporting severe sepsis, you should first code the related organ failure.

B. False—The code for the underlying infection is sequenced before the code for severe sepsis. Additional codes should be reported to indicate the type of organ failure.

2.2 A 7-week-old child is admitted with a diagnosis of sepsis due to streptococcus group B. What codes should be reported?

C. **A40.1** Sepsis due to streptococcus, group B—Category **P36** is found in Chapter 16, which includes conditions that have their origin in the fetal or perinatal period (before birth through the first 28 days after birth).

2.3 A 16-year-old female presents to her physician's office for a well visit and asks for contraceptives because she has been sexually active and is concerned about becoming pregnant. In counseling the patient about sexual activity and sexually transmitted infections, the physician recommends and the patient requests HIV testing. A rapid test kit is negative for HIV. What is the appropriate diagnosis code for the HIV test?

C. **Z11.4** Encounter for screening for human immunodeficiency virus [HIV]

2.4 Codes included in an excludes 2 note are never reported with the codes to which the note applies.

B. False—When an excludes 2 note appears under a code, it is acceptable to use both the code and the excluded code together when appropriate.

2.5 Category **Z16** codes could be reported to show resistance to antimicrobial drugs in addition to which of the following codes?

D. All of the above—Assign a code from category **Z16** (resistance to antimicrobial drugs) following the infection code only if the infection code does not identify drug resistance.

2.6 A child is admitted with pneumonia due to infection by respiratory syncytial virus (RSV). A code identifying infection by RSV must be reported in addition to code **J12.1** (RSV pneumonia).

B. False—Assign only the combination code when that code fully identifies the diagnostic conditions involved or when the alphabetic index so directs.

Chapter 3

3.1 A patient admitted for chemotherapy for Burkitt lymphoma involving lymph nodes of the neck is also treated for nausea with vomiting. What diagnosis codes should be reported?

D. **Z51.11** Encounter for antineoplastic chemotherapy
   C83.71 Burkitt lymphoma, lymph nodes of head, face, and neck
   R11.2 Nausea with vomiting, unspecified

3.2 Following complete resection of a medulloblastoma of the cerebellum a pediatric oncology team is consulted for radiation and chemotherapy planning. What diagnosis codes should be reported?

E. **C71.6** Malignant neoplasm of cerebellum

3.3 You must always start in the table of neoplasms to arrive at the correct code for a neoplasm.

B. False

3.4 *ICD-10-CM* codes for lymphoma include designations of remission or recurrence.

B. False

3.5 After complete excision of a malignant neoplasm, a code for the neoplasm should be reported until all associated treatment is completed.

A. True

3.6 What diagnosis code(s) should be reported for a visit to manage pain in the right lower leg due to an osteosarcoma of the fibula?

A. **G89.3** Neoplasm related pain (acute) (chronic)
C40.21 Malignant neoplasm of long bones of right lower limb

Chapter 4

4.1 A 3-year-old presents to the pediatrician's office with a new complaint of easily bruising and a rash that seems to be spreading. The physician notes that the patient had an upper respiratory virus a few weeks ago but has seemed to quickly recover from that. A CBC is obtained and results reviewed. The physician diagnoses idiopathic thrombocytopenic purpura and instructs the parents to bring the child in for a repeat CBC in 1 week. What diagnosis code(s) is appropriate for reporting this encounter?

D. **D69.3** Immune thrombocytopenic purpura

4.2 The physician diagnoses anemia in hypothyroidism without goiter. What diagnosis codes should be reported?

D. **E03.9** Hypothyroidism, unspecified
D63.8 Anemia in other chronic diseases classified elsewhere

4.3 Transient hypogammaglobulinemia of infancy is reported with code **P61.4** (other congenital anemias, not elsewhere classified).

B. False

4.4 Reporting of sickle cell trait requires documentation of "with" or "without" crisis.

B. False

4.5 Sickle cell thalassemia is classified in the tabular list category **D57** (sickle cell disorders).

A. True

4.6 A child who has a history of acute lymphoblastic lymphoma in remission is found to be anemic at a checkup. What diagnosis code(s) should be reported?

    D. **C83.50** Lymphoblastic (diffuse) lymphoma, unspecified site
       D63.0 Anemia in neoplastic disease

Chapter 5

5.1 A patient with type 1 diabetes who uses an insulin pump is seen in emergency department for ketoacidosis. The patient's pump malfunctioned causing leakage and an underdose of insulin delivery. The patient did not become comatose due to early intervention. What is the appropriate first-listed diagnosis code?

    E. **T85.633A** Leakage of insulin pump, initial encounter

5.2 How many codes are required to report diabetes due to cystic fibrosis with a non-healing ulcer of the right calf?

    D. 3

5.3 Chapter 4 of the tabular list includes codes for reporting transitory metabolic disturbances caused by the infant's response to maternal endocrine and metabolic factors, or its adjustment to the extrauterine environment.

    B. False

5.4 There are 2 categories of codes for diabetes mellitus in *ICD-10-CM*.

    B. False

5.5 Malnutrition codes in Chapter 4 include codes for reporting anemia.

    B. False

5.6 Code **E87.3** is not used to report acidosis in a patient with type 1 diabetes mellitus.

    A. True

Chapter 6

6.1 A teenaged female patient has been referred for mental and behavioral health assessment for chronic bouts of abdominal pain for which extensive workup has shown no physical etiology. Her diagnosis is somatoform pain disorder. What code(s) should be reported?

    A. **F45.41** Pain disorder exclusively related to psychological factors

6.2 Codes in category **F60.3** (borderline personality disorder) would not be reported for the pediatric population.

    A. True

6.3 Codes in the block **F90-F98** (behavioral and emotional disorders with onset usually occurring in childhood and adolescence) are reported only for pediatric patients.

    B. False

6.4 A child has had generalized abdominal pain for 3 days with associated anorexia. The patient will be sent for additional workup, including computed tomography. At the end of this encounter, no further diagnosis is noted. The physician would report codes **R10.84** and **F50.8.**

B. False

6.5 A 17-year-old is seen in the emergency department for injuries incurred when he ran his car off the road and into a wooden fence. His injuries are minor but his blood alcohol level is 95 mg/100 mL and he admits to drinking heavily prior to the accident. Brief intervention and recommendations for further counseling regarding alcohol abuse are provided. The physician should report a code for alcohol use in addition to the codes for injuries incurred in the accident.

A. True

6.6 Using the case from question 6.5 above, the physician would report a code from category **Y90** to specify blood alcohol level.

A. True

Chapter 7

7.1 A child is seen in the office to rule out complex regional pain syndrome II of the right foot due to continued pain following a minor injury. What is the appropriate code?

E. **M79.604** Pain in right leg

7.2 A patient who had Guillain-Barré syndrome 2 years ago presents with continued lack of endurance with any repetitive tasks and feeling that she is tired all the time. She is diagnosed with chronic fatigue as a residual effect of Guillain-Barré syndrome. What code(s) is appropriate?

D. **R53.82** Chronic fatigue, unspecified
    G65.0 Sequelae of Guillain-Barré syndrome

7.3 Polyneuropathy in type 1 diabetes is reported with the code for diabetes sequenced prior to the code for polyneuropathy.

B. False

7.4 A child has had recurrent abdominal pain for several months. The patient has had a thorough workup resulting in no findings of organic cause. The purpose of this encounter is to discuss pain management with a diagnosis of chronic abdominal pain. Code **G89.29** should be reported first, followed by a code indicating the abdominal pain.

A. True

7.5 A 17-year-old with juvenile myoclonic epilepsy is seen in the emergency department for seizures that lasted for more than 5 minutes. The physician evaluates the patient and documents the diagnosis as intractable juvenile myoclonic epilepsy. A code that includes status epilepticus should be reported.

B. False

7.6 A child with childhood absence epilepsy is seen for reevaluation following increased seizure activity. The physician documents the diagnosis as pharmacoresistant childhood absence epilepsy. The correct code for this diagnosis is **G40.A09.**

B. False

Chapter 8

8.1 A child with chronic iridocyclitis has developed a cataract as a complication of the iridocyclitis. What subterm would help you find the code for this cataract in the alphabetic index for cataract?

E. All of the above

8.2 A child is diagnosed with superior oblique muscle paralysis of the right eye. What is the code for this diagnosis?

B. **H49.11** Fourth [trochlear] nerve palsy, right eye

8.3 A 4-month-old child is diagnosed with esotropia of the right eye. The seventh character of the code for this condition designates laterality.

B. False

8.4 The code for neonatal obstruction of the nasolacrimal duct is found in Chapter 16, Certain Conditions Originating in the Perinatal Period.

B. False

8.5 A 5-year-old is diagnosed with myopia. What code should be reported for this diagnosis?

B. **H52.10** Myopia, unspecified eye

8.6 The code for a congenital cataract is included in the tabular index in Chapter 7, Diseases of the Eye and Adnexa.

B. False

Chapter 9

9.1 A child with left ear pain and tinnitus is diagnosed with acute fungal otitis externa of the left ear.

E. **B36.9** Superficial mycosis, unspecified
   H62.42 Otitis externa in other diseases classified elsewhere, left ear

9.2 A teenager complains of loss of hearing in his left ear. The diagnosis is loss of hearing in the left ear due to cerumen impaction. What is the code for this diagnosis?

D. **H61.22** Impacted cerumen, left ear

9.3 A code indicating exposure to environmental tobacco smoke should be reported in addition to codes for otitis media when documentation indicates exposure.

A. True

9.4 What code or codes are reported for acute bilateral purulent otitis media with spontaneous rupture of the right tympanic membrane and intact left membrane?

B. **H66.011** Acute suppurative otitis media with spontaneous rupture of eardrum, right ear

H66.002 Acute suppurative otitis media without spontaneous rupture of eardrum, left ear

9.5 Code **H92.22** would be reported for the diagnosis of a child who sustained a blow to the left jaw and ear resulting in otorrhagia.

B. False

Chapter 10

10.1 A teenager with a family history of ischemic heart disease is diagnosed with essential hypertension. The teenager does not smoke but his mother smokes in their home. What code(s) is reported for this encounter?

D. **I10** Essential (primary) hypertension

Z77.22 Exposure to environmental tobacco smoke

Z82.49 Family history of ischemic heart disease

10.2 Code **I45.6** (pre-excitation syndrome) includes which of the following diagnoses?

E. All of the above

10.3 A diagnosis of myocarditis due to scarlet fever is reported with code **I01.2** (acute rheumatic myocarditis).

B. False

10.4 What code or codes are reported for complete heart block as a complication following surgical repair of a ventricular septal defect?

A. **I97.190** Other post-procedural cardiac functional disturbances following cardiac surgery

I44.2 Atrioventricular block, complete

10.5 Acrocyanosis in a newborn is reported with code **I73.8**.

B. False

Chapter 11

11.1 A child presents to the pediatric clinic with symptoms of fever, runny nose, and cough. A rapid influenza test is performed with a result positive for influenza B. Physical examination reveals serous otitis media of the right ear without rupture of the tympanic membrane. The physician diagnoses influenza type B and serous otitis media of the right ear. What code(s) should be reported for this encounter?

D. **J10.83** Influenza due to other identified influenza virus with otitis media

B97.89 Other viral agents as the cause of diseases classified elsewhere

11.2 A child is diagnosed with hypertrophy of the tonsils and adenoids with chronic tonsillitis and adenoiditis. What code(s) is reported?

C. **J35.03** Chronic tonsillitis and adenoiditis

11.3 Codes for chronic sinusitis specify whether the condition is recurrent.

B. False

11.4 What is the code(s) for croup?

D. **J05.0** Acute obstructive laryngitis

11.5 Codes for acute sinusitis and chronic sinusitis may be reported for the same encounter.

A. True

11.6 Acute streptococcal pharyngitis is reported with which code(s)?

D. **J02.0** Streptococcal pharyngitis

Chapter 12

12.1 A child is diagnosed with acute ruptured appendicitis with peritoneal abscess. What code(s) is reported?

C. **K35.3** Acute appendicitis with localized peritonitis

12.2 A child is diagnosed with eosinophilic esophagitis. What code(s) is reported?

C. **K20.0** Eosinophilic esophagitis

12.3 A child is diagnosed with a paraumbilical hernia without gangrene or obstruction. Code **K42.9** (umbilical hernia without obstruction or gangrene) is reported.

A. True

12.4 Code **K00.6** (disturbances of tooth eruption) is reported for both premature shedding of a primary tooth and for a retained primary tooth.

A. True

12.5 The codes for diverticulitis of the intestines specify the segment of colon affected (eg, rectosigmoiditis) and whether or not there are associated complications.

B. False

12.6 A child who has had a colostomy for 6 months is diagnosed with an uncomplicated small parastomal hernia. What code is reported for the parastomal hernia?

C. **K43.5** Parastomal hernia without obstruction or gangrene

Chapter 13

13.1 A teenager undergoes excision of a foreign body granuloma from the subcutaneous tissue of the right foot caused by a fragment of glass that was retained from stepping on something a year ago. The patient had felt he had something in his foot but could not see it. What *ICD-10-CM* code(s) is reported?

D. **L92.3** Foreign body granuloma of the skin and subcutaneous tissue
Z18.81 Retained glass fragments

13.2 A child reports with an itching rash that began on the last day of a camping trip. He is diagnosed with allergic reaction to contact with poison ivy. What code(s) is reported?

C. **L23.7** Allergic contact dermatitis due to plants, except food

13.3 Diaper dermatitis is reported with code **B37.2** (candidiasis of skin and nail).

B. False

13.4 Allergic contact dermatitis of the eyelid is reported with code **L23.7.**

B. False

13.5 Infantile acne is reported with a code from category **P83.**

B. False

13.6 What code is reported for chronic infantile eczema?

B. **L20.83** Infantile eczema

Chapter 14

14.1 A child who is treated for regional enteritis of the ileum is also diagnosed with Still disease with involvement of multiple joints. What code(s) is reported?

D. **K50.018** Crohn disease of small intestine with other complication
M08.29 Juvenile rheumatoid arthritis with systemic onset, multiple sites

14.2 A teenager is diagnosed with gouty arthropathy of the right ankle and foot in sickle cell disease. What code(s) is reported?

B. **D57.1** Sickle cell disease without crisis
M14.871 Arthropathies in other specified diseases classified elsewhere, right ankle and foot

14.3 Juvenile osteonecrosis is reported with codes in category **M87** (osteonecrosis).

B. False

14.4 Chondromalacia patellae is reported with code **M22.4** not code **M94.269.**

A. True

14.5 Code **M79.601** is the most specific code for diagnosis of pain in the right axilla.

B. False

14.6 What code(s) is reported for acute hematogenous osteomyelitis of the left tibia with major osseous defect?

    C. **M86.062** Acute hematogenous osteomyelitis, left tibia and fibula

    M89.762 Major osseous defect, left lower leg

Chapter 15

15.1 A child is diagnosed with pyelonephritis with vesicoureteral reflux. What code(s) is reported?

    A. **N11.0** Non-obstructive reflux-associated chronic pyelonephritis

15.2 A 13-year-old boy is diagnosed and treated for intravaginal torsion of the left testicle. What code(s) is reported?

    B. **N44.02** Intravaginal torsion of spermatic cord

15.3 Code **N48.1** is reported for candidal balanitis.

    B. False

15.4 Code **N13.6** (pyonephrosis) is reported for conditions in subcategories **N13.1-N13.5** with infection.

    A. True

15.5 Codes **N13.70** and **N13.4** are appropriately reported for vesicoureteral reflux with hydroureter.

    B. False

15.6 What code(s) is reported for diagnosis of painful ovulation?

    D. **N94.0** Mittelschmerz

Chapter 16

16.1 A pregnant 15-year-old is expected to deliver 6 weeks before her 16th birthday. What code(s) is reported for routine supervision of this pregnancy?

    D. Codes in categories **O09.6** (supervision of young primigravida) and **Z3A** (weeks of gestation)

16.2 A 17-year-old girl who is pregnant is seen for concerns regarding a mole on her right shoulder. The diagnosis is nevus right shoulder with incidental pregnancy. What code(s) is reported?

    C. **D23.61** Other benign neoplasm of skin of right upper limb, including shoulder

    Z33.1 Pregnant state, incidental

16.3 Pregnancy in a 16-year-old is always reported with codes in category **O09** as a high-risk pregnancy.

    B. False

16.4 Surgery is performed on a fetus to close a spinal defect. Code **O35.0XX0** (maternal care for [suspected] central nervous system malformation in fetus) should be used on the mother's record.

A. True

16.5 Only one code from Chapter 15 may be reported for each encounter.

B. False

16.6 When a patient is admitted and delivers a liveborn infant with or without complication, what code category signifies the delivery and outcome on the mother's record?

D. Category **Z37** (outcome of delivery)

Chapter 17

17.1 A neonate is started on intravenous antibiotics due to suspected infection transferred during birth due to a localized infection in the mother. Infection in the neonate is ruled out following stabilization and negative culture results. What code(s), if any, is reported for the suspected neonatal infection?

E. None of the above

17.2 A neonate is diagnosed with pneumonia due to aspiration of meconium-stained amniotic fluid. What diagnosis code(s) is reported for this condition?

C. **P24.01** Meconium aspiration with respiratory symptoms

17.3 Codes in Chapter 16 are never reported with codes from other chapters in *ICD-10-CM*.

B. False

17.4 Codes identifying birth weight and gestational age are reported only in the neonatal period.

B. False

17.5 Guidelines for reporting conditions originating in the perinatal period are identical to those for other conditions.

B. False

17.6 Projectile vomiting in a 28-day-old infant is reported with which code(s)?

B. **P92.09** Other vomiting of newborn

Chapter 18

18.1 An infant is diagnosed with congenial goiter. What diagnosis code is reported?

D. **E03.0** Congenital hypothyroidism with diffuse goiter

18.2 A child is diagnosed with rhizomelic chondrodysplasia punctata. What diagnosis code(s) is reported for this condition?

C. **E71.540** Rhizomelic chondrodysplasia punctata

18.3 All codes for congenital conditions are found in Chapter 17 of the tabular list.
   B. False

18.4 A pediatrician is present at a cesarean delivery of a fetus diagnosed with lumbar spina bifida based on ultrasound and alpha-fetoprotein results. On delivery, the neonate is evaluated and diagnosed with spina bifida with lumbosacral meningocele without hydrocephalus. What will be the principal diagnosis on this birth record?
   D. **Z38.01** Single liveborn infant, delivered by cesarean

18.5 Additional codes to identify physical conditions and degree of intellectual disabilities may be reported with codes for Down syndrome.
   A. True

18.6 Unilateral cleft lip status post-reconstruction would be assigned code **Z87.730**.
   A. True

Chapter 19

19.1 Codes for joint pain are included in Chapter 18 of the tabular list.
   B. False

19.2 A 24-month-old is diagnosed with salmonella bacteremia. What code(s) is reported for this condition?
   A. **R78.81** Bacteremia

19.3 Code **R09.01** (asphyxia) is reported for asphyxia due to carbon monoxide poisoning.
   B. False

19.4 A 25-day-old child is diagnosed with respiratory arrest. Code **R09.2** is the appropriate code for reporting this condition.
   B. False

19.5 A child with asthma is seen for wheezing. Code **R06.2** (wheezing) is not reported in addition to the code specifying the type of asthma.
   A. True

19.6 A child undergoing treatment of acute lymphoblastic leukemia is diagnosed with a fever. What diagnosis code(s) is reported?
   B. **C91.00** Acute lymphoblastic leukemia not having achieved remission
   R50.81 Fever presenting with conditions classified elsewhere

Chapter 20

20.1 Codes for pathological fracture are included in Chapter 19 of the tabular list.

B. False

20.2 A 24-month-old is diagnosed with second degree burns of her right thumb and first and second fingers. What is the diagnosis code(s) for the initial encounter for the burns (not including cause of injury codes)?

C. **T23.241A** Burn of second degree of multiple right fingers (nail), including thumb

20.3 In what portion of the alphabetic index will you find reference to the code for accidental poisoning by brown recluse spider bite?

C. Table of drugs and chemicals

20.4 A minor injury to a peripheral nerve associated with a primary injury is not separately reported.

B. False

20.5 All codes in Chapter 19 include seventh characters.

B. False

20.6 A child has a hypertrophic scar on his nose that was caused by an open fracture of his nose. What diagnosis code(s) is reported?

B. **L91.0** Hypertrophic scar
S02.2XXS Fracture of nasal bones

Chapter 21

21.1 External cause codes are reported only with codes from categories **S00-T88.**

B. False

21.2 What external cause code(s) is reported to identify the cause of injuries incurred by a child who rode his tricycle off the front porch of his house (subsequent visit)? (External cause codes only.)

C. **V18.0XXD** Pedal cycle driver injured in non-collision transport accident in non-traffic accident

21.3 In what portion of the alphabetic index will you find reference to the code for reporting a nosocomial condition?

A. External cause of injuries index

21.4 An injury that is caused by an accident on roller skates is classified as a pedestrian accident.

A. True

21.5 Any of the assault codes may be used to indicate the external cause of any injury resulting from suspected abuse.

B. False

21.6 A child is injured by debris in a tornado. Which external cause code(s) is reported first at the initial encounter?

B. **X37.1XXA** Tornado

Chapter 22

22.1 Codes from Chapter 21 are not used to report aftercare during a healing phase of a fracture.

A. True

22.2 What code indicates that a patient has tested positive for HIV but has manifested no signs or symptoms of the disease?

A. **Z21** Asymptomatic human immunodeficiency virus [HIV] infection status

22.3 Codes in category **Z79** (long-term [current] drug therapy) may be reported for which of the following?

E. All of the above

22.4 A diagnosis of tobacco use is reported with code **Z71.6** (tobacco abuse counseling) and a code from category **F17** to identify the nicotine dependence.

B. False

22.5 Z codes are never the first-listed or principal diagnosis.

B. False

22.6 What type of code is sequenced first to indicate a patient encounter is for a fully treated condition that no longer exists but the patient has a personal history of the condition?

D. Follow-up code

≡ APPENDICES ≡

Appendix B: Epilepsy Table

ICD-10-CM CODES FOR EPILEPSY BY TYPE

Category	Description	Related Terms	Not Intractable	Intractable
G40.0	Localization-related (focal) (partial) idiopathic epilepsy and epileptic syndromes with seizures of localized onset	Benign childhood epilepsy with centrotemporal EEG spikes Childhood epilepsy with occipital EEG paroxysms	G40.001 Not intractable, with status epilepticus G40.009 Not intractable, without status epilepticus	G40.011 Intractable, with status epilepticus G40.019 Intractable, without status epilepticus
G40.1	Localization-related (focal) (partial) symptomatic epilepsy and epileptic syndromes with simple partial seizures	Attacks without alteration of consciousness Epilepsia partialis continua [Kozhevnikof] Simple partial seizures developing into secondarily generalized seizures Focal Bravais-Jacksonian Somatomotor Somatosensory	G40.101 Not intractable, with status epilepticus G40.109 Not intractable, without status epilepticus	G40.111 Intractable, with status epilepticus G40.119 Intractable, without status epilepticus
G40.2	Localization-related (focal) (partial) symptomatic epilepsy and epileptic syndromes with complex partial seizures	Attacks with alteration of consciousness, often with automatisms Complex partial seizures developing into secondarily generalized seizures	G40.201 Not intractable, with status epilepticus G40.209 Not intractable, without status epilepticus	G40.211 Intractable, with status epilepticus G40.219 Intractable, without status epilepticus
G40.3	Generalized idiopathic epilepsy and epileptic syndromes		G40.301 Not intractable, with status epilepticus G40.309 Not intractable, without status epilepticus	G40.311 Intractable, with status epilepticus G40.319 Intractable, without status epilepticus

ICD-10-CM CODES FOR EPILEPSY BY TYPE, continued

Category	Description	Related Terms	Not Intractable	Intractable
G40.A	Absence epileptic syndrome	Childhood absence epilepsy [pyknolepsy] Juvenile absence epilepsy Absence epileptic syndrome, NOS	G40.A01 Not intractable, with status epilepticus G40.A09 Not intractable, without status epilepticus	G40.A11 Intractable, with status epilepticus G40.A19 Intractable, without status epilepticus
G40.B	Juvenile myoclonic epilepsy [impulsive petit mal]		G40.B01 Not intractable, with status epilepticus G40.B09 Not intractable, without status epilepticus	G40.B11 Intractable, with status epilepticus G40.B19 Intractable, without status epilepticus
G40.4	Other generalized epilepsy and epileptic syndromes	Myoclonus, epileptic Seizure, grand mal Seizure, petit mal	G40.401 Not intractable, with status epilepticus G40.409 Not intractable, without status epilepticus	G40.411 Intractable, with status epilepticus G40.419 Intractable, without status epilepticus
G40.5	Epileptic seizures related to external causes	Epileptic seizures related to alcohol Epileptic seizures related to drugs Epileptic seizures related to hormonal changes Epileptic seizures related to sleep deprivation Epileptic seizures related to stress	G40.501 Not intractable, with status epilepticus G40.509 Not intractable, without status epilepticus	
G40.80	Other epilepsy	Epilepsies and epileptic syndromes undetermined as to whether they are focal or generalized Landau-Kleffner syndrome	G40.801 Not intractable, with status epilepticus G40.802 Not intractable, without status epilepticus	G40.803 Intractable, with status epilepticus G40.804 Intractable, without status epilepticus

ICD-10-CM CODES FOR EPILEPSY BY TYPE, continued

Category	Description	Related Terms	Not Intractable	Intractable
G40.81	Lennox-Gastaut syndrome		**G40.811** Not intractable, with status epilepticus **G40.812** Not intractable, without status epilepticus	**G40.813** Intractable, with status epilepticus **G40.814** Intractable, without status epilepticus
G40.82	Epileptic spasms	Infantile spasms Salaam attacks West syndrome	**G40.821** Not intractable, with status epilepticus **G40.822** Not intractable, without status epilepticus	**G40.823** Intractable, with status epilepticus **G40.824** Intractable, without status epilepticus
G40.9	Epilepsy, unspecified	**G40.909** Only Epilepsy NOS Epileptic convulsions NOS Epileptic fits NOS Epileptic seizures NOS Recurrent seizures NOS Seizure disorder NOS	**G40.901** Not intractable, with status epilepticus **G40.909** Not intractable, without status epilepticus	**G40.911** Intractable, with status epilepticus **G40.919** Intractable, without status epilepticus

≡ APPENDICES ≡

Appendix C: Signs and Symptoms

Abdominal pain
    Generalized **R10.84**
    Right upper quadrant pain **R10.11**
    Left upper quadrant pain **R10.12**
    Epigastric pain **R10.13**
    Right lower quadrant pain **R10.31**
    Left lower quadrant pain **R10.32**
    Periumbilical pain **R10.33**
Abdominal swelling/mass/lump
    Intra-abdominal and pelvic **R19.00**
    Right upper quadrant **R19.01**
    Left upper quadrant **R19.02**
    Right lower quadrant **R19.03**
    Left lower quadrant **R19.04**
    Periumbilic **R19.05**
    Epigastric **R19.06**
    Generalized **R19.07**
Abdominal tenderness
    Right upper quadrant **R10.811**
    Left upper quadrant **R10.812**
    Right lower quadrant **R10.813**
    Left lower quadrant **R10.814**
    Periumbilic **R10.815**
    Epigastric **R10.816**
    Generalized **R10.817**
Abdominal rebound tenderness
    Right upper quadrant **R10.821**
    Left upper quadrant **R10.822**
    Right lower quadrant **R10.823**
    Left lower quadrant **R10.824**
    Periumbilic **R10.825**
    Epigastric **R10.826**
    Generalized **R10.827**
ALTE in infant **R68.13**[a]
Altered mental status, unspec **R41.82**

Anorexia **R63.0**
Anuria/oliguria **R34**
Apnea, NOS **R06.81**
Apnea of newborn **P28.4**
Ascites, other **R18.8**
Ascites, malignant **R18.0**[a]
Asphyxia **R09.01**
Ataxia, unspec **R27.0**
Atten/conc deficit w/o ADHD **R41.840**
Bacteremia (excludes sepsis) **R78.81**
Breathing abn/breath-holding **R06.89**
Chest pain on breathing **R07.1**
Chest pain, other **R07.89**
Chest pain, unspec **R07.9**
Cheyne-Stokes/periodic breathing **R06.3**
Chills w/o fever **R68.83**
Colic **R10.83**
Cough **R05**
Cyanosis **R23.0**
Cyanosis, newborn **P28.2**
Delayed milestone, childhood **R62.0**
Diarrhea NOS **R19.7**
Diarrhea, neonatal **P78.3**
Dyslexia/alexia **R48.0**
Dysarthria/anarthria **R47.1**
Dysphagia, oral phase **R13.11**
Dysphagia, O/P phase **R13.12**
Dysphagia, pharyngeal phase **R13.13**
Dysphagia, P/E phase **R13.14**
Dysphagia, other **R13.19**
Dysphagia, unspec **R13.10**
Distension/bloating abdomen **R14.0**
Dysuria **R30.0**
Edema, localized **R60.0**
Edema, generalized **R60.02**

---

[a]Secondary code—Report underlying condition first (for apparent life-threatening event in infant, first code confirmed diagnosis and/or use additional codes signs/symptoms).

Enuresis, functional **F98.0**
Enuresis NOS **R32**
Epistaxis **R04.0**
Excessive crying infant **R68.11**
Failure to thrive **R62.51**
Failure to thrive, neonate **P92.6**
Fatigue NOS **R53.83**
Fecal incontinence NOS **R15.9**
Fecal smearing/soiling **R15.1**
Feeding difficulties **R63.3**
Fever newborn **P81.9**
Fever, post-procedural **R50.82**
Fever, post-vaccination **R50.83**
Fever, post-transfusion **R50.84**
Fever presenting with conditions classified elsewhere **R50.81**[a]
Fever unknown origin **R50.9**
Fluency disorder, childhood **F80.81**
Fluency disorder in conditions classified elsewhere **R47.82**[a]
Fussy baby **R68.12**
Gait abnormality, unspec **R26.9**
Growing pains **R29.898**
Halitosis **R19.6**
Hallucinations, unspec **R44.3**
Headache **R51**
Heartburn **R12**
Hemoptysis **R04.2**
Hepatomegaly NOS **R16.0**
Hepatosplenomegaly NOS **R16.2**
Hyperhidrosis **R61**
Hyperventilation **R06.4**
Hypothermia not assoc low environment temp **R68.0**
Hypoxemia/hypoxia **R09.02**
Impulsiveness **R45.87**
Irritability/anger **R45.4**
Jaundice, unspec **R17**
Jaundice, neonatal preterm **P59.0**
Jaundice, neonatal unspec **P59.9**
Local enlarged lymph nodes **R59.0**
Lymphadenopathy, NOS **R59.1**
Malaise NOS **R53.81**
Meningismus **R29.1**

Mouth breathing **R06.5**
Murmur, functional, benign **R01.0**
Murmur, benign in newborn **P29.89**
Nasal congestion **R09.81**
Nausea **R11.0**
Nausea with vomiting **R11.2**
Nervousness **R45.0**
Pain, jaw (mandible/maxilla) **R68.84**
Pain in joint
    Right shoulder **M25.511**
    Left shoulder **M25.512**
    Right elbow **M25.521**
    Left elbow **M25.522**
    Right wrist **M25.531**
    Left wrist **M25.532**
    Right hip **M25.551**
    Left hip **M25.552**
    Right knee **M25.561**
    Left knee **M25.562**
    Right ankle/foot **M25.571**
    Left ankle/foot **M25.572**
Pallor **R23.1**
Palpitations **R00.2**
Persistent vegetative state **R40.3**
Petechiae/spont ecchymosis **R23.3**
Petechiae/ecchymosis newborn **P54.5**
Polydipsia **R63.1**
Polyuria NOS **R35.8**
Postnasal drip **R09.82**
Posture, abn **R29.3**
Rash NOS **R21**
Rales/abn chest sounds (not wheezing) **R09.89**
Renal colic, unspec **N23**
Respiratory arrest **R09.2**
Seizure, simple febrile **R56.00**
Seizure, complex febrile **R56.01**
Seizure, newborn **P90**
Seizure NOS **R56.9**
Seizure, posttraumatic **R56.1**
Shock, cardiogenic **R57.0**
Shock, unspec non-traumatic **R57.9**
Short stature **R62.52**
Shortness of breath **R06.2**

---

[a]Secondary code—Report underlying condition first (for apparent life-threatening event in infant, first code confirmed diagnosis and/or use additional codes signs/symptoms).

Skin mass/lump/nodule/swelling
   Head **R22.0**
   Neck **R22.1**
   Trunk **R22.2**
   Right upper limb **R22.31**
   Left upper limb **R22.32**
   Bilateral upper limbs **R22.33**
   Right lower limb **R22.41**
   Left lower limb **R22.42**
   Bilateral lower limbs **R22.43**
Sleep disorder child NOS **F51.9**
Speech disturbance, unspec **R47.9**
Splenomegaly NOS **R16.1**
Stool, abn **R19.5**
Stridor **R06.1**
Stupor **R40.1**
Syncope and collapse **R55**
Tachypnea, NOS **R06.82**
Tachycardia, neonatal **P29.11**
Tenesmus (rectal) **R19.8**
Torticollis, ocular **R29.891**
Transitory tachypnea newborn **P22.1**
Tremor **R25.1**
Underweight **R63.6** (add BMI)
Urethral discharge w/o blood **R36.0**
Urinary frequency/micturition **R35.0**
Urinary hesitancy **R39.11**
Urinary incontinence, unspec **R32**
Urinary incontinence, functional **R39.81**
Urinary urgency **R39.15**

Vertigo NOS **R42**
Vomiting, bilious **R11.14**
Vomiting, projectile **R11.12**
Vomiting w/o nausea **R11.11**
Weight gain, abn **R63.5**
Weight loss, abn **R63.4**
Wheezing **R06.2**
Test Results
Abdominal imaging abn **R93.5**
Alcohol blood level **R78.0** (**Y90.-** alcohol blood level)
BP elevated w/o hypertension **R03.0**
C-reactive protein, elevated **R79.82**
Echocardiogram abn **R93.1**
Glycosuria **R81**
Head/skull imaging abn **R93.0**
Hemoglobinuria **R82.3**
HIV test nonspecific results **R75**
Hyperglycemia, unspec **R73.9**
Impaired fasting glucose **R73.01**
Impaired glucose tolerance **R73.02**
Abn lead level **R78.71**
Limb imaging abn **R93.6**
Lung field imaging abn **R91.8**
Musc/skel imaging abn **R93.7**
Proteinuria, unspec **R80.9**
Sedimentation rate elevated **R70.0**
TB cell immunity react w/o TB **R76.12** TB skin react w/o TB **R76.11**

Index

A

Aarskog syndrome, 195
Abdominal distention (gaseous), 127
Abdominal pain, 127, 259
Abdominal pregnancy, 171
Abdominal rebound tenderness, 259
Abdominal swelling/mass/lump, 259
Abdominal tenderness, 259
Abnormal posture, 153
Abortion, 171–172
Abrasion, 207
Abscess, 134
Absence epileptic syndrome, 256
Absent nipple, 195
Acanthosis nigricans, 140
Accessory breast, 195
Accessory nipple, 195
Accidental discharge of firearm, 220
Acetonuria, 164
Achilles tendinitis, 150
Acidosis, 48
Acné excoriée de jeunes filles, 139
Acne keloid, 139
Acne vulgaris, 139
Acquired absence of limb, 237
Acquired absence of organs, 237
Acquired deformity of the limbs, 152
Acquired deformity of the nose, 152
Acquired hemolytic anemia, 34
Acquired immune deficiency syndrome (AIDS), 16–18
Acquired short Achilles tendon, 150
Acrocephalopolysyndactyly, 195
Acrocephalosyndactyly, 195
Acrocyanosis, 101
Acute abdomen, 127
Acute bronchiolitis, 111
Acute bronchitis, 110–111
Acute disseminated encephalitis and encephalomyelitis (ADEM), 66
Acute epiglottitis, 109
Acute hematogenous osteomyelitis, 151
Acute laryngitis, 109
Acute lymphadenitis, 135
Acute lymphangitis, 135
Acute myocardial infarction (AMI), 100
Acute myringitis, 94
Acute nasopharyngitis, 108
Acute necrotizing hemorrhagic encephalopathy, 66
Acute nephritic syndrome, 158
Acute non-rheumatic carditis and cardiomyopathy, 98–99
Acute obstructive laryngitis, 118, 248
Acute pharyngitis, 108
Acute rheumatic myocarditis, 105, 247
Acute rhinitis, 108
Acute sinusitis, 108
Acute streptococcal pharyngitis, 118, 248
Acute streptococcal tonsillitis, 108
Acute transverse myelitis, 67
Acute tubulonephritis, 159
Acute upper respiratory infections, 107–109
ADEM. *See* Acute disseminated encephalitis and encephalomyelitis (ADEM)
Adenoid vegetations, 112
Adenoiditis, 112
Adjustment disorders, 58
Adolescent idiopathic genu valgum, 147
Adolescent idiopathic scoliosis, 149
Adult and child abuse, 211–212
Adult osteomalacia, 150
Adverse effects, 45, 211
Agoraphobia, 58
Agranulocytosis, 35
AIDS. *See* Acquired immune deficiency syndrome (AIDS)
Air and space transport accident, 220
Air embolism (traumatic), 212
Airbag injury, 220
Alcohol abuse counseling and surveillance, 235
Alcohol-related disorders, 57
Alcoholic hepatic failure, 125
Alkalosis, 48
Allergic contact dermatitis, 136, 143, 249
Allergic rhinitis, 111
Allergy status codes, 237
Alopecia areata, 139
Alopecia mucinosa, 139
α-thalassemia, 34
Alphabetic index, 3–8
    brackets, 4
    cross-references, 5
    dash, 4–5
    external cause codes, 7
    NEC, 5
    neoplasm table, 6

Alphabetic index, continued
    NOS, 5
    parentheses, 4
    table of drugs and chemicals, 6, 17
Alport syndrome, 159, 195
Alveolar capillary dysplasia, 113
Amaurosis fugax, 69
Amenorrhea, 163
AMI. See Acute myocardial infarction (AMI)
Amyloidosis, 85, 115
Anagen effluvium, 139
"And," 1
Androgenic alopecia, 139
Anemia, 33, 35
Aneurysmal bone cyst, 151
Anhidrosis, 139
Aniridia, 85
Ankylosing spondylitis, 115, 145
Anonychia, 195
Anorexia, 59, 127
Anoxic brain damage, 74
Antineoplastic immunotherapy, 36
Antisocial behavior, 235
Anuria and oliguria, 164
Anxiety disorders, 58
Anxiolytics, 56
Aphagia, 127
Aphakia, 84
Aplastic congenital anemia, 33
Appendicitis, etc, 121
Arnold-Chiari syndrome, 74, 190, 191
Arthropathies, 146
Asperger syndrome, 60
Aspiration pneumonia, 113
Associated glaucoma, 191
Asthma, 112, 113
Astrocytoma, 25
Ataxia telangiectasia, 36
Atresia of the vas deferens, 193
Atrioventricular reentrant tachycardia (AVRT), 99
Atrophy, 67
Attention deficit with hyperactivity, 60
Autistic disorder, 60
Automatic cardiac defibrillator, 99
Automobile accidents, 220–221
Autonomic disorders, 74
AV nodal reentrant tachycardia (AVNRT), 99
AVRT. See Atrioventricular reentrant tachycardia (AVRT)

B

Bacterial meningitis, 65–66
Bacterial sepsis of a newborn, 19, 182
Balanoposthitis, 161
Bartholin gland, 162
Barvais-Jacksonian, 255
Beau lines, 139
Beckwith-Wiedemann syndrome, 195

Behavioral disorders. See Mental, behavioral, and neurodevelopment disorders
Behavioral insomnia of childhood, 235
Behavioral problems, 235
Bell's palsy, 70
Benign carcinoid tumor, 236
Benign essential microscopic hematuria, 163
Benign familial pemphigus, 135
Benign myoclonic epilepsy in infancy, 185
Benign neoplasm of the brain, 236
Bilateral inguinal hernia, 122
Bilateral small kidney, 160
Bilious vomiting of newborn, 185
Biomechanical lesions, 153
Birth process. See Perinatal period; Pregnancy, childbirth, and the puerperium
Birth trauma, 181
Bladder disorders, 161
Bladder-neck obstruction, 161
Blepharitis, 80
Blepharoconjunctivitis, 80
Blepharospasm, 81
Blindness, 86
Blister, 207
Blood and blood-forming organs, 33–40
    code scenarios/examples, 37–39
    immunodeficiency, 36–37
    review test, 39–40, 243–244
Blood transfusion, 36
Body mass index (BMI), 235
Body surface area, 210
Boil, 134
Bone density and structure, 150–151
Borderline personality disorder, 63, 244
Botulism, 70
Brackets, 4, 9
Brain disorders, 74–75
Breast, disorders of, 162
Breast engorgement of newborn, 184
Breast-milk jaundice, 48
Bronchiectasis, 112
Bronchiolitis, 110
Bruising of the scalp, 181
Bulimia nervosa, 59
Bullous disorders, 135
Bullous impetigo, 133
Bunion, 147
Burkitt lymphoma, 25
Burns and corrosions, 210–211

C

Café au lait spots, 140
Calculus of the bile duct, 125, 126
Calculus of the gallbladder, 125, 126
Calculus of the tonsil, 112
Callosities, 140
Calvé disease, 148
Candidal balanitis, 161, 165, 250

Candidal vaginitis, 162
Cannabis, 56
Car accidents, 220–221
Carbohydrate metabolism, 47
Carbuncle, 134
Cardiac arrest, 99
Cardiac murmur, 103
Cardiac pacemaker, 99
Cardiac tamponade, 99
Cardiogenic shock, 103
Cardiomyopathy, 98–99
Cardiorespiratory failure, 115
Carditis, 98
Carotid artery syndrome, 69
Cataract, 84
Category, 1
Cauliflower ear, 152
Causalgia, 73
Cellulitis, 135
Cephalhematoma, 181
Cerebral aneurysm, 101
Cerebral cyst, 74
Cerebral edema, 74
Cerebral infarction, 101
Cerebral palsy, 71
Cerebrospinal fluid leak, 74
Cerebrovascular disease, 101
Cerumen impaction, 91
Cervical duplication, 193
Cervical intraepithelial neoplasia (CIN), 162
Cervicitis, 162
Cervix uteri, 162
Cesarean delivery, 171
Chalazion, 80
Character, 1
Charcot-Marie-Tooth, 70
Chemical-induced diabetes mellitus, 45
Chest pain on breathing, 116
Chiari and Arnold-Chiari syndromes, 190
Child abuse, 211–212
Child in welfare custody, 234
Child sexual abuse, 164
Childbirth. *See* Perinatal period; Pregnancy, childbirth, and the puerperium
Childhood absence epilepsy, 256
Cholecystitis, 125
Cholelithiasis, 125
Choleperitonitis, 124
Cholesteatoma, 91, 93
Chondrocostal junction syndrome (Tietze), 151, 152
Chondrolysis of the hip, 152
Chondromalacia, 152
Chondromalacia patellae, 152, 155, 249
Chondropathies, 151–152
Chromosomal abnormalities. *See* Congenital malformations, deformations, and chromosomal abnormalities
Chronic adenoiditis, 112
Chronic bronchitis, 112
Chronic infantile eczema, 143, 249
Chronic kidney disease, 158, 213
Chronic lower respiratory diseases, 112–113
Chronic multifocal osteomyelitis, 151
Chronic nasopharyngitis, 111
Chronic nephritic syndrome, 158
Chronic obstructive asthma, 112
Chronic obstructive bronchitis, 112
Chronic obstructive pulmonary disease, 112
Chronic parametritis, 162
Chronic pericarditis, 99
Chronic pharyngitis, 111
Chronic rheumatic pericarditis, 97
Chronic tonsillitis, 108, 112
Chronic upper respiratory conditions, 111–112
Ciliary neuralgia, 69
CIN. *See* Cervical intraepithelial neoplasia (CIN)
Circulatory system diseases, 97–105
 acute non-rheumatic carditis and cardiomyopathy, 98–99
 AMI, 100
 cerebrovascular disease, 101
 code scenarios/examples, 103–104
 conduction disorders, 99
 congenital malformations, 191
 diseases of pericardium, 99
 gangrene, 102
 hypertensive heart disease, 99–100
 hypotension, 102
 intraoperative/post-procedural complications, 102
 lymph node disorders, 101
 review test, 104–105, 247
 rheumatic fever, 97
 signs and symptoms, 102–103
 vascular diseases, 101
Cleft lip/cleft palate, 192
Cleft uvula, 192
Clicking hip, 153, 193
Clubbing of fingers, 153
Cluster headache syndrome, 69
Coagulation defects, 35
Cocaine, 56
Cochlear implant status, 237
Cockayne syndrome, 195
Code, 1
"Code, if applicable, any causal condition first" note, 11
"Code also" instruction, 12
"Code first" instruction, 11
Code selection, 12–13
 alphabetic index, 3–8. *See also* Alphabetic index
 guidelines/pointers, 12–13
 sequela, 12–13
 steps in process, 1
 tabular list, 8–12. *See also* Tabular list
 terminology, 1–2
Code structure, 2–3
Cold injury syndrome, 184
Collagen disease, 148

Colon, 10
Colostomy, 127
Colostomy status, 127
Coma, 201–202
Combination code, 2
Communicable diseases, 231–232
Complex regional pain syndrome, 73
Complications of care, 212–213
Concussion, 55, 208
Conduct disorder, 60
Conduction disorders, 99
Conductive hearing loss, 94
Congenital absence of breast and nipple, 195
Congenital alopecia, 195
Congenital anemia, 33
Congenital cardiomyopathy, 99
Congenital central alveolar hypoventilation syndrome, 192
Congenital chordee without hypospadias, 193
Congenital cirrhosis of the liver, 184
Congenital coxa valga, 193
Congenital coxa vara, 193
Congenital deformity of the hip, 193
Congenital deformity of the spine, 193
Congenital deviated nasal septum, 111
Congenital diaphragmatic hernia, 122
Congenital dyserythropoietic anemia, 33
Congenital genu valgum, 147
Congenital hernia of the bladder, 194
Congenital hiatal hernia, 192
Congenital hydrocele, 184
Congenital hydrocephalus, 74
Congenital hypothyroidism, 42, 183
Congenital hypothyroidism with diffuse goiter, 197, 251
Congenital iodine-deficiency syndrome, 42
Congenital malformations, deformations, and chromosomal abnormalities, 189–197
   chromosomal abnormalities, not elsewhere classified, 196
   circulatory system, 191
   cleft lip/cleft palate, 192
   code scenarios/examples, 196
   digestive system, 192
   eye, ear, face, and neck, 191
   genital organs, 192–193
   malformation syndromes, 195
   musculoskeletal system, 193–194
   nervous system, 190–191
   other congenital malformations, 194–195
   respiratory system, 191–192
   review test, 197, 251–252
   urinary system, 193
Congenital nephrotic syndrome, 193
Congenital non-neoplastic nevus, 142, 195
Congenital nystagmus, 191
Congenital pneumonia, 182
Congenital renal cyst, 193
Congenital sepsis, 19
Congenital spondylolisthesis, 194
Congenital stenosis and stricture of bile ducts, 183
Congenital stenosis of the aortic valve, 191
Congenital subaortic stenosis, 191
Congenital syphilis, 115
Congenital torticollis, 149
Congenital unstable hip, 193
Congenital viral pneumonia, 182
Conjunctivitis, 81–83
Connective tissue disease. *See* Musculoskeletal system and connective tissue disease
Contact dermatitis, 136
Contraceptive pills, 172
Contracture of muscle, 149
Contusion, 207
Convulsions of the newborn, 185
Cooperating parties, 1
Corneal disorders, 83
Corns, 140
Coronary artery spasm, 100
Corrosion, 210
Cortical blindness, 86
Cough, 115
Cough variant asthma, 113
Coxa magna, 151
Coxa plana, 151
Cradle cap, 136, 184
Cranial nerve disorder, 70
Crib death, 202
Crigler-Najjar syndrome, 48, 183
Crohn disease, 123, 146
Cross-references, 5
Croup, 118, 248
Cryoglobulinemia, 115
Cryptophthalmos, 191
Cryptophthalmos syndrome, 195
Cutaneous abscess of face, 134
Cyanosis, 142
Cyclopia, 195
Cystic fibrosis, 48
Cystic kidney disease, 193
Cystic meniscus, 147
Cysticercosis, 75
Cystitis and bladder disorders, 161

D

Dacryocystitis, 81
Dash, 4–5
De Lange syndrome, 195
Death, not otherwise specified, 202
Definitions. *See* Terminology
Deforming dorsopathies, 152
Delayed sexual development, 47
Delusional disorders, 58
Demyelinating diseases, 67
Denis classification, 209

Dependence on respiratory (ventilator) status, 116
Dermatitis and eczema, 136
Dermatopolymyositis, 148
Deuteranomaly, 88
Developmental disorders, 60
Deviated nasal septum, 152
Diabetes mellitus, 42–47
Diamond-Blackfan anemia, 33
Diaper dermatitis, 136, 143, 184, 249
Diarrhea, unspecified, 128
Dietary counseling and surveillance, 44, 235
Dietary folic acid deficiency, 33
Digestive system diseases, 119–131
    appendicitis, etc, 121
    code scenarios/examples, 129
    complications of artificial openings of digestive system, 127
    congenital malformations, 192
    diseases of the esophagus, 120–121
    disorders of gallbladder, 125, 126
    disorders of tooth development and eruption, 119–120
    hernia, 122
    intestinal malabsorption, 127
    intraoperative/post-procedural complications, 127
    noninfective enteritis and colitis, 122–123
    other diseases of intestines, 123–124
    other disorders of peritoneum and retroperitoneum, 125
    other gastrointestinal diseases, 127
    perinatal period, 184
    peritonitis, 124
    review test, 130–131, 248
    signs, symptoms, and history, 128
    stomach and duodenal disorders, 121
    stomatitis and related lesions, 120
Discharge of firearm, 220
Dislocation, 207
Dissociative disorders, 58
Diverticular disease of the intestine, 124
Diverticulitis of the intestines, 124, 130, 248
Diverticulum of the bladder, 161
Dorsopathies, 148–149
Doubling of the uterus, 193
Doubling of the vagina, 193
Down syndrome, 59, 196
Drug abuse counseling and surveillance, 235
Drug-induced anemia, 35
Drug-induced diabetes mellitus, 45
Drug-induced hair loss, 139
Drug therapy, 233
Dubin-Johnson syndrome, 183
Dubowitz syndrome, 195
Duodenal disorders, 121
Duodenitis, 121
Dural tear, 74
Dyshormogenetic goiter, 183
Dysmorphism due to warfarin, 195

Dysplasia of the cervix uteri, 162
Dyspnea, 115
Dysuria, 163

E

Ear disorders, 91–96
    code scenarios/examples, 95
    complications of procedures, 94
    diseases of middle ear, 92–94
    disorders of external ear, 91
    loss of hearing, 94
    otorrhagia, 94
    review test, 96, 246–247
Early complications of trauma, 212
Early congenital syphilis, 115
Early fetal death, 171
Eating disorders, 59
Eccrine sweat disorders, 139
ECG. *See* Electrocardiogram (ECG)
Ectopic pregnancy, 171
Eczema, 136
Education maladjustment, 234
Eisenmenger defect, 191
Eisenmenger syndrome, 191
EKG. *See* Electrocardiogram (ECG)
Electrocardiogram (ECG), 103
Emphysema, 112
Encephalitis, 66
Encephalomyelitis, 66
Encounters for attention and aftercare, 232–233
Endocardial fibroelastosis, 99
Endocarditis, 98
Endocervicitis, 162
Endocrine, nutritional, and metabolic diseases, 41–51
    code scenarios/examples, 49–51
    diabetes mellitus, 42–47
    endocrine gland disorders, 47
    excludes 1 note, 41
    malnutrition/other nutritional deficiencies, 47
    metabolic disorders, 48
    overweight/obesity, 48
    review test, 51, 244
    thyroid disorders, 42
Endocrine gland disorders, 47
Enterostomy, 127
Enteroviral meningitis, 66
Enuresis, 61
Environmental tobacco smoke, 92, 236
Eosinophil gastritis or gastroenteritis, 121
Eosinophilic asthma, 113
Eosinophilic esophagitis, 119
Ependymoma, 25
Epidermolysis bullosa, 195
Epididymitis, 161
Epididymo-orchitis, 161
Epigastric pain, 127
Epilepsia partialis, 255
Epilepsy, 67–68, 255–257

Epilepsy table, 255–257
Epileptic spasms, 257
Epiphora, 81
Epispadias, 193
Erythema, 136–137
Erythema multiforme, 137
Esophageal diseases, 120–121
Esophagitis, 119
Esophagostomy, 127
Esotropia, 86
Essential hypertension, 99
Etiology, 4
Excessive menstruation at puberty, 163
Excludes 2 note, 11
Exclusion terms, 10–11
Exercise-induced bronchospasm, 113
Exocervicitis, 162
Exomphalos, 194
Exotropia, 86
Exposure to environmental tobacco smoke, 236
Exposure with hazardous metals, 236
Expressive language disorder, 60
External cause codes, 7
External cause of injury index, 7, 8
External cause of morbidity, 217–226
    code scenarios/examples, 223–225
    external cause status, 219–220
    intent, 218
    legal intervention, 223
    medical and surgical misadventures, 223
    military operations, 223
    operations of war, 223
    other external causes of injury, 221–222
    place of occurrence and activity codes, 219
    review test, 225–226, 253–254
    self-harm and assault, 222–223
    sequelae of previous injury, 218–219
    supplementary factors, 223
    terrorism, 223
    transport accidents, 220–221
External constriction, 207
Extreme immaturity, 181
Extremely low birth weight, 181
Eye disorders, 79–90
    blindness/low vision, 86
    code scenarios/examples, 87–89
    conjunctivitis, 81–83
    corneal disorders, 83
    disorders of lacrimal system, 81
    disorders of ocular muscles, etc, 86
    disorders of optic nerve/visual pathways, 85–87
    disorders of the choroid and retina, 85
    disorders of the eyelid, 79–81
    disorders of the lens, 84
    family history, 87
    glaucoma, 85
    intraoperative/post-procedural complications, 86–87
    iridocyclitis, 83
    juvenile cataracts, 84
    review test, 89–90, 246

F

Facial nerve disorder, 70
Factors influencing health status and contact with health services, 227–239
    code scenarios/examples, 237–238
    encounters for attention and aftercare, 232–233
    family history, 236–237
    health services for examinations, 228–231
    health services in other circumstances, 235–236
    other contact with and exposures to health hazards, 236
    pediatric body mass index, 234
    potential hazards related to communicable diseases, 231–232
    retained foreign body fragments, 231
    review test, 239, 254
    socioeconomic and psychosocial problems, 234
    visits related to birth, 232
    Z codes, 227
Failure to thrive (child), 127
Failure to thrive in newborn, 185
Familial hypophosphatemia, 47
Family history codes, 236–237
Fanconi anemia, 33
Fat embolism (traumatic), 212
Fecal impaction, 124
Feeding difficulties, 127
Feeding problems in the neonate, 185
Female pelvic organs, 162–163
Female post-infective peritoneal adhesions, 162
Femoral hernia, 122
Fetal alcohol syndrome, 195
Fetal growth disorders, 180–181
Fetal hydantoin syndrome, 195
First-listed diagnosis, 2
First trimester, 169
Flatback syndrome, 149
Flushing, 142
Focal hyperhidrosis, 139, 140
Follicular cyst, 139
Follicular mucinosa, 139
Foreign body glaucoma, 231
Foreign body granuloma of the skin, 140
Fracture, 208–210
Fracture aftercare, 210
Frequency of micturition, 164
Functional quadriplegia, 202
Furuncle, 134, 135

G

Gallbladder disorders, 125, 126
Gallstone ileus, 124
Gang-related offenses, 235
Gangrene, 102
Gastritis, 121
Gastroesophageal laceration-hemorrhage syndrome, 121
Gastrointestinal hemorrhage, unspecified, 127
Gastrointestinal mucositis, 127
Gastrostomy, 127
Gastrostomy status, 127
Generalized abdominal pain, 127
Generalized acute peritonitis, 124
Generalized idiopathic epilepsy syndromes, 68
Generalized muscle weakness, 149
Generalized rebound abdominal tenderness, 127
Genitourinary system disease, 157–166
    acute/chronic kidney failure, 160
    breast, disorders of, 162
    code scenarios/examples, 164–165
    cystitis and bladder disorders, 161
    female pelvic organs, 162–163
    glomerular diseases, 157–159
    intraoperative/post-procedural complications, 163
    male genital organs, 161–162
    other diseases of kidney and ureter, 160–161
    renal tubulointerstitial diseases, 159–160
    review test, 165–166, 250
    signs, symptoms, and history, 163–164
    urolithiasis, 160
Genu valgum, 147
Germ cell, 25
Gestational age and fetal growth disorders, 180–181
Gilbert syndrome, 48, 183
Glasgow coma scale, 202
Glaucoma, 85
Glioblastoma, 26
Glioma, 26
Glomerular diseases, 157–159
Glossary. *See* Terminology
Glucose-6-phosphate dehydrogenase deficiency anemia, 34
Glucose-galactose malabsorption, 48
Goat's milk anemia, 33
Goldenhar syndrome, 195
Graft-versus-host disease, 36
Gross hematuria, 163
Guillain-Barré syndrome, 70
Gustilo classification, 207
Guttate psoriasis, 136
Gynecomastia, 162

H

Hair loss, 139
Hallucinogens, 56
Hallux valgus, 147
Hangnail, 135
Hashimoto thyroiditis, 42
Hazardous metals, 236
Headache, 68–69
Health examinations, 228–231
Health services for examinations, 228–231
Health status. *See* Factors influencing health status and contact with health services
Heart and lungs transplant status, 116
Hemiparesis, 71–73
Hemiplegia, 71–73
Hemoglobin disorders, 34
Hemolytic anemia, 34, 183
Hemolytic disease of the newborn, 183
Hemophilia, 148
Hemophilic arthropathy, 148
Hemorrhage of the anus and rectum, 127
Hereditary amyloid nephropathy, 159
Hereditary lymphedema, 195
Hereditary nephropathy, not elsewhere classified, 158, 159
Hereditary spastic hemiplegia, 71
Hernia, 122
Hiatal hernia, 122
High-risk pregnancy, 169–170
Hirschsprung disease, 184, 192
Hirsutism, 139
History of falling, 202
HIV. *See* Human immunodeficiency virus (HIV)
Holt-Oram syndrome, 195
Homelessness, 234
Hordeolum, 80
Human immunodeficiency virus (HIV), 16–18
Hydrocele, 161
Hydrocephalus, 74, 190
Hydronephrosis, 159
Hydrops fetalis due to hemolytic disease of the newborn, 183
Hydrops fetalis not due to hemolytic disease, 184
Hydroureter, 159
Hyperactive bowel sounds, 127
Hyperalimentation, 48
Hypercholesterolemia, 48
Hypersomnia, 59
Hypertensive heart disease, 99–100
Hypertensive kidney disease, 99
Hyperthermia of the newborn, 184
Hypertriglyceridemia, 48
Hypertrophy of the adenoids, 70
Hypertrophy of the breast, 162
Hypertrophy of the tonsils, 108, 112
Hypnotics, 56

Hypochondriacal disorder, 58
Hypospadias, 193
Hypotension, 102

I

ICD-10-CM Official Guidelines for Coding and Reporting, 13
Ichthyosis, 195
Ichthyosis vulgaris, 195
Idiopathic pulmonary hemorrhage, 113
Idiopathic pulmonary hemosiderosis, 113
Ileostomy status, 127
Ileus, unspecified, 124
Immobility syndrome, 149
Immunodeficiency, 36–37
Impacted cerumen, 91
Impetigo, 91
"In diseases classified elsewhere," 4
Inadequate housing, 234
Inadequate parental supervision and control, 234
Inappropriate (excessive) parental pressure, 234
Includes note, 10
Inclusion terms, 10
Infantile acne, 139, 143, 249
Infantile eczema, 143, 249
Infantile idiopathic scoliosis, 149, 194
Infantile spasms, 257
Infantile type polycystic kidney, 193
Infected hydrocele, 161
Infectious and parasitic diseases, 15–22
    coding scenarios/examples, 20–21
    drug resistance, 15–16
    HIV-related illness, 16–18
    review test, 21–22, 242
    sepsis, 18–20
    "use additional code" note, 15
Infectious arthropathy, 145–146
Infectious neonatal diarrhea, 183
Infective myositis, 149
Infective nasopharyngitis, 108
Inflammatory polyarthropathies, 146–147
Inflammatory polyps of colon, 123
Influenza, 109–110
Ingrowing nail, 139
Inguinal hernia, 122
Inhaled steroid therapy, 237
Injectable contraceptive, 172
Injury, poisoning, and other consequences of external causes, 205–216
    adult and child abuse, 211–212
    adverse effects, 211
    burns and corrosions, 210–211
    code scenarios/examples, 214–215
    complications of care, 212–213
    early complications of trauma, 212
    fracture care, 208–210
    Gustilo classification, 207
    how to locate codes, 213–214
    injuries, 207–208
    poisoning, 211
    review test, 216, 253
    seventh characters, 206
    toxic effects, 211
    underdosing, 211
Insect bite, 207
Insomnia, 59
Institutional upbringing, 234
Insulin overdose, 46
Insulin pump malfunction, 46
Intellectual disabilities, 59–60
Interstitial myositis, 149
Interstitial respiratory disease, 113
Intestinal disorders, 123–124
Intestinal malabsorption, 127
Intestinal obstruction of newborn, unspecified, 123
Intracranial and intraspinal abscess and granuloma, 66
Intracranial injuries, 54, 208
Intrauterine contraceptive device, 168
Intravaginal torsion of spermatic cord, 165, 250
Intussusception, 124
Iodine deficiency-related hypothyroidism, 195
Iridocyclitis, 83
Iritis, 83
Iron deficiency anemia, 33
Irritable bowel syndrome, 124
Ischemic heart diseases, 97

J

Jaundice, 183
Jaw pain, 153
Joint disorders, 147
Joint pain, 148, 260
Juvenile absence epilepsy, 256
Juvenile ankylosing spondylitis, 146
Juvenile arthritis, 146
Juvenile cataracts, 84
Juvenile dermatitis herpetiformis, 135
Juvenile dermatomyositis, 146
Juvenile idiopathic scoliosis, 149
Juvenile myoclonic epilepsy, 68, 256
Juvenile osteochondrosis of the head of the femur, 152
Juvenile osteochondrosis of the spine, 148
Juvenile osteonecrosis, 155, 249
Juvenile polyarteritis, 148
Juvenile rheumatoid polyarthritis (seronegative), 146

K

Kawasaki syndrome, 148
Kearns-Sayre syndrome, 71
Keratoconjunctivitis, 82
Keratopathy, 86
Keratouveitis, 83
Kernicterus, 183
Kidney failure, 157, 160

Kidney transplant, 213
Kidney transplant status, 164
Klippel-Feil syndrome, 194
Klippel Trenaunay-Weber syndrome, 195
Knock-knee, 147
Koch-Weeks conjunctivitis, 82
Koilonychia, 139
Kugelberg-Welander disease, 67
Kyphosis, 148, 149

L

Laceration, 207
Laryngismus, 109
Late metabolic acidosis of a newborn, 182
Latent diabetes, 44
Law enforcement officers, encounters with, 223
Leber disease, 71
Left lower quadrant pain, 127
Left sided colitis, 123
Left upper quadrant pain, 127
Legal intervention, 223
Legg-Calvé-Perthes disorder, 152
Leigh encephalopathy, 71
Lennox-Gastaut syndrome, 257
Leukemia, 24–25, 148
Leukonychia, 139
Ligamentous laxity and instability, 147
Light for gestational age, 180
Lipoprotein deficiency, 48
Liver disease, 125
Lobar pneumonia, 110
Localized hypertrichosis, 139
Long QT syndrome, 99
Long-term drug therapy, 233
Lordosis, 148, 149
Loss of hearing, 94
Low birth weight, 180, 181
Low vision, 86
Lowe syndrome, 85
Lung transplant status, 116
Lymph node disorders, 101
Lymphadenitis, 135
Lymphangitis, 135
Lymphoma, 25

M

Macrophthalmos, 191
Male genital organs, 161–162
Malformation syndromes, 195
Malignant pleural effusion, 114
Mallory-Weiss syndrome, 121
Malnutrition, 47
Manifestation codes, 4
Marfan syndrome with aortic dilation, 195
Mastitis, 162
Mastodynia, 162
Mastoiditis, 92
Meckel diverticulum, 192

Meckel-Gruber syndrome, 190
Meconium, 182
Meconium aspiration with respiratory symptoms, 182, 187, 251
Meconium aspiration without respiratory symptoms, 182
Meconium ileus, 48
Meconium plug syndrome, 123
Medical and surgical misadventures, 223
Medical surveillance, 230
Medulloblastoma, 26
Megaloureter, 161
Melanocytic nevi, 142
Melanoma, 26
Meningeal hemorrhage, 101
Meningitis, 65–66
Meniscus derangements, 147
Menstrual cycle, 163
Menstrual headache, 69
Menstrual migraine, 77
Mental, behavioral, and neurodevelopment disorders, 53–64
 anxiety/stress-related disorders, 58
 eating disorders, 59
 excludes 2 note, 53
 intellectual disabilities, 59–60
 mental disorders due to known physiological conditions, 54–55
 pervasive and specific developmental disorders, 60
 psychoactive substance use, 56–57
 schizophrenia, etc, 58
 sleep disorders, 59
 social functioning disorders, 60
 somatoform disorders, 58–59
Mental, behavioral, and other health care needs, 235
Mesenteric lymphadenitis, 135
Metabolic acidosis, 48, 182
Metabolic acidosis of the newborn, 182
Metabolic disorders, 48
Microphthalmos, 191
Migraine, 68–69
Mild cervical dysplasia, 162
Miliaria rubra, 139
Military operations, 223
Misshapen or misplaced ear, 191
Mitochondrial metabolism disorder, 71
Mitochondrial-related conditions, 71
Mittelschmerz, 163, 166, 250
Mixed hearing loss, 94
Moebius syndrome, 195
Molluscum contagiosum, 142
Monoclonal drug therapy, 237
Monoplegia, 71
Morbidity. *See* External cause of morbidity
Motor vehicle accidents, 220–221
Mucocutaneous lymph node, 148
Mucopolysaccharidosis, 194

Multiple sclerosis, 67
Multiple spermatoceles, 161
Muscle disorders, 149
Muscle strain/sprain, 207
Muscle wasting and atrophy, 149
Musculoskeletal system and connective tissue disease, 145–155
    biomechanical lesions, 153
    bone density and structure, 150–151
    chondropathies, 151–152
    code scenarios/examples, 153–154
    congenital malformations, 193–194
    disorders of synovium and tendon, 149–150
    dorsopathies, 148–149
    infectious arthropathy, 145–146
    inflammatory polyarthropathies, 146–147
    intraoperative/post-procedural complications, 152
    muscle disorders, 149
    other acquired deformities, 152
    other joint disorders, 147
    other osteopathies, 151
    review test, 155, 249–250
    signs, symptoms, and history, 153
    systemic connective tissue disorders, 148
Myasthenia gravis, 70
Myelitis, 66
Myelopathy, 75
Myocarditis, 98
Myoneural disorders, 70–71
Myotonia fluctuans, 71
Myotonia permanens, 71
Myringotomy tube status, 237

N

Nail-biting, 142
Nail disorders, 138–139
Nail patella syndrome, 159, 195
Nail shedding, 139
Nasal congestion, 116
Nasal mucositis, 112
Nasal polyps, 111
Nausea, 127
NEC, 5, 10
Necrotizing enterocolitis, 184
Negative life events in childhood, 234, 235
Neonatal aspiration, 182
Neonatal cerebral ischemia, 69
Neonatal cutaneous hemorrhage, 181
Neonatal diabetes mellitus, 183
Neonatal difficulty in feeding at breast, 185
Neonatal erythema toxicum, 184
Neonatal hematemesis and melena, 183
Neonatal hypertension, 99
Neonatal infective mastitis, 162
Neonatal jaundice, 48, 183
Neonatal purpura, 35
Neonatal screening, abnormal findings, 177
Neonatal skin infection, 183, 184

Neoplasm table, 6, 23
Neoplasms, 23–32
    alphabetic index, 25–26
    code scenarios/examples, 29–31
    primary vs secondary, 24
    review test, 31–32, 242–243
    table of, 6, 23
    treatment of malignancy, 26–29
    uncertain behavior vs unspecified behavior, 23, 24
Nephritic syndrome, 158
Nephrogenic diabetes insipidus, 160
Nephrotic syndrome, 158
Nervous system diseases, 65–78
    autonomic disorders, 74
    brain disorders, 74–75
    code scenarios/examples, 75–77
    congenital malformations, 190–191
    demyelinating diseases, 67
    epilepsy/recurrent seizures, 67–68, 255–257
    hemiplegia and hemiparesis, 71–73
    hydrocephalus, 74
    inflammatory diseases, 65–66
    migraines/headache syndromes, 68–69
    myoneural disorders, 70–71
    nerve, nerve root, plexus disorders, 70
    pain, not elsewhere classified, 73–74
    polyneuropathies, 70
    review test, 78, 245–246
    sleep disorders, 69–70
    systemic atrophies, 67
    transient cerebral ischemic attacks, 69
Neuralgic amyotrophy, 149
Neuroblastoma, 26
Neurodevelopmental disorders. *See* Mental, behavioral, and neurodevelopment disorders
Neuroectodermal (peripheral), 26
Neuroendocrine cell hyperplasia of infancy, 113
Neurofibromatosis, 195
Neuromuscular scoliosis, 149
Neuromyelitis optica, 67
Neuromyotonia, 71
Neuropathic bladder, 161
Neutropenia, 35
Newborn. *See* Perinatal period; Pregnancy, childbirth, and the puerperium
Newborn bradycardia, 99
Newborn cardiomyopathy, 99
Newborn coagulation defects, 35
Newborn esophageal reflux, 119, 184
Newborn health examination, 228
Newborn respiratory failure, 115
Newborn sepsis, 19
Newborn tachycardia, 99
Nicotine dependence, 57, 235
Night terrors, 59
Nocturia, 164
Noise-induced hearing loss, 94

Non-neuropathic heredofamilial amyloidosis, 159
Non-obstructive reflux-associated chronic pyelonephritis, 165, 250
Non-rheumatic valve disorders, 97
Non-thermal blister, 207
Non-traumatic hemoperitoneum, 125
Non-traumatic rhabdomyolysis, 149
Non-traumatic slipped upper femoral epiphysis, 151
Non-traumatic subarachnoid hemorrhage, 101
Nondiabetic hypoglycemic coma, 47
Nonessential modifiers, 4
Noninfective enteritis and colitis, 122–123
Noninfective mastitis of newborn, 184
Noonan syndrome, 195
NOS, 5, 10
Nose-picking, 142
Nutritional deficiencies, 47
Nutritional short stature, 47

O

Obesity, 48
Obstructive and reflux uropathy, 159
Obstructive pyelonephritis, 159
Obstructive sleep apnea, 70
Ocular albinism, 191
Official guidelines, 1, 13
Oligoarticular, 145
Oligomenorrhea, 163
Omphalitis, 134
Omphalitis with mild hemorrhage, 183
Onychia, 135, 138
Onychocryptosis, 139
Onychogryphosis, 139
Onycholysis, 139
Onychomadesis, 139
Onychomycosis, 138
Open bite, 207
Operations of war, 223
Ophthalmoplegia, 86
Opioids, 56
Oppositional defiant disorder, 60
Optic nerve hypoplasia, 191
Orchitis, 161
Organic tic, 81
Oro-facial-digital syndrome, 195
Orthopnea, 115
Osseous defect codes, 151
Osteitis deformans, 151
Osteochondritis dissecans, 151
Osteochondrodysplasia, 194
Osteomyelitis, 151
Osteonecrosis, 151
Osteoporosis, 150
Osteosarcoma, 26
Other ectopic pregnancy, 171
Other microscopic hematuria, 163
Otitis externa, 91
Otitis media, 92, 93

Otomycosis, 91
Otorrhagia, 94
Ototoxic hearing loss, 94
Ovarian cyst, 162
Ovarian dysfunction, 163
Ovarian pregnancy, 171
Overactive bladder, 161
Overweight, 48

P

Paget disease, 151
Pain, not elsewhere classified, 73–74
Painful micturition, unspecified, 163
Painful ovulation, 166, 250
Pallor, 142
Palpitations, 99
Pancreatic insulin secretory disorders, 47
Pancytopenia, 35
Panic disorder, 58
Papulosquamous disorders, 136
Paralytic ileus, 124
Paralytic strabismus, 70, 86
Paralytic syndromes, 72
Paramyotonia congenita, 71
Paraphimosis, 161
Paraplegia, 72
Parasitic diseases. See Infectious and parasitic diseases
Parent-adopted child conflict, 234
Parent-biological child conflict, 234
Parent-child estrangement NEC, 234
Parent-foster child conflict, 234
Parental overprotection, 234
Parentheses, 4, 9
Parinaud oculoglandular syndrome, 82
Paronychia, 135, 138
Pathological fracture, 150
Pauciarticular, 145
Pauciarticular juvenile rheumatoid arthritis, 146
Pediatric body mass index, 235
Pelvic cellulitis, 162
Pelvic inflammatory disease, unspecified, 162
Pelvic peritonitis, 162
Pelvic ring fracture, 210
Pemphigus neonatorum, 135, 183
Peptic ulcer of the newborn, 184
Pericardial effusion, 99
Pericarditis, 98
Perinatal intestinal perforation, 184
Perinatal period, 177–188
    birth trauma, 181
    code scenarios/examples, 186
    digestive system disorders, 184
    gestational age and fetal growth disorders, 180–181
    hemorrhagic and hematological disorders, 182–183
    infections, 182–183

Perinatal period, continued
    integument and temperature regulation, 184–185
    maternal factors and complications affecting newborn, 179–180
    other care, 185
    other disorders, 185
    principal diagnosis for the birth record, 178–179
    respiratory and cardiovascular disorders, 182
    review test, 187–188, 251
    transitory endocrine and metabolic disorders, 183
Peripartum period, 172
Peritoneal abscess, 124
Peritoneum, 125
Peritonitis, 124
Peritonsillar abscess, 108, 112
Periumbilical pain, 127
Persistent proteinuria, unspecified, 164
Persistent pulmonary hypertension in a newborn, 100
Personal history of anaphylaxis, 237
Personal history of colonic polyps, 236
Personal history of in situ neoplasm, 236
Petrositis, 92
Phimosis, 161
Phobias, 58
Photoallergic response, 138
Photocontact dermatitis, 138
Phototoxic response, 138
Physeal arrest, 151
Physeal fracture, 208, 209
Physical restraint status, 236
Picker acne, 139
Pilonidal cyst and sinus, 135
Placeholder, 2, 3
Plantar wart, 142
Pleural diseases, 114
Pleural effusion, 114
Pneumococcal arthritis and polyarthritis, 146
Pneumonia, 110
Pneumothorax, 114
Poisoning, 45–46, 211
Polyarthritis, 145
Polyneuropathies, 70
Polypoid sinus degeneration, 111
Pompe disease, 98
Post-concussional syndrome, 54, 55
Post-dysenteric arthropathy, 146
Post-encephalitic syndrome, 54
Post-immunization arthropathy, 146
Post-procedural heart failure, 100
Post-procedural hypertension, 100
Post-procedural musculoskeletal disorders, 152
Post-procedural pneumonitis, 113
Post-procedural respiratory failure, 115
Post-term newborns, 181
Postauricular fistula, 92
Postnasal drip, 116
Postpartum complication, 172
Postpartum depression, 59
Posttraumatic headache, 55
Postural kyphosis, 149
Postural lordosis, 149
Postural scoliosis, 193
Potential hazards related to communicable diseases, 231–232
Potter syndrome, 193
Prader-Willi syndrome, 195
Pre-excitation syndrome, 99
Precocious puberty, 47, 163
Precordial pain, 103
Prediabetes, 44
Pregnancy, childbirth, and the puerperium, 167–175
    caring for pregnant patient, 169
    code scenarios/examples, 173–174
    conditions in the puerperium, 172
    contraceptives, 168
    encounter for delivery, 171
    other encounters, 173
    pregnancy diagnosis and prevention, 168
    pregnancy with abortive outcome, 171–172
    review test, 174–175, 250–251
    spontaneous abortion, 172
    supervision of high-risk pregnancy, 169–170
    trimesters, 169
Pregnancy diagnosis and prevention, 168
Premenstrual syndrome, 163
Premenstrual tension syndrome, 77, 163
Prepuce, 161
Pressure ulcer, 140, 141
Priapism, 161
Principal diagnosis, 2
Progressive external ophthalmoplegia, 86
Protein deficiency anemia, 33
Proteinuria, unspecified, 164
Pseudocoxalgia, 151
Pseudomyotonia, 71
Pseudophakia, 84
Psoriasis, 136
Psoriatic juvenile arthropathy, 136, 146
Psychoactive substance use, 56–57
Psychogenic tachycardia, 99
Psychogenic tic, 81
Psychogenic torticollis, 149
Psychosocial circumstances, 234
Puerperium, 172
Pulmonary interstitial glycogenosis, 113
Puncture wound, 207
Purpura, 35
Pyeloureteritis cystica, 159
Pyknolepsy, 256
Pyoderma gangrenosa, 102, 140
Pyogenic arthritis, 146
Pyogenic granuloma, 140
Pyonephrosis, 159, 165, 250

Q

Quadriplegia, 72

R

Ram's horn nail, 139
Rapidly progressive nephritic syndrome, 158
Rash, 142
Rebound abdominal tenderness, 127
Recurrent and persistent hematuria, 158
Reflux-associated pyelonephritis, 159
Regurgitation and rumination of newborn, 185
Reiger anomaly, 85
Reiter disease (reactive), 146
Relapsing polychondritis, 152
Renal agenesis, 193
Renal dysplasia, 193
Renal osteodystrophy, 160
Renal tubulointerstitial diseases, 159–160
Repeated falls, 153, 202
Respiratory distress of the newborn, 182
Respiratory failure, 115
Respiratory system diseases, 107–118
    acute bronchitis and bronchiolitis, 110–111
    acute upper respiratory infections, 107–109
    chronic lower respiratory diseases, 112–113
    chronic upper respiratory conditions, 111–112
    code scenarios/examples, 116–117
    congenital malformations, 191–192
    disorders in diseases classified elsewhere, 115
    influenza and pneumonia, 109–110
    interstitial respiratory disease, 113
    intraoperative/post-procedural complications, 114
    lung diseases due to external agents, 113
    perinatal period, 182
    pleural diseases, 114
    respiratory failure, 115
    review test, 117–118, 247–248
    signs, symptoms, and history, 115–116
    vasomotor and allergic rhinitis, 111
Retained foreign body fragments, 231
Retinal disorder, 85
Retinitis pigmentosa, 191
Retinoblastoma, 26
Retinopathy of prematurity, 85
Retrolental fibroplasia, 85
Retroperitoneal abscess, 125
Retroperitoneum, 125
Rett syndrome, 60
Reye syndrome, 71, 74
Rhabdomyosarcoma, 26
Rheumatic fever, 97
Rheumatic heart failure, 97
Rheumatic valve disease, 97
Rhinitis, 108, 111
Rhizomelic chondrodysplasia punctata, 194, 197, 251
Rickets, 47
Right lower quadrant pain, 127

Right upper quadrant pain, 127
Robin syndrome, 192, 195
Robinow-Silverman-Smith syndrome, 195
Roger disease, 191
Rotator cuff tear or rupture, 150
Routine postpartum follow-up encounters, 172
Roy-Camille classification, 209
Rubella, 75
Rubinstein-Taybi syndrome, 195
Rule of nines, 210
Ruptured cerebral arteriovenous malformation, 191
Russell-Silver syndrome, 195

S

Sacral alar fracture, 209
Sacral foramina fracture, 209
Salaam attacks, 257
Salter-Harris classification, 209
Sarcoma, 26
Scar conditions, 140
Scarlet fever, 98, 105, 247
Scheuermann disease, 148
Schistosomiasis, 115
Schizophrenia, 58
Schwannomatosis, 195
Schwartz-Jampel syndrome, 194
Sclerema neonatorum, 184
Sclerosing mesenteritis, 124
Scoliosis, 148, 149
Screening for diseases in asymptomatic individuals, 230–231
Screening for infectious/parasitic disease, 230
Screening for malignant neoplasm of cervix, 230
Seborrhea capitis, 136
Seborrheic infantile dermatitis, 136
Seckel syndrome, 195
Second trimester, 169
Secondary autoimmune anemia, 35
Secondary hypertension, 99
Secondary lactase deficiency, 48
Sedatives, 56
"See" instruction, 5
"See also" instruction, 5
Seeking health care. *See* Factors influencing health status and contact with health services
Seizures, 67–68, 255–257
Selection of accurate code. *See* Code selection
Self-harm and assault, 222–223
Sensorineural hearing loss, 94
Separation anxiety disorder, 60
Sepsis, 18–20
Sequela, 2
Sequencing instructions, 11–12
Severe sepsis, 18–19
Sex chromosome abnormalities, 196
Sexual precocity, 47
Sexually transmitted chlamydial infections, 162
Short stature, 47, 153

Shortness of breath, 115
Sibling rivalry, 234
Sickle cell disease, 34, 159
Sickle cell thalassemia, 34, 40, 243
Sickle cell trait, 40, 243
Signs and symptoms, 259–261
    circulatory system diseases, 102–103
    digestive system diseases, 128
    respiratory system diseases, 115–116
Single liveborn infant, delivery by cesarean, 197, 252
Sinus bradycardia, 99
Sinus tachycardia, 99
Sinusitis, 108
Sirenomelia syndrome, 195
SIRS. See Systemic inflammatory response syndrome (SIRS)
Skin and subcutaneous disease, 133–143
    bullous disorders, 135
    code scenarios/examples, 142
    dermatitis and eczema, 136
    infections, 133–135
    intraoperative/post-procedural complications, 140
    other disorders, 140–142
    papulosquamous disorders, 136
    radiation-related disorders, 137–138
    review test, 143, 249
    signs, symptoms, and history, 142
    skin appendages, 138–140
    urticaria and erythema, 136–137
Skin appendages, 138–140
Skin mass/lump/nodule/swelling, 261
Skull fracture, 208
Sleep apnea, 69
Sleep disorders, 59, 69–70
Sleep walking, 59
Slow feeding of newborn, 185
Small for gestational age, 180
Snoring, 116
Social anxiety disorder, 58
Social functioning disorders, 60
Social phobia, 60
Socioeconomic and psychosocial problems, 234
Solitary bone cyst, 151
Solitary cyst of jaw, 151
Somatization disorder, 58
Somatoform disorders, 58–59
Somatoform pain disorder, 63, 244
Sotos syndrome, 195
Spasm-induced angina, 100
Spasmodic torticollis, 149
Sphingolipidosis, 48
Spina bifida, 190, 191
Spina bifida occulta, 194
Spina bifida with hydrocephalus, 74
Spinal muscular atrophy, 67
Spondylolisthesis, 148
Spondylolysis, 148, 149
Spondylopathies, 148
Spondylosis, 75
Spontaneous abortion, 172
Spontaneous bacterial peritonitis, 124
Spontaneous ecchymosis, 142
Spoon nail, 139
Sprain, 207
Staphylococcal arthritis and polyarthritis, 146
Staphylococcal scalded skin syndrome, 133
Status epilepticus, 67
Stealing in the company of others, 235
Stevens-Johnson syndrome, 137
Stevens-Johnson syndrome-toxic epidermal overlap syndrome, 137
Still disease, 146
Stomach and duodenal disorders, 121
Stomatitis and related lesions, 120
Strain, 207
Strange-Vognsen classification, 209
Streptococcal pharyngitis, 108
Stress fracture, 150
Stress-related disorders, 58
Stridor, 115
Subacute osteomyelitis, 151
Subarachnoid hemorrhage, 101
Subcategory, 1
Subcutaneous tissue. See Skin and subcutaneous disease
Subluxation, 207, 208
Subperiosteal abscess, 92
Sudden infant death syndrome, 202
Suicide attempts, 220
Sunburn, 137
Superficial foreign body, 207
Superficial injuries, 207
Suppurative otitis media, 66, 93
Supraglottitis, 109
Supravalvular aortic stenosis, 191
Surgical misadventures, 223
Suspected child sexual abuse, 164
Swimmer's ear, 91
Swyer-James syndrome, 112
Symptomatic myotonia, 71
Symptoms. See Signs and symptoms
Symptoms, signs, and abnormal clinical and laboratory findings not elsewhere classified, 199–204
    code scenarios/examples, 203
    coma, 201–202
    death, not otherwise specified, 202
    functional quadriplegia, 202
    guideline instructions, 200–201
    repeated falls and history of falling, 202
    review test, 204, 252
    SIRS, 202
Synovitis, 150
Synovium, 149–150
Syphilis, 75

System lupus erythematosus, 148
Systemic atrophies, 67
Systemic connective tissue disorders, 148
Systemic inflammatory response syndrome (SIRS), 202
Systemic steroid therapy, 237

T

Table of drugs and chemicals, 6, 17
Table of neoplasms, 6, 23
Tabular list, 8–12
    block-level instructions, 9
    brackets, 9
    category-level instructions, 9
    chapter-level instructions, 8–9
    colon, 10
    exclusion terms, 10–11
    inclusion terms, 10
    NEC, 10
    NOS, 10
    parentheses, 9
    sequencing instructions, 11–12
    subcategory and code level instructions, 9
Tanning bed, 137
Teething syndrome, 119
Telogen effluvium, 139
Tenosynovitis, 150
Terminology
    adverse effects, poisoning, 211
    congenital malformations, 190, 194
    epilepsy, 67
    fetal growth, 180
    genitourinary system diseases, 158, 159
    guidelines and conventions, 1–2, 4
    injuries, 208
    musculoskeletal system diseases, 145, 148
    perinatal period, 180, 182
    skin disorders, 134, 135, 137, 138, 139
Terrorism, 223
Thalassemia, 34
Therapeutic drug level monitoring, 233
Third trimester, 169
Thoracogenic scoliosis, 149
Thrombocytopenia with absent radius (TAR) syndrome, 195
Thumb-sucking, 142
Thyroid disorders, 42
Tietze syndrome, 151
Tobacco abuse, 57
Tobacco abuse counseling, 235
Tobacco use, 92, 236
Tonsillitis, 108–109, 112
Tooth development and eruption, 119–120
Torsion of appendix epididymis, 161
Torsion of appendix testis, 161
Torsion of the testis, 161
Torticollis, 149
Toxic effects, 46, 211, 213

Toxic epidermal necrolysis, 133, 137
Toxic liver disease, 125
Tracheitis, 109
Tracheostomy status, 127
Transient cerebral ischemic attacks, 69
Transient global amnesia, 69
Transient hypogammaglobulinemia of infancy, 40, 243
Transient neonatal myasthenia gravis, 70
Transient retinal artery occlusion, 69
Transitory congenital goiter, 183
Transitory ileus of newborn, 123, 184
Transplanted organ and tissue status, 237
Transport accidents, 220–221
Transverse sacral fracture, 209
Traumatic anuria, 212
Traumatic brain injury, 54
Traumatic compartment syndrome, 212
Traumatic hemoperitoneum, 125
Traumatic ischemia of muscle, 212
Traumatic pneumothorax, 114
Traumatic rhabdomyolysis, 149
Traumatic rotator cuff tear, 150
Traumatic secondary and recurrent hemorrhage and seroma, 212
Traumatic shock, 212
Traumatic subcutaneous emphysema, 212
Trichomonal infections, 162
Trigeminal neuralgia, 70
Trigger finger, 150
Trigger thumb, 150
Trigonitis, 161
Trimesters, 169
Trisomy 13, 196
Trisomy 18, 196
Trisomy 21, 196
Truancy, 235
Tubal pregnancy, 171
Tuberculosis, 116
Tuberculous pleural effusion, 114
Tubulointerstitial disease, 159
Tubulointerstitial and tubular conditions, 159–160
Turner syndrome, 192, 196
Type 1 diabetes, 44
Type 2 diabetes, 44

U

Ulcerative colitis, 123, 146
Ulcerative esophagitis, 119
Ultraviolet radiation, 137
Umbilical hemorrhage, 183
Umbilical polyp of newborn, 184
Underdosing, 45, 46, 211
Underfeeding of newborn, 185
Underimmunization, 232
Unequal limb length, 147
Unilateral cleft lip status post-reconstruction, 197, 252
Unilateral inguinal hernia, 122

Unilateral pulmonary emphysema, 112
Unilateral small kidney, 160
Unspecified nephrotic syndrome, 158
Urolithiasis, 160
Urticaria and erythema, 136–137
"Use additional code(s)" note, 11
Uveitis, 83

V

Vaginal dysplasia, 162
Vaginal intraepithelial neoplasia (VAIN), 163
Vaginismus, 163
Vaginitis, 162
VAIN. See Vaginal intraepithelial neoplasia (VAIN)
Vascular diseases, 101
Vasomotor rhinitis, 111
VATER syndrome, 195
Venous embolism and thrombosis, 101
Ventilator-associated pneumonia, 115
Ventricular septal defect, 191
Vertebra-basilar artery syndrome, 69
Vertical sacral fracture, 209
Vesicoureteral reflux, 159
Vesicoureteral reflux with hydroureter, 166, 250
VIN. See Vulval intraepithelial neoplasia (VIN)
Viral myocarditis, 103
Visits related to birth, 232
Vitamin B_{12} anemia, 33
Vitamin D-resistant rickets, 47
Vitiligo, 140
Volvulus, 124
Vomiting without nausea, 127
Vulval intraepithelial neoplasia (VIN), 163
Vulvitis, 162
Vulvovaginitis, 162

W

Water transport accident, 220
Weaver syndrome, 195
Welding light, 137
Werdnig-Hoffman syndrome, 67
West syndrome, 257
Wheezing, 113, 115
Whistling face, 195
White blood cell counts, 35, 36
Wilms tumor, 26
"With," 2, 3
Woake syndrome, 111
Wolff-Parkinson-White syndrome, 99

X

Xeroderma pigmentosa, 195

Z

Z codes, 227–228. See Factors influencing health status and contact with health services